Friendship among nations

I0093524

MANCHESTER
1824

Manchester University Press

Friendship among nations
History of a concept

EVGENY ROSHCHIN

Manchester University Press

Copyright © Evgeny Roshchin 2017

The right of Evgeny Roshchin to be identified as the author of this work has been asserted by him in accordance with the Copyright, Designs and Patents Act 1988.

Published by Manchester University Press
Altrincham Street, Manchester M1 7JA, UK
www.manchesteruniversitypress.co.uk

British Library Cataloguing-in-Publication Data is available

ISBN 978 1 5261 1644 4 hardback
ISBN 978 1 5261 1646 8 paperback

First published 2017

The publisher has no responsibility for the persistence or accuracy of URLs for any external or third-party internet websites referred to in this book, and does not guarantee that any content on such websites is, or will remain, accurate or appropriate.

Typeset in 10.5/12.5 Adobe Garamond by
Servis Filmsetting Ltd, Stockport, Cheshire

To Sonia

Contents

Acknowledgements

This historical study of friendship has its own history of intellectual friendships and engagements. I owe enormous gratitude to three persons who played a critical role in helping me shape and work on this project. Oleg Kharkhordin provoked my interest in the topic of friendship and assisted in devising the first outlines of this project. Kari Palonen critically read the whole manuscript at all stages of its evolution and inspired me to explore all possible aspects of the topic. Jens Bartelson offered suggestions that led to profound post-dissertation revisions of the manuscript. Pekka Korhonen, Peggy Heller and Kari Saastamoinen kindly read and commented on early drafts of the manuscript. I am deeply thankful to friends and colleagues who read selected chapters and offered suggestions to sharpen the argument: Sergei Prozorov, Quentin Skinner, Nick Onuf, David Konstan, Tapani Turkka and Richard Burke. I am also grateful to professional communities with which I was privileged to collaborate at the European University at St Petersburg, University of Jyväskylä and Queen Mary. My special thanks go to Peter Morley for editing my English prose. Finally, this research would not have been possible without the generous support I received from the Centre of Excellence in Political Thought and Conceptual Change and the Academy of Finland.

Abbreviations

BFSP	British and Foreign State Papers
EAID	Early American Indian Documents: Treaties and Laws
ECCO	Eighteenth Century Collections Online. Gale Group
EEBO	Early English Books Online
EIC	East India Company
FCN	friendship, commerce and navigation
OLL	The Online Library of Liberty
TCIAPA	Treaties, Conventions, International Acts, Protocols and Agreements between the United States and Other Powers

Preface

The history of friendship among nations may seem to be evolving from omni-presence to obsoleteness in the era of complex international regimes and legal regulations. However, even in our time, friendship tends to re-surface whenever there is a will to revise the existing order of things or when regulations fail to regulate. Politics that give birth to various formal arrangements seems to return in the form of friendship to regenerate, challenge or reconstitute the arrangements that had been established before. We see it in turbulent times of the 2020 pandemic, when governments provide help to others, or, aside from the pandemic, when painstakingly slow collective decision-making, particularly in the area of peace-building, is abandoned in favour of uni- or bilateral initiatives to act on a specific issue. Many of such acts are made in the name of friendship. Therefore, in this book I sought to make sense of why there was so much friendship in the world, when the world order underwent major transformations. I was also prompted by the fact that even experienced students of International Relations would be hesitant to define those numerous treaties and declarations of friendship as friendships proper. This skeptical attitude of scholars and wider public was and still is an important driving force for my urge to contribute to the interpretive tradition of International Relations.

Since the first release of this book, I have been asked by my students and colleagues whether the instances of diplomatic friendship are friendships at all. To a great disappointment this may have caused among my interlocutors, the answer has always evaded essentialist interpretation. Everyone will have their own definition of friendship and no consensus on meaning is in sight. Nor is there a point in finding an ideal definition to further apply it to examples from international politics. This book searches for a different answer. One that shows what could be achieved with the support, or under pretext, or just in the name of friendship.

My critics tend to note the conciliatory overtones that friendship may bear. Bringing more friendship into the world seems to some like a pathway to a good peaceful life among nations. This is part of friendship's attraction and for a good reason. However, the other side of the coin is that friendship in politics means a good life for those who take part in it, and, as history shows, not even for all of those who take part. The good life in this context is likely to stand for a certain idea of order brought about by new friendships. Those orders could either be fair to all or favourable to select few.

As history reminds us, friendships sometimes play out differently for friends. Partly, this is why the book does not offer a solution to national egoistic ambitions and power-struggles by advocating greater, deeper, and genuine friendship for the countries and their leaders. Instead, it calls to recognise politics in friendship, to acknowledge rivalries, competition and alternative perspectives that any friendship should in principle celebrate. Although it might be tempting to suggest that friendship could help us build a more benign world order and mitigate conflict, this temptation should be resisted as a matter of both intellectual and political concern. More brutal forms of international politics in the past, accompanying the thirst for expansion and colonisation are no longer with us, but this is no reason to construct oppositions between the uncivilised politics of the past and ostensibly more civil and equitable politics of the present. Today we oftentimes discover how domination takes more subtle forms. By the same token, contemporary friendships may not be used to cede territories, subject nations and manifest superiority as they were in the era of imperial expansion. Yet, these friendships are not void of politics.

We ought to discover the past friendships with their rough edges not for the sake of our own high moral grounds but for the sake of critical re-inspection of what friendship helps to achieve in our time. This is the reason behind the need to uncover the forms of political friendships practiced in international politics throughout its key transformations. It is a need to dig out of political dust what was abandoned in friendship alongside with the reasons it was abandoned. At the same time, the rediscovery of abandoned practices and concepts is not a hunt for lost treasures. When we encounter the unexpected or the deviant in what we know as utterly familiar, there is a chance we might wish to re-examine what we know. This was my main motivation when I undertook to trace friendship among nations back to earliest examples of this practice, to uncover the ways it was conceptualised in the classical and more recent books of history, political philosophy and law.

If types of political friendship that a reader takes away from the uncovering of intricate and nuanced historical trajectories seems grim, it should only help us see the politics of friendship from a new perspective. A perspective that helps us to notice that political friendship is open to contingency, and not just permanency, to compromise, negotiation and contract, and not just natural affection and emotions, to power, contestation and inequality, and not just equality and reciprocity.

Friendship among nations guides the reader through the ways friendship was used in the language of international politics and theory. Friendship is one of those basic concepts, like peace, love, liberty, power, or state, that help us see the different ends they could be put to serve and how politics is always part to it, hence the reference to Hans Morgenthau's influential work in the title is not completely accidental. This is due to the long history of such concepts in the language that our societies speak. Such longitude gives us a privilege to observe them over time and across contexts. The latter are oftentimes discrepant and incommensurable, which brilliantly highlights the fact that what we mean to say is not always the same as what people in other historical times and political circumstances would have meant to say using exact same words. What is more, given this amenability to change, what we say reflects the power politics of times long gone. There is a certain irony inscribed in the fact that we use the tools of the power politics, which we are not always aware of. The irony is twofold when tools with such baggage are used to wage our own rhetorical battles.

Finally, it is worthwhile to underline that this book speaks to a genealogical tradition of International Relations. In its use of rhetorical and linguistic approaches it highlights the work of power *through* language, when political and commercial regimes based on friendship agreements were enacted with words, and *in* language, when one concept of friendship was replaced with another by a winning party. This is the type of critical contribution that linguistic approaches in social sciences may hope to achieve: they draw our attention to the fact that some of our conceptual constructs are constructed in the politics of a more or less distant past. Thus, probably the only political lesson we can hope to learn from history is not one that helps us solve or avoid problems, but one that helps us look differently at our values and politics.

Evgeny Roshchin
St Petersburg, 2020

Introduction

The problem

This book is about friendship between sovereign political agents, whose role in the modern world is performed by states. However, not all the political friends that feature in this book fit contemporary ideas about state and sovereignty, unless we anachronistically describe as states agents acting on behalf of aggregate entities or representing their own realms in the classical and early modern periods. This book therefore focuses on relations of friendship that bind together whole polities. What this book is not about are international networks of individuals forged, for instance, during student exchange programmes; NGOs advocating international friendship; relations between sister-cities and regions belonging to different states; and friendship of peoples, unless represented as sovereign actors in the international realm.

Friendship among nations or friendship between states constitutes a distinct kind of friendship. It has a global reach and millennia-old history, but still it remains tremendously paradoxical. We commonly hear leaders of states professing friendship towards one another. For example, US president George W. Bush and Russian president Vladimir Putin famously called one another friends, but this did not have a significant impact on relations between the two great powers, and the relationship had to be 'reset' under Barack Obama. The European Union Neighbourhood Policy was enacted with reference to the idea of a 'ring of friends'. Observers portray some countries – for example the US and the UK – as good old friends. Elsewhere, web pages are inundated with this type of acclamatory friendship rhetoric. However, such rhetoric does not stop at proclamations. Turning to more formal and binding practices, we find an astonishing number of friendship treaties that states and their historical predecessors concluded throughout documented diplomatic history. A key protagonist in recent international history was the Soviet Union, whose friends, surprisingly or not, instantly turned into cold-hearted neighbours, at best, once the superpower dissolved. Apart from bilateral friendships, the world has seen multiple attempts to posit friendship as the true foundation of a properly organised international community, ranging from the World Alliance for Promoting International Friendship through Churches (1914–1947) and Woodrow Wilson's description of the statute of the League of Nations in terms of friendship, to the United Nations *Declaration on Principles of International Law Concerning Friendly Relations and Cooperation among States*. In fact, making formal friendship is as old as the hills in world history. But despite, or perhaps because of, the universality of the practice, a common popular attitude is to question whether the statesmen and – women involved really mean what they say. As 2013 was marked by a protracted row over alleged US monitoring of the communications of private citizens and state leaders seen as America's best friends in Europe, thus effectively undermining any claims of trust built among friends, the implied answer certainly is that all such friendship rhetoric is lip service. Such friendships are rarely, if ever, perceived as true friendship.

Despite prolific discourses and a multiplicity of concluded treaties, this suspicion towards friendship is not uncommon among students of international relations (IR). In fact, friendship as a term is shared by virtually all the languages of rival theories of IR, including Realism (Dunne and Schmidt 2001; Morgenthau 2005: 183; Snyder 1997: 32; Waltz 2000: 10). However, hardly any school of thought turns friendship between states into a separate object of analysis, presuming that egoistic concerns for their own constituencies and attempts to increase their own security and material gains in the competitive environment render the world of states no place for serious friendship. In light of this interpretation, it is not surprising that the subject of friendship is anything but conventional, and thus it remains understudied (Wendt 1999: 298).[1] Therefore, speaking seriously of friendship between states risks being labelled unrealistic, naïve or wishful thinking. In this sense, academic and non-academic discourses often share the same assumptions about the nature of international friendship: namely, they juxtapose it with familiar examples of friendship between individuals that imply a high degree of emotional attachment, sincerity, trust and refraining from seeking advantages from the relationship.[2]

From this perspective, there are only two basic roles, not necessarily mutually exclusive, that friendship can play in the discourses on international relations. The first is as an anthropomorphic metaphor for the relations between states. Here, international friendship cannot be claimed to be friendship in the full sense of the word, but within these limitations it may refer to various kinds of cooperative, peaceful or benevolent relations between states. This includes Carl Schmitt's famous definition of the political as the distinction between friend and enemy (1996: 26), which migrates into a realist understanding of international

---

[1] For an overview of the emerging field of friendship studies see Devere and Smith (2010); the Journal *Amity* was launched in 2013 in an attempt to start filling this gap.

[2] For an example of such post-war idealist and religious argument defending friendship between nations see Dickinson (1927: 440).

politics. The second role involves significantly more than merely metaphorical language. It functions as a constituent part of a normative argument seeking a change in international relations that would transform their foundations from fear and conflict to trust, cooperation and sincere friendship. Some realist thinkers even go so far as to imply a remote possibility of the first function giving way to the second. For instance, Arnold Wolfers in *Discord and Collaboration* proposed that 'close and effective interstate amity as among allies should tend to promote emotional friendship' (Wolfers 1962: 33; see also Snyder 1997: 146 for similar observations).

However, there is an emerging area of scholarship that takes the second role of friendship in international politics seriously and tries to portray such relations in terms of trust, reciprocity, respect, mutual help, care and genuine emotional attachment (see, for instance, Eznack and Koschut 2014; Schwarzenbach 2009: 254–261). Were it not for the popular concept that appeals to friendship are metaphorical in nature and popular suspicion of statesmen and -women who stress their 'true' friendship, such scholarship would have promised an entirely new perspective on the (im)possibility of international anarchy. It can be achieved by refocusing attention on the basic structures of international partnerships and agreements (Onuf 2009: 8–9), on ways of mitigating anxiety in international politics instead of plunging into a vicious circle of security dilemmas (Berenskoetter 2007), on means of building regional peace instead of balancing (Oelsner 2007); and, more generally, by providing a structural role as friends (instead of 'enemies' or 'rivals') for states that share a single set of political values and economic priorities and thus express commitment to a single international community and culture of cooperation (Wendt 1999: 298–299).

Such a portrayal of international politics involves a good deal of anthropomorphism and inevitably moralisation of international friendship, because its expected elements are derived from the model of friendship between individuals and its related code of ethics. Certainly, proponents of this approach admit that 'exploring political friendship as analogous to personal friendship does not involve an attempt to equate or identify political relationships between entities such as countries, states or peoples with personal relationships between individuals' (Lu 2009: 43). Some also claim that the analogy cannot be complete because states 'are ontologically incapable of having feelings' (Digeser 2009a: 324–337; 2009b: 28–32). Nevertheless, the model of friendship between individuals serves as a convenient vantage point for this approach to 'provide a normative account of political friendship as a moral good among peoples with which we can evaluate and criticize some current practices of international friendship' (Lu 2009: 43). The model of individual friendship thus prompts observers to cast international friendship in deeply moral terms, thereby providing standards against which we can make normative judgements about the depth, partiality and sincerity of diplomatic relations. Such normativity has become an intrinsic element in this thriving scholarship, and possibly in our overall (post-)modern understanding of international friendship. On the one hand, this perspective serves as a guideline for those defending a critical and reformist stance towards the vectors of international politics and provides a checklist of criteria for those seeking to analyse overlooked friendly relations between states; on the other, it simultaneously infuses many others with insurmountable scepticism about states' ability to comply with high moral standards.

Indeed, no matter how strictly one posits the reservations about the limits of the analogy, critics of this emerging scholarship have noted that speaking seriously about the concept of friendship in the realm of international politics is bound to entail the risk of 'over-analogy and moral fetishism'. This is due to incongruent types of reciprocation between persons and countries, and to stand-ards of impartial public morality and partial morality in private life assigning an inherent moral value to a chosen person (see Keller 2009: 60–65). By and large, it is a familiar argument upon which even such diverse classic writers for con-tending IR traditions as Norman Angell and E.H. Carr could agree. Both Angell and Carr insisted on the difference between individual and state morality; the latter cannot include things such as love, hatred and other intimate emotions. Thus, Angell discards the analogy between state and individual as false, because self-sacrifice, while praised among individuals, is something that states cannot afford. Moreover, it is psychologically impossible to have affection for millions of people living in a different country (1913: 370–376). Similarly, Carr admits that moral impulses are possible in high politics and that states can be altruistic, but only when they can afford it. This being rare, he notes that even individu-als often expect states to be immoral and to prioritise the welfare of their own citizens, thereby discriminating against others. For this reason, Carr dismisses as misplaced the idea of the famous eighteenth-century jurist Christian Wolff that nations should love other nations as themselves (Carr 2001: 143–151).

In fact, this debate over the applicability of friendship and the limits of analogy – which divides observers into the believers of the emerging school of friendship studies and non-believers who are prepared to speak of friendship among states only metaphorically – stems from a common basic assumption intimated above. Both sceptics and believers view friendship along the lines suggested by the ideals of private relations with the ensuing moralisation of all relations so labelled. The difference between these two supposed poles is a matter of degree: some are more prepared to take the analogy seriously and some less, but both see friendship as a moralised practice inherent in human nature. This is the reason why we may feel uncomfortable when relations between states or their leaders are described in terms of friendship. It is also why we cannot account for the prolific rhetoric and institutionalisation of friendship in diplomacy and international politics at large. This sums up the impasse of modern thinking about friendship among nations. A theoretically and politically important question is why we have such an impasse at all and why we have come to recognise an ethical perspective on friendship as the only meaningful way of talking about it.

Questioning the present

The question of how natural this political and disciplinary impasse is, and in fact how contingent it is upon visions of modern international society, can be answered by contrasting it with distant yet recognisable past and other disciplinary domains. The sense of paradox is augmented once we look for conceptions of friendship in fields such as histories of classical political thought and Roman law, in which friendship is not at all an unusual subject and is not a matter of critical valuation of political situations under scrutiny.[3] This is not because relations between political communities in the ancient world were radically better than in our own time, but rather because ancient political practice contained different concepts of friendship that were not necessarily connected to the domains of ethics and normative judgement. Thus, what the modern impasse indicates is nothing less than a conceptual rupture between the past and the present signifying a range of political choices about what should belong to the modern international society of sovereign states and what is bound to be unintelligible. Granted an evolving nature of international society, questioning the conditions that maintain such a rupture becomes a pressing intellectual and political concern.

This study ventures to investigate the nature and conditions of the conceptual change(s) that rendered the classical and presumably alternative concept(s) of friendship virtually unknown and irrelevant to present-day scholarship. In so doing it will explain why friendship is one of the most popular concepts in diplomacy, international law and politics, and yet cannot be analysed as anything other than a moral phenomenon. In other words, this study will offer a perspective on friendship that explicates its functions within the overall international order and the reasons why it was lost in past academic, philosophical and diplomatic debates. It will demonstrate how contingent this loss was on the political rationality of those debates and why the recovered perspective may help us to understand the continuing practice of making friendship among states, as well as the rhetoric of friendship used on some occasions to praise diplomatic engagement and on others swiftly bent to become a morally powerful instrument of critique.

---

[3] Terms such as 'international', 'foreign' and 'treaty' would be utterly anachronistic in an analysis of ancient political practice. Therefore, all instances of such terms henceforth do not represent an attempt to make the phenomena of the ancient world fit our modern categories. Rather, my use of the terms is analytical and only helps the reader to identify the subjects and areas referred to in the analysis.

At least two objections can immediately be raised to the relevance of contrasting friendships of the moderns and ancients. First, today's political and social realities are fundamentally different from those of the ancients. Thus, their conceptual apparatus may not be adequate to grasp the subtleties of modern or post-modern political practice. Secondly, classical teachings on friendship such as Aristotle's *Nicomachean Ethics* or Cicero's *On Friendship* are still parts of our intellectual heritage and appear on curriculums of political theory. Hence, the claim that the concept has been lost might be without substance.

However, the problem of contemporary scholarship lies precisely in its selective focus on classical ethics of friendship. References to authority of the classical injunctions on ethics may not only affirm an all too powerful narrative in the history of political thought, but also frame and constrain our own discussion of contemporary friendship. This original prioritisation of the ethical dimension of friendship is one of the key means to perpetuate a theoretically constraining impasse about political friendship. By grounding our visions in ancient ethical theories, solidified by tradition, we make a choice that helps us overlook a range of other political and international friendships. Thus, current political theorising about friendship tends to ignore a plethora of classical views and references to, for instance, contractual and legal friendship. This is despite the fact that historians and jurists considered these works canonical at least until the seventeenth century, when, as I shall maintain, the ethical and normative perspective on friendship established an intellectual monopoly. Thus, the scope of currently prevailing understanding of friendship and the ways we speak about it might not necessarily be of our own making. Certain present-day wisdoms and observations were formulated in earlier epochs and debates, and we simply take them for granted as standards for our own conduct. In doing so, we adapt a number of ancient relics to present-day practice and make them actual elements of our lives at the level of both language and behaviour.

For instance, Aristotle's notion of friendship is no doubt an artefact of his own time and for this reason alone can be deemed alien to our own culture. However, it inevitably becomes an integral part of our social reality and normative code by way of learning, teaching and citing in scholarly and didactic narratives. Of course, classical teachings are rarely received in one complete package. Theories and concepts are dissolved into constituent elements and appropriated selectively according to the vision and aims of the interested agents. At this point we should ask why it has become natural for contemporary political theorists and IR scholars to look at the writings of Aristotle, Cicero and others for ethical and normative perspectives on friendship, and why it has become *the only way* of understanding the concept (for an exception see Smith 2011). At the same time, if we admit that inter-national friendship seen from an ethical and normative perspective fails to convince a significant number of observers, we should also ask whether this perspective, popularised in the early modern era, prevents us from conceptualising forms of political/'international' friendship familiar to classical authors, their early modern interpreters and modern historians of Antiquity.

Thus, in an attempt to understand the nature of existing theoretical impasse, in this book I follow modern scholarship in tracing conceptions of political friendship back to classical authors. However, I then offer an alternative geneal-ogy that highlights what a theoretical choice, privileging the discussion of ethics, can tell us about our contemporary international society. This alternative geneal-ogy starts with restoring legitimacy to what is commonly discarded as irrelevant, that is, conventional practices described by the Aristotelian concept 'friendship of utility' (Aristotle *NE* VIII, 3–6). I argue that this *political* concept of friend-ship from classical heritage was still available to sixteenth- and seventeenth-century European theologians, jurists and philosophers, who commonly glossed upon its ancient and contemporary application. Re-affirming the plurality of perspectives on political friendship in the classical as well as in the early modern period is key to revealing the contingency of the contemporary divide that exists between sceptic and normative arguments. In fact, reconstructing such plural-ity would be a precondition for a genealogical investigation that would identify points at which it discontinues and a conceptual change occurs that inaugurates a whole new way of thinking about friendship between modern sovereign states that ultimately overrides a political argument by ethical concerns.

The argument

The central argument of this book is that our current understanding of friendship between states, and international society in general, is informed by a profound conceptual change that occurred in the seventeenth and eighteenth centuries. As a result of this change, the alternative concepts of political friendship deployed according to the rules of particular rhetorical genres, ranging from discussions of treaty terms to celebrations of heroic friendships, were effectively replaced with a master ethical and 'naturalistic' perspective. This study posits that central to understanding the transition to modern international society and the formation of early international regimes is the identification of such discarded perspectives on political, contractual and pragmatic friendship. This currently discarded con-cept can be found not only in ancient political thought; but it was also a conven-tional element of a less distant past: learned juridical and political discourses of early modernity recognised friendship as one of the central diplomatic practices, as a type of relationship that is conditional upon negotiated terms and obliga-tions, and as having implications for the exercise of sovereign/supreme power in relation to various political agents.

This book argues that the loss of pragmatic and contractual understanding of friendship in the seventeenth and eighteenth centuries has left today's scholar-ship without the proper means to account for the persisting diplomatic practice of making friendships and its political effects. It is this conceptual change that allowed, for example, the jurist Christian Wolff in the eighteenth century to put forward the claim that nations ought to be friends and love each other. Re-description of the concept in terms of natural and moral demands was part and parcel of political projects that sought to attach a greater legitimacy to the emerging 'society' of absolutist states. This political rationality had set up an idealistic and normative framework for future generations to theorise friendship among nations, while giving good reasons for contemporaries and later thinkers such as E.H. Carr to remain sceptical.

Recovering a lost perspective on political friendship can help us see how this concept accommodates the issues of power in unequal relations of a divided world and the contingency of forged friendly ties to political circumstances. Thus, it would help us understand friendship as a political agreement, the terms of which could be negotiated, re-negotiated and, possibly, declared void depending on the dynamics of a political situation. Re-introducing this concept would demonstrate that diplomatic rhetoric of friendship is not just lip service, leading us to castigate it as insincere, bogus and unworthy of a serious discussion, but an essential part of generating legitimacy, both domestically and internationally, for the agreed upon policies. The debate opened in this way may eventually transcend the opposition of realism and idealism over the issues of international friendship and rhetoric. As the offered genealogical conceptual history[4] will demonstrate, concerns over power are inherently linked to the uses of friendship in intellectual debates and diplomatic practices (often, but not always, institutionalised).

Focusing on the nexus of concepts and diplomatic practices is central to the argument of this book, as it shows how deeply friendship was woven into the institutional fabric of an early modern international society, how diplomatic use of the concept helped to constitute the nascent institutions and how it may still be employed in international politics. The book will identify the constitutive functions of friendship, that is, sets of practices designated by the concept domestically and internationally. Highlighting political friendship in the constitution of pre-modern polities challenges a powerful Westphalian narrative about the monopolisation of authority by the sovereign state and recognition of state sovereignty as a foundational principle of a new international system. Identifying the use of friendship in diplomatic relations with similar European polities and polities outside Europe, deemed 'uncivilised' in colonial discourses, will indicate how instrumental this concept was for ensuring the sanctity of agreements in the New and Old Worlds, drawing dividing lines between competing loci of author-

---

[4] Conceptual history is a term used predominantly in continental Europe to refer to approaches focusing on the history of concepts. In what follows I will use both terms interchangeably.

ity, facilitating the colonisation of North America and India, and the emergence of new independent states.

This book suggests that without an insight into the institutionalisation and conceptualisation of friendship, research into the expansion of the international society prompted by the founding fathers of the English School (see Bull and Watson 1984) would remain incomplete. The study of the concept of friendship will cast a critical light on the fundamental institutions of international society, such as international law, diplomacy and great power management (on institutions of anarchical society see Bull 2002: 71). The status of 'international law' has been one of the most disputed subjects since John Austin's qualification of international law as international morality (Austin 1885, 1: 231–232). This qualification corresponds to a central IR assumption about anarchy at the international level: there is no central lawgiver, nor an ultimate adjudicator, nor a supreme power that would ensure law enforcement (for a classical distinction of hierarchical and anarchical political orders see Waltz 1979: 114–116). Most influential attempts to rescue international law from this intellectual assault turned to the idea of (international) society, law as a recurrent and observable societal practice, and law as intersubjectively held ideas, that is, to the understanding of law as existing 'between' states rather than law commanded from 'above' (Koskenniemi 2002; Nardin 1999; Oppenheim 1905; Suganami 2008).

However, the nature of international law and obligation remains a politically contested matter. No consensual definition of international law seems to be in view. Against the backdrop of such discontent, Friedrich Kratochwil in his recent 'meditations' suggested that, instead of looking for a definition, it is best to think of international law as a language game and see what it does and how it is played (Kratochwil 2014: particularly 68–74). In this broadly constructivist agenda the focus shifts towards the performative and illocutionary, rather than representative, functions of language and rhetoric. For it is maintained that these functions make certain rules legal and binding (see Onuf 1989: 77–87).

This study focuses on the early modern period when religion and kinship were no longer able to offer rule enforcement; hence alternative tools facilitating compliance were in high demand. It is argued that contractual friendships were among key diplomatic instruments to maintain the binding character of new political arrangements and, thus, to substitute for a lack of central authority. Therefore, it is not accidental that already the Renaissance diplomacy witnessed a sharp rise in friendship agreements (Lesaffer 2002). The authority of friendship could be augmented by nothing other than references to an existing record of making friendships and rhetoric with which relevant audiences were persuaded to observe friendly duties. This study will demonstrate how friendship became constitutive of legal regimes that would be fully developed by way of specialisation only under a modern system. A number of duties and rights pertinent to commerce and navigation, and to a more traditional area of alliance-making, were accepted by states and princes as a result of formal friendly arrangements, which indicates how instrumental were these extra-legal, although contractual, political means.

Contractual friendship in diplomacy challenged the distinction of anarchy and hierarchy on yet another count. As will be argued, political and contractual friendships were not always made on equal footing. In fact, contrary to a common expectation of equality in friendship, diplomatic relations bearing this name underpinned international hierarchies and the whole project of European colonisation. The rhetoric of friendship proved sensitive to the roles friends needed to perform either by explicitly recognising the superiority of one friend over another or by making parties accept arrangements under which one party would enjoy greater rights over certain critical issues, but not necessarily all (e.g. possession or control over a certain territory or a right to independent foreign policy). In this sense, the study not only posits that the modern international system is compatible with hierarchical orders (cf. Keene 2002; Lake 2009) but also demonstrates how it was brought about and legitimised by rhetoric of friendship in European colonial projects in North America and India in the seventeenth to nineteenth centuries.

This is exactly what research in history of concepts helps us achieve by looking at the peripheries of dominant and habitual perspectives both in space and time. Thus, it would be difficult to ascertain the role of friendship in contemporary international society if one only looked at how, for instance, the Soviets proclaimed friendship and brotherhood with China or members of the Warsaw Pact. Looking at the historical and geographical 'margins' of our international society can help us identify practices and principles of modern rules and institutions that nowadays are shuttered by rhetorical recognition of formal state sovereignty. As this study is about concepts, their contestation and negotiation, it will concentrate more on the history of the British Empire and the foundation of the United States of America. Britain was a relative latecomer in the colonisation project, and faced in North America circumstances very different from those in South America. Coercion, which was the key instrument in the Spanish conquest, could not be employed to the same effect in the North. Other means, including numerous agreements of friendship with native peoples, had to be found (for a comparison of Spanish and English colonisation see Acemoglu and Robinson 2013: 20–26). This is the main reason why this study will trace English diplomatic and colonial practices, which I also recognise as one of the main cultural and intellectual limitations of this book.

Changes in the language of 'international' agreements are always more incremental than changes motivated by radical turns in intellectual debates, as the former are predicated on the acceptance by parties of an agreement which, in turn, is achieved by couching the subject in recognisable terms limiting the opportunities for contending interpretations. This language, deployed at the peripheries of European society, has for much of European colonial history retained elements of contractual friendship and their utility to the institutions and norms that make up this society (in international nomos friendship replicates a relationship between constituent and constituted power so acutely analysed by Giorgio Agamben in case of sovereignty, law and exception; see Agamben 1998: particularly I: 1–4; 2005: 88). The expansion of European society required negotiating with members-to-be or those to whom membership was denied what had already become an unnoticeable, naturalised norm in relations among members of 'civilised' society. While in the European society of states ideas about rules were increasingly seen in terms of natural law, at the periphery rules and compliance often hinged on contingent agreements, in which binding force stemmed from political friendships. For this reason the focus on concepts and linguistic practices reveals that 'contractual' and 'contingent' arrangements were as important to the emergence of European society of absolute states as was a shift to 'naturalistic' theories of law in intellectual debates (cf. Reus-Smit 2009: 104–106). The conceptual change featuring in these debates was one of the reasons why political and legal theory failed to recognise that peripheral practices of building imperial orders and constituting new states proliferated on such curious grounds as political friendship.

One reservation is due, however, about the link of friendship to contract. The contractual concept of friendship that this book seeks to recover with the view to reappraise the constitution of international order does not build on the idea of contract in a strict sense, in which parties make reciprocal promises that can be enforced by law/a law-enforcing agency. Clearly, in international friendships no one other than friends themselves or 'friends of friends' can enforce obligations. Therefore, the attribute 'contractual' in the concept of contractual friendship denotes only a number of elements that pertain to the idea of a formal contract and grasps only those parts of the language game that emphasise the agreed upon, promised or merely assured obligations. Thus, what this concept will illuminate for the reader are ways in which polities and rulers sought to oblige one another and amplify an accepted/imposed obligation by its subsequent legitimation. If such friendship does not presuppose external sources of enforcement, we are led to consider 'extra-legal' ways to ensure compliance; hence the politics of language games constituting friendly obligations and international orders becomes of ultimate importance.

Studying concepts

Language and politics

Ever since the linguistic turn in social sciences, texts have been understood as forms of contingent political action. Language is therefore not a neutral medium or container of objective means to express views or describe political phenomena, but is a political tool and manifestation of politics (Austin 1975; Ball 1997; Rorty 1989: chap. 1; Skinner 1989a). The basic assumption behind this understanding, in Peter Winch's famous formulation, is that 'the concepts we have settle for us the form of the experience we have of the world' (Winch 1990: 15; see also Pitkin 1972: 121). It further means that, in order to portray some phenomenon in a positive or negative light – or simply as existing rather than as imaginary – and thereby try to direct public reactions in a profitable way, a political agent has to choose words accordingly and manipulate their application to the case in question.

If politics is about rival interpretations of events and actions couched in carefully selected terms and styled to provoke certain public reactions, we should not assume that language and its constitutive elements are neutral phenomena secondary to politics. Instead, the concepts we have and their application will always be inherently contested by contending political parties. It does not mean that regularities in the use of concepts are impossible, because this would render communication equally impossible. Linguistic conventions are by nature expressions of a temporary social and political status quo, while the politics of contending factions consist in challenging these conventions or extending their application to new cases (for more on these arguments see Skinner 2002a: chapters 4, 8).

My next assumption is that political agents – to the ranks of which I include diplomats, political theorists, jurists, philosophers, publicists and the like – try to win approbation from their immediate audience as a way to achieve their aims. Therefore, the use of concepts and formulation of arguments is contingent upon the specific circumstances of the agents, while their aims are always audience-adjusted. I share this underlying assumption with the burgeoning literature of 'contextualist' international studies, much of which is informed by Quentin Skinner's methodological works on linguistic action (see *inter alia* Armitage 2000; Bell 2007; Jahn 2006; Keene 2002, 2005; Tuck 1999): The concepts and corresponding arguments should not then be taken as responding to eternal truths or describing the essence of eternal phenomena, even if their authors try to appropriate this role for them. Instead, the use of concepts and arguments is tailored to a specific situation of an actor and can be interpreted by way of close scrutiny of the context.

Claims such as this became a major challenge to theories that try to assemble very heterogeneous intellectual contributions made millennia apart under one umbrella of ostensibly universal questions of human nature, power, interest and war. What has become a 'contextualist' and 'historiographic' turn in international relations primarily focusing on international political thought (Armitage 2013; Bell 2002; Holden 2002) effectively questioned the construction of such IR teleologies, or 'Whig' histories (cf. Butterfield 1965), whose main political function was to add legitimacy to contemporary arguments about the nature of politics at the expense of historical accuracy.

Concepts and meaning

Insofar as concepts are inherently contested and used to advocate a specific idea or course of action, we cannot presuppose that concepts have a fixed meaning accessible to anyone regardless of their background. Along the lines of Ludwig Wittgenstein's observation that 'the meaning of a word is its use in the language', it is argued that the meaning of a concept is played out in particular language games (see Wittgenstein 2001: para. 7, 43). Put differently, in a given political context a concept would be used by actors with a view to defend their own distinct, sometimes intersecting but frequently conflicting, views and aims. With these underlying assumptions, fixing the meaning of a concept would be a daunting task.

This is not to say that actors have a free hand in ascribing meaning to a concept, because they need to make sense to their audience in the first place. Statements such as 'war is peace' would only make sense in a particular context, that is, that of George Orwell's '1984'. Thus, to deliver a message successfully an actor would need to follow recognisable linguistic conventions and choose from an available range of things that could be done with the concept in a particular context and time (Palonen 2003: 41; Skinner 2002a: 101–102). The study of concepts would therefore require scrutinising the prevailing conventions, or language games, of a period: who plays the game, by what rules, and to what effect.

To this end, this book will not be searching for the most accurate definitions of 'ethical', 'natural' and 'contractual' concepts of friendship in past contexts, nor will it offer any such. Instead, it will identify the rules of political language games that make up the concepts in question. It will focus on the terminology of friendship (e.g. words that refer to the concept of friendship such as '*amicitia*', '*societas*', '*amitié*', 'amity' and 'friendship'), vocabulary that attributes to friendship certain qualities (e.g. adjectives that describe its psychological, ethical or legal nature), grammar that defines the range of actions that friendship could be made to perform (e.g. verbs that demonstrate how actors make, maintain and use friendships), and any other regularities that indicate the presence of rules, or linguistic conventions, which make the rhetoric of friendship and its comprehension by the relevant audience possible.

Words that help express a concept are basic indicators that research in the history of concepts would need to trace (for a similar methodological injunction in *Begriffsgeschichte* see Richter 1995: 44). As Skinner observed, concepts that a society possesses are predicated on the corresponding vocabulary with which these concepts could be discussed with consistency (Skinner 2002a: 160). Words are not the same as concepts that constitute the edifice of politics and political thought. But an arrangement of words that follows a loosely defined pattern would reflect a social and political status quo and a possession of concept by a particular society (Skinner 1989a: 8). For this simple reason, political action that goes beyond the bounds of what is acceptable, yet builds on a number of values associated with the status quo, would require its advocates to rhetorically modify the linguistic conventions that regulate the application of concepts relevant to such an action. By the same token, isolating a corresponding conceptual change would hinge on a basic contrast of the past convention with what has established itself as a novelty, rather than an aberration, in the use of friendship in discourses of and about international politics.

To make a strong case for a change, that is, render it politically significant, studies in conceptual history start by reconstructing what was conventional in the first place. This book will guide a reader through a documented story about the alternative ways of using the concept and 'doing things' with friendship. In other words, it will demonstrate which conventional alternatives to a 'moralised' friendship had existed before they were side-lined and made incomprehensible in modernity. To this effect the book selects a number of examples ranging from classical to modern sources to show how exactly these distinct uses of friendship figured in political rhetoric and what difference they made.

For instance, to identify how exactly the term '*amicitia*' was involved in a 'contractual' language game in diplomatic sources of the late medieval–early modern period, this study will scrutinise a range of associated words (i.e. verbs and adjectives) that were used across a body of various 'treaties' and pacts and thus were part of 'contractual' language. A detailed scrutiny of the vocabulary used by the parties in specific contexts would be prerequisite to establishing linguistic conventions in corresponding genres and tracing their incremental transformations over extended periods of time. It is on the grounds of identified regularities that contractual vocabulary of friendship will be isolated. The selection will thus be a matter of observation, rather than a preconception of what counts as contractual; hence, some expressions, such as 'mutual' or 'constant friendship', found in treaty texts and legal commentaries, which may seem to a modern reader as pertaining to an altogether different vocabulary, would be identified as a manifestation of friendship's 'contractual' meaning. A reconstructed contractual convention will indicate how friendship performed a binding function in the absence of any established international regimes and courts. It is this convention that had to be modified, even if incrementally, for impersonalised actors, such as modern sovereign state and empire, to integrate it into the system of binding relations cemented by numerous friendships and further transform it into the rules of contemporary international society.

By no means do changes in vocabularies and rhetoric, which makes use of them, follow a uniform pattern in heterogeneous language games. As a newspaper columnist and an incumbent minister are likely to discuss budget cuts in different terms, likewise Aristotle's *Nicomachean Ethics*, Hugo Grotius's *The Rights of War and Peace* and a corpus of early 'international' pacts used friendship according to the rules of language games that were not necessarily identical. Some of these games comprised histories and accounts of existing practices and customs; others regulated ways to raise philosophical questions about the nature of genuine friendship and provided room for rhetorical responses; yet others, for example formal agreements, displayed stricter rules that only allowed customary copying of specific terms in recognisable statements. This has important implications for the patterns of use and dynamics of conceptual change: whereas some games allow for a conceptual change necessitated by a new philosophy or a trend in political thought, others display a more incremental trajectory of conceptual adaptation and modification. The latter is typical of diplomatic conventions in drafting 'international' agreements, which proved crucial for the history of contractual friendship. Due to a degree of inertia in legal customs and 'regimes' among nations, this domain conserved elements of conspicuously contractual friendship in the modern world.

Key to understanding different 'international societies', as well as the legitimacy and authority they ascribe to rules, is which of these games they recognise and whether these games can intertwine by occasionally building on the tropes and arguments of each other. Friendship is one such indicator of language games unfolding in modern European society and, by extension, global international society, showing how rules are negotiated, enacted and cemented. For instance, in early modern Europe it was possible to overtly negotiate the scope and subject of friendship – perhaps an unthinkable practice in contemporary friendships; it was equally legitimate to praise the virtues of a friend who had no interest in practical outcomes of the relationship; and, more importantly, on occasion actors could employ 'ethical', that is, extra-legal, arguments to cement the terms of an 'international' pact and exhort their counterparts to observe them. The interplay of these linguistic games gives us clues as to how polities 'oblige' others, why a friend should have 'duties', why we expect reciprocation in friendship, and the means of inaugurating binding 'regimes' and agreements in the formative junctures of international societies that may have lacked central authority to enforce 'law'. The power of this clue is hard to overestimate should we only contrast juridical narratives of the sixteenth century – allegedly mediating a transition to a modern international society – , which recognised the utility of friendship-making in relations among polities, to the juridical arguments of the eighteenth century that lacked any such recognition and posited friendship as a product of nature and the natural foundation of society. The shift from one linguistic game to the other is ultimately a subject of conceptual history and international political theory. This is also the agenda that contextualist studies of concepts share with an IR constructivist literature stressing the role of rules in international politics (see Onuf 1989).

Genealogies and conceptual change

Contested concepts

Describing historical events and processes is the task commonly performed by historians. International political theory is interested in historical changes not for their own sake but for what these changes say about the present-day knowledge of international politics and the role of power in formation of such knowledge. Since the 1980s international political theory and political theory have developed and incorporated a range of methodological tools to analyse changes in language, both historically and politically. At the forefront of this research are variations of contextualism, including the history of concepts, and genealogy. These aim at critical re-evaluation of currently prevailing principles and values, and at creating room for re-consideration of marginalised alternatives. The aim is predicated on commitment to anti-whiggish and anti-teleological writing of history (for an opposition of 'whiggism' and 'usable past' see Kratochwil 2014). These approaches engage with the past by way of contextualisation and subsequent identification of the contingency of beliefs and ruptures in political traditions.

This book will practise a particular combination of the history of concepts and genealogy connected by the idea of rhetorical contestation. In doing so it will build on insights from genealogical research and Quentin Skinner's methodological injunctions. As this is not a conventional technique in international political theory, a few explanations are due as to how the two combine and what difference it makes politically. The history of concepts, as a research programme, seeks to demonstrate what change in the meaning of concepts is about and how it can be political. Political theorists argue that the aim of the history of concepts is *par excellence* political (for an elaboration of this argument see Palonen 2002) in the sense that it demonstrates how the past might inform our own thinking or how concepts and institutions forged in past ideological battles might be constitutive of policies made in the present. In this way it reveals contingency of political beliefs and identifies alternatives that can help us reflect upon and reassess today's prevailing social conventions and their normative agendas (ibid.: 103).

The factors of contingency and contestation in the use of political concepts can be assessed only by way of detailed scrutiny of the context in which these concepts are used. Placing concepts in context means that we show how they are used in specific documents and by particular authors. Such an exercise allows shifting one's perspective on concepts from that of metaphysical units to one of practical tools helping to express the user's views and opinion. This shift is instrumental to arriving at a basic understanding that all concepts are necessarily contested by their users either at the level of definitions or at the level of innovative application in political rhetoric.

As Skinner maintained, concepts and values are amenable to rhetorical re-description, thereby admitting no standard or stable meaning of a particular concept (Skinner 2002a: 182; Palonen 2003: 163). Thus, all claims about the contingency of concepts are not about 'mere' contingency, but imply a demon-stration of alternatives formulated in the lexicon of their protagonists. It appears, then, that any concept held for whatever reason to be dominant is in fact a mani-festation of its approval and acceptance by the relevant audience. This, however, does not eliminate the possibility of alternative ways of formulating and using the concept that may well have been in circulation in the same period and that, after retrieval, can tell us as much about the political context as the dominant account.

Skinner, an influential protagonist of this approach (see, for instance, Skinner 1989b), in his later essays adopted the term 'genealogy' to describe a type of his-tory of concepts he is doing (Skinner 2009, 2012), but the task of such research he had already formulated in *Liberty before Liberalism* (1998). It consisted, he wrote, in recovering alternative 'perspectives' and bringing his reader to 'rumi-nate' what was recovered for her (Skinner 1998; for ways in which this task draws upon Weberian and Nietzschean thought see Palonen 2003: 25, 2005; Skinner 1999, 2006). Basically, Skinner expects his readers to do the thinking themselves when presented with unfamiliar past perspectives on a subject and account of conceptual change (Skinner 2002a: 88).

Effective history

Skinner's approach was questioned by a number of critics. One of the key criti-cisms concerns the problem of political relevance, for it is not always clear how exactly such a conceptual genealogy links past debates to present-day knowledge and politics. Skinner's original contribution to theory consisted in destabilising the existing teleological histories or traditions. It proved to be a blow to the pil-lars of contemporary theories with their teleological, self-legitimating interpreta-tion of history. However, destabilisation by means of contextualising historical accounts does not always effectively engage contemporary debates. This is one of the reasons for some contemporary genealogists, who build on Nietzsche's obser-vations, to see this result as unable to make any difference. For them, Nietzsche's genealogy must aim at radical 'debunking' of current beliefs, which Skinner's genealogy allegedly does not deliver (an argument put forward by Lane 2012).

Skinner himself admits that his studies are not meant to totally debunk a system of thought or morality, as was the aim of Nietzsche's *Genealogy of Morality*. Instead, it is the reader who should do her part of the job. Translating this debate into the question of relevance for the audience of political and inter-national theorists means that genealogical research needs to make a clear connec-tion between unsettling the past and contesting present-day knowledge. Thus, what needs to be emphasised is the task of writing what is called an 'effective history', that is, history that engages present-day theories and ideologies. Being effective is a political dimension of the genealogical investigation into the history of friendship. The genealogical effect of this study will consist in equipping the reader with the means to render meaningful those friendships in world politics that seem incomprehensible, bizarre or insincere. It will also reopen contemporary debates privileging ethical, normative and emotional aspects of friendship by explicating the room for power and politics in friendship. It is for this reason that I take as a starting point the above-described contemporary discussions of international friendship and their classical authorities on the subject of friendship. Reconstructing a conceptual alternative in the past will eventually help us see how friendship was used politically in critical junctures in the history of the international system. Only in this sense can one claim that this genealogical approach delivers on the aim of debunking. And only this kind of relationship to the present makes a genealogical approach 'effective' in the Nietzschean and Foucauldian understanding of the term (Foucault 1991,2002; Saar 2008: 298).

One problem with a genealogical history of concepts is that making sense of past statements may run into the fallacy of presentism. Therefore, any attempt to examine present-day political arrangements by way of showing historical contingencies needs to address a problem of translation: the language games of past debates may not be comprehensible to contemporary audiences or may not speak directly to our problems. Although translating the observables into categories of analysis may help our comprehension, it may also unintentionally produce a presentist bias and cause misrepresentation of vital knowledge of the past (for the effects of such presentist bias see Bartelson 1995: 66–67; Richter 1995: 132). Insofar as we do not aim to reproduce historical texts in full and in original language, there is no unequivocal solution to the problem of presentism (for more on this problem as well as for its ingenious qualification as 'original sin' of historians see Syrjämäki 2011). Nevertheless, there are ways at least to mitigate the effects of such bias and keep the results 'falsifiable'. One of these ways is in recognition of 'perspectivism' rather than 'objectivism' of any research orientation (Max Weber was among the first to defend this principle in social sciences, see Weber 2004). Thus, the main aim of this study will consist in identifying a conceptual alternative that can help us make sense of political friendship. As such, this aim does not presuppose the recovery of the past context in full, and thus leaves the argument open for modification or even refutation. Similarly, this study is not about tailoring past concepts to present-day needs and adapting them to a teleological or continuist interpretation of history. Instead, it will recover only one of the possible perspectives and thus cannot claim to recover a full history of friendship among nations, which is way too broad a field geographically, chronologically and thematically to be covered in one book.

Furthermore, presently genealogy, similarly to the history of concepts, stands more for a research programme than for a philosophical task (Vucetic 2011).

By recognising an inextricable knot of power and knowledge (Foucault 2002) it works as a reminder of the fact that our interest in the past is driven by present-day concerns. Apart from this well-known self-exposition, it also holds commitment to identification of the strange and unknown, rather than a confirmation of tradition. Its ultimate task is to render strange the conventional. However, it is up to an author to determine what would be sufficient for achieving this task. Therefore, in its quest to question the currently prevalent ethical naturalistic perspective on friendship, this book seeks to uncover what used to be its powerful alternative, the loss of which, as will be demonstrated, was informed by the power struggle over the basic concepts of contemporary international society. If a crucial alternative, vital to the constitution of contemporary society, is identified in the scope of undertaking, then there is no need to exhaust the degrees of strangeness; that task could be left to further studies aiming to extend the horizons of our thinking.

Following this precept the study will unfold the current ideas of friendship back to their self-styled intellectual origins, that is, the ethical works of Aristotle and Cicero, situate these 'origins' within relevant contexts and language games by way of contrast to legal discourses and historical narratives, and then identify political choices and ideological principles that determined the selective use of classics in a historical juncture that is conventionally held as constitutive to modern international society. Thus, the periods examined in this study are nothing new for the textbook chronological canon of IR theory, as nearly every textbook identifies Thucydides, Niccolò Machiavelli and Thomas Hobbes as classical realist thinkers (Donnelly 2013: 34–36; Jackson and Sørensen 2010: 60–65; Lebow 2013: 60). A closer contextualist reading of these periods shows how selective existing canons are in focusing primarily on power, state and sovereignty for the purpose of increasing their own legitimacy, while overlooking potentially destabilising arguments, values and lexicon shared by the political agents of the past. Whereas Thucydides, Machiavelli and Hobbes are important figures in the conceptual history of friendship, the arguments they contribute to the relevant debates indicate how essential this concept was for understandings of 'power', 'sovereignty' and 'security' in the wider context of historical narratives and theorising of the law of nature and nations, as well as political philosophy. It is therefore critical even for realist thought to analyse classical arguments in context to see what was at stake in discussions of the phenomena in which it is primarily interested.

Furthermore, instead of a 'tradition' of thinking about friendship, in what follows the reader will encounter an analysis of contending visions and politically motivated conceptual choices. For this reason alone, it is critical for our investigation to start with a scrutiny of friendship uses in most popular classical works to be able to see which of the main *topoi* remained popular or in some demand among authors who we usually take as the founding fathers of modern

international thought. As the Renaissance and early modern thought were creatively appropriating Antiquity, it is instructive to single out basic conventional
uses that classical sources made of friendship. Hence, the genealogies of phenomena such as friendship are often bound to start in the classical period to be able to
explain the rupture, if any, with the modern world (cf. Skinner 2000a).

   The type of genealogy and history of a concept I propose in this book combines
intellectual history and diplomatic practice. Thus, it examines how friendship
figures not only in historical and philosophical narratives but also in diplomatic
pronouncements and in treaty texts. This is key to understanding whether the
lenses of juridical and political theory lost the political practice of friendship
from their focus, and, if so, when and how this might have happened. If one
only traced the history of words back to Antiquity, the case of friendship would
have displayed an astonishing and, perhaps, unmatched conceptual continuity
stretching over two millennia. It would have looked like nations always used
the corresponding term in diplomacy. Indeed, there was no period in recorded
history when friendship was not used in politics among nations. The only thing
that varied was the words expressing the term: a Greek '*philia*' in ancient Greece
and medieval Byzantium, a Latin '*amicitia*' in Rome and throughout the Middle
Ages in Europe, a French 'amitié' in the period of Francophone diplomacy, and
the English words 'amity' and 'friendship' in a later Anglo-Saxon diplomatic tradition. In addition, many other vernacular languages in the early modern period
quickly supplied relevant diplomatic agencies with their own terms.

   In what follows I will seek to reconstruct this practice with the aim to demonstrate a long diplomatic alternative to the philosophical reflection on the ethics
of friendship. However, neither of the alternatives remained intact throughout
the history of diplomacy. The use of friendship in intellectual reflection and
diplomatic practice underwent many nuanced transformations, and looking at
these helps us see to what ends friendship was used in different contexts. These
ends could have been descriptive, normative, constitutive or contractual. Not all
of these were captured in intellectual reflection. Thus, in order to properly reconstruct the conceptual alternative, I will scrutinise the main conventional ways
of using friendship in the formative junctures of past and modern international
societies. This scrutiny will contain specific examples of treaties, pacts and letters
using friendship and its corresponding vocabulary. What will transpire from
such scrutiny is an ensemble of distinct speech acts and terms performing unique
functions in often-incongruent contexts, all of which make up a variety of forms
that the alternative concept of friendship took in different regions and over time.
Despite the multiplicity of forms and uses, many of them share a number of
conventional elements that make them part of the same conceptual 'world'.

   These elements include a range of negotiated subjects: local 'regulative
regimes' regarding commerce, law and territory; the status of great powers and
hierarchy; recognition of new members of international society. It will become

clear that continuity in the custom of using friendship in diplomacy is about the utility of friendship in constituting political forms and 'regimes' under the condition of international 'anarchy'. At the same time, behind the curtains of continuity our analysis of diplomatic speech acts will demonstrate how the use of the term varies across contexts. Changes in diplomacy may be incremental and gradual, as diplomats have to refer to, and thereby reproduce and construct, 'traditions' and customs. This explains why certain diplomatic instruments are routinely borrowed with degrees of uniformity and survive through history. But it does not always explain the contingent circumstances in which the instruments are employed. By looking into such invocations we will identify the discrepant functions in the corresponding international orders that friendship was put to perform. It is from these functions, which diplomacy assigned to friendship in specific periods, that one could reconstruct its context-specific meaning. As a result of such exposition the history of friendship will reappear as a 'discontinuous continuity' reflecting changes in international societies themselves.

Rhetoric, continuity and change

Conceptual continuity can be part of intellectual reflection, too. Many disciplines are predicated on the construction and perpetuation of a 'tradition', which legitimises a certain system of teaching. Thus, Friedrich Kratochwil noted the importance of the past and 'tradition' in law, where knowledge of the past is 'handed down' to settle the problems of the contemporary world (Kratochwil 2014: 68–69). The thirst for political and disciplinary legitimacy will be in the spotlight of this study. Deliberate attempts to legitimise certain principles and rules require the use of rhetoric in context. As a result, conceptual continuity and change will be understood as products of rhetorical strategies employed either to maintain the status quo or bring about change. Looking at concepts as rhetorical tools will explain how the corresponding terms remained parts of conventional theoretical vocabulary but at a certain point in time ceased to capture the practice of contractual friendship in the analysis of international politics.

The point of change is a matter of central concern for any international and political theory. This study will inquire into the conceptual change that friendship underwent and explicate how this change may be constitutive to the foundations of modern international society. From the perspective of rhetorical use of concepts in particular disciplines (arguments, more often than not, are formulated polemically to refute opponents or earlier beliefs and use amplification techniques to persuade the audience), the genealogist's task will be in identifying the contexts in which the use of the alternative concept of friendship was appropriate, and the arguments which managed to change its range of reference predominantly to ethics and normative discussion.

This book will identify one central period of rhetorical re-description in the early modern period that produced the currently prevailing normative and 'naturalistic' perspective on friendship. Rhetorical analysis of this period will examine authorial arguments, their relevant contexts and language games before and after the conceptual change. It will do so in order to show how the new perspective related to and superseded previous concepts of friendship, and outline its effects on subsequent diplomatic, legal and political theory and practice. It will show in which works it was common to make use of friendship, how early modern authors (jurists, philosophers, poets, etc.) borrowed from the classical tradition and from which sources they typically borrowed, and why at some point it became expedient within the same fields to borrow arguments and examples from drastically different contexts and build normative rather than descriptive arguments.

Contextual and rhetorical analysis will indicate how the use of friendship was contingent on various factors, such as power positions in particular political settings and the entrepreneurial needs of merchant, colonial, state and other agencies. Depending on such circumstances, actors could choose which rhetorical strategy to deploy, which set of values to endorse and which terms to use. This amounts to a simple observation that in such heterogeneous circumstances values and concepts cannot be the same. Concepts are constantly rhetorically described and re-described, and thus can be interpreted with the help of classic rhetorical figures. One such figure is the *paradiastole*, which allows agents to substitute one thing for another within the range of reference of the same concept. Once such re-description is identified in a historical context, we may claim to have observed an instance of conceptual change (see Skinner 1996: 150–151; 2007: 163). However, to claim that a change in the use of a concept had taken place it is essential to demonstrate whether the innovative use became a convention, that is, was taken up as an authoritative and common use within a particular field or discipline. Therefore, the book will pay attention not only to an innovative use of concepts but also provide examples of what was conventional and how novelty gradually became a convention.

Rhetorical analysis allows for integrating power into the understanding of conceptual change. Political actors use concepts and arguments to defend certain values or a course of action which are often opposed by the parties maintaining alternative views. Thus, concepts that become prevailing and conventional, side-lined and marginalised, or re-described to refer to a different set of practices and values, are necessarily reflections of the changes in the political status quo indicating losses and victories in rhetorical battles. This study will thus attempt to connect specific uses of concepts with particular political outlooks, genres of argumentation and thematic contexts. Establishing this connection is necessary to identify political functions that both innovative and conventional statements, uses of concepts and doctrines may perform. Such a political rationality is not always self-evident, for things are often taken for granted or simply as a matter of custom which emerged in response to a concrete problem long ago and subsequently solidified into routine practice. Reconstructing the alternative concept of friendship may help us see exactly this: the power positions and sets of values that we do not tend to notice or take as problematic due to the 'naturalised', ethical concept of friendship integrated into contemporary ideas about international society. However, in declaring this aim one final caveat is due: this study is not about the thought of particular authors and its development; rather, it concerns the history of arguments and uses of the concept to which those authors contributed.

Structure

In the first chapter I analyse a number of classical sources and their use of terms such as *philia* and *amicitia* expressing the concept of friendship. This analysis posits that ancient Greece, Rome and other Mediterranean powers possessed at least two concepts of friendship, which were used conventionally and legitimately. The first conventionally referred to a set of ethical relations binding together two or more individuals. This concept is familiar to modern audiences primarily from Aristotle's *Nicomachean Ethics* or Cicero's *On Friendship*, and is a commonplace starting point for discussions of friendship in IR. The second, usually overlooked, captures political relations between members of the same political community, such as kings, cities and peoples. As such, the second concept could be free from the burden of ethical standards, and could refer solely to political relations marked by degrees of contingency and pragmatism. When such relations went wrong, the agents involved could well appeal to standards of ethical friendship in order to legitimise their present situation and future conduct. But in many more cases the second concept designated the establishment of political and legal order based on a political contract of friendship on specific terms. This contractual and contingent nature of political friendship was manifested in a number of classical works ranging from Thucydides to Titus Livy and the legal landmark of the sixth century, the *Digest of Justinian*. In fact, this concept was also identified in the *Nicomachean Ethics* as friendship of utility, but has been discarded by modern scholars as an inferior type of friendship. This chapter restores friendship of utility in its own right by identifying its conventional use and a range of political practices it helped to explain.

The second chapter plays a key role in recovering a perspective on contractual political friendship that was abandoned in the formative period of modern international politics. In contrast to the common critique of the instrumental use of friendship, this chapter outlines sixteenth- and seventeenth-century arguments that used the concept to portray actual power and legal relations. For the authors of these arguments, the use of friendship was not a matter of masking unjust social and political arrangements; rather, it was one of the concepts commonly used to describe 'non-institutionalised' – and on occasion 'institutionalised' –

political relations, which took a variety of forms. For them friendship was a contingent power resource that could be mobilised, negotiated, contracted and consequently breached. For this reason it was an inherently particular concept that could designate both equal and unequal distributions of obligations between partners. In this chapter I trace the incremental changes in the vocabulary of diplomatic documents, in both Latin and early vernacular versions, in order to identify contractual manifestations of friendship terms at the level of the grammar of 'international' politics. I demonstrate how deeply the concept was entrenched in the historical and juridical discourses of the period, and how authors of treatises used it conventionally to refer to certain types of treaty specifying a number of binding obligations concerning trade, alliances, neutrality and territorial integrity. In the absence of the institution of state sovereignty and developed international trade and navigation regimes, protracted legal debates highlight that agreements about friendship in the early modern period played an analogous role to these contemporary institutions. The residues of this institution and a degree of path dependency explain why the diplomatic practice of making formal friendship treaties or merely naming counterparts as friends still persists in the contemporary world. It is also this context that sheds light on our tendency to conflate, indeed for good reason, friendship with alliance or trade partnerships.

In the third chapter I show that Humanist authors of the early modern period indeed possessed at least two alternative concepts of friendship expressed using the same terms. The second concept – highly moralised and normative – was no less prominent in political and philosophical discourses, and no less important for the understanding of modern European international perspectives. Moralist discussions of political friendship and its defence of virtue indeed provide completely different perspectives, as they draw attention to the contradiction between duties of office and duties to a friend, problematic relations between ruler and ruled, and possible compromises of both power and friendship. More importantly, however, moralist discourses highlight the emerging set of values for the European 'republic' of commonwealths. Virtuous friendship was envisioned by a range of authors from Erasmus to English republican writers of the revolutionary period as a foundation of a proper international constitution. I also argue that Humanist authors first formulated a critical argument against princely friendship, for when contrasted with ideals of genuine and sincere friendship their friendship was often portrayed as feigned and detrimental to the good of the European 'republic'. Nonetheless, in early modern political thought the contractual concept and moralised normative concept of friendship co-existed, while their rules of application helped political agents to substitute one range of reference for the other when circumstances suggested such a rhetorical manoeuvre. This chapter also seeks to stress that the later conceptual change did not consist in a linear chronological replacement of the old contractual concept with a new one.

The fourth chapter is central to the argument of the book, as it analyses the seventeenth- and eighteenth-century debates that conditioned the change in the identified prevailing perspectives on friendship. It explores the reasons why the contractual and contingent concept of friendship disappeared from learned philosophical, juridical and political discourse. The main reason for this turn in conventional arguments about friendship can be found in the great debate regarding the natural condition of men and natural law, to which Thomas Hobbes, his followers and opponents were the key contributors. The debate spilled over into theories of natural law and the law of nations, where the identity of the concept of friendship needed to be established in relation to rival theories of the state of nature and the nature of man that in turn presupposed an alternative reasoning for the popular trope of the social contract and visions of the nature of sovereign power. The chapter surveys great works in the history of international law and moral political philosophy, and shows how friendship became the exclusive feature of the natural condition, and why the power of normative prescription for friendly conduct was derived from particular interpretations of nature and human sociability. Having been submitted to the authority of natural law and presented as a moral regulator for an emerging society of sovereign states, the concept of friendship, this chapter postulates, gradually disappeared from the range of conventional legal statements on international treaties. This century-long episode in juridico-philosophical debate had a profound effect on how generations of modern scholars tended to see friendship among nations – basically dividing them into two camps of ardent proponents and inveterate sceptics that prefer the 'Hobbesian' conception of international political culture.

The final chapter shows the consequences of such rhetorical conceptual re-description for our interpretations of the extensive use of friendship in modern and late modern diplomacy. I argue that the 'naturalised' and 'moralised' concept of friendship fails to grasp a vast domain of political relations that conditioned contemporary commercial relations, as well as the rise and consolidation of the colonial world. It is only in light of the contractual and contingent concept of friendship recovered in the first two chapters that we can comprehend an array of functions friendship performed in bringing about modern trade regimes, the British colonies and empire in North America and India, and last but not least the sovereignty of the newly created United States of America over native American tribes. More specifically, this chapter analyses collections of treaties from the seventeenth to the nineteenth centuries, and traces how friendship agreements facilitated the launch of commercial relations and associated legal arrangements. Thus, I trace the relations of friendship to institutions of international law such as the Friendship, Commerce and Navigation Treaty and 'most favoured nation' status. In this chapter I also analyse how friendship agreements contributed to the colonisation processes in North America and India by allowing first settlements, mediating ideas of political order, justifying relations of equality and inequality, and helping to seize territories from and affirming sovereignty over native tribes and local rulers *en masse*, thereby producing complex structures of imperial power.

1

The ambivalence of ancient friendship

In this chapter I set out to highlight common ways in which classical literature uses the concept of friendship in the context of relations with foreign powers. I do not aim to analyse the whole corpus of ancient Greek and Roman literature. The task of this chapter is much more modest. It will deal with a small number of classical authors who were invoked, often in an eclectic manner, in early modern literature on the law of nations, and later in international relations, as intellectual authorities or sources of information in attempts to describe historical norms or patterns of political conduct. The task of this selection is to postulate the existence of conceptual instruments used to describe the common practice of making and breaking political friendships. However, given the specific aim of this chapter, it will not account for all nuances of conceptual application in classical works that sometimes are centuries away from each other.

Making these instruments more visible in classical literature and later debates will help us to identify an alternative perspective on international friendship that, for reasons that will be set out below, failed to become part of today's scholarship in IR and politics. However, this failure is no reason to believe that this perspective is irrelevant to today's theory. The historical circumstances and political rationality that contributed to its failure do not have the power of universal law, and what was discarded by one generation of scholars can be reactivated by another if found expedient. I do not mean to argue that the alternative perspective could have existed independently of the familiar ethical and normative accounts of friendship. In fact, as a number of classical texts demonstrate, different perspectives on friendship could have been intertwined or separated when political circumstances and the creative powers of a particular author demanded. For this reason, in the following discussion of the overlooked contractual concept of friendship, I shall also pay attention to the links between this concept and the ethics of personal and public relations.

One of the first tasks of the conceptual historian is to select a term or terms that express the concept in question. The history of international friendship is no exception. In fact, in the case of friendship this task might be more complex than it seems. This is due first of all to our focus on sources originally written in

Greek and Latin. In both languages, several related terms were used to designate
the phenomenon of what we could call a political friendship. Thus, a few words
on terminological clarification are required before we can start our conceptual
inquiry. In ancient Greek sources, the various forms of political friendship were
designated by *hetaireia*, *xenia* and *philia*. The term '*summakhia*' is also often
mentioned with *philia*, but in contemporary language it is commonly translated as alliance. As David Konstan maintains, from at least the sixth century
BC, '*philia*, along with *summakhia*, was a normal word for a treaty or alliance
between states'. According to him, *philia* could designate peaceful relations,
whereas *summakhia* means active confederation or alliance (Konstan 1997: 83).
This is the conceptual pair with which I shall be mainly concernedbelow, as it
refers to public political friendships made by individual entities, city-states or
peoples, rather than by individuals belonging to different tribes or cities.

The survey of conceptual use in Greek sources will not include the term
'*xenia*', which referred to friendly relations with people from foreign countries,
despite numerous attempts to associate the origins of diplomacy with the practices of making *xenia*. This is due to the nature of the relations described by the
term. A typical example would involve a travelling stranger requesting that the
noble owner of a house receive him as a guest and become friends with him.
Plutarch describes this situation in *Solon*, when Anacharsis as a stranger knocked
at Solon's door and said that he 'had come to make ties of friendship [*philian*]
and hospitality [*xenian*] with him' and, when Solon remarked that friendships
should be made at home, offered to make himself a 'friend and guest' (*philian
kai xenian*) at Solon's home (Plutarch, *Solon* V, 2).[1] In Konstan's interpretation, this term was mainly used to refer to personal friendship (predominantly
of kings and aristocrats) (Konstan 1997: 83), which is essentially different from
the subject of this book, which is friendship between aggregate entities.[2] Further
confusion might arise over the use of *philia* and *hetaireia* in the context of the
inner political life of the *polis*. By the fifth century BC, the *philoi* constituted a
powerful resource in the political life of Greek city-states. Relations within such
groups were often described with the term '*hetaireia*'. However, according to
Konstan, this term was mainly used to 'designate the aristocratic clubs that were
politically active in Athens' (ibid.: 60–61). Thus, the limited application to the
specific circumstances of city life makes an analysis of *hetaireia* largely irrelevant
for the purposes of this book. In Latin sources, the use of the term '*amicitia*' is

---

[1] A nineteenth-century translator of Xenophon's *The Anabasis; or, Expedition of Cyrus*, J.S.
　Watson reflected on the contemporary reception of the term *xenia*: 'I have translated this
　word by *guest-friend*, a convenient term, which made its appearance in our language some
　time ago. The *xenoi* were bound by a league of friendship and hospitality, by which each
　engaged to entertain the other, when he visited him', p. 4, fn.3.
[2] Gabriel Herman (2002: 6–9) defines *xenia* as a ritualised personal relation, which, however,
　can bind together whole social groups – for example elites – belonging to different cities.

more homogeneous and stable as far as friendly relations between peoples are concerned. However, the following exposition will also identify its links to terms such as '*amor*', '*concordia*', '*societas*' and '*foedus*'.

Friendship in ethics

Friendship understood as an ethical phenomenon was a central theme in ancient discussions of life in the political community. In this context we can find many observations on what constitutes friendship among individuals, what is good and what is detrimental to friendship, what conditions feeble and lasting friendships, the circumstances in which they are formed and who can become friends. Since such discussions of friendship occasionally took the form of narratives on friendship between different cities and peoples, it is all the more important to start by reconstructing the main themes in the ethics of friendship. Given the scope of ancient contributions to this discussion, I shall mainly, but not solely, focus on Aristotle and Cicero, who were among the most popular sources for *loci communes* on friendship among early modern political theorists and moralists and who remain the key intellectual authorities on this subject in the modern debate.

The most elaborate discussion of friendship in the classical period can be found in Aristotle's *Nicomachean Ethics*. In this work Aristotle classified friendship into three types: *of virtue* (sometimes translated as excellence), *of pleasure* and *of utility*.[3] In philosophy friendship of virtue is considered as the best form of friendship and, thus, is taken as a moral ideal to which every friend should aspire. This attitude also seems to be shared by scholars of international relations, who see such friendship as a solution to the modern vices of inter-state politics driven by security concerns. This friendship is usually portrayed as durable and as preventing conflict, whereas the other two types – of pleasure and of utility – are considered to be of lower rank and often dismissed as having negative connotations for a good moral person.

In fact, disregarding friendships of pleasure and utility simply on the grounds of moral inferiority is not entirely fair to Aristotle's account. He does introduce a qualitative scale of friendship by claiming that friendship of virtue is the most complete or perfect (*NE* VIII, 3/1156b5–15), which has prompted his interpreters to undervalue the other types. He also seems to treat all three types of friendship as essential social practices; even if friendship of virtue is worth praising, the other two are no less important social bonds in the life of the city. This is first of all due to the limited scope of 'perfect' friendship. Friendships of

---

[3] To avoid any possible misreading and anachronism, it should be stressed here that 'virtue' in this context designates the morally excellent, rather than the art of achieving something required of a particular social role, while 'utility' does not necessarily mean economic calculation, but refers to a general idea of expediency.

virtue, as Aristotle observes, are rare; they 'require time and familiarity' (ibid., 3/1156b25–30), and most importantly are uncommon, since it is impossible to have profound familiarity and shared experience with lots of people (ibid., 6/1158a10–20). This is a crucial limitation on extending this type of friendship to larger groups of friends, and even more so to relations between cities.

Despite these limitations, friendship of virtue has a strong moral appeal for those who see it as a way to a happy life in the form of lasting, joyful and peaceful social relations. Such relationships are conditioned by the friends having a degree of likeness and equality of virtue, and by their inclination to wish good to a friend for the friend's own sake, rather than in expectation of some benefits (ibid., 3/1156b10–15; 5/1157b25–30). Therefore, in friendship based on virtue and mutual love there is no room for complaints and quarrels (ibid., 13/1163a20–25), making this the least political form of friendship, for politics is always about discontented parties challenging undesired outcomes.

In his most famous work on the subject, *On Friendship*, Cicero also connects virtuous friendship to love. He finds the origin of the former in the latter, and thereby opposes this understanding of friendship to the idea of friendship of utility:

> The Latin word for friendship – *amicitia* – is derived from that for love – *amor*, and *love* is certainly the prime mover in contracting *mutual affection*. For as to material advantages, it often happens that those are obtained even by men who are courted by a mere show of friendship and treated with respect from interested motives. But friendship by its nature admits of no feigning, no pretence: as far as it goes it is both genuine and spontaneous. Therefore I gather that *friendship springs from a natural impulse* rather than a wish for help: from an inclination of the heart, combined with a certain instinctive feeling of love, rather than from a deliberate calculation of the material advantage it was likely to confer. (Cicero 2001, VIII: 26; emphasis added)

In this argument, friendship is conceived solely as genuine and true, as admitting only sincerity and benevolence while discarding all possibility of pretence for the purpose of gaining benefits. Cicero also points out another key property of friendship: genuine friendship is a product of nature, and as such is the opposite of advantage-seeking relations, which cannot cement friendship due to the shifting nature of utility (ibid., IX). In this sense, the moral goodness of friendship does not allow for friendship of degrees and thus for various types of friendship – what is not good is simply wicked and must be condemned. Stoic philosophers (see, for instance, Seneca's Epistle IX) and their followers in Renaissance debates also cultivated the ideal of such virtuous, disinterested love/friendship for another, for whom one could even die. We can find similar arguments in accounts of what we would now call international politics. Dio Chrysostom's (40–120 AD) classical maxim on 'foreign' policy, which suggests that a policy of friendship should be preferred to one of hatred, since it would be disgraceful to fail in actions inspired by the spirit of benevolence, is one example (Dio Chrysostom vol. IV: 40, 23). The virtuousness of friendship was then re-actualised as a powerful trope in early modern critiques of 'corrupt' conduct among princes (e.g. by Erasmus), particularly against the backdrop of religious wars and the declining authority of the Roman Church.

Modern scholars seem to follow the tendency to idealise friendship of virtue and disinterested love as the 'true' form of friendship capable of delivering a happy life, while ignoring 'instrumental' or 'defective' forms (see, for instance, Berenskoetter 2007: 665; Smith Pangle 2003: 43). However, this is one of the major problems in modern interpretations of friendship in Aristotle, particularly those approaches concerned with politics, since it does injustice to the other forms of friendship that he discusses. In privileging the 'best' and the question of what friendship 'ought' to be, it is easy to overlook how things actually are and the purposes that the ignored practices might serve.

As mentioned above, Aristotle does not seem to condemn forms of friendship that could be qualified as incomplete compared with virtuous friendship. Friendships of pleasure and utility are not enduring and have other drawbacks, but nonetheless comprise significant parts of the social order and people's personal worlds. They perform an important function of self-satisfaction, and in some cases of achieving a common good. Here I shall omit discussion of friendship of pleasure as pertinent to intimate relations between a small circle of individuals and thus irrelevant to the aim of the present chapter, and focus on the implications for politics of utility-based friendship.

The crucial role of friendship of utility is manifested in Aristotle's observation that 'friendship seems too to hold states [cities] together, and lawgivers to care more for it than for justice; for unanimity [*homonoia* – concord] seems to be something like friendship, and this they aim at most of all, and expel faction as their worst enemy' (*NE* VIII, 1/1155a20–25).[4] Friendship among fellow citizens is friendship in the political sense, that is, friendship of utility rather than of virtue. Community and friendship of utility seem to be mutually conditioning phenomena in Aristotle. As he further explains, 'political community seems originally to have come together and to continue for the sake of what is useful, since it is this that legislators aim at, and it is said that what is useful, in common, is just' (ibid., 9/1160a10–15). Aristotle complements this observation by arguing that there are forms of political friendship corresponding to three forms of polity (monarchy, aristocracy and property-based timocracy), based on the different models of equality/inequality and ideas of proportionality. With the exception of democracy, deviant types of polity (tyranny, oligarchy) contain little justice and do not allow for much friendship (ibid., 11/1161a10–30 – 1161b1–10).[5]

---

[4] For a discussion of the Greek use of *homonoia* as a political ideal see de Mauriac (1949).
[5] See also Max Weber's observations on the political organisation of the Greek *polis* as a gathering of citizens enjoying equal rights and on an alternative authoritarian organisation

Thus, friendship of utility manifested in a political arrangement can be perfectly advantageous for all the parties involved, as it might facilitate provision for such common goods as security, public order and space to excel in virtues. The realisation of long-term advantages following from common public procedures might be the sole reason for the endurance of political community, and might not require the participants necessarily to become virtuous, as is sometimes suggested (Lu 2009: 53). As Aristotle noted, friendship of utility is even better illustrated by alliances between cities (*poleis*), which people also call 'friendships' even though the main reason of international alliances (*summakhia*) is expediency (*NE* VIII, 4/1157a25–30). The scope of such friendships is inevitably narrower than that of friendship between fellow citizens, but they clearly indicate the legitimacy of friendship in making short- and long-term advantage-seeking strategies within and between cities.

Of course, friendship as a concord between citizens that secures justice and the integrity of the city became a popular trope and normative ideal among those who saw the good of city or republic, and later the state, as the chief priority, rather than politics within and between political communities. In fact, friendship as concord might be one of the feasible alternatives to monarchical power that is ostensibly capable of containing competing political forces and keeping cities together. For instance, Cicero emphasises the value of friendship and concord for the city by contrasting them with their antipodes and at the same time by comparing, somewhat hyperbolically, family bonds to those of the city:

> Nay, if you eliminate from nature the tie of affection, there will be an end of house and city, nor will so much as the cultivation of the soil be left. If you don't see the virtue of friendship and harmony [*amicitiae concordiaeque*], you may learn it by observing the effects of quarrels and feuds. Was any family ever so well established, any State so firmly settled, as to be beyond the reach of utter destruction from animosities and factions? This may teach you the immense advantage of friendship. (Cicero 2001, VII: 23)

This link between friendship and concord, as will be demonstrated in subsequent chapters, as well as the link to the term 'love', appeared to be intensively articulated in medieval and early modern political discourse. However, in line with Aristotle's observations, I wish to emphasise not so much the absolute value of concord and integrity, but the legitimacy and practical aspects of friendship of utility, that is, political friendship.

There also seems to be a difference between political friendship with collective bodies or with individual political friends, on the one hand, and personal

---

based on the model of *oikos* and patrimonial power (Weber 1978: particularly 261, 381, 1013, 1071); in the latter organisation the forms of dependency leave little space or necessity for making additional friendship ties.

friendship that might develop into friendship of pleasure or virtue, on the other. In his study of the idea of 'the king's two bodies', Ernst Kantorowicz noticed an important distinction, maintained by the ancient authors, between personal friends of rulers and friends of kings and political entities. For instance, Plutarch's *Alexander* (47, 9) stresses the difference between Hephaestion, *a friend of Alexander*, and Craterus, *a friend of the king*. Similarly, Aristotle in his *Politics* (III, XVI, 13/1287b) mentions those who are friends to kings and to their government (for the observation see Kantorowicz 1957: 498). Another type of political friendship is with large bodies of people, such as described in Xenophon (c. 430–354 BC), who maintains the possibility of personal sincere friendship towards both Lacedaemon and particular individuals (*Hellenica* II, I, 7). Meanwhile, in Sallust we can find advice to 'cultivate the friendship of the Roman people at large rather than that of individual Roman citizens, and not to form the habit of bribery' ('*ut potius* publice *quam privatim amicitiam populi Romani coleret neu quibus largiri insueceret*'; *The War with Jugurtha* VIII, 2). Such distinction draws another line between the understanding of political friendship as a public relationship, which still embraces the idea of utility, and personal friendship following the trajectories of virtue or pleasure.

The ethics of friendship of utility is such that it is always conditional, that is, it only lasts as long as friends are able to provide benefits (*NE* VIII, 8/1159b10–15; see also Curtius VII, I, 26–27 on the mutual benefits resulting from political friendship: '*amicitiam … fructus percepisse confitear*' ('friendship [we] sought from it and gained from it great fruits')). For a similar reason, friendship of utility, which is also a political friendship, cannot prevent conflicts between friends. Complaints arise when friends, for whatever reason, no longer receive what they expect (something that, according to Aristotle, is not possible in friendship of virtue; *NE* VIII, 12/1162b5–15). Aristotle points out that there are two kinds of friendship of utility, similar to written and unwritten 'justice'; the corresponding complaints are thus made on similar grounds. The first type of friendship resembles a legal agreement with fixed terms, and a complaint is made when one friend does not receive a benefit from the relationship he contracted, which is usually the case in commercial intercourse. The second type of friendship is more like an unwritten rule, and the complaint is made when a person does not receive equal or proportional benefits according to his expectation (ibid., 13/1162b20–35).

For complaints to be successful in the eyes of either a political counterpart/friend or one's own constituency, they should be couched in efficacious rhetorical arguments. According to Aristotle, there are three types of rhetoric: deliberative, forensic and epideictic. He emphasises that political rhetoric deals with what is expedient or harmful (*Rhetoric* I, III, 1358b), and adds that deliberative rhetoric can only treat subjects that are in people's power to change, which include such contingent matters as peace, defence and war (ibid., 1359b–1360a). Thus, deliberation over political friendship between *poleis* or the expediency of such friendship appears to be one of the key subjects of political rhetoric. The argument that I wish to make here is that the explication of habitual practices or the ethics of political friendship, as opposed to the valorisation of virtuous friendship, sheds more light on both pre-modern and modern friendships between cities, peoples and states. As we shall see below, only in light of this analysis of utility-based/political friendship can we comprehend the co-existence of moral and contractual arguments about friendship between cities and peoples in classical political rhetoric.

Friendship and political association

Contemporary controversy over meaning
The complex character and multifaceted nature of friendship have spawned heated debates, particularly in non-English contemporary academic literature, on the origins and meaning of the concept (expressed by the terms *'philia'* and *'amicitia'*) in relations between political communities in ancient Greece and Rome. The debates have revolved around whether friendship in this context stands for merely benevolent relations or for specific obligations resulting from a treaty, whether it constitutes a distinct type of treaty or is its subject, and whether it is not a euphemism for 'international' *clientela* under the Roman Empire (for an overview of the predominantly German debate see Cimma 1976: 23–32). These questions arise when we consider certain extant ancient histories and orations – a source that does not figure often in modern discussions of international friendship.

It has been suggested that friendship became an expedient political concept framing relations between ethnically distinct communities in the classical world. In fact, making friendships could have been a means of overcoming the limitations of relations based on blood ties and, possibly, on 'natural' distrust and hatred (Paradisi 1974: 318–319). Bruno Paradisi even argues that the Roman use of friendship certifies recognition of the counterparty and its capacity to contract political relations with Rome (ibid.: 308). Whether the Romans and Greeks employed the same diplomatic practice and described it with the same concept of friendship remains an open question.

Erich Gruen argues that the diplomatic concept of friendship was not an original invention of the Romans, who initially preferred a solemn *foedus* (treaty of union) as a form of 'international' union. He maintains that Rome acquired this concept in the course of relations with other political entities (before the third century BC, the concept was used rather rarely and mostly by other parties; Gruen 1986: 54–55). Comparison of the use of *philia* and *amicitia* and descriptions of the relations to which the terms referred, according to Gruen, demonstrates the affinity of the two conventions. It also suggests that the modes of establishing friendly relations could stem from the Greek pattern. This explains the presence of popular Greek formulas such as 'to offer friendship' and 'to accept friendship' in Roman practice (ibid.: 59–72).[6]

One of the key issues in debates over both Greek and Latin usage of the terms is the extent to which friendship can be considered a type of diplomatic agreement or a contracted relationship with a number of binding obligations. This is in fact a crucial problem, and solving it would help to determine the concept's principal domains of designation: whether it is a moral component of ancient diplomacy indicating what ought to be done to achieve the good life *or* whether it is a practical tool that facilitates international political, military and commercial intercourse as it is and does not necessitate the exercise of virtues. It is difficult to argue in favour of just one of these alternatives, given the variety of contexts in which the terms were used (such as agreements on military alliances, peace treaties or mere diplomatic communication; Gruen 1986: 68) and linguistic norms of usage. Those who wish to defend the interpretation of friendship as an expression of disinterested benevolence and sincere affection have to explain the apparent connection between friendship and the concept of treaty/agreement, which implies negotiated terms. Moreover, the link to agreement can also mean that the terms are not always proportional and may be used to subjugate one of the parties, particularly in the context of Roman expansion. On the other hand, those who insist on the meaning of friendship as a diplomatic instrument or formal treaty have to face the fact that a definition of friendship as a treaty is missing and there are histories in which friendship is simply praised and not related to any specified conditions.

Gruen admits that *philia* did not necessarily designate relations between equal partners, but this does not mean it was appealed to in order to cloak aggression or affirm someone's power. Rather, he says friendship was used to convey benevolence and to express the readiness of the stronger power to protect the weaker (ibid.: 75; Sue Elwyn also points out this feature of friendship and its consequent transfer to Roman usage: Elwyn 1993: 262–266). In the Latin usage of the third and second centuries BC, Gruen argues, *amicitia* did not designate an instrument of imperialistic policy, since *amicitia* agreements did not contain specific obligations, and were mainly informal and did not imply forms of dependence or clientele (Gruen 1986: 76–78; Christian Baldus similarly claims that *amicitia* refers to 'a relation of friendship without any further concrete engagements': Baldus 2004: 120).

However, with the increase in Roman military might and Roman expansion, many cities and kings preferred to protect themselves by becoming *amici* of

---

[6] Maria Rosa Cimma also observes a shared linguistic convention in the accounts of specific cases of concluded friendships in both Greek and Latin sources: it consists of describing a political actor with the formula 'friend and ally' – *philos kai summakhos* in Greek and *amicus ac socius* in Latin (Cimma 1976: 43).

Rome. This was one of the reasons why Rome so often embarked on the Greek practice of 'accepting into friendship' (Gruen 1986: 86). Although this practice eventually coincided with the growing dependence of neighbouring peoples on Rome's power, Gruen insists that the term '*amicitia*' itself did not designate relations of subordination (ibid.: 90).

An alternative view, as argued by Paul Burton, holds that the Romans transferred their social standards of friendship, which included unequal relations, onto their relations with other peoples. Burton emphasises – *pace* Ernst Badian, Gruen and, partly, the interpretation of friendship suggested here – that the relations of *clientela* and *amicitia* should not be confused, although sometimes they represented intersecting models (Burton 2003: 341–344). Instead of *clientela*, the Romans used the discourse of *amicitia* in the international sphere, particularly in the process of building the empire. This discourse and the corresponding informal relations, according to Burton, implied something more than *clientela*, which explains the moralising and emphatic language of diplomatic interactions, their sincerity and reciprocity, and the fluctuations in the status of the parties. This model turned out to be a 'congenial and flexible method of negotiating … the prevailing chaos of the Mediterranean international system' (ibid.: 365).[7]

The alternative view also suggests that friendship was indeed a product of agreement, or could have been a special type of treaty. In Cimma's reading of the corpus of classical texts, diplomatic *amicitia* had to be negotiated and agreed upon by the parties involved. In many cases there was no formal agreement, but friendship was still not an expression of mere benevolence. In contrast to previous scholarship, Cimma argues that diplomatic friendship was not necessarily a tool for overcoming 'natural enmity', but rather a flexible contractual instrument that could have been invoked in a number of situations. It is assumed that the parties would normally agree on conditions, even if a formal agreement were not concluded. Given the scope and variety of situations in which friendships were reportedly made, Cimma proposes to distinguish between three types of agreements about friendship: a treaty of friendship (*foedus amicitiae*), the main goal of which is friendship; a treaty in which friendship is one of the possible clauses; and treaties that produce friendship when implemented (Cimma 1976: 80–85).

Cimma also admits that evidence for the status of the treaty of friendship *per se* and the exact formula of its conditions is inconclusive. Her solution for tackling the ambiguity in the sources is to track down two distinct types of terminological usage: generic and technical. The generic use of friendship would correspond to

---

[7] See also Konstan (1997: 136–137, 147) for a slightly different argument that friendship between superiors and inferiors in the Latin usage is a euphemism for patronage relations; and Paradisi (1974: 332–333), who argues that Roman friendship corresponds to 'international vassalage'.

mere proclamations of friendship, regardless of any specific agreements. In this case, friendship would designate only benevolent relations. The technical use of the term, on the other hand, would refer to all situations in which the authors mentioned agreements and their juridical implications. The conditions of such 'juridical' friendship should then be derived from the reported situation (ibid.: 84–91).

Such terminological differentiation provides a handy tool for qualifying the divergent and sometimes ambiguous uses of friendship in classical works. However, this interpretation can be modified still further to include Aristotle's definition of political friendship as friendship of utility, with two forms resembling written and unwritten laws. It helps to identify the 'generic' diplomatic friendship-as-mere-benevolence as a form of friendship of utility. This in turn explains the ease with which complaints and references to the norms of virtuous conduct are made – an unthinkable practice in Aristotle's understanding of virtuous/'benevolent' friendship – when the expectations of one party are unmatched by the policies of the other. It also highlights how morality and politics could well intermingle in one concept.

In the following my purpose is not to resolve the debate over the meaning of diplomatic friendship either generally or in relation to a specific historical power. Instead, I shall utilise the key extant sources on relations between political communities to demonstrate the links between political/diplomatic friendship and its semantic field and vocabulary, the thematic contexts and situations in which actors employ the concept, and the rhetorical tropes that frame such usage. In doing this, I shall explicate a number of legitimate ways to use the concept of friendship in political accounts that constitute a viable alternative to the virtuous and normative theorising that prevails today. As will become evident in chapter two, this conceptual alternative constituted an authoritative source for sixteenth- and seventeenth-century jurists and political philosophers for reflecting upon and systematising 'international' politics, and to sharply demarcate their conceptual use from that of political moralists who advocated virtue and the naturalness of the relationship.

Friendship, alliance and treaty

The alternative to friendship of virtue and disinterested benevolence manifests itself most conspicuously in the context of 'foreign' relations with peoples and cities in the classical world. These are political relations *par excellence*, and could include issues such as establishing relations with a new country, making a treaty or building an alliance against a third party. In the modern understanding, such political relations should be conditional and result from negotiations and compromises that accommodate all or some of the complex preferences of political actors. A similar understanding of a political agreement constituted a paradigm for the political and diplomatic friendship represented in both Greek and Latin conceptual worlds.

One of our major sources for Greek foreign relations and their agreements is Thucydides's *The History of the Peloponnesian War* (431 BC). Thucydides uses the term '*philia*' frequently in his description of the foreign relations of the Greeks and their treaties. In this context the term is closely linked to the terms 'alliance' (*summakhia*) and 'ally' (*summakhos*), as well as to the concept of 'agreement' (*spondai*). Notably, in Thucydides's account of negotiated, concluded and broken alliances, *summakhia* and *summakhos* appear to be the prevailing terms (see also Aristotle's observation on *summakhia* as *philia* above). On several occasions, Thucydides mentions parties seeking, obtaining or gaining someone's friendship and alliance. Thus, when presenting the rationale for the Boeotians to make alliance with the Argives and then to ally together with the Lacedaemonians, he writes that the latter would prefer to be friends and allies (*philous kai sumakhous*) of the Argives and were prepared to invoke the enmity of the Athenians by breaking their treaty (*spondon*) with Athens (Thucydides V, XXXVI, 1; see also the description of the calls for friendship and alliance (*philian kai summakhian*) voiced in Sicily against Athens in VI, XXXIV, 1–2).

In his account of Greek diplomacy, the concept of friendship is frequently linked to the notion of contract and treaty involving specific obligations between the contracting parties and their allies (Thucydides V, XLI 2–3). Many historical accounts mention the diplomatic norm for cities and peoples to conclude friendships: in Dionysius of Halicarnassus's account (around 60–7 BC), friendship appears together with the treaty or as a type of treaty (see examples in VI, 21, 2; VI, 95 1–2); Plutarch also reports that Theseus made friendship (*philian*) between the Athenians and the Cretans (Plutarch, *Theseus* XIX, 7). All of these contribute to the understanding of friendship as a treaty or agreement. However, when Thucydides presents treaty terms, it is the conditions of *spondai* and *summakhia* that are spelled out (V, XLVII).

The conditionality of friendship and political agreement becomes even more apparent in a later source – Polybius's *The Histories* (second century BC), in which he uses the term '*philia*' to refer to the name or type of agreements that the Romans made with Carthage: 'The first treaty between Rome and Carthage dates from the consulship of Lucius Junius Brutus and Marcus Horatius. ... The treaty is more or less as follows: "There is to be friendship [*philian*] between the Romans and their allies [*summakhois*] and the Carthaginians and their allies on these terms"' (Polybius III, 22, 4–5; see also III, 29, 7). This quotation includes a typical formula specifying the terms of the agreement: 'there is to be friendship on the following conditions' (see also the preliminaries of the friendship treaty with the Romans in Polybius I, 62, 8–9). As mentioned above, this is not the only possibility; there are many instances in classical sources in which the link between the treaty and the condition of friendship and alliance is articulated without specification. For instance, Herodotus mentions peoples that just become friends and allies (*philotyta te kai symmakhien*) (Herodotus 1960: II, 181). Similarly, Andocides's *On the Peace with Sparta* refers to a pact of friendship (*philotyta*) that becomes an alliance (*symmakhian*) (1968: 30).

In Latin histories and orations, the term '*amicitia*' is similarly connected to the concepts of treaty (*foedus*) and alliance/partnership (*societas*). Sometimes, the connection is close enough for these terms to be used interchangeably; this is reflected in modern translations, which as a result sometimes render *amicitia* as alliance. The association of *amicitia* with *foedus* is crucial to contrasting diplomatic political relations with relations based on virtue and mere benevolence. This conceptual linkage appears in many historical accounts in the form of *amicitia ac foedus* or *amicitiae foedus* (Tacitus, *The Annals*: II, LVIII; Ammianus Marcellinus – a fourth-century Roman historian – XVII, XIV, 1).

The diplomatic relationship reflected by the term '*amicitia ac foedus*' entails a number of actions illustrating that it was by nature deliberate, conditional, negotiated and limited in scope. First, *amicitia ac foedus* can be requested by a party. Sallust gives examples of parties in need *asking for* this agreement with Rome ('*amicitiam et foedus petentibus*') and of the Senate and people of Rome *granting* the treaty of friendship, when deserved ('*foedus et amicitia dabuntur, cum meruerit*') (Sallust, *The War with Jugurtha* CIV, 4; also CXI, 1). Naturally, if someone is in a position to accept requests and grant agreements, there should be a possibility to *reject* friendship ('*repulsum ab amicitia*', ibid. CII, 13). Secondly, the literature abounds in examples of contracted or formed *amicitia*. Julius Caesar makes use of *amicitia populi Romani* in this way in his *Commentaries on the Gallic Wars* in the context of alliance-making. For instance, the Ubii people (a Germanic tribe) are reported to have 'formed an alliance [*amicitiam fecerant*]' with Caesar and asked for his military help (Caesar IV, 16; see also Curtius IV, VII, 9–10 for '*amicitiaque coniuncta*' ('after concluding friendship with them')). Thirdly, and similarly to modern treaty practice, such friendship agreements could be renewed (*redintegrata*) (see Tacitus, *The Annals* XIII, XXXVII). Finally, friendships could be breached and annulled when the political situation and actors' choices dictated. For instance, Cimma demonstrates the possibility of breaking a treaty of friendship with examples from *Punica* by Silius Italicus (ca. 28–ca. 103) ('*soluto foedere amicitiae*'; XVII, 70–75). Even if many examples of contracted friendship did not bring about a formally written agreement – a possibility discussed by Aristotle – the connection to the concept of treaty evident from the usage of these terms indicates the contractual and inherently pragmatic nature of political friendship between communities. This also means that the relationship is immanent to the contingent situations that contain much room for doing politics tactically and strategically.

These possibilities are buttressed by the close links between *amicitia* and *societas*, which often contributes to a terminological confusion. Many scholars insist on a strict distinction between the two relationships designated by these terms (Bederman 2001: 159). The argument against conflation is that *societas* stands for active military alliance, while *amicitia* does not always include this possibility (Lesaffer 2002: 81). However, the distinction between *societas* and *amicitia*, and the latter's connection to *foedus*, should not cause *amicitia* to be confused with peace (*pax*), because there are instances of friendships being made without a prior conflict between the parties and also of peace agreements being concluded but not followed by friendship (Cimma 1976: 66).

For the purposes of this chapter, it suffices to emphasise the possibility for friendship to be associated with alliance as a politically beneficial enterprise, even if benefits could easily become disadvantages. This semantic link can be identified even in Cicero. For instance, in his *Oration against Verres*, friendship is used in the form of *amicitia populi Romani*, that is, political friendship of many and among many. It is also often used with 'ally' and 'alliance' (*socius* and *societas*) in the formula 'friend and ally of the Roman people'. The few examples in the Latin text include *societatis populi Romani atque amicitiae, societatis amicitiaeque, perpetua societate atque amicitia* (Cicero 1913–21; *Orationes in Verrum* II, 36, 88; IV, 29, 67; IV, 33, 72 accordingly). In *History of Rome*, which was to become one of the main authorities on the subject of friendship treaties for early modern authors on the law of nations, Titus Livy uses the same formula '*amicitia populi Romani*', when mentioning the 'loyal friendship' of the Hernicans to Latins (see, for instance, Livy 1905: VI, 2). The conceptual linkage between *amicitia* and *societas* in Livy's account appears to be conventional too: for instance, he notes that envoys could be sent to the Romans to ask for friendly alliance or 'treaty together with friendship and alliance' ('*foedus ictum, cum amicitiam ac societatem*'; VII, 27).

The contexts and the ways in which these authors use the concept suggest that friendship could be conceived more as a political and public relationship than as a virtuous individual or familial relationship based on affection and 'natural benevolence'. As Bruno Paradisi, quoting Cicero's *Oration against Verres*, observes, *amicitia* belongs to the same range of diplomatic instruments relating peoples and cities to Rome as *societas, sponsio, pactio* and *foedus* (1974: 339). This is what constitutes the public nature of such a relationship – its principal participants are political communities (cities, kingdoms, peoples), although sometimes the relationship was portrayed as being arranged by people acting on behalf of these units. The benefit of such a friendship-alliance engagement with a strong party would have been obvious and immediate. For instance, in the above example from Caesar, the aim for the Ubii of making friendship with Rome was simply to bring the Roman army to the banks of the Rhine and thereby demonstrate to others that the Ubii 'might be safe under the fame and friendship of the Roman people [*uti opinione et amicitia populi Romani tuti esse possint*]' (Caesar IV, 16). In a similar vein, Augustus mentions in *The Deeds* (c. 14 AD) an embassy sent to him from King Phrates of the Parthians to seek his friendship (*amicitia*) though the Romans had not previously defeated the Parthians in war. Augustus adds an important observation that during his principate many peoples experienced the good faith of the Romans without any embassies and friendship (*amicitiae commercium*; Augustus 32). All of this indicates that friendship and embassies required more particularised engagements and secured benefits.

From Tacitus's *The Annals*, we can see that the conditions of political friendship could have been more specified, strict and even detrimental to the parties involved. A typical obligation of the *amicitia ac societas* relationship was to provide aid to allies (*socii*) (see Tacitus XII, X). In other cases, obligations might not have been specified in the formal agreement, but the conditions for making and securing an informal friendship could be conveyed to the counter-agent as an ultimatum. Thus, Tacitus reproduces the message of the Germanic Tencteri tribe to the people of Cologne: 'to secure for ever our friendship and alliance [*amicitia societasque*], we demand that you take down the walls of your colony, the bulwarks of your slavery' (Tacitus IV, LXIV). The language that classical works use to describe this and similar situations demonstrates the conventionality of the link between friendship, alliance and treaty in diplomatic practice and rhetoric, along with a handful of political possibilities that such diplomatic friendship could accommodate. We can see that it can be based on a treaty and on an informal agreement, and that its terms can be specified or just implied. Regardless of the degree of formality that every such agreement contains, on all occasions it seems to reflect the particularity of the political settings achieved. Thus, friendship is necessarily dictated by the contingency of the political situation, and in this sense is conditioned by the strategic and tactical calculations of the participants.

Friendship and complaints

No matter how pragmatic the diplomatic relations described by the concept of friendship, it would hardly have been such a popular and appealing concept had it not engaged the idea of moral virtue. The Aristotelian idea of complete or perfect friendship, as well as Stoic ideals of friendship (see Hutter 1978: 128–129), provided an admirable, although rarely attainable, standard for social conduct. Even in the case of daily engagements with 'common' friendship or political friendship, the actors' ideas of proper conduct towards these mundane friends might be haunted by considerations of virtue (see Xenophon's *Cyropaedia* III, 28 on juxtaposing necessity and sincere goodwill in friendship). Thus, it would be facile to dismiss all 'mere' proclamations of friendship as lacking good faith and sincere benevolence. Indeed, some political actors can adhere to the proclaimed ideal of friendship with others as long as this course of action is unimpeded by circumstances that might inflict major losses or even a possibility of self-sacrifice.

Such situations highlight the limits of transition from political friendship to friendship of virtue. Sometimes, political rationality suggests that it is best for the actor's own good and security to leave the relationship than to remain faithful. When this happens, the betrayed parties tend to level bitter complaints against their betrayers – a phenomenon constitutive of friendship of utility and, by extension, political friendship. Accusations and complaints are most likely when concluded friendships follow the pattern of 'unwritten justice' and create a relationship based on unspecified terms and open-ended to boot. We can suppose that political actors in certain situations find it more expedient to leave friendship unspecific, and expect thereby to widen the window of opportunity in the course of further action, while justifying the friendly union by invoking publicly commendable ideals of virtuous relations. However, when such political friendships dissolve, it is easy for the disadvantaged party to appeal to the same ideals of virtue; accusing the other side of a perfidious breach of those ideals also helps to explain away the failure and justify a new course of action (see also Bederman 2001: 277 for observation on parties apologising for broken agreements).

This explains a popular mode of argumentation that appears in the literature regarding dissolved or negotiated diplomatic friendships. The 'fuzziness' of the proclaimed relationship of political friendship allows the actors to easily abandon the idea of political contract and capitalise on the commended image of virtuous friendship. Thucydides demonstrates the transition to this genre of argumentation and rhetoric with a speech that the envoys of the Mitylenaeans delivered to the Lacedaemonians and their allies. The speech draws the analogy between diplomatic relations of communities and commended models of friendship between individuals, involving the ideals of justice, honesty and similitude of opinions:

> We will first discuss the question of justice and rectitude, especially as we are *seeking an alliance* [*summakhias*]; for we know that neither does *friendship* between men [*philian idiotais*] prove lasting, nor does a league between states [*koinonian polesin*] come to aught, unless they comport themselves with transparent *honesty* of purpose towards one another and *generally are of like character and way of thinking*; for differences in men's actions arise from the diversity of their convictions. (III, X, 1; emphasis added)[8]

The question of true friendship between political actors can also involve ideals of harmony and mutual confidence, as follows, for example, from Sallust (*The War with Jugurtha* XXXI, 23–24). However, what the authors and their characters in the narrative attempt to arouse people's emotions about are the

---

[8] In this case *koinonia* should rather be interpreted as communion, intercourse or cooperation; see also Konstan (1997: 83). Sallust in *The War with Catiline* also stresses the necessity of shared understandings of what is good and evil as a basis of firm friendship (*firma amicitia*), XX, 3–4.

violated terms of a political contract. This is the most usual rhetorical means of reinforcing an accusation of mistreating allies (*socii*): refusing to provide help or inflicting damage in other privileges. Titus Quinctius's accusatory reply to the tyrant Nabis, in Titus Livy's *History of Rome*, lists a number of such injuries to a contracted friendship as alliance:

> 'At all events,' you say, 'I have not injured you directly or violated your friendship and alliance' [*amicitiam ac societatem*] … What acts, then, constitute a violation of friendship [*amicitia*]? These two, most of all – to treat my allies [*socios*] as enemies, and to make common cause with my enemies. Both of these things you have done. Though you were our ally you seized by force a city in alliance with us, namely Messene, which had been admitted to our friendship [*in amicitiam nostrum acceptam*] and enjoyed precisely the same privileges as Lacedaemon. And further, you not only concluded an alliance with Philip, our enemy … In open hostility to us, you infested the sea round Malea with your piratical barques, and have seized and put to death almost more Roman citizens than Philip … Forbear henceforth, if you please, to talk about your loyal observance of treaties [*fidem ac iura societatis*]; drop the language of a citizen and speak as a tyrant and an enemy. (Livy 1905: XXXIV, 32, 14–20)

Likewise, Cicero's *Oration against Verres* rebukes the latter, *inter alia*, for his behaviour towards a friend and ally of the Romans. Cicero tries to convince his audience that it would be very harmful for the Roman people were the Roman praetor not punished for his actions. He does so by posing rhetorical questions on how foreign nations perceive his actions, namely whether those nations would think it is contrary to friendship 'that a guest of the Roman people has been plundered? a friend and ally of the Roman people insultingly driven out?' (IV, 30, 68). He continues by giving an example of Verres's atrocious behaviour towards Sopater, a magistrate of the people of Tyndaris. And he deploys irony as he tries to make his audience despise Verres for arbitrarily executing this 'ally and friend of the Roman people' (IV, 40, 86).

The problem of faithfulness to an agreement is what brings to light the nature of political friendship. Self-sacrifice, deep empathy, honesty, goodwill and disinterested benevolence towards the other party can all be the ornaments of political friendship. The actors can even be supposed to truly excel in these virtues. However, frequent cases of dissolved friendships provoking accusations and reproaches make it obvious that political friendship involves a combination of *virtue* and *contract* (formal or informal) as its two inalienable components. Failure to comply with the written or unwritten terms of an agreement creates a basis for complaint; the low specificity and greater reliance on 'mere' honesty and benevolence of such an agreement create more opportunities for rhetorical appeals to virtue of friendship as a way to strengthen one's case. On the other hand, the combination of virtue and contract, rather than virtue alone, makes political friendship a convenient instrument for reacting flexibly to constantly changing political agendas, for recruiting new allies and pursing new courses of action. Thus, we can presume that only the contingent proportion of virtue and contract explains the praiseworthiness of each particular diplomatic friendship.

Asymmetry in political friendship

Another difficult challenge for the interpretation of friendship from the perspective of virtue originates from the issue of power and disproportionate power capabilities. Why do parties agree to or impose unequal relations on others and still call themselves friends? The easiest answer to this question would define friendship as a euphemism for clientela or imperialism, thus dismissing the question altogether. However, this would neglect the prominent practice of Roman diplomacy and rhetoric. I argue that it is still legitimate to consider friendship between unequal parties as political friendship on the assumption that this relationship is by definition conditional. The combination of conditions and virtue discussed above actually includes the possibility of contracting disproportionate friendship. The principle of diplomatic symmetry is a modern invention, while the classical world was familiar with the legitimate practice of making agreements on unequal terms. In fact, as Arthur Nussbaum points out, equal treaties played no significant role in the long history of ancient Rome (Nussbaum 1952: 680 and fn. 10), and in this sense are different from the modern canons of international law. Nevertheless, unequal terms could have been accepted voluntarily by a weaker party because they did not necessarily infringe on that party's freedom and dignity.

The conventionality of the link between friendship and inequality of the parties, however symbolic, is perhaps best captured in the passage from Livy's *History* in which he recounts a request for Roman help from the Campanians, who were besieged by the Samnites:

> Senators! the people of Capua have sent us as ambassadors to you to ask for a friendship which shall be perpetual, and for help for the present hour. Had we sought this friendship in the day of our prosperity it might have been cemented more readily, but at the same time by a weaker bond. For in that case, remembering that we had *formed our friendship on equal terms* [*aequo amicitia*], we should perhaps have been as close friends as now, but we should have been less prepared *to accept your mandates*, less at your mercy. Whereas now, won over by your compassion and defended in our extremity by your aid, *we should be bound to cherish the kindness bestowed on us* if we are not to appear ungrateful and undeserving of any help from either gods or men. (Livy 1905: VII, 30, 1–3; emphasis added)

Other arguments follow the same logic. These were meant to convince the Romans to make the Campanians their friends and allies. Quite typically, to gain this friendship the ambassadors' speech was rather submissive. Were the treaty to be granted, they argued, it would increase Roman wealth and power as the Campanians would become their obedient allies. As has been demonstrated elsewhere, Roman authors conventionally registered these relations of inequality and dependency and added specific adjectives to underline the status of friends (White 1978: 81–82). The Campanians' appeal thus highlights at least two possibilities open to parties seeking Roman friendship. First of all, they could contract a friendship on equal terms. Secondly, even if they had to choose between annihilation and the treaty, they could voluntarily agree to the status of an inferior friend and follow Roman mandates.

The seemingly either–or alternatives available to a party that has to make a choice between peaceful submission or an attempt to fight for an equal role is reflected by Polybius, who reproduces Aristaenus's speech to the Achaeans on policy vis-à-vis Rome:

> it was impossible to maintain their friendship [*philian*] with Rome, by holding out the sword and the olive branch at one and the same time. 'If,' he said, 'we are strong enough to face them and can really do so, very well; but if Philopoemen does not venture to maintain this … why striving for the impossible do we neglect the possible?' … 'Therefore,' he said, 'either it must be proved that we are capable of refusing compliance, or, if no one dares to say this, we must readily obey all orders.'
> (Polybius XXIV, 12, 1–4)

Accepting an inferior position to Rome did not always result in a total loss of liberty and transition to the state of slavery. The virtue of such unequal political friendship could have been in the preservation by Rome of the weaker party's dignity and freedom. This is demonstrated by both Roman jurists and historical accounts. Thus, Tacitus in his history mentions the fierce tribe of Thracians, who 'sent envoys with assurances of their friendship and loyalty [to Rome]', which could be continued 'if they were not tried by any fresh burden'. A new burden in their interpretation would doom them 'to slavery as a conquered people', which they can only face with 'swords and young warriors and a spirit bent on freedom' (*The Annals* IV, XLVI).

Another possibility following from unequal friendship with Rome was to become its province. Cicero's *Oration against Verres* describes the origins of this process by referring to how Sicily became a province of Rome: 'of all foreign nations Sicily was the first who joined herself to the friendship and alliance of the Roman people [*Sicilia se ad amicitiam fidemque populi Romani adplicavit*]. She was the first to be called a province; and the provinces are a great ornament to the empire' (Cicero II, 2, 1). He continues by commending the cities of the island for being faithful to this friendship and alliance ever since.

Again, these accounts demonstrate the perfect compatibility of friendship with engagements that seem to incur loss in political status. Such political friendship could still have brought benefits to some parties in the form of aid and protection, and to others in the form of glory and expansion. Furthermore, if a party escaped the prospect of annihilation, its liberty would be preserved and it would receive some sort of benefit, making it easier for this party to invoke the commendable ideals of friendship and present it as such to relevant publics.

Titus Livy's classification of treaties

The links connecting friendship with the idea of formal or informal contract and the associated idea of conditionality, which, as we saw above, can accommodate the disproportionate share of the parties' duties and promises, are registered in the classical typology of treaties constructed by Titus Livy in *History of Rome*. This work, together with the observations of the Roman jurist Pomponius (second century AD) in the *Digest of Justinian* (533 AD), to which we shall return below, are often referred to as the two central sources containing systematising passages on international treaties concluded in Antiquity (Baldus 2004: 114). Livy's classification is not just of antiquarian value for those interested in the history of Antiquity; for its systematisation of ancient treaty practice it became a central *locus communis* for early modern scholarship on the law of nations and nature, and in this way contributed to the persistence of the conventions of political friendship recovered in this chapter. Livy's classification includes three types of agreements used to make friendships:

> There were three kinds of treaties [*foederum*] by means of which States and monarchs came to terms with one another [*paciscerentur amicitias*]. In one case the conditions were dictated to those who had been vanquished in war … In the second case powers who have been equally matched in war form a league of peace and amity on equal terms [*aequo foedere in pacem atque amicitiam uenirent*] for then they arrive at a mutual understanding in respect of claims for indemnity, and where proprietorship has been disturbed by the war, *matters are adjusted either in accordance with the former legal status or as is most convenient to the contracting parties*. The third class of treaties comprises those made by States which have never been enemies and who unite in forming a league of friendship [*amicitiam sociali foedere inter se iungendam coeant*]; *no conditions are either imposed or accepted, for these only exist between victors and vanquished* … These were terms [imposed/unequal] on which to make peace with Philip their enemy, not a treaty of alliance with Antiochus, who was their friend [*amico societatis foedus ita sanciendum esse*]. (Livy 1905: XXXIV, 57; emphasis added)

This classification cements the argument for the conditionality of political friendship by associating it with a type of treaty (*foedus*), and emphasising the preceding process of negotiation – and, perhaps, compromise – and the conventionality of unequal relationships. This quote does not directly identify the first type as *amicitia*. However, the formulation of the object of classification and the emphasis on equal terms in the definition of the second type are enough to assume the possibility of publicly recognised unequal agreements on friendship. A degree of ambiguity in this classification is sometimes used to make the case for the impossibility of unequal friendships. This alternative interpretation draws on another powerful and well-known statement on political friendship from Quintus Curtius: 'friendship is strongest among equals [*firmissima est inter pares amicitia*] ... Do not believe that those whom you have conquered are your friends. There is no friendship between master and slave [*Inter dominum et servum nulla amicitia est*]' (*History of Alexander* VII, VIII, 27–29). Being a strong argument for equality in friendship, this formulation is a rhetorical attempt to win better terms of agreement for the Scythians. If the treaty were to be enduring and beneficial, it could only be so were both parties equal. However, in itself such a formulation implies that the opposite, that is, an unequal friendship, is still a feasible alternative.

In fact, political friendship contracted to emphasise the inequality of the parties seems to be ubiquitous in the sources. Reports of parties vanquished in war being admitted to friendship, or of recognition of primacy in friendship out of respect, and contrasts with equal friendships made voluntarily are common for Sallust (*The War with Jugurtha* XIV, 5) and Tacitus (*The Annals* XII, X). In a similar vein, Dionysius of Halicarnassus in his *Roman Antiquities* describes Roman relations and treaties with other cities and peoples. He mentions Tarquinius, who accepted the submission of the Sabines and made a treaty of peace and friendship with them (Dionysius vol. III: 66, 3). Later, Tarquinius is said to have gained supremacy over the Latins and sent ambassadors to their cities 'to invite them also to enter into a treaty of friendship and alliance with him' (ibid. vol. IV: 49, 1).

These treaties were apparently based on unequal terms for the parties, which sometimes implied the other party's direct submission to Rome. Reports of those cases were made in both Greek and Latin. Thus, the concept of contractual political friendship, including friendship on unequal terms, was made available to early modern scholarship through studies of both Roman law and Greek history. This usage of the concept appeared to later readers as a linguistic and rhetorical tool designed to bring about, fix and legitimise various power constellations (such as alliances, empires) that were not necessarily favourable to all the parties involved.

Friendship and postliminium: legal implications

Inequality in the Roman context does not mean loss of freedom. It reflects in the symbolic recognition of the unequal power of Rome's counterparts and sometimes in disproportionate legal obligations. The *Digest*, a compilation of Roman law, epitomises this use of friendship in Rome's dealings with 'foreign' peoples and cities. The 'juridical' use of the concept is manifested in the context of the application of the right of *postliminium*. In his discussion of this issue, the jurist

Proculus (first century AD) directly links friendship to the issue of equality/
inequality and consequently to the definition of a free people:

> A free people is one which is not subject to the control of any other people; a *civitas
> foederata*, one which has either entered into friendship under an equal treaty [*aequo
> foedere in amicitiam venit*] or under a treaty [which] includes the provision that this
> people should with good will preserve the *majestas* of another people. It has to be
> added that that other people is to be understood to be superior, not that [the feder-
> ated] people is not free; and insofar as we understand our client [states] to be free,
> even if they are not our equals in authority, dignity or power, so also those who
> are bound to preserve our *majestas* with good will are to be understood to be free
> [*liberos*]. (The *Digest* 49, 15, 7, 1)

Notably, this definition of a free people includes the status acquired upon entering various types of *foedera*, one of which is friendship concluded on unequal
terms. Thus, in this passage friendship again stands for a type of treaty. Moreover,
Proculus finds it necessary to add an adjective 'equal', thereby saving a logical
opportunity for other types of friendship to bring about unequal relations, with
implications for the status of a free people. Besides, Proculus emphasises that the
term 'free' does not necessarily mean 'equal'; a free people in such relations could
be unequal to the other in terms of authority and power, and might even need
to recognise it explicitly, although without damaging its free status (this also
follows from the above example from Tacitus, *The Annals* XII, X). From these
formulations we can also infer that a friendship agreement remains a matter of
voluntary consent of the parties, except for those cases when treaty conditions are
dictated by a victor in war or when the very condition of inequality is represented
as slavery, as the example above from Curtius demonstrates.

The discussion of the right of *postliminium* further highlights the legal implications of friendship treaties. One of the main authorities on the subject of *postliminium* is the Roman jurist Pomponius, who was widely cited by early modern
writers on the law of nations. Due to his and Livy's authority for early modern
authors, and the links between friendship and legal obligations that become
apparent in his definition of *postliminium*, it is crucial to reproduce it here:

> The right of *postliminium* applies both in war and in peace. 1. In war, when those
> who are our enemies have captured someone on our side and have taken him into
> their own lines; for if during the same war he returns he has *postliminium*, that is,
> all his rights are restored to him just as if he had not been captured by the enemy.
> Before he is taken into the enemy lines, he remains a citizen. He is regarded as
> having returned from the time when he passes into the hands of allies or begins
> to be within our own lines. 2. *Postliminium* is also granted in peacetime; for if we
> have neither friendship [*amicitiam*] nor *hospitium* with a particular people, nor a
> treaty made for the purpose of friendship [*foedus amicitiae*], they are not precisely
> enemies, but that which passes from us into their hands becomes their property,
> and a freeman of ours who is captured by them becomes their slave, and similarly if

anything of theirs passes into our hands. In this case also *postliminium* is therefore granted. (The *Digest* 49, 15, 5)

This definition registers conventional diplomatic practice and explicates the specific obligations that the parties to contracted friendship undertook to observe towards each other. For instance, observance of *postliminium* had implications for the property rights of citizens, as well as for safe merchandise. Invoking friendship thus included an appeal to the effective political and legal order to which the parties to this agreement belonged. As we shall see in subsequent chapters, the right of *postliminium* also became a salient topic in discussions of alliances and obligations towards allies in the sixteenth and seventeenth centuries. The reason why *postliminium* became one of the main *topoi* invoked in discussions of friendship in early modern legal discourse was that this concept helped to solve the uncertainties arising in political and legal conduct in the absence of universally operating rules and laws.

Conceptual continuities in the Middle Ages

In the remainder of this chapter I shall try to demonstrate that the alternative understanding of political friendship recovered above and its conceptual means of expression can also be identified in early medieval Greek and Latin literature. Bruno Paradisi maintains that in the Middle Ages several changes took place in the ways friendship was practised as compared with the ancient world. He argues that, due to the proliferation of imperial and monarchical forms of power, friendship also changed its prevalent form from friendship among peoples to friendship among kings (Paradisi 1951: 333–334; see also Epp 1999: 177–178). In fact, this form was anything but new; it just became more popular than friendship between peoples. Also, the concept was used differently in that it did not refer to detailed treaties, but instead pointed to more general cooperative relations between the political agents (Paradisi 1951: 337–338). In this sense the dividing line between the use of friendship in accounts of personal and public relations starts to become blurred, since the latter loses its specified contracted form. This conceptual development parallels the idea of 'the king's two bodies', since the separation of the office from the person and friendly relations between the holders of that office was not yet complete; on the contrary, we could claim that friendly relations were established by virtue of having a body politic (for a discussion of the problem see Kantorowicz 1957; henceforth, I shall mention personal forms of friendship with the reservation regarding their political nature, unless otherwise specified). Paradisi puts forward yet another important observation, namely that friendship was gradually integrated into the Christian doctrine of peace and hence often gives way to concepts of *pax*, *amor* and *concordia* in the conventional use (Paradisi 1951: 372).

One of the best illustrations of *concordia* taking the place of *amicitia* is *Variae epistolae* (537 AD) by Flavius Magnus Aurelius Cassiodorus, an Ostrogothic statesman. On many occasions where previous convention would have dictated the use of *amicitia*, Cassiodorus uses *concordia*. The kings in this work are said to seek and desire *concordia*; sometimes he even uses it together with *amor* to strengthen its bonds (I, 1, 2; V, 2, 3). Cassiodorus reproduces the text of a petition that the senate of the city of Rome sends to the Emperor Justinian (ca. 534–535 AD), which mentions *pax* and *foedus* and also assures and affirms the need for *concordia* (XI, 13). Notably, the letters in the *Variae* constitute parts of the documentation produced by the Ostrogoths; in this sense the Ostrogoths not only succeeded to the Roman power in the region but also had a grasp of Roman conceptual apparatus. Much later we find examples of the term appearing in agreements concluded by the pope with secular powers in the region. The text of the peace of Beneventum (1156) between King William I of Sicily and Pope Adrian IV uses the terms *pax* and *concordia*, while the 1177 treaty between Pope Alexander III and Emperor Frederick I uses the term *pax* (*Fontes* 1995: 386–389).

Paradisi's observations only partly apply to linguistic conventions and legitimating discourses in another part of the Eurasian continent, that is, to the growing Byzantine Empire, where the use of the term *philia* prevailed. The works of two prominent historians of Justinian's time, Procopius of Caesarea (c. 500–c. 565 AD) and Agathias of Myrina (c. 536–582/594 AD), demonstrate that the use of friendship to constitute and legitimate political inequality remains a conventional part of these later accounts, too. This is illuminated in a passage from Procopius's the *Persian War*, in which the Colchians appeal to the Persians:

> But at a later time it came about that our ancestors, whether neglected by you or for some other reason ... became allies of the Romans. And now we and the king of Lazica give to the Persians both ourselves and our land to treat in any way you may desire. And we beg of you to think thus concerning us: if, on the one hand, we have suffered nothing outrageous at the hands of the Romans, but have been prompted by foolish motives in coming to you, reject this prayer of ours straightaway, considering that with you likewise the Colchians will never be trustworthy ... but if we have been in name friends [*philoi*] of the Romans, but in fact their loyal slaves ... receive us, your former allies, and acquire as slaves those whom you used to treat as friends [*philois*], and shew your hatred of a cruel tyranny ... by acting worthily of that justice which it has always been a tradition of the Persians to defend. (Vol. I: II, 15, 16–19)

Here the Colchians complain precisely about unequal friendship with the Romans by hyperbolically comparing their status as friends to that of slaves. The argument of the Colchians as presented by Procopius in fact registers two models of friendship: both were possible (as the case of the Colchians shows), but not always acceptable to all parties. Having first presented themselves as parties in a model of unequal friendship in which they had to submit to the will of the Romans, they continued by arguing for a model based on more equal and just relations. These two models of friendship were amenable to rhetorical re-descriptions condemning one state of affairs and favouring another – strategies used by contractors before, as we saw from Curtius's example. This is evident in a passage about Justinian sending a letter to a Persian king, Chosroes and trying to convince him not to enter war. One of the rhetorical devices aimed at persuading Chosroes is an appeal to the ideal that true friends who seek to preserve the existing 'order of things repel even those charges against their friends [*philous*] which are most pressing' and, alternatively, 'those who are not satisfied with established friendships [*philias*] exert themselves to provide even pretexts which do not exist' (ibid., II, IV, 23).

Similarly to the recovered conceptual use oscillating between virtue and contract, these Greek authors also associated friendship with agreement, and not with appeals to virtue alone. When Chosroes, according to Procopius, decided to march with his army through Roman territory, the Roman envoys asked him to treat the Romans as his friends (*philon*) on this journey. In exchange, Chosroes requested a noble hostage from the Romans 'to make this *compact binding*, and in order that they might carry out their agreement' (ibid., II, XXI, 26 emphasis added). Agathias in his *Histories* makes a similar report about the Goths seeking and making friendship with the Franks, and as a result losing their territories to the Franks (I, 6). Procopius's *Gothic War* registers examples of conferring the status of friend. For instance, the status of *Gothois philoi* is reported to be given, along the lines of the Roman historical accounts, to those who chose to be loyal to the Goths when they besieged Rome and who let them enter the city. As a reward they were granted the offices of those who had not been willing to give the Goths anything (VII, XXI, 16–17). The following events made the Gothic king Totila request that Justinian preserve peace with him, despite developments in Italy, and offer in exchange to call him 'father' and to be his ally (VII, XXI, 21–25). Although Justinian rejected this offer on the grounds that it was his general Belisarius who was entitled to make such an agreement, it is indicative that the report of this event showed the willingness of the Gothic king to submit to the emperor. Another aspect worth noting is the invocation of the 'family' metaphor. Even if it were fruitless in this case, as we shall see below it proved operational over centuries of diplomatic relations. However, the appeal to the 'father–son' model was less frequent than that to the 'brother–brother' model.

According to Procopius's account, the Germanic peoples seemed to follow the Roman customs of making friends. Agathias mentions that the Franks also used Roman laws and understood treaties similarly (I, 2). Thus, both the Goths and the Franks apparently were familiar with different forms of friendship that could be contracted with other peoples. On some occasions they were reported to have made unequal friendships; on others, as in Agathias's praising of Frankish customs, they made friendships on equal terms as a means to preserve public peace, particularly when Frankish armies matched each other in power (ibid.).

Perhaps one of the best examples illustrating the use of friendship and family metaphor in managing imperial affairs is a later Byzantine source, Constantine Porphyrogenitus's *On the Administration of Empire* (948–952). This work demonstrates several different ways of employing friendship. On the one hand, it follows the Roman custom of making friendships with the barbarians on the imperial borders so that they could protect the empire from other tribes. On the other hand, friendship is also used in portraying a homogeneous Christian polity that excludes heathens (on the re-association of the concept of the 'barbarian' with the border of the Roman Empire, although not on natural principles, and on the opposition of the Christians and heathens, see Koselleck 2004: 168, 169–180, respectively). This function is evident in Constantine's quasi-'primordial' account of community:

> For just as each animal mates with its own tribe, so it is right that each nation also should marry and cohabit not with those of other race and tongue but of the same tribe and speech. For hence arise naturally harmony of thought and intercourse among one another and friendly converse [*philias*] and living together; but alien customs and divergent laws are likely on the contrary to engender enmities and quarrels and hatreds and broils, which tend to beget not friendship [*philei*] and association but spite and division. (Constantine 13, 180–185)

This idea of a political community is supplemented with instructions that Christians should avoid marriage with heathens (ibid. 13, 140). Together with presenting this political ideal, Constantine also uses friendship to describe and advise on policies towards barbarians. Making friendships in this account could be compared to a medieval checks-and-balances system containing various barbaric tribes in their hostile aspirations: 'If the ruler of Alania is not at peace with the Chazars, but thinks preferable the friendship of the emperor of the Romans, then, if the Chazars are not minded to preserve friendship [*philian*] and peace with the emperor, he, the Alan, may do them great hurt' (ibid. 11, 3–6). This use of friendship follows customary Roman practices in dealing with the barbarians on the borders of their provinces.

Constantine's account of relations with the barbarians follows convention in making room for asymmetrical or unequal friendships. The rulers of neighbouring peoples could make oaths of loyalty and fight against the emperor's enemies. Inequality is realised not only in the services that the parties provide towards each other; it is also articulated in Constantine's vision of their symbolic relationship to him: 'But since the curopalate is our faithful and upright servant and friend, at his request let the frontier of Phasiane be the river Erax or Phasis' (ibid. 45, 156–158). A letter sent to the Frankish emperor Lothair I in 843 by the emperor Michal III seeking an alliance against the Saracens is another example of an attempt to make friendship in which the Byzantine emperor would be superior to his counterpart. In this letter, Michal III suggests that *philia* should be firmly established between his majesty and his beloved son (*Fontes* 1995: 267). However, apart from hierarchy in relation to the emperor, Constantine's narrative also contains examples of friendships without any self-evident signs of inequality. He reported, for instance, that the Iberians have always maintained 'loving and friendly relations with the men of Theodosioupolis' (Constantine 45, 65).

I argue that these contrasting uses of the concept describing different political contexts should not be taken as contradictory or as a result of inconsiderate and indiscriminate use of the concept. Quite the contrary: the divergent uses still correspond to the classification of friendship agreements proposed by Livy, which registered these contrasting friendships as equally legitimate customary practices. The evidence from these select Byzantine authors shows that friendship was a concept that could be invoked in a number of politically important *topoi*: treaty-making, political equality/inequality in voluntarily maintained relations, and public obligations to friendship compacts.

Similarly, contracted friendship continued to be a popular diplomatic tool in the western part of Europe in the Middle Ages. In 921, Charles III, the king of the West Franks, and Henry I, the king of the East Franks, made a treaty of friendship in which they mutually recognised each other's rights to their respective territories, thus settling the issue over Lotharingia. Specifically, the document starts with the proclamation that it is made in the name of God, and then states that princes sought and made '*pactum ac societatis amicitia*'. It was followed by the promise to be friends (*amici*) with each other and by the oath that '*amicitiae firmitas inviolabiliter observaretur*' (*Fontes* 1995: 488).

Besides being invoked in this Frankish settlement, the term *amicitia* was later used when settling issues arising in relations between the German emperor and the French king. For instance, the 1310 treaty between Emperor Henry VII and King Philip IV of France, which is claimed to mark the emancipation of France from the Holy Roman Empire, also starts with the confirmation of '*tres granz amitiez et les affections*' (ibid.: 448). Previously, Emperor Frederick II and King Louis IX of France in the 1227 alliance treaty had confirmed and renewed '*confederationem et amicitiam*' (ibid.: 410). Later, in 1355–1356, in the 'family alliance' between Emperor Charles IV and King John II of France, the text used the formula '*unionis et amicitiae gratam concordiam*' (ibid.: 424). It is important to note that the 1310 treaty of friendship has also a clause containing a promise from the emperor to oblige those princes whom he appoints in lands bordering France to swear an oath of benevolence and alliance to the king of France. This appeared to be a critical implication of friendship agreements for medieval societies. Making friendships often involved third parties (friends and allies of the contracting parties) upon whom the agreed terms were also extended. In this way, contracted friendships made a significant contribution to the operation of the medieval political order.

Randal Lesaffer pointed out this element in friendship (*amicitia*) agreements of the late Middle Ages and Renaissance (Lesaffer 1997: 83). He also suggested that the *amicitia* agreement had the following juridical implications: it involved an obligation not to provide help to the other's enemies and not to use violence in solving conflicts arising between the parties; it extended the obligation to sustain peace to allies of the parties; and it included the subjects of the princes, meaning that the rule of law would apply to them, especially when they travelled to the 'friendly' dominion (Lesaffer 2002: 91, 94). Thus, friendship agreements appeared to play the role of an instrument providing political and legal order. This is particularly important in medieval societies; as many scholars have demonstrated, kings and emperors did not have a monopoly of power in their dominions, meaning that the dividing line between 'internal' and 'external' was rather blurred (see Lesaffer 2004: 15–16; Ziegler 2004: 151).

However, the absence of a clear demarcation line between 'internal' and 'external' did not mean a disordered anarchy, as contrasted to the modern order of the sovereign state. Even if rulers and their subjects in the Middle Ages could 'declare war and conclude peace with each other 'as if' each were subject to 'international law'', these ways of conduct, as Otto Brunner observes in his study of feuds and lordship, were 'in strict accordance with legal procedure' (Brunner [1939] 1992: 14). In such a complex matrix of political power, friendship and peace, Brunner argued, were central categories defining kinship groups and communities of law (ibid.: 18). Brunner's study shows that a feud declared against separate political agents and whole polities immediately involved friends of the challengers. Friends (*amici*) were obligated to assist in a feud by providing aid and counsel (ibid.: 49). A basic obligation of a friend, as Brunner puts it, was 'to treat his friend's enemy as one who stood outside the peace', which included prohibitions on provision of 'house and hearth, food or drink' to a friend's enemy, as well as on letting a friend's troops pass through one's own territory (ibid.: 53; see similar provisions in The Peace of Augsburg § 14, 1555). In this sense the concepts of ally and friend in Brunner's study have an overlapping meaning and could be used interchangeably. However, what is worth emphasising is that friendship was a category capable of grasping a complex mix of social, political and legal relations and thus allowed for a diversity of uses. The concept of friendship could be used to describe various predominantly voluntary relations between equals and non-equals, allies and kindred, public/international actors and private individuals, all of which were part and parcel of the social-political order of medieval Europe.

Scholars have noted the scarcity of 'international' friendship agreements during the Middle Ages, although they never disappeared completely. However, in the Renaissance, with the disintegration of the moral and political ideal of *respublica Christiana*, the number of friendship treaties multiplied (Lesaffer 2002: 94–96). One of the major factors that buried this ideal was bitter rivalries between Spain, France, the Holy Roman Empire, the pope and Venice, among others. In addition, the recognition of papal and imperial authority was far from unanimous. The same factors, together with the threat posed by the Turkish sultan, constituted a political context for the renewal of friendship-making practice. Negotiations of offensive and defensive alliances, alliance and peace treaties in the late fifteenth and sixteenth centuries customarily invoked the concept of friendship (see, for instance, Lesaffer 2004: 11–13[9]). Perhaps it is not surprising that the concept of friendship, already so well entrenched in the system of maintaining medieval political and legal order, appears so frequently in agreements aimed at establishing a political order among quasi-sovereign princes.

Instead of a comprehensive study of the concept of friendship in the ancient and medieval world, a task well accomplished by other scholars, this chapter has attempted to recover an understanding of political friendship and the conventional ways in which it was expressed that have often remained unnoticed in modern interpretations of international friendship. Taking friendship of virtue as a desired ideal against which past and present practices of friendship are contrasted tends to prioritise the question of what *ought to be* over the question of what *is*. This analytical and normative choice thus dismisses and leaves unaccounted for a large body of friendship agreements in the contemporary and classical worlds for reason of their non-compliance with the expected exercise of virtue. However, this analytical perspective misses an important element in the constitution of the international order, and fails to account for how political actors practise, describe and legitimise their relations.

Conventional ways of applying the concept to political relations between communities in classical literature stem from a basic understanding of political friendship as based on utility and on the promise of particular benefits for participating parties. Along with friendship based on virtue, such friendship constituted a legitimate practice maintaining the classical social and political order, and thus cannot be discarded as somehow false or immoral. The perspective of contractual and inherently conditional friendship offers us a grip on a series of the key diplomatic practices in the classical world. These practices are highlighted in major rhetorical *topoi* in the history of friendship such as 'friendship treaty'-making events, the classification of friendship treaties, issues of equality and inequality, alliance-making and imperial expansion, and the obligations that followed from voluntarily contracted friendships. This perspective does not

---

[9] On the same subject see also Mattingly (1988: 148–165); and for a detailed overview of the events, negotiations and references to *amicitia* in southern Europe and the Levant see Setton (1976: 36, 180, 218).

exclude the possibility of the rhetorical and practical exercise of virtue. As I have
tried to show, the application of the concept of friendship was conditioned by
the intrinsically linked ideas of virtue and contract, the varying proportions of
which determined the choice of vocabulary and rhetorical figures used by the
participating actors in situations of making new friendships and breaking old
ones. The alternative modes of conceptual usage and argumentation excavated
from classical literature will bring us to and explain the intellectual 'origins' of
the early modern convention of employing the contractual concept of friendship.
It is only in connection with the classical *loci communes* that we can manage to
identify this alternative 'tradition', and explain its intelligibility and co-existence
with familiar accounts of ethical friendship.

2

Early modern friendship: politics and law

Horizontal and hierarchical power relations within a community

Medieval Scholastic scholarship and its intellectual agenda shaped by ideas of a universal order were irrevocably challenged by the Reformation and the consequent segmentation of Europe, a process accelerated by rivalries among major political powers. The demand for intellectual tools to account for manifested contingency and the particularity of political situations necessitated a turn to a powerful alternative able to be sensitive to the experience of particular 'nations': the classical tradition, Hellenic and Roman (for the contrast between the universality of medieval thought and the particularity of the classical tradition see Pocock 2003: 6–14). The flourishing of political and legal thought in Italian and northern European humanism was to a large extent driven by the rediscovery of classical authors and the new techniques used to interpret them (see Skinner 2000a). Humanists' punctilious study of original sources – and in particular the significance that they attached to the language used by the authors, and their attempts to divine those authors' underlying intentions – were among the principal factors that explain why many classical linguistic conventions and tropes permeated Renaissance and early modern literature.

This was also the main channel through which conventions regulating the use of friendship in ancient sources migrated to early modern political thought. In this chapter I shall make a case for the enduring persistence of the political contractual concept of friendship – that is, the modes of friendship of utility reconstructed in the previous chapter – and its key place in early modern political and legal thought. As I shall demonstrate, the concept of political friendship was rearticulated in theories of the internal arrangement of and relations between political communities. This casts a new light on the political and social order at the dawn of the sovereign state and modern international regimes.

The 'Aristotelian' idea of friendship 'in a political sense', or friendship as a basic agreement about the nature of a polity and co-existence, is an easily identifiable trope in Humanist discourses on the constitution of polities, literary works and political rhetoric. Many Humanist authors display an understanding of friendship as a distinctive and constitutive element of political community. This idea is articulated in Thomas Hoby's translation of Baldassare Castiglione's *Il Libro del Cortegiano* (1561), which provides an account of the deeds of Alexander the Great:

> To breake and to ende controversies emonge his subjectes ... To provide so, that the Citye may be all *joyned together and agreeinge in amitye*, lyke a private house, well peopled, not poore, quite and full of good artificiers ... and all men, as one people, *that shoulde live in amitye and agreement together*, under one government and one lawe. (Hoby 1900: bk IV, p. 332, emphasis added; for a similar use see also James I's *Basilikon Doron* [1603] 2001: 31)

The link between amity and agreement, as articulated in this quote, is crucial for the 'Aristotelian' vision of the political community, because it establishes the paradigm for implementing justice. Humanist authors seem to converge on the centrality of concord, as an opposition to open conflict, to the idea of political co-existence. In this sense, there is a patent correspondence between the ancient framing of friendship as similitude of opinion about the political order – in the sense of the realisation of the common interest in being friends and abiding by collective rules rather than holding a uniform opinion on every item on the political agenda – and the Humanist praise of civic concord. Edmund Spenser asserts this ideal of friendship as civic concord by introducing a special character into his poem *The Faerie Queene* (1596; Book IV, 'Of Friendship'): '*Concord* she cleeped was in common reed, Mother of blessed *Peace*, and *Friendship* trew, They both her twins, both borne of heauenly seed' (Spenser 1935: 130; ch. X, xxxiv; Thomas Stanley similarly defines amity as concord of life, 1655: 93). Walter Dorke makes an even stronger claim when he reiterates Cicero's dictum (see chapter one) almost verbatim in his *Tipe or Figure of Friendship*: 'without Friendship no house can be wel guided, no Citie well gouerned, no Countrey safe preserued, no State long continued, no nor anie thing in the use of man rightly ordered' (Dorke 1589: 8; for an analogous argument see Leslie 1584: 6). This is to a large degree the language of civic virtues, which is not always comprehensible and shared by the modern rationalised perception of politics.

However, the idea that friendship is central to a political community is also prolific in the anti-Aristotelian intellectual tradition, which offered a new science of politics based on study of the ideas of necessity and political interests. Rather than a continuing defence of a set of natural human and republican virtues, this tradition looked to other intellectual authorities, such as Thucydides, Tacitus and Polybius, as sources of specific historical cases and arrangements (Tuck 1993: 26–28, 94–119). Thus, *Les Six Livres de la République* (1576)[1] by French

---

[1] Below I shall refer to the edition *The Six Bookes of a Commonweale. A Facsimile reprint of the English translation of 1606, Corrected and supplemented in the light of a new comparison with the French and Latin texts* (1962).

Catholic jurist and theorist of sovereignty Jean Bodin, a work best known for laying out an early modern conception of sovereignty, portrays itself as drawing on the best laws of commonwealths then extant, rather than speculating about ideal or imagined polities (Bodin 1962: 3). Seemingly, the turn to historical precedents as a way to acquire a better understanding of how power can be exercised in reality – when considerations of virtue might not be the first priority – opened even more opportunities to access the contractual concept of political friendship identified in the first chapter.

This is one of the reasons why Bodin, while advocating the concept of indivisible sovereignty, still finds room for the *topos* of friendship as a distinctive element of political community. Only lawful political communities, according to Bodin, are kept together by ties of friendship – as opposed to, for example, gangs that may also have social life and social relations, but lack real friendship. In Bodin's formulation, pirates 'seeme to liue in neuer so much amitie and friendship together, and with great equalitie to diuide the spoile ... yet for al that they ought not to be of right called societies and amities, or partnerships' (ibid.). Bodin also invokes historical cases of solidarity being sustained among the subjects of princes by means of friendship, specifically mentioning Lycurgus's command to maintain and cherish small societies and communities called *philitia* as an example of such basic forms of solidarity, and stressing that 'amitie and friendship was the onely foundation of all humane and ciuill societie' (ibid.: 363). Similarly, he explained the stability of the Venetian government: 'that which hath most maintained their seignorie against the commotion of the citisens, is the mutuall amitie and concord of the gouernours and gentlemen among themselues; and the sweetnes of libertie, which is greater in that citie than in any other place of the world' (ibid.: 427).

The conventionality of friendship as political cohesion was such that we even encounter it in the rhetoric of the key political actors. For instance, Henry VIII of England used this seemingly odd phrase in an address to his Parliament and ultimately his own subjects: 'although I with you and you with me are in this perfect love and concord, this friendly amity cannot continue' (Henry VIII 1545). Yet, this conception of public political relations seems perfectly in line with Humanist thought. In this context, the conjunctions 'love and concord' and 'friendly amity' are definite markers of the public and political nature of friendship, while the relationship itself resembles a quasi-constitutional political agreement regarding the basic rules of political community, or civil concord.

Aside from the idea of friendship as civil cohesion, Humanist literature articulates another form of utility-based friendship, namely friendship as a resource of power available to particular parties. In the early modern context, the key figure of such relations of friendship was the prince. The very status of the prince raises a puzzling question for both early modern and modern writers: if a prince's associates cannot be at the same level of political hierarchy and are thus unequal to him, does it not render their status of friends a mere euphemism for medieval vassals? We have encountered this question before, when discussing Roman practices; the same problem appears relevant for the early modern period. Allan Silver and Gerd Althoff seem to concur that the necessity for a prince to have political friends among his subjects as a means of maintaining social order corresponds to the vertical model of 'vassalage'. The relationship itself was thus not a matter of choice and may have lacked modern personal emotional attachment (Althoff 1999: 94; Silver 1997: 48–49). Jonathan Dewald, however, maintains that sixteenth- and seventeenth-century friendship combined medieval and modern conceptions, implying the co-existence of two different types of friendship: among formal equals, and between those of unequal status ('horizontal' and 'vertical' friendship, in Dewald's formulation) (Dewald 1993: 108–110). This holds true in respect to the 'international' realm, where kings who were formally equal in dignity could have a duke (e.g. a duke of Burgundy), who was of lower rank, as a party to friendly relations. Thus, the vertical pattern of friendship might not have fitted vassalage relations entirely: although the disparity of the parties to the friendship was acknowledged, inferior friends could well remain outside vassalage structures and enter the relationship voluntarily.

Nevertheless, descriptions of princes as relying on a group of friends for the purpose of maximising power and achieving certain political goals are common in a range of sources from the early modern period. For instance, Thomas More's *The History of King Richard the Third* (1513) provides a vivid account of vertical friendship serving a particular political goal: 'the Lordes whiche at that tyme were aboute the kyng, entended *to bryng him vppe to his Coronacion, accompanied with suche power of theyr frendes,* that it shoulde bee harde for him to brynge his purpose to passe' (More 1997; emphasis added). Certainly, such political friendship could be beneficial to both the superior and inferior parties, since helping a lord to secure a grip on power could bring material or other advantages to his associates as well. But although this benefits both parties, the historical accounts also register the subordinate status of friends to a prince by listing them alongside semantically close categories: 'friends, alies, clyents, and servants' (see Beacon [1594] 1996: ch. 3; similar roles are assigned to a prince's friends in the historical accounts of Francis Bacon and Jean Bodin). As Henry St John, Viscount Bolingbroke, remarked in *Idea of Patriot King* (1738) on Queen Elizabeth's friendships: 'she had private friendships, she had favourites: but she never suffered her friends to forget she was their queen; and when her favourites did, she made them feel that she was so' (1997: 288).

The paradigm of friendship as a resource of power was also open to appeals to virtuous conduct, indicating the degree of voluntariness in political allegiances. These appeals were usually made in discussions of issues such as fidelity and duties to one's friends. Roger Ascham's *A Discours and Affaires of the State of Germanie* (1570) refers to a historical episode in which one of the foes of Duke Maurice of Saxony (1521–1553) commented out of spite:

> he that could finde in his hart to betray his frend Duke Henry of Brunswicke, his nigh kinsman Duke Fredericke, his father in law the Lansgraue, his soueraigne Lord the Emperour, his confederate the French kyng, *breakyng all bondes of frendshyp*, nature, law, obediēce, and othe, shall besides all these, deceaue all men if at length he do not deceaue hym selfe. (Ascham 1904: 167–168; emphasis added)

This remark on the betrayal of friendship highlights a whole array of possible political friendships with peers and symbolic superiors. The lamenting mode of expression demonstrates that friendship was not an entirely contractual concept. Even if such political friendships were made with some consideration of the anticipated benefits, the ethics of fidelity and loyalty to a friend remain an integral part of political friendship. The two components of the relationship might not always have synchronised, but this mismatch was not necessarily illogical, as explained in the previous chapter.

The use of friendship in Humanist literary and political works shows that early modern thought regained the concept of political friendship as both basic political concord and a resource of power that particular groups or actors could exploit. This was by no means a monolithic conception drawing on the available ancient ideals, as no such universal ideal existed in the classical sources. Instead, the concept of political friendship was informed by reference to distinct intellectual and political traditions of argumentation, ranging from Aristotelian and Ciceronian civil virtues to Sceptic studies of the historical practices of the best and worst forms of commonwealths. Thus, while containing subtle nuances in the various competing intellectual traditions, the concept of political friendship was a key element in all early modern visions of the constitution of polities – visions that had not yet been shaped by the regimes of a sovereign state (for a critique of the idea of 'sovereign state' in the early modern period see Spruyt 1994) and ideologies of nationalism (see the classic studies by Gellner 1983 and Hobsbawm 1990). The variety of conceptualisations of political friendship and its intrinsic links to the network of power relations is indeed the first element to be determined if we wish to understand the reception of the concept in Humanist thought and legal scholarship focusing on relations among polities.

Contractual friendship and alliance in diplomacy

Amity and its range of reference

The rise of legal Humanism had a profound impact on the formulation of the principles regulating relations between and among polities. In contrast to universalist conceptions of human nature and belonging to Christendom, Humanist authors turned to the study of historical precedents from which principles of legal practice and alternative modes of political conduct could be devised and justified. Thus, ancient history and the systematisation of laws of a particular commonwealth were at the heart of debate and ideological interpretation (Skinner 2000a: 207–208). Similarly to the internal constitution of communities, this method also shaped the conceptual application of friendship in accounts of encounters between various semi-independent and dependent communities. It is in works on the history of particular dynasties and treatises on historical legal norms and practices that the contractual concept of friendship identified by classical authors is most vividly rearticulated.

The *Oxford English Dictionary* cites Francis Bacon's essay *Of Friendship* (1612) as one of the earliest uses of the word 'friendship' (OED vol. VI: 194–195), but the examples given in the essay concern mainly private relations among individuals. The same dictionary designates political or public friendship by the word 'amity', which dates back to the thirteenth century (OED vol. I: 404) and is linked to the Latin tradition of using *'amicitia'* to designate friendly relations with strangers. Uses of 'amity' in English sources thus often, but not always, contain important markers of public and political engagement in relationships of friendship. The genealogical entry point suggested by the OED therefore deserves attention and a brief exploration.

Bacon (1561–1626), an exponent of a new Humanist tradition in Richard Tuck's terms (1993: 108), in his histories of the kings of England does indeed give examples of political compacts of friendship that strongly resemble the Roman practice. For instance, in *The History of the Reign of King Henry the Eighth* he mentions Henry VIII as pragmatically entering 'peace and amity with France, under the assurance not only of treaty and league, but of necessity and inability in the French to do him hurt' (Bacon 1998: 222). *The History of the Reign of King Henry VII* provides even more examples of the usage of the term. Bacon also conventionally inserts conceptual couples of friends, confederates and allies when reporting on the meeting of the English king and French ambassadors ('inclinations also of the two Kings in respect of their confederates and allies have severed', ibid.: 74), or when describing James III of Scotland as a 'true friend and confederate' of Henry VI (ibid.: 84).

Bacon also makes use of an already familiar conceptual couple 'concord and amity' when describing relations between England and Scotland: 'for the good of this whole island and the knitting of these two kingdoms of England and Scotland in a strait *concord and amity* by so great obligation' (ibid.: 127). These passages clearly evince the role of amity as a public relationship between countries and their kings, but they also emphasise that such amity cannot be affected by the conduct of the kings' subjects. This in itself signals monopolistic claims to authority:

My lords, … the King our master is tender in any thing that may but glance upon the *friendship* of England. The *amity* between the two Kings no doubt stands entire and inviolate. And that their subjects' swords have clashed, it is nothing unto *the public peace of the crowns*; it being a thing very usual in auxiliary forces of the best and straitest *confederates* to meet and draw blood on the field. (ibid.: 75; emphasis added)

These are marks of a distinct register in political rhetoric, regulated by its own rules of conceptual usage. The distinct rules of conceptual application that Bacon's historical narrative captures in these examples, constitute a linguistic game that seemingly preserves the alternative concept of political contractual friendship available to classical authors in their description of foreign encounters. Etymological traces of the term 'amity' also show that the game in which Bacon's historical narrative of political friendships is involved had been formed through a protracted process of medieval diplomatic circulation of the Latin term '*amicitia*' and its incremental adaptation to vernacular political vocabulary. The etymology of contemporary language, in fact, points in the same direction as the outline of medieval conceptual continuities presented in the previous chapter: the understanding of linguistic conventions that regulated the use of political friendship by early Humanist thinkers requires reconstruction of the genealogical trails of the term in late medieval diplomatic sources and their transmission to the early modern language of politics.

The Christian Latin language of 'love-diplomacy' and its vernacularisation
The *amicitia* that underlies the tradition of 'amity' seems to be a key term in the diplomatic vocabulary of the late Middle Ages and Renaissance. However, as has been argued elsewhere (Paradisi 1951), medieval diplomatic vocabulary was tailored to express the shared Christian religion and a concomitant sense of brotherhood and unity. A common religion and language – Latin – account for this linguistic register being imbued with terms such as '*amor*', '*dilectio*' and '*concordia*' (Paradisi 1974: 372), even if their insertion into the semantic field of political friendship was not entirely new, given previous links between friendship and concord and the obvious commonality of the etymological roots of '*amicitia*' and '*amor*' in classical discourse. What, however, could have been new was the political reality of a Christian communion of believers who were in principle all – princes not excepted – brothers, sisters and friends in Christ. The basic relationship within this communion would have been love and glory. In theory, the Pauline society of believers is apolitical; it mitigates the divide caused by identity, because the constitutive relation within it is to God and in God, rather than towards other believers (see the discussion of the 'Pauline' non-identity in Ojakangas 2011). This would have been different from the civic and political relations that articulate otherness, which is bridged and mitigated by means of friendship. However, this Christian ideal had an intricate relationship with the

diplomatic language of Christian princes in which it was supposedly couched. '*Amor*', '*dilectio*' and '*concordia*' did indeed widely permeate the diplomatic vocabulary, but they never succeeded in replacing the phraseology of friendship/ *amicitia*; even more paradoxically, their application was often regulated by the same linguistic conventions as the discourse of political friendship. Thus, when combined they formed a curious language – and one that is perhaps hardly comprehensible from a modern perspective – of unity and at the same time disunity, both apolitical and political.

How did the idea of Christian love and concord express itself in the language of diplomacy that guides princely conduct? The most basic linguistic expression of this phenomenon was the regular and, as sometimes maintained, exclusive appearance of '*amor*', with all its religious connotations, in diplomatic correspondence and agreements between European monarchs. From the twelfth century onwards, some historical sources referred to '*amor*' as the *desired* or *reached* agreement. One example is an agreement between Richard I of England and Philip II of France that states: '*Et uterque nostrum alteri bonam fidem, & bonum amorem se servatorum promisit; ego Philippus Rex Francorum, Richardo Regi Anglorum tanquam amico & fideli meo*' (Rymer I, I, 20, 1189[2]); another is the *Charta Regis Scotiae*: '*quod in perpetuum bonam fidem ei servabimus partier & amorem*' (ibid. I, I, 150, 1244). Given the spiritual and political prominence of the Church, one cannot fail to notice how frequently, and perhaps more naturally than anywhere else, the term is used in papal bullas and other clerical documents that constituted an essential part of medieval diplomacy.[3]

'*Concordia*' was another term from the Christian discourse that could in principle have been substituted for '*amicitia*' in diplomatic jargon, given its wide circulation. Some scholars even tend to conflate the use of '*amicitia*' and '*concordia*' in medieval 'treaties' by equating both with amity (for examples of translating '*pace et concordia*' as 'peace and amity' see Ziegler 2004: 153, 158). Such conflation might be due either to an anachronistic conception of all historical diplomatic agreements as treaties of peace and (widely and vaguely understood) friendship, or to linguistic conventions regulating the use of Christian concepts in the realm of diplomacy. For instance, this convention explains the use of the term in an early English Alliance (Confederatio) with Flanders against France that contains the couple '*pax aut concordia*' (Rymer I, I, 30, 1197; the connective '*aut*' here means that categories are disjoint but not exclusive) and dictates its inclusion in the same range of contracted relations as 'peace' and 'treaty' in an

---

[2] References to Thomas Rymer's *Fœdera* collection are made in the form 'Rymer A, B, C, D' in which A stands for the volume number, B – for the part number, C – for the page number, D – for the year of the cited document.

[3] It appears, for instance, in such phrases as '*religionis amore principium acceperunt*' in a letter of Pope Adrian IV, see ibid. (I, I, 5, 1154); and '*laborare velitis nostris precibus & amore*' in *Super dicto Negotio ad Cardinales* (ibid. II, III, 9, 1328).

agreement between the English and French monarchs: '*Pax, Amicitia, Fœdera, & Concordia*' (ibid. VI, I, 89, 1515). However, like '*amor*', '*concordia*' also has clear Christian associations, as is apparent from the frequency with which it appears in bullas. The Christian connotations of '*concordia*' and the interrelationship with the linguistic conventions of its application merit a separate investigation, although such an inquiry falls outwith the limits of this book.

If translated literally in this context as 'love', '*amor*' retains a paradoxical link to friendship (*amicitia*) through the way in which the principal participants of this relationship were named. The Christian concept of love apparently contains an inherent tension between its various connotations that scholars have attempted to clarify since Augustine's dismissal of the strict distinction between '*dilectio*', '*caritas*' and '*amor*' in respect to good and evil affection (*De Civitate Dei* XIV, VII). Thus, rather than 'lovers' ('*amatores*'), which would probably have invoked an improper erotic context, Christian princes engaging in diplomatic relations called one another '*amici*' (friends), even if it was a choice accentuating the nature of Christian love as unconditional, emphasised by the formulas '*amicus in Christo*' and '*carissimo amico*'/'*amico suo carissimo*'. As such, this vocabulary is tied to the idea of the community of believers as friends in Christ and to the concept of universal '*caritas*', which is nonetheless difficult to apply to the type of relations that could be sought and negotiated by the mundane powers. Such relationships are more comprehensible if described by a hypothetically narrower '*amor*' deprived of erotic connotations. These limits in conceptual application indicate the possibility for pragmatic and contingent action, which is expressed and described by related vocabulary found in the language of diplomacy among Christians.

It comes as little surprise, therefore, that the prolific vocabulary of Christian love is effectively appropriated by diplomatic linguistic conventions reflecting and promoting pragmatic relations contracted for particular political ends. In fact, late medieval '*amor*' assumes the same place in the grammatical structure of diplomatic statements as '*amicitia*', thereby merging the meaning of a possibly universal affection with the contractual linguistic convention. What is surprising in this conceptual development is that '*amor*' does not completely replace the classical master noun in diplomacy – '*amicitia*' – despite their possibly conflicting ideological functions and contexts of application. The flexibility of Christian diplomatic language was such that it allowed the terms to be used simultaneously and interchangeably in the same documents and even statements. Thus, the message that the use of both terms conveyed to relevant audiences could have been virtually the same.[4] This linguistic convention attained its apotheosis in the

---

[4] The following are typical examples of expressions from the fifteenth and sixteenth centuries: '*bonus Amor mutuus & Amicitia*' (Rymer IV, II, 68, 1414), '*Amicitiæ mutuæ & Amoris Fœdere solidius connectantur*' (ibid. IV, IV, 28, 1421), '*intimo Amore, Fide & Amicitiarum*

'treaty' of love (e.g. in the form '*amoris foedera*'), which in itself demonstrates the complex intertwinement of ideological and political practices in the conceptual apparatus under Christendom. Notably, contracted 'love' was a common element not only in princely diplomatic politics, but also in relations between powers spiritual and temporal.[5] In this sense, the natural affection and common Christian disposition was conveniently subsumed by the language game of advantage-seeking relations in the context of inter-princely relations.

The permeation of '*amor*' in medieval discourse had a tangible impact on the development of vernacular diplomatic vocabularies. In the fourteenth century, diplomatic documents composed in French and circulated between the English and French commonly rendered '*amor*' as '*amour*'. In most cases, '*amour/amur*' also effectively replaced '*amicitia*'.[6] Similarly to the conventions of Latin diplomacy, the parties to documents composed in French called each other '*Amiz*'. However, by the late fifteenth and early sixteenth century, '*amour*' disappears almost completely from French diplomatic formulations, ceding its place to '*amyte*' and '*amytie*'[7] (despite that some documents composed in Latin still contained '*amor*'). French political actors were not the only ones whose correspondence used '*amor/amour*', as the term also appeared occasionally in documents exchanged with other European powers.[8]

In turn, these tendencies in Latin and French vocabularies conditioned a somewhat contradictory choice of terms in the first agreements and other documents composed in early modern English. One of the first documents written in English and appearing in Rymer's *Foedera* makes use of both 'love' and 'friendship'. The instructions given to the bishop of Lincoln, Sir William Coggeshale

---

Foedere conjuncti' (ibid. V, IV, 220, 1506) and '*Amore & Amicitia, quæ inter Nos est*' (ibid. VI, I, 14, 1510; VI, III, 86, 1543). The overlapping meaning and use of the terms translated into their inconsistent appearance in diplomatic correspondence. Examples of such inconsistency can be found in the documents exchanged between the king of England and duke of Burgundy in 1419. Some used expressions containing both terms: '*ipsum Amoris, & Affectûs mutui, ac speciales Amicitiæ Foederibus invicem copulari*' (*Confirmatio, pro Parte Regis, Foederis cum Duce Burgundiæ*, in ibid. IV, III, 144, 1419); while others retained just one: '*De & super Ligis, Confœderationibus, Alligantiis, & Amicitiis, generalibus vel particularibus, realibus sive personalibus*' (*Instrumentum Ambaxiatorum Burgundiæ super Confœderatione præmissa*, in ibid. IV, III, 144, 1419).

5 In 1442 the alliance was suggested to Pope Eugene IV, the text of which proclaims '*Foedus seu Confœderationem & Alligantiam reiprocæ Dilectionis & Amicitiæ contrahere*' (see *De Foedere cum Eugenio Papa*, in ibid. V, I, 111, 1442).

6 For the use of the word '*amur*' see ibid. (II, III, 9, 1328); for the terminological couple '*Amour & Alliance*' see ibid. (III, II, 19, 1360); for the appearance of the term in the extended diplomatic formula '*a bonne Paix, Transquillite, Amour, & Alliance*' see ibid. (IV, III, 27, 1417).

7 See the 1468 treaty with Burgundy, ibid. (V, II, 153, 1468).

8 See later documents on the relations with the king of Denmark: '*amore & benevolentiæ affectione refertissimus*' and '*ad sinceri Amoris cultum ejusque conservationem pertinere queant*' (ibid. VII, I, 203, 1598).

and Nichol Bildeston, who were sent as emissaries to the duke of Bavaria and to other German princes and cities to request auxiliary forces to assist England in its conflict with France, read: 'They shall declare … howe the sadde Love, Pees, and Accorde, that continually hath been betwix the King's Progenitours, and also him and the said Elizours and Duc Henry'; later, however, we also come across 'friendship': 'to considre the grete Charge that he hath born many Yeres continuing his Werres, and shew him such Frendship now as they wol desire of him in cas semblable' (ibid. IV, IV, 45, 1421). It is noteworthy that the clause on the augmentation of the Christian faith among Christian princes appears separately in this document.

'Love' is still a rare, if not aberrant, occurrence in English diplomatic correspondence during this period. The first documents written in English often copied French terminology. For instance, Edward IV's proposal of peace and abstinence from war that ambassadors were instructed to convey to the French king uses the French '*amyte*' to refer to a binding agreement: 'and, over that, thei shuld make a private *Amyte* betwixt them both, *bynding* them to a mutuell Assistence in Case any of them both were be their Subgects wronged or disobeied' (ibid. V, III, 65, 1475; emphasis added). Given the Latin and French origins of the word '*amyte*' and its dual etymological relation to the concepts of love (*amor*) and friendship (*amicitia*), the English experienced certain difficulties in finding a uniform term to designate the diplomatic relationship they were contracting. The problem became even more acute after the Reformation. While '*amitié*' gradually replaced '*amour*' in French copies of the documents concluded and exchanged with the English authorities, the English copies often used variations of 'frendship', 'friendship', 'frendshippe' of Germanic origin and 'amitie' and 'amity', sometimes even in the same document (ibid. VII, I, 96, 1592; VII, II, 206, 1615).

The overall tendency in diplomatic vocabulary of the late fifteenth and sixteenth century, however, was to avoid extensive use of 'love' and related terminology in diplomatic exchanges. The changes brought about by the Reformation and the temporal authorities' monopolisation of power over worldly affairs (Jackson 2007: 38–49; Skinner 2000b: 14–19) required contriving the conceptual means that would secure the intelligibility and efficacy of interaction between independent and distinct polities. The connotations of universal and unconditional love were seemingly of no avail to the emerging system of the balance of power. The incremental conceptual change from 'love' to 'friendship' is clearly manifested in the vernacularisation of Latin vocabulary in early modern English translations. Richard Hakluyt's *The Principal Navigations Voyages Traffiques & Discoveries of the English Nation* (1598–1600) is instructive in illustrating this process and the ways in which the late medieval conceptual apparatus was understood and adapted to early modern conventions. It contains a collection of documents in the form of correspondence, agreements, charters and licences, all originally written in Latin and then rendered into early modern English. What is indicative of the conceptual change is the choice of words for translating such Latin terms as '*dilectio*', '*concordia*', '*amor*' and '*amicitia*' in diplomatic contexts.

Hakluyt, for instance, reproduces the text of the 1157 League between Henry II of England and Frederick Barbarossa Holy Roman Emperor, which in Latin uses expressions such as '*salutem, & veræ dilectionis concordiam*', '*amplectimur, pacis & amoris invicem dignatus estis fœdera inchoare*' and '*inter nos & populos nostros dilectionis & pacis unitas indivisa, commercial tuta*' (Hakluyt 1903: 316–318). The English translation in Hakluyt's work shows that the Christian Latin 'love' vocabulary ('*dilectio*' and '*amor*') was either unfit or incomprehensible and had thus to be adapted to the emerging modern diplomatic language, its conception of the international agreement, and the rules for naming and wording. Thus, an English translation renders these expressions as, respectively: 'wishes health and concord of sincere amitie', 'to beginne a league of peace and friendship betweene us' and 'an indivisible unitie of friendship and peace, and safe trade of Marchandize' (ibid.). Two elements are worth emphasising here: the term '*amor*' is translated as 'friendship', while '*dilectio*' in the first instance becomes 'sincere amitie' and in the second 'friendship'.

A 1216 (possibly 1217) letter from Henry III of England to Haquinus (Haakon IV) of Norway also contains a conventional Christian '*pacis & dilectionis*' in the expression '*desiderantes fœdus* pacis & dilectionis *libenter nobiscum inire, & nobiscum confœderari*'; in this case it is translated as 'desirous to begin and conclude betweene us both, a league of peace and amitie' (ibid.: 320–321) to remove the Christian '*dilectio*'. A century later, in 1313, Edward II uses the term '*amicitia*' in a letter to Haquinus (Haakon V Magnusson) in the peculiar combination: '*delinquentium societate non fuerunt, aliqualiter ulciscantur, vestram* amicitiam affectuose *requirimus & rogamus*', translated as 'nor have had any society with the saide offenders … you would of your *love and friendship*, command the foresaid pledges to be set at libertie' (ibid.: 340–342). A very similar translation appears in a second letter of Edward II (ibid.: 344); in a third, '*amicitia*' is translated solely as 'love and friendship' based on the model of the previous two letters (ibid.: 348). This third letter contains the postulation '*inter nos & vos, notròsque & vestros subditos hinc inde foveri desideramus mutuam* concordiam & amorem', which is translated as 'that mutuall concord and amitie should be maintained and cherished between your and our subjects on both parts' (ibid.: 345, 348).

What had previously been 'love' under Christendom had to be transformed into and recognised as friendship (expressed with words either of Latin or Germanic origin) for the sake of the conceptual stability of early modern 'sovereign' diplomacy. These translations show that the medieval '*dilectio*' and '*amor*' no longer fitted the concept of the public 'international' agreement. Instead, '*amitie*' had to be used, even if the original sources lacked the word '*amicitia*'. As such, 'love' did appear in these translations, but it was used to translate the personal disposition of a king towards his counterpart and his subjects, expressed in the original as '*amicitia affectuose*' or merely '*amicitia*', as opposed to the state of public relations or international compact. Despite the appearance of 'sincere amitie', it follows from comparison with the Latin terms that '*amitie*' is predominantly used to refer to public agreements and relations with foreign princes.[9] These conceptual and terminological transformations were by no means unique to northern Europe. Politics in Byzantium and eastern Europe witnessed analogous conceptual developments: Muscovite Rus' had for a long time used '*liubov*' (love-friendship) as its diplomatic master noun, adapted from the Greek '*philia*' (which had a double designation – love and friendship – as well as strong Orthodox Christian connotations) and Greek diplomatic conventions. By the late seventeenth century, the strong connotations of Christian unconditional love and intimate feelings necessitated the replacement of '*liubov*' with the more fitting term '*druzhba*' (friendship), which is still in use (see Roshchin 2009).

The intricate presence of two words – 'amity' and 'friendship' – standing for friendship in early modern English allowed speakers to employ, when necessary, their subtle and elusive distinctions to accentuate, in addition to the reached public agreement, the personal affection of a monarch for his or her counterpart or his or her disposition to the overall state of affairs. Such is the example of an edict made by James I in June 1603, which declares: 'Although we have made it knowen by publike Edict, That at our entrance into these our Kingdomes of England and Ireland, we stood, as still wee doe, in *good amitie and friendship* with all the princes of Christendome' (Edict of James I 1603; emphasis added). The edict also designates to whom it applies, and mentions 'any subiect of any princes in league, or amitie with us'. The conceptual borderline between 'amity' and 'friendship' is unquestionably fuzzy and far from constituting a definite rule. The different etymological origins of the two words also allow them to be perfectly synonymous and refer to the same phenomenon. Nonetheless, the oscillation between the connotations attached to one concept, expressed by two distinct terms, makes intelligible such conjunctions as 'amitie and friendship' and 'friendly amitie' present in early modern sources.

Vernacularisation of the common Christian vocabulary of 'love' and the para-doxical loss of 'love' in this process shows that the concept ceased to perform its political function of pacifying and holding the Christian world together. In the context of the polity-bound exercise of sovereign power and religious strife, the

---

[9] There are multiple examples in the original sources of this period, such as the expression 'Peace you haue broken, and olde amity' from the story about the Battle of Flodden in the reign of Henry VIII (*The Mirror for Magistrates* 1960 (1587 Ed.): 490), showing the link between the concepts of public agreement and amity.

idea of universal love – as well as love as an intimate relationship between prob-
able competitors – was difficult to accommodate in the conceptual vocabulary of
diplomacy. The parties continued to appeal occasionally to love in their expressions of fidelity to a common Christian faith, but only as a means to augment
the agreements into which they entered. Besides, the advantages of love were also
emphasised when contrasted with the state of hostility between monarchs. The
rhetoric of exhorting the parties to proper conduct added another key political
function to the concept of love and later friendship: in building an opposition
between the condemned and desired states of affairs, '*amor/amicitia*' could be
used to promote, justify and legitimise certain political acts.[10]

The history of the curious combination of love and friendship in diplomatic
vocabulary highlights the problematic co-existence of the particular and universal claims to authority in European politics. On the one hand, the language of
love served the ends of the Christian community of believers and their common
political space; on the other, the language game that in practice subsumed the
vocabulary of love preserved the space for political contingency, local particularity and compromise. This game eventually ushered in the replacement of
'love' with diplomatic 'friendship' as a corollary to the centrifugal processes in
Christendom (for the argument on the problematic and contending claims to
authority under the allegedly imperial setting of the Middle Ages see Osiander
2001: 129–136). This political rationality explains the resurgence of '*amicitia*'
and its vernacular analogies in the Renaissance diplomacy in northern Europe –
and even more so in the south, as follows from Randall Lesaffer's observation of
the similar increasing frequency of occurrences of '*amicitia*' in treaties concluded
between Italian powers from the early fifteenth century onwards (see Lesaffer
2002: 94–95; 2004: 36–37).

The resilient linguistic convention of political friendship: contract and alliance
It is time to inquire into the nature of this convention of diplomatic friendship,
the features and elements that made its application distinct, and the reasons why
it evolved from the late Middle Ages into early modern diplomatic language in
such a way as to become one of the most popular international instruments. In

---

[10] In 1475 the French and English kings made an agreement of friendship, *Appunctuamenta
de Amicitia*, in which '*amor*' refers to the relationship between the kings and is contrasted
with war and hostility, which ought to cease to exist: '*sic quòd, quamdiu vixerint, Guerræ,
Bella, & Hostilitates inter eos omninò Cessabunt, ymmò & Benivolentiâ & Amore Se & Sua
mutuò pertractabunt*' (Rymer V, III, 67, 1475). Similarly, in the Treaty of London that
James I concluded with Spain in 1604, violations of ancient friendship, which in James I's
understanding were due to personal quarrels between the monarchs, are found inexpedient
particularly because the ancient friendship had been daily cemented by love and good
offices: '*vincula disrumperent, ac veterem amicitiam, novis semper ac indies cumulatis amoris
ac benevolentiae officiis excultam, violarent*' (Davenport 1917: 251, Doc. 27).

other words, this is a question about what constitutes friendship as a political and legal concept in the domain of diplomatic text. A peculiar feature of conceptual history in studying a conceptual change and use of concepts in a corpus of diplomatic texts consists in employing a very wide range of methodological tools to evaluate the perfomativity of a text, and of particular statements and concepts. The style of writing diplomatic documents does not allow for the use of rhetorical figures – the main driving forces in Skinnerian analysis of conceptual change – to prevent even a minimal contestability of the conveyed meaning. Nor can the use of friendship be analysed by isolating individual parts of speech with the aim of establishing the illocutionary or performative effects of the statements in the Austinian style (see Austin 1956–1957).

To understand a conceptual change in diplomatic – and 'shared' *par excellence* – language, it is all the more important to broaden the scope of analysis to utilise a set of techniques scrutinising the rules of application of specific terms. Regardless of various preconceptions of the idea of a contract or a commended ideal of friendship, the following analysis will identify the links from '*amicitia*' to the subject of the documents in which it is used, to its range of reference or neighbouring semantic fields, and to the adjectives *and* verbs associated with this noun. Only this methodological breadth is capable of making sense of the otherwise repetitive nature of diplomatic texts and highlighting the nature of linguistic convention.

Despite the proliferation of terms with strong Christian connotations and common assumptions about the prevalence of '*amor*' (see Paradisi 1951; 1974: 372), late medieval diplomatic agreements and exchanges contain a number of examples of '*amicitia*' designating political agreements, even if use of the term before the mid fourteenth century remains rare. The princes of southern Europe, for instance Castile and Sicily, were among the first to popularise its use in diplomatic practice; after a while, it became customary in diplomatic exchanges between English and other northern European princes as well. In documents from the twelfth and thirteenth centuries, '*amicitia*' is used as a part of emerging formulas that were to become diplomatic cliché in early modernity. One of the first signs of '*amicitia*' becoming a part of such a stable diplomatic formula is its repeated inclusion into 'treaty' formulations proclaiming a state of friendship: '*promissimus ergo vobis ... terra & mari pacem & perpetuam amicitiam nos fideliter servaturos*' (Rymer I, I, 21, 1190).[11] Other signs of the re-emerging formula are the recurring use of '*amicitia*' with related terms such as '*foedus*', '*societas*', '*confoederatio*' and '*pax*'.[12] This semantic field of the concept was evident in ancient

---

[11] See also '*quod nos facimus & firmamus pacem, & veram amicitiam cum*' (ibid. I, II, 40, 1201).

[12] For instance, the terminological couple '*pax & amicitia*' appears in the king of Navarre's *Carta*: '*quod nos facimus & firmamus pacem & veram amicitiam*' (ibid. I, I, 40, 1201); other

historical accounts, and seems to have migrated through the process of copying to the late Middle Ages.

The innovation of the late Middle Ages included the broadening of diplomatic instruments associated with '*amicitia*'. Whereas earlier documents contained parsimonious and narrower titles and terminological associations such as '*foedus et amicitia*' or '*societas et amicitia*', the diplomatic language of the fourteenth century opened up the convention to change. From the fourteenth century onwards, the formula extends to include a wide range of related terms, including corresponding nouns and adjectives. In this sense the agreement with the Doge and People of Genoa (*Conventiones cum Duce & Populo Januensibus*) is a typical example: '*Confoederationes, Amicitias, Conventiones, Remissiones, Pacta, & Pacem perpetuam*' (ibid. III, I, 13, 1347). Together with the growing number of references to '*amicitia*' and its extensions (and in this sense the dispersion of the diplomatic cluster of terms around it), the period also witnessed the dissociation of the classical terminological couple of '*societas*' and '*amicitia*', with direct implications for contemporary customs.[13] '*Societas*' lost its own ideological battle and was replaced by '*liga*' and '*alligantia*'. Thus, the new associations that '*amicitia*' formed were '*Liga & Amicitia*' and '*Amicitia & Alligantia*'.[14] Diplomatic linguistic conventions seem to have allowed for the separate and the conjoint use of the terms: '[Quoscumque] *Tractatus, Confoederationes, Pacta, Conventiones, Alligantias, Amicitias, Pactiones, Promissiones, Fœdera, & Ligamina...*' (ibid. III, II, 61, 1362). Consequently, participants in this relationship were no longer termed '*socii*', but rather '*alligati*' (ibid. III, I, 66, 1351).[15] The term was rendered in early French documents as '*alliez*' (see *De Amicitia & Alligantiis inter Reges Angliae & Franciae*, ibid. III, II, 19, 1360), and in early English diplomatic documents became 'Allies' (ibid. IV, IV, 45, 1421). As we shall see, the association of

terminological couples include *societas, confœderatio* & *amicitia* from 'Litera Regis Norwegiæ de antique amicitia observanda, &* contra Theotonicos Regnum invadere conjurantes': '*mutuæ societatis & amicitiæ inter vos & nos, transmissis, vestræ fraternitatis excellentiæ grates referimus speciales; attentius deprecantes ut confœderationes & amicitias antiquas ... observare velitis cum effectu*' (ibid. I, IV, 87, 1286); for *fœdus & amicitia* there is also *De Fœdere cum Imperatore*: '*nos sibi in amicitia & mutuo fœdere jungi voluit*' (ibid. I, II, 100, 1227).

[13] For a more detailed analysis of the diverting conceptual trajectories of '*societas*' and '*amicitia*' see Roshchin (2013).

[14] The former were common for the agreements with Castile, for example '*Necnon ad Ligam & perpetuam Amicitiam, inter ipsum Regem & suos Subditos, & Nos & nostros Subditos, Ineundum*' (Rymer II, IV, 151, 1343); see also *Ad Regem Castellæ, super Tractatu & Matrimonio antedictis*: '*Necnon de Ligis & Amicitiis, inter Nos & Domos nostras Regias ineundis, & mutuis Auxiliis hinc inde præstandis*' (ibid. II, IV, 186, 1345).

[15] See also the agreement of friendship (*Appunctuamenta de Amicitia*) between France and England, 1475: '*Amicitiam, Ligam, Intelligentias, atque Confœderationem Inivimus, Contraximus*', in regard to which the following should be done: '*Amicitia, inter antedictos Principes, ut præmittitur, contracta, minimè Violentur seu Rumpatur; sed talia, contra dictam Amicitiam sic attemptata*' (ibid. V, III, 67, 1475).

friends and allies had important legal implications, particularly in respect to the concept of *postliminium* and its attached liabilities.

In fact, this subtle terminological replacement frames the irretrievable conceptual association of friendship with alliance in most contemporary international theory and practice since Hans Morgenthau (2005: 193–204), with attempts to emancipate friendship from the burden of this relationship being an exception rather than the rule (see Berenskoetter 2007; Onuf 2009). The emphasis on more active political and military bondage and obligation, predating the modern classification of offensive and defensive alliances, was evident in French vocabulary as the combination 'love and alliance' (see the titles '*amour & alliance*' above). The political context of the affirmed conceptual association was indeed that of dispute settlement and pursuance of interests, often commercial, by means of securing alliances. However, the synonymy of friendship and military alliance was not always apparent and implied. As noted by Brunner, friendship in the Middle Ages could have an independent designation of a local community of order, to which some party could be in the role of perpetrator (Brunner 1992: 52). It also follows from the links that friendship had in this corpus of documents to the concepts of enmity and enemy: namely these links show that the relations were not necessarily antonymous, even though *adversarius* did appear in corresponding treaties.

An increasing number of late medieval feuds and inter-princely contentions meant a collateral politicisation of the relation between orderly friendship and disorderly enmity. This politicisation actualised the opposition between friendship (representing the community of law) and enmity (representing the state of feud) in the medieval politico-legal establishment, and re-introduced the context of alliance-building into the concept's immediate range of reference. As a rhetorical means of reinforcing the opposition between friends and enemies, international compacts repeatedly used the formula '*Amicorum Amicus & Amici, & Inimicorum Inimicus & Inimici*' to frame a prince's relations not only to his counterpart but also to interested third parties (Rymer V, IV, 220, 1506). The opposition was amplified by the internal structuring of documents related to peace agreements, in which proclamations of friendship were followed by the cessation of hostilities and enmity.

Granted the issues of throne succession and religious strife – with its absolutisation of the enemy – the conceptual opposition probably reached its utmost intensity following the Reformation. The wars between Elizabeth I of England and Philip II of Spain at the end of the sixteenth century constitute one of the key political instances of bringing together the ideas of friendship and active military alliance. Papers relating to the negotiations between Elizabeth I and Henry IV of France over their policies towards Spain show that 'friendship' was now used to justify and, in fact, to demand alliance-building. Thus, Elizabeth I wrote in one of her messages:

> And if the *French King* shall procure Peace both with his Subjects, and expell the
> *Spaniards* out of his Countrey, and yeld to her *Majestie* such Frenship against the
> *Kinge of Spayne* ... by ayding of her against *Spayne*, as she hath done to him against
> the same *King of Spayne*, she shall not mislike that he make Peace with his Subjects.
> (ibid. VII, I, 96, 1592)

This document, produced in the midst of the ongoing war in France and rivalries
between England and Spain, perfectly illuminates the utility of friendship (e.g.
in the form of 'friendship against') to princely discourse on alliance-building and
the provision of help, allowing it to be used in arguments that justified, substantiated and demanded a certain course of action. Elizabeth I also employed other
justificatory tools, by comparing her aid to that of other 'Frends in Christendom'
and by pointing out to Henry IV that his status of 'a Christian Prince' obliges
him not to make peace with the Spanish king. 'Friends in Christ/Friendship in
Christendom', as noted earlier, was a powerful rhetorical trope drawing on the
previous ultimate, but fading, politico-religious ideal of medieval Europe.[16] The
power of this ideal could still be sensed in the course of religious wars in the
European continent. For instance, The Peace of Augsburg (1555), which formally put an end to the religious conflict between Catholics and Lutherans in the
Holy Roman Empire, contains an order to subjects previously cleft by religious
intolerance to treat each other in *true friendship and Christian love*.[17]

While putting forward the image of the community of believers, in princely
diplomacy friendship in Christ was also made to refer to a collective stand against
the enemy of the faith. The Reformation ushered this community into the realities of conflicting and mutually exclusive visions of the world that sanctioned the
formation of local and rival groupings between Christian princes and their alliances with 'infidels'. Thus, the universal ideal of being friends within a common
Christendom is now particularised, even if inadvertently, in political rhetoric to
serve the needs of individual princes laying claims to being defenders of both the
true faith and the interests of their realms (see also Lesaffer 2004: 29–33).

In terms of its juridical identity, the application of '*amicitia*' in this period
remains somewhat ambiguous, although it was commonly listed among other
pacta, *conventiones* and *confœderationes*: it could have meant both a particular
type of treaty and the subject of a treaty. In some documents the term refers to

---

[16] In addition to '*amicus in Christo*', the late medieval and early modern periods witnessed
references to the general condition of friendship between Christian princes: '*Ad Honorem
Dei, evitationemque effusionis Sanguinis* Christiani, *pro quiete ac bono Pacis perpetuò dura-
turis, De, pro, & super* Alligantia *& perpetua* Amicitia *inter Nos*', Alliance with Burgundy (in
ibid. IV, II, 40, 1413); or, to give another example: '*Amicitiam omnium Christianorum
Principum*' (ibid. VI, I, 113, 1516). For a detailed discussion of the use of rhetoric in early
modern diplomatic letters, see Mack (2002: 177–188).

[17] See § 14: '*rechter Freundschafft und Christlicher Lieb meynen*', at www.westfaelische-
geschichte.de/que739.

the type of treaty either in the document heading[18] or in the body of the text.[19] This type of treaty was also mentioned as such in notifications sent to third parties.[20] Nevertheless, available examples of the conjunction of 'amicitia' and 'foedus' in diplomatic documents are inconclusive regarding the independent status of friendship as a treaty.

This indeterminacy remains equally equivocal in the structure of the sentences connecting the noun to an associated set of verbs. Setting aside the attempts to finally resolve the issue of whether 'amicitia' refers to an independent type of treaty, a survey of associated verbs highlights the nature of the designated relationship with significantly higher certainty. Late medieval diplomatic charters and letters revealed the beneficial status of friendship, as they typically contained promises to be on the same side as friends or expressed the desire to be friends with another party.[21] Nevertheless, alongside such demonstrations of desire, there are expressions that indicate how and why 'amicitia' could be understood as a *contracted agreement* as early as the twelfth and thirteenth centuries. The range of verbs associated with 'amicitia' points to the voluntariness, temporariness and conditionality of the designated relationship: the parties commonly entered into, resumed, observed, preserved and united in friendship.[22] The same vocabulary was employed in the fourteenth and fifteenth centuries, which were marked by an increased circulation of the term in diplomatic discourse. As the utility of diplomatic 'amicitia' gained wider recognition, the parties resorted to language that resembled the language of modern agreements, albeit couched in Latin terms: friendship could be fostered, made stronger and firmer; parties could promise to maintain and preserve friendship treaties permanently; they entered, agreed upon, contracted and concluded friendships; parties could indissolubly unite in a compact of friendship, and also undertake mutual obligations.[23]

[18] For example, '*Fœdus* & *Amicitia innovata inter Henricus Regem Angliæ* & *Philip. Regem Franciæ*' (Rymer I, I, 17, 1180).

[19] For example, in the agreement with the duke of Bavaria: '*in amicitia* & *fœdere mutuo specialius adjungi*' (ibid. I, II, 100, 1227).

[20] For example, '*pacis* & *amicitiæ Fœdus*' was mentioned in the epistle sent from Richard I of England to Pope Clement III (ibid. I, I, 22, 1190).

[21] See, for instance, '*asciscant sibi de suis amicis communiter*' (ibid. I, I, 20, 1182) and '*amodò volumus esse amici*' (ibid. I, I, 16, 1177).

[22] See '*amicitiam innovavimus*' (ibid. I, I, 17, 1180); '*amicitiam nos fideliter servaturos*' and '*in amicitia adjungi*' (ibid. I, I, 21, 1190); '*amicitia inter nos* & *vos perpetua perseveret*', '*amicitiam observare*' and '*in amicitia jungi voluit*' (ibid. I, I, 50, 1212).

[23] See '*de mutua amicitia confovenda*' (ibid. II, IV, 151, 1343); '*recolentes amicitiam solidam*' and '*augeri amicitiæ mutuæ firmitatem*' (ibid. II, IV, 151, 1343); '*Attemptata ex utraque parte debitè, quantum ad Nos ... mutuam Amicitiam inter Nos* & *dictum Regem... perpetuò confoveri, cupientes*' (ibid. III, I, 7, 1347); '*amicitiae foedera conservare cupimus*' (ibid. III, I, 29, 1348); '*Amicitias, Pacta inierunt* & *fecerunt*' (ibid. III, I, 13, 1347); '*Unitatis* & *indissolubilis Amicitiæ Fœdere conjungatur*' and '*Unitatis* & *Amicitiæ nexibus antiquitus mutuo jungebantur*' (ibid. III, II, 60–61, 1362). See also examples from the fifteenth century:

This is by no means an exhaustive list; it is simply the case that these expressions appear to be exemplary of the speech acts made in the surveyed corpus of diplomatic documents. The phrasing of these expressions, the use of specific verbs and their regularity in the corpus of diplomatic texts provide sufficient evidence for the interpretation of friendship (*amicitia*) as an independent, negotiated and contracted political relationship, for the purpose of which the compact was made. In some cases the parties chose to name their agreement as a friendship compact; in others it was referred to as a compact type.

The contractual aspects of friendship become even more salient if we take into account the range of clauses that follow these perlocutionary proclamations of friendship and the obligations that parties to friendship agreements incur (for an overview of the obligations incurred by '*amicitia*' see Lesaffer 2002: 91). This is perhaps not surprising, given that the object of the survey is the language of international agreements themselves. However, these examples are helpful in pointing out that references to friendship in late medieval agreements were not so much about affirmation and confirmation of some value or a normative ideal, but more about a particular type of contracted relationship, as reflected in the language games unfolding around the concept.

Binding conditions of friendship were often meant to ensure predictability of action and the unity of the parties in their conception of order (for instance, by means of clauses accentuating the obligated condition: '*ac speciales Amicitiæ Fœderibus invicem copulari*', Rymer IV, III, 144, 1419). This is probably one of the most basic tasks that the contracted diplomatic instrument should have performed in the absence of a commonly recognised authority and unstable allegiances among various dukes and barons who tended to change sides in the frequent conflicts of the pre- and post-Reformation periods. Such a function thus resembles the discursive practices that helped the ancient Roman Empire expand by allying peoples without demanding the surrender of their 'free' status, even if, as Arthur Nussbaum observed, Roman treaty practice was not formally incorporated into medieval and early modern treaties (Nussbaum 1952: 680–681). It is also no surprise that the tying and binding functions of the concept commonly referred to on the eve of what came to be termed the Westphalian system were later rearticulated in those regions (e.g. America) where the laws and customs of 'civilised' conduct had not been elaborated and enforced in practice, and in regions undergoing a rearrangement of the political order.

As already noted, the fourteenth century was marked by more frequent asser-

---

'*bonus Amor mutuus, & Amicitia, atque grata Conversatio nutriri, augmentari, firmari, & continuari possint*' (ibid. IV, II, 68, 1414); '*Amicitiæ contrahere, inire, facere, atque firmare*' (ibid. V, I, 111, 1442); and '*perpetuam Pacem, Amicitiam, Alligantiam, & Confœderationem, pro Nobis... Ineverunt, Fecerunt, Concordaverunt, Contraxerunt, & Concluserunt*' (ibid. V, II, 146, 1467).

tions of friendship and its listing among other types of treaties and leagues in documents relating to 'foreign' relations; the same tendencies continued into the fifteenth and sixteenth centuries. However, once the instrument of friendship became an accepted and widely implemented norm, the grammatical rules for using the term '*amicitia*' gradually started to change. Notably, by the late sixteenth and early seventeenth centuries, the practice of composing diplomatic documents lost the need for a range of verbs emphasising the contractual and binding nature of friendship. Sometime between the fifteenth and sixteenth centuries, diplomatic linguistic conventions started to transform in a way that emphasised the value and quality of the reached agreement, rather than the fact of contracting. As concluded friendships, pacts and alliances became increasingly common, diplomatic instruments started to emphasise their own sincerity, integrity, firmness, sanctity and true nature with corresponding adjectives in the opening lines of the text.[24] In the early seventeenth century, such rhetorical means of reinforcing and ornamenting friendship became a stabilised and ritualised convention.[25] The Treaty of Friendship and Peace (*Tractatus firmæ Amicitiæ, & Pacis perpetuæ*), or the Treaty of Madrid, made between Charles I of England and Philip IV of Spain in 1630 and ending England's costly involvement in the Thirty Years' War (1618–1648) demonstrates a whole range of qualities with which the parties could rhetorically celebrate and reinforce the contracted friendship in the midst of protracted and multi-sided religious conflict:

> First, it was and is concluded, settled, and accorded, that from this day forth, there shall be a good, sincere, true, firm and perfect amity, league, and perpetual peace, which shall be inviolably observed and kept, both by land and by sea and fresh waters, between the Most Serene King of the Spains and the Most Serene King of Great Britain, and all their heirs and successors, and all their kingdoms, countries, dominions, lands, peoples, vassals, liegemen, and subjects, now being or which hereafter shall be, of whatever condition, rank, or degree they may be, so that the aforesaid vassals and subjects must henceforth favor each other mutually, and render each other mutual services, and treat each other, mutually, with sincere good-will.[26]

[24] See, for instance, *Appunctuamenta* [agreement] *Amicitiæ perpetuæ inter Regem & Ducem Burgundiæ*: '*bona, sincera, vera, integra, perfecta, firma, sancta, & perpetua Pax & Amicitia, Liga, Confœderatio, & Unio, per Terram, Mare, & dulces Aquas*', in Rymer (V, IV, 40, 1474); and *Tractatus Amicitiæ cum Francisco Rege moderno*: '*Inprimis, quòd bonæ, sincera, firmæ, & perfectæ sint & inviolabiliter habeantur Pax, Amicitia, Fœdera, & Concordia*', ibid. (VI, I, 89, 1515).

[25] The convention normally required enumerating qualitative adjectives in the first articles of the 'treaties' to amplify the contracted condition of friendship, as exemplified by the Treaty of Madrid between Spain and England in 1604: '*conclusum, stabilitum, et accordatum fuit et est, ut ab hodie in antea, sit bona, sincera, vera, firma, ac perfecta amicitia et confoederatio ac pax perpetuo duratura, quae inviolabiliter observetur, inter*', in Davenport (1917: 252, Doc. 27).

[26] Translation in ibid. (312, Doc. 35). Compare to the original: '*Primo conclusum, stabilitum & concordatum fuit, & est, ut ab hodie in antea sit bona, sincera, vera, firma & perfecta*

This range of adjectives, which varied depending on the customs of a particular power, strengthens the contractual language and obligations undertaken by linking them to the realm of morality and rendering morally repugnant alternatives of league, amity and peace. The extended formula, ritualised through practice, of morally acceptable friendship and associated terms was also meant to ensure the credibility and legitimacy of all subsequent contracted agreements, despite their frequent ruptures and short lives. Seemingly, the transition from the semantic field of verbs to the semantic field of adjectives amplifying the commendable moral nature of friendship eventually led to the devaluation and dwindling of elevated rhetoric and increased parsimony of usage in modern friendship treaties. Lesaffer even goes so far as to claim that during the seventeenth and eighteenth centuries, references to '*amicitia*' in treaty preambles 'became standardized and deteriorated to quite meaningless commonplaces' (Lesaffer 2004: 36–37).

Apart from elevated rhetoric, the Madrid treaty article indicates the unique application of the concept of friendship. Along the lines of discussion in the beginning of this chapter, it has horizontal and vertical dimensions pertaining to the power hierarchies within a claimed or actual realm. The contract of inter-princely friendship bound together a complex mix of politico-social realities: units more or less fixed in space (e.g. 'kingdoms, countries, dominions, lands, peoples') and those active agents who had the potential of setting these units in motion (e.g. 'heirs and successors' and 'vassals, liegemen, and subjects, now being or which hereafter shall be, of whatever condition, rank, or degree they may be'). This feature of medieval and early modern treaties was identified by Lesaffer, who linked it to the peculiarities of the heterogeneous medieval and early modern political system, in which princely vassals could perform independent political roles and make agreements with the prince himself (see Lesaffer 2004: 16–18). Karl-Heinz Ziegler makes a similar observation by stating that 'powers of lesser rank were also participants of international relations as subjects of international law, as far as they were able to wage war and conclude treaties' (Ziegler 2004: 151).

The diplomatic language game shows that, despite the universalist ideas of a common Christian universe, the late medieval concept of friendship retained in this specific context the link to an idea of a political compact or contractual instrument. Friendship as a political compact was employed to address the problematic contingency of late medieval and Renaissance politics. The manifesta-

---

amicitia, & confederatio, ac Pax perpetuo duratura, quae inviolabiliter observetur inter Serenissimum Regem Hispaniarum & Serenissimum Magnae Britaniae Regem, eorumque Hæredes ac Successores quoscumque, eorumque Regna, Patrias, Dominia, Terras, populos, homines, ligios, ac subditos quoscumque praesentes, & futuros cujuscumque conditionis, dignitatis & gradus existant, tam per terram, quam per mare, & aquas dulces, ita ut praedicti vassali & subditi sibi invicem favere, & mutuis prolequi officiis ac honesta affectione invicem se tractare habeant' (ibid.: 309).

tion of contractual language and the association with terms such as 'treaty' and 'league' show that friendship was more than a mere proclamation of benevolent attitudes. The conventions of its application indicate that it specifically meant to enact the complex regional orders binding together princes, their territorial realms, vassals and allies.

Friendship in the law of nations

One way to explicate formal diplomatic language is to delve into the definitions and linguistic conventions provided by commentaries and contemporaries' reflections on the practice, which add an argumentative perspective to the pre-scriptive linguistic conventions discussed so far. Indeed, Bacon's use of the concept of friendship can be understood not only against the backdrop of centuries of diplomatic practice; but it also sits well in the discourses of his predecessors and contemporaries on law and the philosophy of government. Renaissance and early modern discourses on the law of nations and nature offer a distinct and clear range of reference for the concept. Contributions from various philosophical and juridical traditions overlap in linking friendship to ideas of contracted agreement, an 'international treaty' open to classification and specific duties that a contract obliges parties to pay. These ideas contain further implications for political equality and inequality, spatial order and territorial integrity that I shall turn to in the rest of this chapter.

The recurrent connection of friendship to alliance or league in diplomatic documents manifests itself similarly in learned discourses by theologians and jurists. Focusing on an individual concept, such as friendship, helps us to see the subtleties of knowledge transfer from one epoch to another, subtleties that cannot always be explained by the prevalence of an 'ism', like the popularity of Stoicism or Scepticism (see Tuck 1993). Schematic explanations analysing the influence of a particular author or mode of argumentation are often insensitive to the concepts and practices that are borrowed by custom or unintentional copying of classical sources. This, however, remains an important and often unaccounted-for channel for transmitting classical practices into early modern settings, and could explain the presence of a conceptual means to denote contingency and particularity within theoretical claims about the universality and unconditionality of certain phenomena.

This helps us to understand the linkage of friendship and alliance in the teachings of Francisco de Vitoria, one of the founding fathers of the School of Salamanca of jurists and theologians. In *De Indis* (1539), while discussing the 'titles whereby the Indians might have come under the sway of the Spaniards', Vitoria points out that Spain has justified grounds for deposing those 'barbarian' rulers who through force and fear try to make subjects who have converted to Christianity 'return to idolatry'. Curiously, this interference in the affairs of native rulers is justified not only on the grounds of common religion and the preservation of faith, but also on the grounds of 'human friendship and alliance [*amicitiae et societatis*], inasmuch as the native converts to Christianity have become friends and allies of Christians [*amici et socii Christianorum*]' (Victoria 1917: 158, 264). Although he substantiates this claim by referring to Galatians 6 – in which St Paul advises to 'do good unto all men, especially unto them who are of the household of faith' – and thus to the universal bonds of all brothers in Christ, Vitoria still resorts to the terminological means available in classical sources to describe contingent and contractual political relations. Notably, the understanding of '*societas*' as an alliance with Rome, rather than a holistic community, is registered in Christian works as early as St Augustine's *The City of God* (2002: III, 1), which rescues Vitoria's activation of this vocabulary from the status of aberration in the Christian tradition.

Vitoria uses the conceptual couple of 'friends and allies' in yet another, but related, context. The final title that allows Spain to acquire dominion over 'barbarians' and their lands is vested, according to Vitoria, in the '*causa sociorum et amicorum*'. As opposed to the first example, in which the Spaniards allied with converted Indians against their errant rulers, in this case 'friends and allies' are mentioned in the description of alliances that the Spaniards can make with Indian rulers who wage just wars against other Indian rulers. As a result of these wars, Spain may share in the rewards with its allies and thus acquire new territories. In the structure of Vitoria's arguments, friendship and alliance are thereby also linked to the extension of Spanish territorial possessions.

What is important in this regard is that Vitoria explicitly invokes the practices employed by the Romans in extending their empire. He writes that the Romans helped their friends and allies in waging just wars against wrongdoers, and thereby came into the possession of new provinces (Victoria 1917: 160, 266–267). Having cited Christian authorities (e.g. Sts Augustine and Ambrose) approving the Roman Empire, Vitoria preserves the Roman conventional political compact '*amicitia et societas*', and the overall justificatory function of political friendship, in affirming dominion over new territories within the horizon of viable options for those reflecting on the acquisitions happening in the New World. This is not to argue that Vitoria advocated the Spanish conquest and natural inequality of natives and Spaniards. In fact, the Dominicans defended the idea of natural equality and opposed the Spanish subjugation of indigenous peoples (see Fernández-Santamaria 1977: 62–80; Skinner 2000b: 168–171; Tuck 1999: 68–75).

Nonetheless, the understanding of friendship as a possible political contract and alliance was something that the Thomists shared with their rivals among the ranks of Humanist jurists and theologians. It provided a conceptual means for establishing not only the spatial political order in the newly discovered world, but also among the old European powers centralising their structures of authority. Thus, Jean Bodin's *Six Livres* makes a similar linkage between friendship and contracted instruments regulating relations among commonwealths and princes, such as 'alliance', 'league' and 'confederation' (Bodin 1962: V, VI). In a move akin to Humanist scholars, Bodin invokes the classical tradition and builds his account of international practices on examples of treaties, leagues and friendships from Titus Livy, Plutarch and other ancient authors. Naturally, his exposition accommodates the classical linguistic rules of conceptual application and related thematic commonplaces.

Bodin thus describes the Roman customs to disarm and take hostages from among those 'with whom they had not ioyned in league, nor contracted friendship vpon equall tearmes' (ibid.: 615). He also uses the expression 'to contract a league of friendship' (ibid.: 629) and notes the renouncement of friendships before declarations of war (ibid.: 635). Bodin then reproduces this language of the Roman histories in accounts of more recent events; for instance, in discussing whether faith should be kept with the enemies of Christendom, he mentioned that 'the Emperour Charles the fift made a league of friendship by his Ambassadour *Robert Inglish* with the King of Persia' (ibid.: 628). The chapter on treaties and alliances in the *Six Livres* thus most explicitly exhibits the '(neo) Roman' convention of using friendship to refer to 'international' relations among sovereign actors; this is a type of friendly relationship which does not spring from human nature and natural disposition, but rather is purposefully contracted for a limited application.

Bodin's book was soon translated into Spanish and English. It is noteworthy that the first translation into English, by Richard Knolles in 1606, did not discriminate between the terms 'friendship' and 'amitie' in passages on alliances and compacts: Knolles could, for example, choose to write, 'a league of perpetuall friendship made betwixt Philip of Valois and Alphonso of Castile', and continue by discussing the 'perpetuall league and amitie' that was maintained between Scotland and France (ibid.: 634). He even compounded the terms when translating Bodin's classification of alliances and rendering one of the types as an alliance of 'amitie and friendship' (ibid.: 633), although the French text used simply '*amitié*' (cf. Bodin 1986: 220).

In light of the peculiar vernacularisation of diplomatic terms and the translation of Bodin's treatise, it is instructive to look at early modern translations of classical works on the subject for their choice of terms and rearticulation of the contractual concept of friendship in vernacular political languages. Philemon Holland's 1600 translation of Livy's *History* indicates a somewhat stricter distinction in its choice of terms to designate different types of friendship. Livy's oft-cited passage on the three types of 'treaties' ('confederacies and associations') by which 'States and Kings ordinarily conclude league and amitie one with another' uses mainly 'amitie' (Livy 1600: XXXIV, 57). An exception is made for the third type: 'when they that never were enemies, meete and conferre together about concluding some friendship, by way of solemne alliance and societie' (ibid.: 884). Note the greater vagueness assigned to this type by the expression 'some friendship', and the contrasting formulation in the next sentence qualifying Antioch for this type of friendship and treaty with the Romans: 'and not to draw a contract of amitie and association with Antiochus, a friend at this present' (ibid.: 885), despite the Latin terms used in these passages. However, in a later translation (1686) of the *History* the distinction has already vanished, as the translators render '*amicitia*' as friendship in the passage on the types of treaties only once and in regard to the third type: 'when those that never were Enemies came together to contract a mutual Friendship by a League of Alliance' (Livy 1686: 648; note also that '*societas*' is already being expressed as 'alliance').

The distinction between 'friendship' and 'amity' has remained blurred since then, and the terms have been used interchangeably. Nevertheless, the tradition of historical accounts continued to display certainty in using the terms to designate the public, conditional and contracted nature of concluded friendships as political compacts. This linguistic convention of historical narrative survived for about two centuries, and manifested itself in the great histories of the Enlightenment. Such expressions as 'to enter into an alliance and friendship' and 'to enter into strict amity' were common in descriptions of public and contracted political relations.[27] Historical narratives by David Ramsay, Hume and Gibbon also use other verbs in conjunction with 'amity' and 'friendship' to emphasise the particular and contractual nature of the relationship; these verbs include 'obtain', 'acquire', 'cement', 'destroy', 'restore', 'renew', 'confirm', 'maintain', 'prevail' and 'to render durable'.

Yet another element linking the use of friendship to the concept of a political compact in eighteenth-century historical narratives is its coincidence with the specification of binding terms or conditions, as had also been the case in Bodin's text. Thus, Hume's history of Richard I mentions the English king's agreement with Tancred, who had seized power in Sicily: Richard 'stipulated by treaty to marry his nephew, Arthur, the young duke of Britanny, to one of the daughters of Tancred. But before these terms of friendship were settled, Richard ... had taken up his quarters in the suburbs' (Hume 1983: I, X). Such examples are legion, though specific phrasing may diverge to reflect the particularity of historical practice and the narrators' sources. The binding nature of contracted relations could be emphasised by Ramsay's references to 'the ties of ancient friendship', which was an important gesture in communication with native Americans (see Ramsay [1789] 1990: ch. VII); similar expressions appear in Gibbon (see

---

27 The examples of such expressions are in Edward Gibbon's *The History of the Decline and Fall of the Roman Empire*, 1776 (1906: vol. III, ch. XVIII), David Hume's *History of England*, 1754–62 (1983: vol. I, ch. I; vol. II, ch. XIX) and Charles Montesquieu's *Persian Letters* (1777: vol. 3, letter XCV).

Gibbon 1906: vol. I, ch. VII; vol. V, ch. XXXI). The heterogenic phraseology of friendship cannot, however, conceal a number of regularities in the use of specific contractual vocabulary, indicating the concept's limited application to something that had been entertained only by qualified parties and contracted for specific political ends. Thus, in historical narratives friendship compacts are sometimes not even conceived in terms of moral commendation, but are rather presented as instruments for achieving certain political goals and judged accordingly by their effects. In this sense, the conventional uses of these late historical narratives corresponded to the use of the concept in treaties of the period, particularly those concluded with indigenous peoples.

Treaty classification and political inequality in the law of nature and nations

Social and political change in Renaissance and Reformation Europe was articulated in a variety of new political practices and complex priorities for alliance-making that transcended the conditions of joint action for the sake of common faith. New political circumstances, manifested in a greater number of concluded agreements and compacts, required a new vocabulary, new conceptual means of description and reflection, new taxonomies and new definitions. The classical tradition provided an almost ready-made collection of theoretical and conceptual means for Humanist writers to conceive of this flourishing heterogeneity and multiplicity of political forms. This tradition offered diplomatic and juridical discourse the concept of friendship of utility in the form of a political compact tightly linked to the ideas of 'treaty' and 'league'. As described in the previous chapter, the classical tradition also registered political friendships or 'friendship treaties' made on unequal terms. Hence, the question of whether this dimension of the concept had any currency for early modern political and juridical thought must be the subject of a separate exploration, with implications for the idea of the sovereign equality of actors in the emerging Westphalian system.

Early modern authors in the law of nature and nations tradition, highly sensitive to the practicalities of new inter-princely conduct, eagerly appropriated tropes, commonplaces and specific terms from classical literature. Pierino Belli (1502–1575), a lawyer and diplomat experienced in the affairs of the Roman emperor and the duke of Savoy, employs multiple categories, taxonomies and cases available in a number of sources ranging from Roman historians and jurists, through the Bible and the *Digest* of Justinian, to contemporaneous authors. The authority of these sources and their language thus become an effective means of amplifying the author's own arguments and the legal system as a whole.

In his comprehensive treatise on the rights of war, *De Re Militari et Bello* (1563), Belli employs these sources in an analysis of numerous contemporary conflicts among Christian princes and also with infidel rulers. The agreements that usually accompanied these conflicts, either *a priori* or *a posteriori*, reconstitute an already familiar linguistic and political context for the application of friendship in the new historical epoch. Belli's work introduces Titus Livy's classification of friendship compacts as a *locus classicus* for early modern legal treatises concerning public treaties. Belli reproduces all three types given by Livy: (1) friendship compacts with terms imposed on the vanquished party by the victor; (2) friendship compacts concluded on equal terms by parties evenly matched in war (*equo fœdere in pace & amicitia veniunt*); and (3) friendships concluded on equal terms by parties who have never been enemies (*amicitiam sociali fœdere conueniunt*) (Belli 1936a: 122; 1936b: 279–280).

Belli focused primarily on the first two types, which he applied to situations dating from only a few years before his treatise. He compares the first class of treaty with the peace 'which the Emperor Charles imposed upon the Duke of Saxony and other Germans who sided with the Duke', while the second type refers to pacts concluded between the emperor and his challenger the king of France (Belli 1936b: 280). The way in which this juridical classification is formulated shows the revitalised utility of the concept of friendship in grasping the contractual political relations between actors whose rights and power positions may not necessarily be equal or may vary contingently in the dissolving *respublica Christiana*.

This is also evident from Belli's other examples of agreements outside the context of classification. For instance, he mentions that Solomon contracted friendship and 'neighbourhood' with the king of Egypt (*amicitiam & affinitatem contraxit*) (Belli 1936a: 44). Further in the same chapter, he corrects the proposition of Spanish author Joannes Lupus by stating that the clause of the leagues and compacts (*foedera*) 'that the contracting parties shall hold the friends of all as friends, and the enemies of all as enemies' should apply only with the reservation 'without doing injustice' (Belli 1936b: 94). Thus, with the precondition of justice, friendly obligations can also apply to third parties. As we shall see, this dispute became a matter of prolonged juridical debates in which the scope of friendship was to be significantly extended.

Attuned with the postulates of the Roman jurists, Belli puts forward a suggestion that accentuates the degree of freedom available to those who joined in an agreement of friendship with a possibly more powerful party. Even in cases of 'unequal' friendship, inferior political allies retain their freedom, unlike a conquered and captive people (*dediti, captivi*). To convey this meaning, the jurist also invokes the classical link between friendship (*amicitia*) and alliance (*societas*): 'Allies are those who are bound to us by a friendly compact [*fœderati* sunt qui nobis *amicitia & societate* sunt iûcti], and yet are themselves independent – whether they have entered the compact on even terms, or whether it has been agreed that one party by courtesy recognize the authority of the other' (Belli 1936a: 41; 1936b: 87; emphasis added).

As the translation of the treatise shows, this proposition refers back to *Digest* 49, 15, 7 in which the jurist Proculus makes an observation regarding treaties of friendship and alliance that involve either a recognition of one nation's superiority over another or a proclamation of their equality. The recognition of inequality in friendship in fact offered a legitimate perspective on the emerging international order, which lacked a universal moral and political authority, but contained complex social hierarchies that had to hang together within a network of agreements and informal relations.

Discussing political inequality either on its own terms or as part of wider considerations of treaty taxonomies did not seem unacceptable to early modern scholarship. Indeed, many authors conventionally employed the classical concept of political friendship to bring up this idea and connect it to the freedom that an inferior counterpart could still enjoy.[28] This is not to say that all of them had the same intentions in writing their texts with the help of these concepts. Authorial intentions varied from defending the rights of individuals and property rights to defining the lawful agency to contract treaties and wage wars. Thus, the intentionality that the concept of friendship was used to support in each work was not necessarily the factor that conditioned the meaning and application of the concept. The persistence of contractual political friendship in treatises on *jus gentium* and *jus belli* from the sixteenth and early seventeenth centuries was due rather to the authority of the classical sources and their utility in providing new perspectives on the subjects of war and authority in the formative period of international law and the modern international system.

This is one of the key reasons for the conventional appearance of the term '*amicitia*' in the context of Livy's classification of 'international' agreements. Another legal adviser, Spanish author Balthazar Ayala, whose work was held in high esteem by Hugo Grotius and whose main concern, as stressed by Schmitt, was defining the 'just war' and 'just enemy' (Schmitt 2003: 153), invokes the same context and range of reference when using the concept of friendship (*amicitia*). In *De Jure et Officiis Bellicis et Disciplina Militari Libri III* (1582) Ayala reconstructs the classification of friendship treaties from various classical *loci communes* (including Livy, Dionysius of Halicarnassus and the *Digest*) in his chapter on treaties and truces, which had as its main purpose to define legitimate sovereign authority to conclude treaties.

In contrast to Belli, Ayala prefers to discuss remote historical cases. He draws attention to the issue of inequality in treaties concluded by Rome. Even when expounding treaties concluded between the parties equally matched in war

---

[28] In this sense, the taxonomies of treaties that included unequal friendship, in which one of the parties explicitly or implicitly recognised the superiority of the other, ran counter to republican ideals of freedom and their reception in the realm of princes and commonwealths (for a comparison see Pettit 2010; Skinner 1998).

('*aequo foedere in pace atque amicitia*'), Ayala emphasises that this category of treaties should also include cases in which Rome's superiority is recognised by the other party. Thus, he uses such phrases as '*Imperium, maiestatemque P.R. gens Aetolorum conseruato*' or '*alterum populum superiore esse*', whereas in the case of unequal treaties proper he uses '*deditii*': '*in ditione populi Romani essent*' and '*Romanis dedite*' (see Ayala 1912: 75). He justifies this extension of the category on the grounds that Rome neither imposed any conditions on the other party nor deprived it of anything, thus implying a degree of retained liberty. The third category of treaties, which basically copies that described by Livy, includes cases in which parties who were never enemies bind themselves together with an alliance and friendship, though such an act presupposes spelling out the conditions of the alliance (ibid.: 74). Ayala also amends Livy's classification by adding treaties under which a city or a province is taken under the protection of a foreign ruler or joins another's realm on certain conditions. In this case, the treaty also includes recognition of the superiority of one people over another, with the latter remaining free. According to Ayala, this is the meaning that Cicero attached to the phrase '*majestatem comiter conservare*' ('majesty courteously preserved'; ibid.: 75). Nonetheless, while questioning Livy's arguments, Ayala's descriptive techniques remain within the limits of the 'ancient' convention of using friendship in the context of treaty classifications as well as in the affirmation of international superiority and inequality.

The same thematic association of friendship and treaty classification can be found in the work of the Dutch jurist often said to be the founder of modern international law, Hugo Grotius (for more on Grotius's 'mathematical' method and principles for distinguishing a natural human community and voluntary associations see Eikema Hommes 1983). The occurrence of the conceptual association in his work has a more direct bearing on modern theories of international relations. This is due to Grotius's authority in modern scholarship, particularly in the so-called English School, as an author of the conception of 'international society' based on shared rules of conduct; some have understood this as a society of states (Bull 2002: 27–30), while others have been prepared to see a greater heterogeneity of participating actors (Wight 1966: 101; 2005: 46–49). As an intermediate 'solidarist' conception of international society located between the Machiavellian and Kantian traditions, the Grotian One provides room for a culture of shared rules that apply exclusively to the conduct of legitimate, presumably sovereign authorities (for more on Grotius's significance for international relations see Suganami 1992; Wight 1991).

Limiting Grotius's theory to the conduct of actors that enjoy absolute sovereignty proved to be problematic: as Edward Keene has demonstrated, Grotius added several exceptions that indicate a theory of sovereignty as in fact divisible (Keene 2002: 44, 58). Further to this is the assumption that Grotian sovereignty could be divided but at the same time should be definite (Tuck 1991:

520). Grotius's international actors reveal their sovereign status in various aspects of international interaction ranging from the definition of a legitimate ruler with whom a treaty can be concluded, to principles for erecting fortresses and foreign rulers' acceptance of portions of populations into their dominion. What contemporary theory often overlooks is that Grotius chooses to present and justify these rules of sovereign conduct by using the concept of friendship, but not yet sovereignty. Another problem in modern-day interpretations of Grotius's thought stems from the ambiguity of the concept of international society attributed to him and the term '*societas*', which continue to be the subject of critical re-examination (Keene 2001; Roshchin 2013). That is why it is crucial for the purposes of this study to view the work of Grotius and other jurists of the age not so much as theorists of modern international politics, but as a repository of pre-existing legal customs and linguistic conventions (Roelofsen 1997).

Grotius's treatise *De Jure Belli ac Pacis* (1625) throws new light on the *topos* of treaty classification and thereby on the subject of friendship compacts and their relation to political inequality. Similarly to Ayala, Grotius picks up the topic in his chapter on public treaties (*De federibus ac sponsionibus* II, XV) and their legitimate contractors. In subchapter IV he reproduces the classification of treaties found in Livy with the purpose of amending it. Among the three types is one compact in which the contracting parties who have never been enemies 'enter into an Alliance, without giving or receiving Laws on either Side [*amicitiam sociali federe*]' (Grotius 2005: II, XV, IV). Not all modern translations of this passage, including the one used here, are subtle enough to convey the exact meaning of the '*foedus*' made for the purpose of alliance. Grotius meant precisely a *contracted* political association in the form of '*amicitia*' and '*societas*'. This is the type of agreement that grasps the contingent nature of political relations. Grotius, however, leaves some room for uncertainty as to whether friendship is indeed a matter of contract and negotiation, or in fact a relationship immanent to nature. This is because he does not offer an extended commentary on friendship treaties *per se*, and does not stretch the term to describe other types of treaty, including those implying subordination.

This is a key moment in the history of friendship, even if the typology seemed of marginal importance to the 'founder of international law'. Grotius further emphasises the distinction between natural and human voluntary law, the latter comprising internal civil law and the law of nations (ibid.: I, I, X; I, I, XIII and XIV). In the law of nations this distinction divides treaties only into two main categories, as opposed to the three found in Livy: those that do not add anything to the law of nature and those that do. The first category is based on the assumption that there is a natural relation between all mankind and includes, for instance, treaties made upon the conclusion of war that proclaim freedom of commerce and principles of hospitality (ibid.: II, XV, V). The second includes treaties concluded on equal and unequal terms; these could be leagues, offensive and defensive alliances, or confederacies, among which he mentions Greek '*summakhia*' and Roman '*societas*' (1625; 2005: II, XV, VI). These certainly could be made on equal and unequal terms. However, although Grotius refers to Livy and other ancient authors when specifically discussing confederates of unequal status, he does not use the term '*amicitia*' in explicating this status, preferring instead terms such as '*inaequale foedus*', '*clientes*', '*subditi populi*' and '*socii*' (Grotius 1625: I, III, XXI). Thus, even if the practical inequality of sovereign authorities is still a recognised possibility in Grotian 'international society', while the term '*societas*' could still refer to limited interest-based associations (Roshchin 2013), the *topos* of treaty classification no longer affirmed the possibility of unequal friendships between sovereigns. The identification of friendship in Grotius's account either as part of the universal law of nature or as part of voluntary human law will be further determined in the course of this chapter.

The *topos* of treaty classification as modified by Grotius reappears in other eminent jurists of the law of nations. One such is the English jurist Richard Zouche, whose authority in the history of international law was partly due to his innovative treatment of *jus gentium* (the law of nations) as *juris inter gentes* (law among nations) – the title of his treatise is *Juris et Judiciis fecialis, sive Juris inter Gentes* (1650) – which contributed to the further furcation of international law from other fields of law. Zouche takes up the subject of public treaty and legitimate authority to contract such a treaty with a conventional reference to Livy. Thus, he defines a treaty as a contract that binds peoples together by the will of supreme authority, when those who are at peace with each other and who were never enemies unite in friendship and a treaty of alliance ('*ad amicitiam, sociali foedere inter se conjungendam coeunt*'; Zouche 1911, Latin volume: 1, 4, 4). This reference and definition raise the question of the extent to which friendship can be identified with the treaty. The confusion is exacerbated by Zouche's comment stressing the contractual nature of friendship: 'For although friendship and alliance may sometimes exist on grounds of personal or real relationship, yet they are usually strengthened by the closer bond of a treaty of solemn contract' (Zouche 1911: 25). He also points out that the conditions and terms of such treaties must be defined. In this manner he seems to discuss treaty types, but the initial association with Livy's 'definition' leaves the relationship between friendship and the idea of a general treaty inconclusive. Thus, when Zouche continues by defining equal and unequal treaties (*foedera*) and adding the 'classical' dictum that a party accepting disadvantageous treaty terms also 'has to recognize the other as his superior and respect his sovereignty readily' (ibid.), it is impossible to say whether these treaties and alliances are absolutely independent of political friendship.

Given the emphasis that these authors put on the original link between friendship (*amicitia*) and treaty (*foedus*), their recognition of the topic in the classical sources and their admittance of the contractual nature of friendship, as manifested in specified binding terms and conditions, the possibility of friendship as an instrument of maintaining formal political inequality cannot be dismissed altogether. What needs to be further explicated, however, are the themes and contexts constituted by these legal terms, and thus the extent to which the concept of political friendship was rooted in the realm of voluntary law in the sixteenth and seventeenth centuries.

Law and the place of virtue: Gentili vs Bodin

Alberico Gentili (1552–1608), an Italian-educated Humanist jurist who taught at Oxford and practised in the High Court of Admiralty in England, was one of the central figures in the discussion of rights of war, diplomacy and actual international customs. Grotius himself admitted Gentili's authority for his theoretical arguments, and moreover structured his own treatise similarly to Gentili's. Gentili's treatment of the issue of public friendship, or friendship in relations among rulers, appeared to be quite unconventional in comparison with other jurists of the period. He deals with the subject most extensively in the chapter 'Of friendship and alliance' (*De amicitia & societate*) in his seminal *De Iure Belli Libri Tres* (1589). What makes Gentili's treatment of the subject and use of the concept unconventional is that he draws attention to friendship *per se* and to its relationship with contractual obligations and justice, as opposed to attempts to suggest another typology or to confirm an existing one. Thus, he starts his discussion with the provocative rhetorical questions: 'Will not therefore an agreement about friendship, which makes nations friends, furnish something greater? Or does the agreement regarding fraternity also imply that the parties to it are joined by as great a friendship as if they were brothers?' (Gentili 1933b: 387).

The analogy made by the question evokes the classical problem of the relationship of contract and virtue within the semantic field of the same concept, that is, the relationship of friendship of virtue and friendship of utility in Aristotelian terms discussed in the previous chapter. The inherent tension between these components can be readily employed, as we have already seen in classical authors, to challenge and give a new twist to an existing custom, or sometimes just a local agreement. Having raised these introductory questions, Gentili proceeds to argue against Jean Bodin's suggestion that a contract of friendship does not lead to provision of aid:

> Bodin is also proved wrong by the constant usage of the Romans, who invariably considered it their duty to make war in behalf of their friends. If this is not so, what is gained by that agreement and that title of friendship? Certain it is that among private individuals, if one friend did not lend aid to another, he would seem to have inflicted a severe wound upon the laws of friendship. Why should it not be the same with states (*publicis personis*)? (Ibid.; Gentili 1933a: 633)

Indeed, the chapter on treaties between princes and commonwealths in Bodin's
Six Livres considered the question of when it is proper to provide aid to friends
and allies and when not, thereby demonstrating the conditionality of friendship.
Bodin referred to a *locus communis* using the example of the Campanians asking
Rome for help against the Samnites, who were attacking them, and appealing
to their '*amicitia ac societas*' with the Romans (see the quotation from Livy VII,
30, 1–3 in chapter one). To substantiate his statement further, Bodin reproduced the reply of the Roman Council: 'The Senate holds you of Campania to
be worthy of succours, but it is fit so to ioyne friendship with you, as a more
auntient league and societie may not be violated: the Samnites are linkt vnto vs
in league, and therefore we denie you armes against the Samnites' (Bodin 1962:
633). By means of this conventional reference, complemented with an example
of a league between France and Switzerland, Bodin proposed his resolution to
the problem of providing help to friends and allies:

> But it may so fall out, that three princes being in league, one may make warre
> against the other, and require aid of the third. In this case there are many distinc-
> tions. If the treatie of alliance be but of amitie and friendship, it is most certaine that
> he is not in that case bound to giue any succours, if the treatie imports a defensiue
> league, he must aid the most auntient ally by a precident alliance: If the associats
> be of one standing, he owes succours vnto him that is vnited vnto him by an offen-
> siue and defensiue league. If it be offensiue and defensiue of all parts, he must not
> succour neither the one nor the other: but he may well mediat a peace.(Ibid.)

Bodin also provided examples – more or less commendable, in his view, but all
drawn from historical fact – of different types of neutrality and policies towards
allies. In fact, as Skinner has pointed out, this treatment of the Roman sources
might have been due to the new approach to methodology shared by the con-
stitutionalist authors of sixteenth-century France that privileged the study of
'national' histories and customs over Roman law. This approach did not take the
authority of Roman law for granted; rather, it advocated its further explication
(see Skinner 2000b: 270–271, 290–291).

This 'neo-Roman' treatment of friendship and treaties of alliance, as well as
the principles of providing help to friends and allies, appear to have discomforted
Gentili's understanding of friendship among nations. In fact, Gentili's rhetorical
questions targeted the issue of justice in keeping faith with contracted obligations and dealing with friends and allies. The trajectory of these arguments again
ties the conceptual history of friendship to discussions of just war through the
provision of aid to an ally. We encountered this connection before in Vitoria's
arguments. Later, another Spanish theologian and philosopher, Francisco
Suárez, replicated the connection when concisely addressing the subject of
friends and allies in his dispute on war in *De Triplici Virtute Theologica* (1621,
XIII). Suárez argues that the sufficient cause of waging a just war arises when a

wrong is 'inflicted upon allies or friends' (*fœderatos siue amicos*). Suárez chooses to refer to the authority of Aristotle to substantiate his claim: 'For a friend is a second self' (*NE* IX; Suárez 1944a: 804; 1944b: 817).[29]

These arguments were often delivered by distinct rhetorical devices and belonged to rival theological and Humanist traditions, which contained further distinctions in their relationships with classical heritage. For instance, Gentili's discussion of friendship, as framed by his introductory questions, is entirely redirected towards situations and circumstances in which friends should or should not provide aid. This move might have provided grounds for later jurists for whom Gentili was an authority to limit themselves solely to the postulation of necessary, but inevitably general, friendly obligations. However, Gentili himself stressed that he was not speaking of an ideal friendship invented by philosophy, in which all the possessions of friends are considered to be held in common, but only 'of friendships of which our law takes cognizance; that is, those within the experience of mankind' (Gentili 1933b: 388). This thought must have been dear to the jurist mind-set, as it was later rearticulated by another English jurist John Selden, who stressed the necessary reservations to the philosophical dictum especially in regard to common property over things, for instance, dominion over seas: 'Which communitie notwithstanding derogate's nothing at all from the Dominion here in Question; unless any will bee so unadvised as to affirm, that the Laws of friendship (wherein Philosophers say all things are common) ... may overthrow private Dominion' (1652: 148).

Hence, Gentili's exposition mainly concerns the duties of a friend, who at the same time is a contracting party, in a situation in which wars or conflicts break out between princes who are both friendly to his or her realm. This involves questions of whether it is just to provide aid to one of the parties, to both or to none; or whether priorities should be set in providing aid to friends (Gentili 1933b: 389–396). In this sense, the discussion of the topic comes close to Bodin's line of argumentation, but unlike the Frenchman's accentuation of the precedence of alliances and their types, Gentili stresses the justice of choice. Suárez's argument is different, but not entirely inconsistent with Gentili's attitude, since the logic of his exposition suggests that friendship should belong to the category of *iura gentium* that 'were introduced by tradition and custom ... rather than by any written constitution' (Suárez 1944b: 377), even though he amplifies his statement on friends by invoking Aristotelian ethics. Despite the distinct philosophical and juridical identities of the contributors to this discussion, and notwithstanding their attempts to deduce general principles or otherwise to draw attention to the

---

[29] In fact, the invocation of Aristotle marks another *locus classicus* for a more ethically oriented discussion of friendship, as distinct from political compacts, that was held by the earlier theologians and canonist jurists. See, for instance, John of Legnano's treatise *De Amicitia*, fourteenth cent. (Lignano 1584).

rationality of specific policies by means of problematising the meaning of friend-ship, the linguistic convention appears constant in preserving the concept's link to the issue of contractual obligations towards parties to the treaty as well as to third parties.

Friends' obligations from a legal perspective

The parsimonious contractual diplomatic vocabulary and the ideas of political compact, obligations and treaty classification that we have discussed so far all contribute to one political concept of friendship that was used to secure the exercise of authority over lands and seas (on the Roman law thesis of sovereignty as *dominium* see Kratochwil 1995; for a refinement of this thesis see Holland 2010). The contractual nature of friendship and its inclusion into a legal regime prescribing rules for the internal life of a realm and its policies towards other powers and legal aliens is best manifested in public laws concerning commerce and in scholarly discussions of *postliminium* in the context of the law of war. Indeed, Renaissance and early modern jurists revitalised the Roman conven-tional linkage between allies (*socii*), friends (*amici*) and *postliminium*; the most authoritative source of this linkage is the definitions of *postliminium* provided in the *Digest* (see chapter one). Traces of this conceptual linkage can be identified as early as the recognised inaugural work on the law of treaties, *Tractatus de con-federatione*, by the fifteenth-century Italian jurist Martinus Garatus Laudensis, who makes a reference to Paulus's discussion of *postliminium* (*Digest* 49, 15, 19, 3) as the restoration of captives upon their arrival in the domain of an allied or friendly power, without elaborating on this norm (Garatus Laudensis 2004: Q. XXXVIII, p. 428).

Much later, the debate on *postliminium* and its possible implications for policies that sovereigns should pursue towards their friends/allies involved many eminent figures in the history of international law. Despite the comparison mentioned earlier with friendships between individuals and public persons, Gentili rearticulates the *topos* of *postliminium* at the opening of his posthumous *Hispanicae Advocationis Libri Duo* (1613) by questioning one of its key compo-nents. Specifically, Gentili's main aim in the chapter 'Whether there is *postlim-inium* in the domain of a common friend' was to argue in favour of the meaning of 'our' (*noster*), when attached to 'friend',[30] as meaning 'common' (*communis*) to belligerent parties, to the effect that law could be enacted when the interests

---

[30] Even if Gentili demurred from the commonly held opinion of the time, for example by Baldus, the wording of this expression goes back to Pomponius's dictum in *Digest* 49, 15, 5, 1: '*tunc autem reversus intellegitur, si aut ad amicos nostros perveniat aut intra praesidia nostra esse coepit.*' Translation: 'He is regarded as having returned from the time when he passes into the hands of allies or begins to be within our own lines.'

of the belligerents clash in the territory of a common friend. This means that the status of a friend is not a mere expression of benevolence; instead it involves a 'legal regime' that establishes the terms of personal freedom and property relations with the subjects of a friend (Gentili 1921b: 3–5; obligations in friendship are mentioned in his earlier *De Legationibus, libri tres*, see Gentili 1585: 37). Gentili also ties the term 'friend' to '*socius*' (ally), highlighting the political nature of public obligations (Gentili 1921a: 2–3).

The reason for making this association and proposing the meaning 'common/ shared' for 'our friend' was to offer a solution to a specific political situation and defend Spanish interests in the realm of England, which by the will of James I was a friend and ally of both Spain and Holland, which were at war with each other at the time of Gentili's writing. Arguing against a Portuguese jurist Antonius da Gama, Gentili raised the question of whether 'certain Lusitanians' captured by Spain's Dutch enemies and brought to England should not become free by virtue of the friendship that their home country had with England. Advocates of the Dutch interest would argue that Dutch property and spoils should remain secure in the realm of a formal friend. However, Gentili raised doubts about the applicability of this law, on the grounds that a realm might have formal friendship not only with Holland (or 'our', from the Dutch perspective), but also with an enemy of Holland. The doubt born of England's friendship with both belligerent parties could in itself be, in Gentili's opinion, grounds for beneficial action towards the prisoners.

The problematic role of a friend that maintained friendly relations with warring parties may have sown the seed for the concept of neutrality within friendship, but this seed needed plenty of time to grow. Thus, Grotius's discussion of *postliminium* also discusses people's liberty to move between dominions and the restoration of their rights (chapter 'Of the Right of Postliminy', 2005: III, IX). Grotius had different tactical reasons for raising this issue, but he nevertheless also demonstrates the legal nature of political friendship that engenders the right of *postliminium*. Grotius, as the *topos* suggests, cites the definition of *postliminium* given by Pomponius and many other classical authorities, and in so doing also proposes a definition of friends and allies in whose territory the right of *postliminium* applies. Grotius's interpretation of classical sources clearly differs from the tenor of Gentili's message. For Grotius, an '*amicos nostros*' to whose territory a person comes in safety performs rather the role of an active ally: 'Friends, or Allies [*amici aut socii*], are not to be taken simply for those with whom we are at Peace, but those who join with us in the same War [*partes in bello*]' (ibid.: III, IX, II; 1625: 646). As if in reply to the case made by Gentili, Grotius adds that 'But among those who are Friends, but not engaged in the same Party, Persons taken in War, change not their Condition (of Captivity) unless by a special Article and Agreement' (2005: III, IX, II).

Richard Zouche joins this line of inquiry by further linking friendship to shared legal 'regimes' and the issue of contested ownership rights in wartime. When discussing the status of contending princes in the chapter 'Of Status among Belligerents', Zouche defines as unfriendly those with whom a prince has no friendship or legal intercourse, and hence no legal instruments to seek recompense for any damages (Zouche 1911: 37). Zouche often refers to the 'Roman' juridical understanding of friendship as collateral to smooth commercial relations, and conventionally considers the juridical *topos* of friendship and *postliminium* in the context of problems related to ownership rights. In the section 'Of Questions of Ownership between Belligerents', Zouche addresses a number of common issues related to property rights in the state of war. He explicitly refers to the passages cited above from Gentili and Grotius, framing them as a debate over the question of *postliminium* and whether it applies solely to friends or allies. In this discussion Zouche seems to take the side of Gentili; when assessing the second treaty between the Romans and the Carthaginians, he argues that it is not decisively against Gentili's position 'because treaties often contain superfluous provisions on matters which would otherwise be legally secured' (ibid.: II, VIII, 2 or 121). Thus, in Zouche's interpretation, *postliminium* may apply in the domain of a friend who is not openly on the side of the enemy and in whose domain the captives are in safety.

This discussion indicates that jurists in the early seventeenth century still maintained a 'Roman' understanding of friendship as a law that required a contract and secured rights of property and freedom in specifically designated spaces (mainly territories belonging to the contracting parties). The restoration of rights that public friendship could bring to captured subjects was predominantly encapsulated by the Roman concept of *postliminium*. But this was not the only possible connection between friendship and legal regimes. Another English jurist, John Selden, articulated this type of 'Roman' conceptual linkage, in his dissertation annexed to *Fleta* (1647). Selden cited Tacitus's *Annals* (XII, 32) in explaining that the goal of Camulodunum, the first Roman colony in Britain, was to provide aid in the case of rebellion and to imbue allies with respect for the laws (*imbuendis sociis ad officia legum*). According to Selden, it therefore followed that 'as many of the *Britains* also as were Associates to the *Romans*, either as their Friends, or as being by the Fate of War subdued or reduced under their Power, were then to be trained up to the Offices or Observation of the Duties prescribed by the Imperial Law' (Selden 1771: IV, II; p. 57). Among this generation of jurists, the firm connection between friendship and legal 'regime', and more particularly to *postliminium*, is to a large degree due to the significance of Roman law and classical sources for making an informed judgement (see Nussbaum 1952: 684–685).

The conceptual linkage of friendship to law and the obligations of allies gradually started to erode in learned discourse at the close of the seventeenth century, although the convention was not transfigured completely and the change was far from abrupt. The German jurist Johan Textor's treatise *Synopseos Juris Gentium* (1680), which contributed to the emergence of a 'positivist' tradition of international law, shows that friendship continued to belong to the domain of legitimate juridical knowledge. However, his use of the concept differs from that identified in the treatises by Belli, Gentili and Zouche. For instance, Textor no longer mentions any concrete duties or obligations implied by a friendship contract, nor does he discuss friendship together with issues related to the affirmation of authority. Instead he uses the formula 'the law of common friendship' ('*lege communis amicitiae*'; Textor 1916a: 106) and thereby sustains the logical connection between friendship and positive international law. Thus, he states that 'some kinds of promise and obligation are proffered by way of doing kindness, and come from *the law of friendship*. In them we give the use of our property or our services gratuitously' (Textor 1916b: 130; emphasis added). This statement, however, deviates from early conventions in that it omits any specification of the obligations in question. Nevertheless, it is significant that it still links the law of friendship to the use of property.

Textor's treatise could be said to belong to the earlier convention of treating friendship as a voluntary political relationship, but at the same time it breaks away from the conceptual couple 'friend/ally' that constituted that convention. He reasserts the divide between private and public friendships (*publicam amicitiam*) when arguing that sacrifices made for a friend are rather the result of affection pertinent to some individual friendships and do not follow from the law of nature (Textor 1916a: 108; 1916b: 282). This sets up the limits for applying the analogy of interpersonal friendship based on affections. In this sense, there is the logical space for the application of this analogy, as in Gentili's description of 'public persons'; however, the figure of interpersonal friendship is not used to completely substitute for contracted 'international' friendly relations, as was to happen soon afterwards in discourses on the law of nations and nature.

The important conceptual separation of friends and allies – an inextricable couple in earlier convention – occurs when Textor introduces the concept of neutrality, defined as equal friendship with contending parties. The introduction of 'neutrality' in turn had significant implications for debates on the application of *postliminium* involving such renowned jurists as Gentili, Grotius and Zouche. In Textor's treatise, friendship with contending parties is presented as one of the main qualities of the mediator or neutral party: 'A formal requisite is the *equality of the friendship* of the neutral Prince or State towards the foes; that is, he must not adhere to one more or less than to the other' (Textor 1916b: 274; emphasis added; see also p. 278). Thus, the mutual friend is '*nec pro hoste nec pro socio*' ('neither held for an enemy nor for an ally') (Textor 1916a: 105). This is a considerable conceptual innovation by comparison with the classical convention and its early modern revival. At the same time it is a solution – in the form of an adaptation of vocabulary to political change – to the impasse, identified by

Gentili in the interpretation of a friend exclusively as an active ally of one party, which further multiplied in continued wars and alliance-making by European powers.

Dutch jurist Cornelius van Bynkershoek maintained a similar view in *Quaestionum Juris Publici Libri Duo* (1737), in which he also insisted on the principle of equality of friendship (*aequalitas amicitiae*) to the belligerent parties (Bynkershoek 1930b: 61). Francis Hutcheson, a Scottish philosopher, in *A System of Moral Philosophy* (published posthumously in 1755) also sides with this view in discussing the laws of war, connecting the concepts of a neutral state and a mutual friend by stating that a state is not obliged to provide assistance to or declare just the cause of one of the parties in a civil war if it was previously in friendship with that state (Hutcheson 1755: 357). At the same time, 'a common friend' ought to prevent any hostile acts between the conflicting parties on that common friend's own territory (ibid.: 361). Of course, a friend deprived of preferences towards and making no distinction between parties to a conflict represents a case that stands a short distance from the idea of 'universal friendship' promulgated by later law of nature thinking. This kind of friendship is then used to justify, and sometimes even require, the non-action of a mutual friend.

However, Bynkershoek makes an important reservation regarding the concept of friend that explains its more passive political role and dissociation from juridical discussions of *postliminium*. He bluntly distinguishes friends from allies: when discussing the status and role of *non hostes*, or neutral parties, he contrasts allies and 'simply friends' who are not bound by a treaty and are independent of both belligerents: 'these I have called simply "friends" to distinguish them from allies (*sociis*) and confederates (*foederatis*)' (Bynkershoek 1930a: 70; 1930b: 62). This understanding of friends as neutrals with whom a party is at peace has a further effect on Bynkershoek's interpretation of *postliminium* and the corresponding debates. He expressly joins with Grotius, and refutes Gentili, in interpreting the right of *postliminium* defined in the *Digest*:

> He who returns to the territory of an ally [*foederatos*] has the right of postliminy because he seems to have returned to his own country, since allies constitute as it were one nation with us ... Therefore, I would interpret the term 'friends', as used by Pomponius, as being friends in the highest degree, that is to say, those who are in alliance with us against the same enemy; and when Paulus speaks of 'friend or ally' [*Regem socium vel amicum*] I would interpret the phrase as meaning: 'friend, that is to say, ally', otherwise he might have used only the word 'friend'. It is only among allies and because of the actual alliance [*societatis*], that the right of postliminy obtains. (Bynkershoek 1930b: 91)

This is an important affirmative statement as it sheds light on the juridical status of friendships. In Bynkershoek's opinion, only the status of a friend-as-ally has implications for the safety of the friend's property and captives returning to the friend's territory. However, not all friends are allies. Neutral parties, that is to say 'mere friends', are not bound by the obligations of an alliance treaty; thus, the right of *postliminium* does not apply in their territory. In this interpretation, friendship as non-alliance emerges as a phenomenon pertinent to the domain of natural human sociality and hospitality, and is not a volitional and political activity. This transformation is central to this study and will be fully explained in chapter four, but even at this point it is clear that the scholarly discourse of the eighteenth century is reluctant to portray 'mere friendship' as regulated by contractual obligations. As there are no rules without exceptions, Bynkershoek's earlier *De Dominio Maris Dissertatio* (1702) is still more ambivalent in using the concept of friendship when discussing property rights. In his argument with the Turks he refers to a contract of friendship as a means of preserving property rights in foreign territories: 'For it is by virtue of such a compact that the convention of one state is ratified by another, since, otherwise, friendship could not possibly exist between men who cared for their possessions' (Bynkershoek 1923: 34).

Notably, the distinction between friend-as-ally and 'mere friend' as a neutral party parallels another crucial development noted by Carl Schmitt in *The Nomos of the Earth*. Schmitt pointed out that equal friendship, or neutrality, with both belligerent parties became possible with the elimination of the question of *justa causa* in waging a war. This in turn corresponded to the formation of an order based on the sovereignty of states, expressed in the recognition of their equal rights to wage wars in an orderly fashion and recognise the neutrality of non-belligerent members of this society (Schmitt 2003: 165–167). This obviously allows for a more multifaceted political reality than that presupposed by the strict friend/enemy antithesis in Schmitt's earlier work *The Concept of the Political*. As applied to the conceptual transformation of friendship, this development is evident when, for instance, the views of Vitoria and Bynkershoek are contrasted. Vitoria pictured an engaged role for a friend who joins one party in a just war and then acquires titles to the lands of the defeated party; this role would fit the concept of friend-as-ally, but would definitely contradict the concept of neutrality as equal friendship put forward by Bynkershoek.

The equation of friends and neutrals did not become an unequivocal moral and political standard, as the issue was continually emphasised and given new twists in debate. For instance, Plumer Ward argues that connections between states 'improved into very strict ties of amity, often ending in a departure from that impartial neutrality which in the abstract they preserve towards one another' (Ward 1795: 189). In this respect the convention remained heterogeneous, as authors continued either to associate friends with allies or to distinguish between the two, even if the understanding of strict friends and allies could have been informed by a much higher moral standard. The opposition to Ward's view can be found in a later piece by the American jurist Henry Wheaton (1836), who, with reference to Bynkershoek, maintains that 'the neutral is the common friend' of parties that happen to be at war (Wheaton 1878: § 414). The same is true of another natural law proponent, James Lorimer, who states in *The Institutes of the Law of Nations* (1883–1884) that a neutral party remains a 'mutual friend' to belligerents after the proclamation of neutrality. Moreover, he argues that neutrality cannot be a relation of indifference: 'An attitude of indifference between rational entities … bound together as they are by the links of reciprocal rights and duties, if it can be called a relation at all, is an anti-jural relation' (Lorimer 1883–1884: 129). Thereby, he revitalises the link between 'juridical' and friendly relations so familiar to the ancient and early modern jurists, but in so doing he no longer discusses the specific duties and legal obligations of friends.

The debate over these 'technical' issues between key thinkers in the history of jurisprudence and politics among nations appears crucial for the understanding of the contractual nature of international friendship. Early modern scholarship on the law of war seems conscious of the legal 'regime' launched by a formal agreement of friendship between sovereigns. Obligations of friendship constituted law in an international realm and had to be observed in relation to the subjects of friends and their enemies in the course of a specific war. Eighteenth-century scholars extenuated the link between contractual friendship and active alliance in their attempts to specify the concepts of mutual friend and neutrality; this could have closed further discussion of the juridical nature of friendship, had the concept not also been a popular tool in juridical language not directly related to military contexts.

Lines, spaces, dominion and laws

Carl Schmitt attributed a central role in the emergence of classical European public international law and order to the 'amity lines' agreed upon in the sixteenth century by Spanish and Portuguese rulers. These 'amity lines' not only delineated the space free for appropriation by these European powers, but also indicated the limits beyond which the established European system of law and order was suspended. In Schmitt's dramatic portrayal, the uncontrolled 'ruthless conflict' and piracy beyond these lines performed an important constitutive function, in the sense of being antithetic, of maintaining the zones of normal order (Schmitt 2003: 94–96). This ingenious finding of the pre-global geopolitical function of friendship often distracts attention from its more popular function of delineating territorial orders closed for appropriation and producing concrete legal regimes of interaction between individual European powers within Europe. This could be anachronistically termed as a regional peace instrument, if peace is understood as a community of law.

In fact, even early Spanish and Portuguese treaties aimed to preserve peace and love-friendship as a primary political and legal arrangement between them. These monarchs similarly appealed to the value and sanctity of the union, peace and concord, friendship and love that existed between them: '*por bien de paz e concordia e por conservagion del debdo e amor que entre los senores*' (treaty concluded at Vitoria, 1524; Davenport 1917: 122, Doc. 13). On another occasion, before presenting claims to the Moluccas islands (now part of Indonesia) the monarchs also expressed the desire to preserve their mutual love: '*teniendo la voluntad que sienpre tuvo e tiene a la conservagion del gran debdo y amor que ay entre el y el dicho senor Rey de Portogal*' and confirmed that the love and good offices that they show to each other and that preserve their friendship and union are well received: '*Primeramente, que del amor que el dicho senor Rey tiene, y buena voluntad que muestra, a la conservagion de la amistad y verdadera unyon de entre su Magestad y el dicho Serenisimo Rey*' (see the draft of an unconcluded treaty, 1526, ibid.: 133, Doc. 14). Later, when introducing the agreement on the disputed islands and other lands and seas, they saw it as being done in the service of God and for the preservation of their love '*y al bien de sus rreinos y por conservagion de la hermandad, debdo, y amor que entrellos ay*' (Saragossa treaty, 1529, ibid.: 150, Doc. 15). The use of the concept in these Spanish–Portuguese treaties thus sanctions the division of space, with subsequent implications for the legal order attached to different sides of the dividing lines. This particularly applies to the alleged oral agreement of Cateau-Cambrésis (1559) regarding the 'Indies' that set geographical limits ('amity lines') for the application of treaties (see ibid.: 219–221, Doc. 21); according to Schmitt, this had a profound impact on the division of political space onto zones where moral and legal principles legitimately operated and where they could be suspended.

Notably, at the same time as Spain and Portugal were helping to draw 'amity lines' by appealing to friendship when settling disputes over certain lands and seas, those who marched in the vanguard of the discovery of and actually encountered the New World also made appeals to friendship, thereby transmitting the European idea of friendship as a contractual political instrument to indigenous communities. A good example of this practice is Magellan's expedition, which reportedly concluded friendship treaties with indigenous people. One such treaty of '*paz y amistad*' was allegedly concluded with the 'kings of the Moluccas' in 1521 (see extracts in *Colección de los viages* 1837: 295–296). Thus, even in the early stages of the great European discoveries, there are signs that explorers used friendship to engage indigenous peoples in orderly relations. The utility of friendship may have been due to various factors. The nuances of European diplomatic customs and contracts could easily be lost in the type of translation that the first interpreters could offer for the kind of friendship that explorers wished to make. Local rulers may well have understood this kind of friendship as a sort of cordial relationship that two persons make out of special disposition towards each other. The likelihood of such an understanding does not, however, undermine another key diplomatic function that friendship agreements performed – namely that they proved to be an expedient conceptual carrier of political and legal order that also acquired a particular spatial anchorage in the New World. It is by concluding peace and friendship treaties that European powers in the course of their spatial advances brought about and moulded various kinds of political order, as well as defined its geographical limits.

Contemporaneous authors of Humanist political pamphlets and discourses seem also to have realised the bearing that political friendship had for the security of concrete territorial legal and political arrangements. This is one reason why at the time they presented friendship as a vital requirement for the commonwealth to survive. Even Erasmus, often an adamant critique of princely friendships, makes such a claim in his observation on public treaties:

> The good and wise Prince will make every effort to keep peace with all men, but especially with his neighbours, who, if incensed, can do most harm, but as friends are most useful; nay, without mutual intercourse with them, the State cannot even exist. Moreover, it is easy to establish and maintain friendship between peoples who are linked by community of language, propinquity of territory and similarity of character and customs ... there are some [nations] so captious, so perfidious and insolent, that, even as neighbours, they are useless for purposes of friendship. (Erasmus 1921: 48)

In this passage Erasmus puts forward a common idea of having friendships with those who surround oneself, but in his interpretation this idea extends to all surrounding territories and peoples. The usefulness of friendship in this respect lies in maintaining commerce and preserving alliances. Although Erasmus is known for his criticism of existing practices of friendship, it is notable how his Humanist dictum on neighbourhood policies and friendship resembles the notion of the community of law and the contracted concept of friendship in bringing about peace, order and mutual advantages for its members. Similarly, Thomas Starkey's *A Dialogue between Cardinal Pole and Thomas Lupset* (1529–1532) presented friendship as the main instrument in the 'international' realm. Starkey claimed that friendship with surrounding nations is one of the three main requirements for a commonwealth to exist and to prosper (the two others being population size and good internal laws and order). Starkey placed friendship against the backdrop of a gradually dissolving Christian community at the core of his image of an ideal political commonwealth. In particular, he stated:

> yf ther be no lake of necessarys for the sustenance of the pepul, ... yet yf the same cuntrey lake the *frenschype* of other joynyd therto, and be inuyronnyd and compassyd aboute wyth ennemys and fowys, lying euer in wayte to spoyle, robbe, and destroy the same, I can not see now that cuntrey can long florysch in prosperyte. Wherfor the *frenschype* of other ys no les requyryd then ryches and abundaunce of other thyngys necessary. (Starkey 1871: 50; emphasis added)

Friendship thus appears as one of the basic legitimate tools that not only help to maintain the civic concord and integrity of the commonwealth, but also secure its survival in the external environment. The actualisation of friendship in moralist and juridical discourses points to its expediency while other instruments of medieval law and political order were fading away. The orderly and friendly environment could have been a matter of moralist concern shared by Erasmus, More or Starkey, but it was equally a matter of practical necessity and pragmatic calculation by power-holders, as the author of the dialogue *A Discourse of the Common Weal of this Realm of England* ([1581]; attributed by some to John Hales, by others to Thomas Smith) explains in his account of continental neighbourhood policies:

> we stand not in like case as fraunce or flaunders, that youe speake of; yf they haue not vent one waie, they may haue it an other waie alwaies, for firme lande is rounde abowte theim in maner; yf they be at warre with one neighbour, they wil be frendes with an other, to whose countries they maie send theire commodities to sell. (Lamond 1929: 93–94)

The permeation of friendship into discourses on the security and well-being of the commonwealth is due precisely to its association with the production and arrangement of positive legal regimes regulating sovereign encounters, preserving rights of dominion over a realm and stipulating the conditions of commercial intercourse. The legal implications of 'amity' (and consequently '*amicitia*') are made clear particularly in commentaries on English Common Law. That the term belongs to legal vocabulary is evident from commentaries by English jurist Edward Coke (1552–1634) on the *Magna Carta* of 1215 and on the statutes preceding and following this major document.[31] In a commentary on the chapter on the rights of merchants and their status he glosses: 'all Merchant strangers in amity (except such as be so publiquely prohibited) shall have safe and sure conduct in seven things' (Coke 2003: 874). The link is reiterated in the work of another influential jurist Mathew Hale (1609–1676), who, in a classification of 'leagues' that is no longer Roman, singles out 'leagues of simple amity'. These leagues, he maintains, often include 'liberty of mutual commerce and trade, and safeguard of merchants and traders in either's dominions', although the degrees of such liberty depend on the conditions of a particular contract (Hale 1736: 160).

As opposed to a more abstract discussion of the applicability of *postliminium*, the public contract of amity here appears to have a concrete bearing on the organisation of commerce by granting foreign merchants certain rights in the

---

[31] Coke's use of 'friendship' and 'amity' also shows a subtle difference in the relations designated by these terms. Coke used 'friendship' predominantly to describe private relations among individuals, whereas 'amity' is used in most contexts where public and legal relations are discussed.

English realm. This is in no way an innovative interpretation of legal amity: similar titles for foreigners to trade in the English realm were rather common in contemporaneous legislation. For instance, such a clause is even inserted into an Ordinance of the Lords and Commons of the Long Parliament, which contended at the time for authority within the realm, proclaiming it 'lawfull for all foreigners and strangers in amity with this Kingdom to have free Trade and Commerce, to and from the city of London' and other places, provided they pay duties and customs and do not bring arms to the enemies of the Parliament (*An Ordinance*, 30 August 1644). Such an understanding survived at least for another century when it was rearticulated, although in a more rudimentary form, in William Blackstone's *Commentaries on the Laws of England* (1765–1769). Among offences against the law of nations, Blackstone first singled out 'committing acts of hostilities against such as are in amity, league, or truce with us, who are here under a general implied safe-conduct: these are breaches of the public faith', which may interrupt commerce and provoke war (Blackstone and Tucker 1996: 68).

Alongside protection for foreigners whose sovereigns were party to the treaty, amity also meant being subject to the laws of the realm and the jurisdiction of the sovereign. This is vividly illustrated in Coke's treatise *Institutes of the Lawes of England*, which includes a commentary on issues of high treason and makes particular reference to the following: 'And all Aliens that are within the Realme of England, and whose Soveraignes are in amity with the King of England, are within the protection of the King, and doe owe a locall obedience to the King' (Coke 2003: 958); and: 'The tryal against an Aliennee, that lived here under the protection of the King, and amity being between both Kings, for High treason, shall by force of this Act of 1 & 2 Ph. & Mar. be tried according to the due course of the Common Law' (ibid.: 1008; for similar statements connecting amity to the questions of protection and jurisdiction see Hale 1736: 59). By virtue of being such an instrument, amity constituted one of the sovereign's key prerogatives in foreign policy-making.

Failure to observe contracted amity could incur deadly consequences for the perpetrators. James I, for example, used breach of amity as grounds for his proclamation against Walter Raleigh in 1618, in which he accused Raleigh of disobeying the order to refrain from any hostilities towards 'the territories of any Princes in amity with us', and of having 'broken and infringed the peace and amity which hath been so happily established [with the King of Spain]' after Raleigh ransacked the city of St. Thomé during his mission to South America (cited in Anderson 1787: 361). Ironically, before his earlier imprisonment Raleigh had been prosecuted by Edward Coke in 1603.

Public amity also served as the grounds for restraining freebooters during the reign of James I. To observe concluded amity and thereby affirm his own authority, the king imposed limitations on their conduct: 'That all such our men of warre, as be now at Sea, having no sufficient Commission as aforesaid, and have taken, or shal go to Sea hereafter, and shal take any the ships, or goods of any subiect of any princes in league, or amitie with us, shall bee reputed and taken as pirates' (Edict of James I, 1603).[32]

As can be seen in these passages, the legal regime of public amity extended to issues of navigation and sovereign authority at sea. John Selden, who according to Schmitt believed that law and power existed only on *terra firma* and was thus unable to grasp the new maritime *nomos* (Schmitt 2003: 175, 180), in fact provides an additional insight into the spheres of sovereign jurisdiction regulated by the laws of amity. In *Mare Clausum* (1635), translated as *Of the Dominion, Or, Ownership of the Sea* (1652), Selden refers to amity when discussing specific legal issues concerning, for instance, fishing licences and disputes over property rights at sea, which constitute the essence of 'the possession of the English Sea'. Selden's overall aim was to defend the idea of the English king's dominion over adjoining seas, within certain limits. The politico-legal concept of amity in his treatise referred to the agreements and practices that recognised the spatial limits of English authority: 'The limits related to both place and time: So that according to agreement, the Foreiner in amitie might not fish beyond these Limits' (Selden 1652: 358).[33]

Selden then uses the term when articulating another related principle of recognition of dominion over designated territorial waters, namely the maritime practice of 'striking sails'. According to him, this practice dictated that all ships entering waters under the dominion of a foreign power should lower their sails in acknowledgement of that foreign power's authority. Failure to do so would qualify as treason, and the ships would cease 'to bee protected upon the Account of Amitie'. Even if the owner of the ships later proves that 'the same Ships and Goods do belong to the friends and Allies of our Lord the King', the persons responsible for misconduct, as Selden points out, would still be punished for rebellion (Selden 1652: 402). Hence, Selden's commentary suggests that, by virtue of entering into an agreement on amity, foreign sovereigns were duty bound to recognise the authority of the English monarch over the surrounding sea within defined limits, while their subjects were obligated to obey the laws of England and recognise its jurisdiction once in the designated territory. In exchange for such recognition and by the terms of the agreement, 'foreigners in amity' would receive the protection of the English monarch. However, Philip

---

[32] Similar instructions, according to Slingsby Bethel, were issued to Dutch seamen: 'All Captains and Commanders of men of War, both private and publick, give security before they go to Sea, not to wrong the Subjects of any Nation in Friendship with the States' (Bethel 1681: 136).

[33] In fact, contrary to Schmitt's supposition, research on the history of claims to sovereignty over seas and limitations on fishing that contributed to the idea of '*mare clausum*' shows that these were novel seventeenth-century legal arguments (Fulton 2005: 66).

Meadows disagrees with Selden's opinion and argues that the practice is not about the recognition of sovereignty at sea. Instead, it signifies two basic things: 'Cultus Superioris', that is, showing respect to those superior in degree; and 'Symbolum Pacis & Amicitiae', that is, showing that the parties are bound by an agreement of peace and amity/friendship (used interchangeably). The recognition of sovereignty that Selden infers from this practice is unsubstantiated, as the crowns are in 'parity and equality of Degree' and thus cannot afford such recognition. Moreover, in the case of the English Channel, these arguments imply that no recognition of sovereignty can be claimed, because the English king no longer possessed both shores (Meadows 1689: 17–19).

In the context of an argument on the 'closed sea', Selden also contributes to the debate on the rights of friends of England who are enemies of each other. In his opinion, dominion over the seas includes 'prescribing of Laws and Limits to Foreiners, who being in Hostilitie one with another, but both in amitie with the English, made Prize of each other in this Sea' (Selden 1652: 285). This relates back to the case, discussed by Gentili, of the Spanish captives of the Dutch, but in principle applies to many other cases of property seized from the ships of enemies and friends. In fact, the tradition of regulating this matter had long been familiar to English law; for example, there are regulations dealing with the same subject from the first half of the fifteenth century: 'Merchandises taken in Ships of the King's Enemies, though belonging to *Foreigners in Amity* with the King, shall not be restored' (*The Statuses* 1763: 580; emphasis added). This interesting legal collision of interests remained a central topic in the seventeenth century. Thus, Richard Zouche similarly raises the question of whether it is lawful to seize goods belonging to a friend from an enemy's ship or, *vice versa*, whether a friend's ships carrying the goods of an enemy can be captured (Zouche 1911: 122–123). He suggests that if the goods can be used in war, then they should not be returned.

In developing the topic of being friends with two parties in conflict with each other, Selden takes up the case of the Spanish–Dutch controversy in the English seas and offers his solution, to the effect that the dominion of England would also be evident in the settlement of this case. He opens up the discussion by recognising the status of contending foreign nations, which are 'in amitie with the English' (Selden 1652: 363). He then goes on to refer to James I's proclamation of 1604 setting up 'the limits', that is, the distance from the English coast, within which safe passage and protection were granted in equal degrees to all foreigners in amity. Selden seeks to defend the exclusive dominion of England not only within these limits, as other jurists seemed to have interpreted the proclamation, but also extend it over the wider 'British Sea', even if with a thinner regulatory regime. This attempt, the grounds for which are not always found satisfactory by later histories of law (Fulton 2005: 48–51), clearly illustrates the intrinsic link of amity to the construction of regulatory regimes or a community of law attached to a specific territory not bound by land borders: 'whilst hee [the king] commanded a keeping of the peace within these Creeks or Closets, did, as *Arbiter*, permit those that were in amitie with him, but enemies among themselves, to make prize of one another, in the rest of the Sea; yet not without som qualifications or restrictions added concerning use of the more open part of the Sea' (Selden 1652: 370).

While referring to Gentili's arguments in defence of Spanish interests harmed by the Dutch, Selden tries to show the exceptionality of the case, but simultaneously infers from both practice and Gentili himself that English dominion of the surrounding seas is much wider, even if some regulations are limited to certain lines.[34] In this sense the 'closed seas' and disputed territoriality are as much the subject of juridical and political concern as issues arising from the remote 'open seas'. Both types of spaces had to be drawn and regulated by legal instruments, such as amity, that could ensure protection for subjects within certain territorial limits. A party's removal from a relationship of amity would imply the absence of protection of property rights and exposure to the free exercise of arbitrary power even within the realms of those who were not formal enemies.

Curiously, Hugo Grotius, the author of *Mare Liberum* (1609), who defended the right of Dutch sailors to free navigation against the Portuguese policy of closed seas in the East Indies – the argument that Selden refutes in *Mare Clausum* in the section on territorial seas – also later recognises sovereign dominion over territorial waters and the sanctity of territorial social orders. In *De Jure Belli ac Pacis*, Grotius mentions friendship in the context of territorially bounded realms and the principles of their relations. Notably, friendship as a type of league or treaty only figures in Grotius's discussion of whether the validity of a treaty is questioned as a result of invasion or usurpation. He cites T. Quinctius's address to the tyrant Nabis to advance the maxim that making 'friendship and confederacy' (*amicitia & societas*) is only possible with a lawful and just ruler, adding that usurpation shall not cause any damage to previous treaties concluded with established authorities (Grotius 2005: II, XVI, XVIII). Towards the end of his treatise, in the chapter 'Concerning the publick Faith whereby War is finished; of Treaties of Peace, Lots, Set Combats, Arbitrations, Surrenders, Hostages, and Pledges', Grotius devotes two subchapters to friendship and friendly obligations (ibid.: III, XX, XL, XLI), pertaining to what today might be called the domain of 'state sovereignty', although he does not use the term 'sovereignty'. In his argument Grotius draws a parallel between friendship and law:

[34] Again Philip Meadows makes it clear that the king's dominion and jurisdiction are limited to the lines defined in the sea chart and proclamation by James I. According to Meadows, these coastal parts of sea constitute part of the country and are different from the High Sea; hence, they fall under the jurisdiction of common-law courts, while the latter comes under the jurisdiction of the Court of Admiralty. It is within the former that by will of the king 'all Hostilities betwixt Foreigners in War one with another, but in Amity with *England*, forbidden' (Meadows 1689: 43).

Thus those Things that are done contrary to Friendship, do break that Peace which was contracted under the Condition of Friendship; for what the Duty of Friendship alone may require from others, ought also here to be performed by the Right of Covenant [*Sic quæ contra-amicitiam sunt, rumpunt pacem quæ sub amicitiæ lege contracta est: quod enim inter cæteros solius amicitiæ officium exigeret, hic etiam pacti iure præstandum est*]. And to this (tho' not to every Peace, for there are some not on the same Account of Friendship, as *Pomponius* observes,) we may refer many of those Things, which Civilians advance concerning Injuries and Affronts done without force of Arms. (ibid.: III, XX, XL; for the Latin version see Grotius 1625: 745)[35]

The parallel thus becomes rather literal, since it allows for friendship to be contracted and regulated by specified rules. However, there is also a possibility for friendship to remain at the level of mere 'friendship duties' that seem to follow the dictates of natural law. To further clarify the status of the concept in this context I shall look at its range of reference, namely at examples of acts that, according to Grotius, are contrary to friendship:

But cruel Threatnings, without some new Cause given, are inconsistent with Friendship [*amicitia pugnant*]; and hereto I will refer the Building of strong Places on the Frontiers, not so much for Defence as Offence, and an unusual raising of Forces, if there be just and apparent Reasons to think that they are prepared against him with whom we have made Peace. (Grotius 2005: III, XX, XL)[36]

In light of these examples it is possible to conclude that the customs and laws of public friendship not only recognise particular territorial limits or frontiers, but should also aim to assure the counterpart that a formal friend poses no threat to territorial possessions. It is worth emphasising that the argument is made not for the abstract condition of peace as absence of war, but in recognition of territorially bound political order, which in itself contributed to the individualisation of such orders and the nascent territorial expression of modern state sovereignty. The next subchapter in Grotius's treatise, 'Whether to entertain Subjects and Exiles be contrary to Friendship', further substantiates this point:

To receive particular Persons as are willing to remove from one Prince's Territories into another's, is no Breach of Friendship [*non est contra amicitiam*]; for this Liberty is not only natural, but has something favourable in it … But we have already proved, that it is not lawful to receive whole Towns, or any great Multitudes, who made a considerable Part of the State from whence they came. (Ibid.: III, XX, XLI; Grotius 1625: 746)

[35] Following Grotius, George Dawson recapitulates for his audience the idea that things done against 'the Laws of Hospitality, Amity and Friendship' break peace concluded for these purposes (Dawson 1694, IV: 11).

[36] Along the same lines Meadows brings up the example of Queen Elizabeth's warnings to Henry IV of France against stationing an 'unusual' fleet in the seas next to England for it would 'weaken the Amity and good Assurance betwixt the two Crowns' (Meadows 1689: 23).

These arguments in Grotius's treatise are important, as they highlight the remaining utility of political friendship to produce and re-produce spatial politico-legal orders in the early modern period. This is not to claim that the concept and the terms that express it were used identically throughout two centuries of diplomatic exchanges and across the vast areas of the Old and New Worlds. In the course of great discoveries and European rivalries outside the European continent, friendship agreements could well be used to delineate general spheres of influence, while the arguments made by jurists such as Grotius, Selden and Zouche demonstrate that the concept of friendship referred to a customary diplomatic instrument that facilitated relations between and the exercise of supreme political authority within concrete territorial units (and stretching out to territorial waters). In this context friendship enacts a number of specific legal 'regimes' that provide for rights and duties in fields such as navigation through foreign waters, trade in foreign ports and lands, the law of prize, war conduct within special zones/dominions, recognition of borders and authority, and so on.

In this chapter I have pursued one main goal: recovering a very particular political concept of friendship. In the first chapter we observed a number of linguistic regularities in the classical sources that allowed us to identify – in addition to the familiar concept of friendship that belongs to the realm of ethics and virtue – a concept of friendship that was part and parcel of the political-juridical lexicon. This chapter has demonstrated that late medieval and early modern sources pertaining to loosely defined domains of diplomacy, 'high politics', law and jurisprudence equally contributed to the survival of the contractual political concept of friendship. Certainly, it would be far-fetched to claim that the classical 'tradition' of contingent and contractual friendship – if there were a coherent 'tradition' in the first place – simply continued or was imported in one package into the early modern period. But what can be argued is that early modern authors were absolutely familiar with the juridical and political concept of friendship that I identified in the classical period, albeit they invoked the concept to pursue their own tactical aims and further their specific arguments. For this reason the use of classical authors and relevant passages on friendship is always selective and cannot represent a comprehensive tradition of any sort.

Nevertheless, the concept of friendship that I have recovered in the context of early modern arguments concerning diplomatic exchanges, matters of the law of nations and issues of political authority within and outside a realm, has a very specific range of reference and is expressed with its own distinct vocabulary, and these are comparable to the classical *topoi*. First, early modern political discourse related the concept of friendship to the social and political practices of maintaining order and exercising authority within a political unit. Secondly, the political and juridical treatises of the time conventionally connected friendship to a type of political compact, which is tightly linked, but not reducible, to the concept of alliance. Thirdly, and more importantly, in the contexts of juridical arguments on the law of nations, the concept of friendship was used to refer to a number of what we would today call 'legal regimes' regulating commerce, property and personal rights, rules of navigation, recognition and respect of territorial possessions. In this context, the application of the concept required a largely contractual vocabulary (particularly verbs and adjectives). As opposed to contemporary 'rhetoric' of friendship, this type of diplomatic friendship involved concrete obligations and had serious material consequences. Fourthly, references to the concept were common in the contexts of drawing dividing lines between different types of political orders, whether quasi-global or between traditional European dominions. As such, this shows how the concept helped in constituting orders while encountering multiple competitors or creating political divides, on the one hand, and forging contingent political groupings on the other. Thus, the consensual and cosmopolitan ideals that we may wish to associate with international friendship are effectively challenged by these early modern perspectives on diplomatic practices.

Overall, this range of reference indicates how significant and practical the concept was in crafting the foundations of the early modern law of nations, the principles of sovereignty and the co-existence of the nascent European society of sovereign states (even if the concept of the sovereign state had not gained currency by this time, while the main parties to agreements were 'crowns', 'monarchs', 'kingdoms', 'nations' and 'dukes'); how contingent and limited contractual arrangements such as friendships were, how they could vary to include vertical and horizontal political relations, and relations between equal and unequal powers undertaking symmetrical and asymmetrical obligations. This recovery not only sheds a new light on our contemporary understanding of international friendship, but also registers an alternative way of seeing and practising friendship in the period when most of the foundations of contemporary international society were forged. Recognition of this alternative practice should then stimulate further critical reappraisal of the role of 'sovereignty' in this period, as well as issues of territoriality and international law. Specifically, the recovery of a contractual and highly political concept of friendship further complicates the understanding of peace and community under the allegedly imperial order of the late Middle Ages, the transition from this supposedly homogeneous system to the heterogeneous system of sovereign states, and the problematic, far from abrupt consolidation of the sovereign state.[37]

---

[37] In this sense, the analysis of arguments and their linguistic commensurability with the Roman *topoi* contributes to research in International Relations and political theory on the role of neo-Roman language and thought in the early modern period – Onuf (1998), Skinner (1998), Tuck (1999) – and rejoins the challenges to the Westphalian legal and political orthodoxies effectively posed by the studies of Beaulac (2000), Krasner (1999), Kratochwil (1995) and Osiander (2001).

At this stage it is legitimate to raise the question of whether friendship as a contractual diplomatic instrument was the sole tool that political philosophers and jurists could reflect upon in their arguments, and whether they referred to other sorts of relations and appealed to ethical standards of friendship, given the significance of ideas of a shared community of Christian faith and heritage. Indeed, this question is engendered by the juridical and legal texts themselves. The hints of an alternative convention could be seen already in appeals to Christian love in diplomatic exchanges and to the value of friendship asserted by Erasmus, as well as in the juridical debate initiated by Gentili. Yet perhaps Grotius ultimately provides an excellent example of how, by means of rhetoric, the borders between contractual and ethical concepts can be shifted and their application modified to make a more convincing case for the author. Grotius explicitly compares public political friendships and friendship between individuals conceived along the lines of another classical concept of ethical friendship:

> For what *Cicero* said of private Friendship, may be fitly applied to publick [*Nam quod de privatis amicitiis dixit Cicero, ad has publicas non minus recte aptes*]. That all the Duties of Friendship are to be observed religiously at all Times, but especially when it has been renewed by a Reconciliation. (Grotius 2005: III, XXV, VII; 1625: 786)

By invoking the authority of Cicero, Grotius in fact amplifies the transfer of the ideals of private friendship onto the relations of public persons, who are thereby constituted and legitimised as independent political entities and 'great individuals', and whose obligations towards each other are cemented by this very comparison. At the same time, this rhetorical transposition demonstrates that the vocabulary of legal contract is not entirely isolated from the sphere of private relations for, as Grotius shows by means of this rhetorical figure, one concept of friendship, that is, the ethical, can be applied, at least partly, to an unusual state of affairs – public political relations.

The analogy itself points to two crucial elements in such rhetorical arguments. First, Grotius's use of the concept of friendship allows it to be a part of natural law, even if understood in terms of self-preservation and utility (for arguments on minimal sociability and self-preservation in Grotius see Tuck 1987: 109–113) and a voluntarily contracted law of nations, which is particularly evident when he articulates the difference between the general duties of friendship and voluntarily established laws. Nonetheless, the presence of the concept of friendship in the domain of natural law, as the fourth chapter of this book will demonstrate, played a major role in conceptual transformation initiated by the next generation of jurists. Secondly, the analogy indicates that the normative discourse contemporaneous to debates, to which Gentili and Grotius contributed, contained a readily available concept of ethical friendship that apparently could be legitimately borrowed for making arguments even about legal matters. In fact, as the next chapter will demonstrate, like classical argumentative contexts, early modern discourse displayed a set of linguistic conventions that regulated the use of friendship in ethical arguments about the conduct of agents towards each other and normative arguments about politics at large. The ethical and contractual concepts of friendship served their own purposes, but could occasionally intersect in the rhetorical battles waged in the period.

3

The ethics of friendship in early European diplomacy

Surprising as it may sound, Humanist discourse in early modern Europe operated with a range of linguistic conventions that signalled the existence of a concept of friendship that was not only distinct from but also often entirely excluded the possibility of the contractual concept discussed in the previous chapter, despite sharing its key terms – 'friendship' and 'amity'. The conventions that determined its distinct conceptual identity stemmed from the realm of ethics and morality, which many believe to be alien to the realm of politics despite the assertions of some prominent politicians. Even in early modern Humanist discourses, the normative prescriptions and thinking in terms of ideals differed essentially from the language of contingently made and broken agreements. One of the central questions that this chapter will seek to answer is whether this ethical perspective on friendship was incompatible with the idea of politics, even politics framed in moral terms. This question needs answering, given that discourses about the ethical standards of friendship occupied as much space in public debate as legal statements on friendship – if not significantly more.

In fact, early modern discourses on ethics and moral norms in friendship represent an invaluable vantage point for reappraising current ideals of friendship between nations and their leaders. It would certainly be a naïve anachronism to compare the friendships professed at summits by present-day state leaders (and any awkwardness we may feel) with the ethical predicaments identified by early modern Humanist writers in the collision of friendship and politics. Nonetheless, this discourse is instrumental for elucidating the ways in which ancient ideas about the ethics of friendship translated into the early modern moralisation of friendship and understandings of the constraints that this entailed for political roles.

The ethical concept of friendship is never strictly separated from the performance of political roles, for discussions of ethical principles and moral norms always take place within the framework of a particular political regime, societal arrangement and culture. It is therefore essential to contextualise the moralist arguments of Renaissance authors in order to highlight the political rationality of high moral standards of friendship appealing to past and modern publics.

Indeed, turning to an early modern moralist discussion opens up various perspectives on political phenomena and practices that are fundamental to the emergence of the modern political system. In particular, the debate highlights the problematic overlap between friendship and the duties of office, indicates the obstacles for friendship between ruler and ruled, and raises the question of whether power can be compromised through ties of friendship. Most importantly, though, the moralisation of friendship signals that this alternative concept referred to one of the normative foundations of the European 'republic' of sovereigns.

Certainly, the European 'republic' of mainly monarchical courts at the dawn of the Reformation and during the religious wars of the sixteenth century can be spoken of as such only metaphorically. Discourses on Europe as one republic or commonwealth started to emerge in the seventeenth century and reached their apogee in the eighteenth, embracing such figures as Giovanni Botero and, most prominently, Emer de Vattel (see Deudney 2007: 139–142; Gulick 1967: 11; Pagden 2013: 282–308). Sixteenth-century Europe was probably too sundered by religious conflict to constitute a single entity. However, the metaphor of a republic, applied to this period as well as the seventeenth century, is only meant to capture the basic shared morals of Christian princes and ideals of friendship in circulation at the time; this seems to have been a normative concept that helped this peculiar republic hang together. In a sense, the European 'republic' represented the inverse of another compound republic of the post-1648 period, namely the German Bund, which, according to Peter Haldén, had a 'republican' institutional structure but lacked the normative concepts that could legitimise this order (Haldén 2011: 18). Conversely, the European 'republic' possessed normative concepts, even if it lacked an explicitly republican institutional structure, if, and only if, for the moment we ignore the institutional juridical implications of friendship highlighted in the previous chapter. This perspective provides a clue to the role of friendship in projects of perpetual peace in Europe. It is no coincidence that this friendship had to be personal and normative, as it was contingent on the monarchical political constitution of the 'republic'. The value attached to monarchical friendships was seriously challenged, as we shall see, by republican commonwealths and their ideologies, as well as by a belief in the corruption of princely friendships.

The ideal of friendship forged in Humanist discourse was different from the democratised standards produced by the rising commercial societies and the French and American revolutions. Early modern Humanist discourses of friendship derived from a high moral standard and noble ideas of virtue that amounted to a very exquisite concept of friendship. Thus, language centred on virtue and language centred on contract make it possible to reconstitute the 'Aristotelian' framework of friendship of utility, pleasure and virtue in the early modern context. It can in fact be posited as a framework for both moralist and juridical

Humanist discourse, because the moralist discourse on friendship of virtue is often, if not always, connected to an alternative conception of friendship of utility. However, in this discourse the alternative is conceived not as a practised social norm and institution, but as a condemnable corruption of virtue, that is, a vice. Therefore, discussion in this chapter will inevitably revolve around the theme of virtuousness and genuineness, vicissitude and corruption. It is this unequivocal vector of conceptual relation that later on conditioned a major transformation of international friendship. However, to better understand the change, which will be scrutinised in greater detail in the next chapter, we need first to identify which political norms and moral issues became central to Humanist discourse on friendship in the sixteenth and seventeenth centuries, and how these scholars' understanding contributed to the ideological underpinnings of the emerging international system by linking personalised princely friendships to issues of alliances, commercial relations and sovereign authority.

Equality and virtue: the noble standards

The appealing ancient ideal of friendship rooted in virtue became a key theme in the prolific Renaissance discourse on the subject. Humanist authors seem to have pushed the value of 'true' and 'perfect' friendship even further than Aristotle himself intended. While Aristotle's account admits all forms of practicable friendship, Humanist authors tended to prioritise the true form – that is, friendship of virtue – while disparaging other types of friendship as not proper. Such opinions were widely shared across Europe. Key contributions to the discourse were available in Latin and various vernaculars, into which important works were promptly translated. One of the key authorities on the subject in the northern Renaissance was Michel de Montaigne, whose essay 'Of friendship' advocated friendship of virtue, or friendship for its own sake, as the only true form, and denigrated the other forms of friendship identified by Aristotle (Montaigne 1613: 92–93). Montaigne's work was soon translated into English, as was that of some of his associates. For instance, Pierre Charron carried on Montaigne's line of thought by elevating the standard of virtuous friendship and emphasising its value not only to private life, but also to society at large. For both thinkers, Aristotle's study of friendship constituted the primary frame of reference. Like Montaigne (ibid.: 90), Charron refers to Aristotle's observation that lawmakers should care more about friendship than justice. He also modifies the classification of friendship of 'the ancient', which in his opinion did not capture actual social practices. Comparing the types of friendship based on their various roots (nature, virtue, profit, pleasure), he maintains that virtue is 'the more noble and the stronger, for that is spiritual, and in the heart as friendship is' and 'vertue is more liberall, more free, and pure, and without it the other causes are poore, and idle, and fraile' (1608: 430).

The argument made for virtuous friendship involved a requirement, slightly varying among moralist authors, for a number of prescriptions and standards, coupled with the dismissal of certain social practices. Turning the discussion onto these inevitably produced a set of limitations on friendship in politics or conceivable political friendships. The values that constituted the core of friendship of virtue in Humanist discourse included, but were not limited to, likeness and similitude of thinking and attitudes, faithfulness, plainness, sincerity, reciprocation and trust (for these moral dicta see, for instance, Barclay 1631; Brinsley 1612; Corrozet 1602; Montaigne 1613). Thomas Elyot's famous treatise *The Boke named Governour* (1531), which echoes Erasmus in seeking to provide moral instruction for a ruler, offers 'the true discription of amitie or frendship' (ch. xi) that directly cites Aristotle and Cicero and reasserts the postulate that friendship is a virtue that requires 'perfecte consent of all thinges', similitude and trust. Elyot also makes a point of repeating Cicero in that '*amicitia*' comes from Latin '*amore*', and adds that it received an English name 'frendshippe or amitie' (Elyot [1531] 1992: II, XI: 11–28; note the interchangeable positions here of 'friendship' and 'amity'). In stressing consent among friends, Elyot honed in on a very popular Aristotelian trope on friendship in the literary sources of Tudor England – 'one soul in bodies twain' (for more on this see Mills 1937).

Adamant demands for honesty, sincerity and plainness of hearts and minds in true friendship naturally formed another central and antonymic image in moralist debate: the image of feigned or pretended friendship. Thomas Churchyard elegantly expressed this popular trope of suspicion in his verse 'Of fained frendshippe':

> In fréends are found a heape of doubts,
> that double dealyng vse,
> A swarme of sutche I could finde out,
> whose crafte I could accuse:
> A face for loue, a harte for hate,
> those faunyng freends can beare,
> A tong for trothe, a hedde for whiles,
> to fraude the simple eare. (Churchyard 1580)

Another popular trope expressing the same 'problem' in discourse on friendship was the idiom of a 'wolf in sheep's clothing', stemming from the biblical theme of false prophets (see Cornwallis 1600–1601: essay 6 'Of friendship and factions'; Shannon 2002: 214). The moral pathos of such denunciations was pure and simple: one should not use friendship to seek profits and favours from friends; and by the same token friends should beware of such pretence. Naturally, the valorisation of this moral requirement clashes with the old idea of friendship among socially and politically unequal parties (e.g. father and son; prince and subject). As Charron puts it, disparity 'hindreth that inwardnes and familiaritie and entire communication, which is the principall fruit and effect of friendship, as likewise because of the obligation that is therein, which is the cause why there is lesse libertie and lesse choice and affection therein. And this is the reason why men giue it other names than of friendship' (Charron 1608: 431). It is on these grounds that Aristotle's typology of friendship was challenged and the prospects for political friendship effectively undermined.

If this is the horizon of true friendship, then we cannot but exclude a crucial dimension that it had comprised in the thought of classical authors and a strand of contemporaneous thinking regarding the constitution of community and the diversity of practice in the law of nations – namely that a power-holder, and particularly the holder of princely office, became a central problem in moralist discourse. Whereas in the classical tradition, applying the concept of friendship to the description of cooperative and enjoyable relations between unequal parties could be integral to the vision of normal politics, from the moralist perspective this relation would be no more than a corrupt practice of seeking advantages from the other party, which cannot escape flattery, pretence and insincerity. The problem is exacerbated by the highness of the office, because, as William Cornwallis summarises: 'For Princes, or great fortunes I think it much more vnsafe, since they cannot easily determine, whether they loue them, or their fortunes, whether this league be entered for a mutuall safegard, or for the ones particular, and it is the more daungerous, since the name of a common good authoriseth this breach' (1600–1601: essay 6).

The figure of the prince, in fact, highlights a number of obstacles to the emergence of true friendship. Laurie Shannon's detailed study of the literary sources of the period documents the popularity of this theme in a number of authors. She demonstrates how common it was for the authors to deny the possibility of true friendship between the commander and the commanded (Shannon 2002: 129, 138). Insofar as friendship is understood as 'one soul in two bodies', it entails limitations on the public capacity of princes who happen to engage in friendly relations with another person. Likeness of minds and fidelity to a friend mean that the prince-as-friend may fail to be impartial as a sovereign to his socially and symbolically inferior friend. Thus, privileging a friend may turn the prince into a tyrant vis-à-vis his other subjects. Furthermore, if the prince has to take into account his friend's feelings and will, he will no longer be a true sovereign unhindered in his exercise of power. To be a true friend, a sovereign therefore has to retreat into his private capacity, and possibly abandon his public duty, since abdicating the status of a superior releases 'friends' from the need to seek favours through blatant flattery (see discussion in ibid.: 158–159).

The standard of social (in)equality in friendship is neatly captured by John Lyly's term 'half-friendship'. In Lyly's *Endymion* (1591), the character Sir Tophas rejects the idea of friendship with boys (pages), saying that '*amicitia* … is *inter pares*', and offers them the status of 'half-friends' (Lyly 1902a: 26). While this is certainly a satirical episode, it nonetheless highlights the problem. In another play by Lyly, *Euphues and his England* (1580), we can find a seemingly commended portrayal of equal friendships. In a letter to Euphues, Philautus asks: 'haue I broken the league of friendship?' (Lyly 1902b: 147); in reply Euphues writes: 'For aunswering thy suite I am not yet so hastie, for accepting thy seruice I am not so imperious, for in friendeship there must be an equalitie of estates, & be that may bee in vs, also similitude of manners' (ibid.: 150). These satirical and straightforwardly normative statements on equality as a prerequisite of true friendship, which they strive to bring about, in fact indicate the social promi- nence of the opposite of their ideal. We may contend that the whole discursive trend to condemn friendship among unequal parties indicates the existence and perceived problematic nature of such a social practice.

Possibly to moralists' chagrin, the practice was also registered in the politi- cal realm by key political theorists. Jean Bodin, for instance, notices tensions between the idea of equality and friendship in at least two dimensions of political life already mentioned. First, political thinkers sought to problematise the ideal of equality. For instance, Jean Bodin notices tensions between the idea of equal- ity and friendship in at least two dimensions of political life already mentioned. He argued against the utopian idea (specifically as proposed by Thomas More) that things and goods should be divided and kept in equal shares in the com- monwealth. Dividing things equally among the members of the commonwealth, according to Bodin, is unjust and in fact ruins it: 'To say, That equalitie is the nurce of friendship; is but to abuse the ignorant: for it is most certaine, that there is neuer greater hatred, nor more capitall quarrels, than betwixt equals: and the iealousie betwixt equals, is the spring and fountaine of troubles, seditions, and ciuill warres' (Bodin 1962: 570).

In line with this observation is the idea that the English author Francis Bacon puts forward in his essay *Of Followers and Friends* (1597): 'There is little *friend- ship* in the world, and *least of all between equals*, which was wont to be magni- fied. That that is, is between superior and inferior' (Bacon 1964: 139; emphasis added). Bodin and Bacon thus turn the normative dictum upside-down and locate the source of peril precisely in equality between friends, thereby making the problem of inequality/equality particularly acute and salient in the discourse of the period.

Secondly, Bacon and Bodin raise the issue of friendship, although with differ- ent emphases, between a prince and his subjects, the improbability of which was stressed in moralist accounts. Bacon, perhaps sensing the moralist problem of abusing friendship for the sake of the advantages that an office-holder can bring, remarks in the essay *Of Friendship* (1612): 'It is a strange thing to observe how high a rate great kings and monarchs do set upon this fruit of *friendship* whereof we speak ... For princes ... cannot gather this fruit, except ... they raise some persons to be as it were companions and almost equals to themselves' (ibid.: 75;

emphasis added). On the one hand, this observation illustrates the sovereign's burden, but on the other it also indicates the possibility of friendship, however fragile, between unequal parties. Such phrases as 'raise some persons' or 'almost equals' in this quotation grasp the inherent power asymmetry in and the downward vector of this social relation (as it is the sovereign prince who grants the status of 'friend' to his inferiors). If we assume that promotion to the status of friend of a prince does not eliminate the sovereign status of the latter, then the power asymmetry is bound to remain in this type of friendship.

Bodin approaches the issue of friendship between prince and subject from a slightly different angle. In addressing the topic of doing justice, he recommends the prince do justice by himself, rather than delegate this function to magistrates, since it will maintain and nourish 'the vnion and amitie of the Princes with the subiects' (Bodin 1962: 500[1]). From this perspective, the inequality and power asymmetry in friendship is seen as an integral part of the idea, discussed in the previous chapter, of maintaining the unity and governability of the princely realm.

The idea that social ties and solidarity are maintained by means of friendship, combined with the idea of coercive justice, curiously re-emerged later in Gottfried Wilhelm Leibniz's 'mirror of princes'-type essay *Le Portrait du Prince* (1679), in which he maintained that societal ties are established by three political virtues: justice, friendship and valour. It would have been possible to maintain society solely by friendship, but due to the weakness of human nature and the artificial division of goods, which Leibniz deems to be held in common by nature, people arrived at the necessity of preserving the social order through the use of justice, which princes, as depositaries of power, are there to maintain (Leibniz 1981: 98). In England arguments were also made to present friendship as the bonds of political community, although virtue was put in the forefront of this Aristotelian trope. Thus, Elyot stresses that the nature of man is in 'humanitie', 'whiche is a generall name to those vertues, in whome semeth to be a mutuall concorde and love' (Elyot 1992: II, VIII, 10–11). Further he adds that benevolence extended to the whole country may be called charity, but when it concerns one person it could be 'named love or amitie' (ibid.: 17–19). Two centuries later, Lord Bolingbroke was still trying to picture the unity of men in society as a public friendship resting on the principle of like thinking about political affairs. He further rhetorically connects friendship to a more general allegiance to the constitutional foundations of political community: 'when persons are spoken of as friends to the government, and enemies to the constitution, the term friendship is a little prostituted ... Such men are really incapable of friendship; for

---

[1] A similar meaning of the role of amity is conveyed in Humphrey Crouch's *The Parliament of Graces* (1642: 3), written at the beginning of the English civil war and stating that 'Amity' had left England as a result of dissent and war.

real friendship can never exist among those who have banished virtue and truth'
(Bolingbroke [1733–1734] 1997: 89). Virtue in this case lay in endorsing constitutional means of governing, rather than in supporting the arbitrary, albeit
profitable, rule of a prince. Thus, the transformed Aristotelian trope connecting
friendship and justice/government as the cornerstones of political community
survived well in a period in which conceptions of sovereign state power appeared
to hold sway.

However, such attempts to see friendship comprising equal and unequal relations as a normal element of political life were gradually marginalised by prolific
moralist oppositions of sincere vs insincere, equal and true vs unequal and untrue
friendships. For instance, in John Locke's seminal first *Treatise of Government*
(1689) the word 'friendship' is used to designate exclusively relations between
equal individuals. 'Friends and Equals' were explicitly opposed to 'Jurisdiction
and Superiority'; in this context Locke, in fact, writes about brotherly relations
(see Locke 2003: I, § 118: 226; I, § 135: 239–240). The word 'amity', which
was used by both earlier and contemporaneous thinkers to designate the phenomenon of publicly contracted friendship, is simply absent from Locke's text.
Such statements further reinforce the ethical dimension of political friendship,
which would later allow for stronger statements on the impossibility of friendship among states.

Indeed, seventeenth- and eighteenth-century discourse contained a handful of
statements positing the incommensurability of friendship and inequality. George
Wither, for instance, argued in his pamphlet *Friendship* (1653) that inequality
is incompatible with friendship, and particularly with political friendship: 'Now
in Relations which have not that equality, as *Father* and *Son*, and the like, or
Politick Relations, as *King* and *Subject*, the inequality and aw created thence quite
destroyes possibility of *Friendship*; and this incapacity of the greatest happinesse
here, is the sharpest *Thorn* in a *Kings Crown*' (Wither 1653: 7).

An even more hyperbolic comparison arguing the incompatibility of inequality and friendship appears in E.G. Gent's *A Discourse of Friendship*, which contends that no friendship is possible between prince and slave, as it would involve
an unacceptable diminution of honour on the part of the former (Gent 1676:
42–43; on equality and reciprocity in friendship see also Johnson 1792: 411).
Most of these discourses contributed to the idea of the impossibility of friendship
between people of different ranks, and between commoners and power-holders.
Moralist authors rendered reciprocal exchange of offices, love and honorary sacri-
fice an insuperable obstacle for political and social relations admitting inequality.

Further moralist arguments widened the divide between the concepts of
friendship and politics. Certainly, the discourse preserved room for the genre of
personal instructions to foster friendships for the reason of their usefulness in a
person's life. But the prevailing theme of argumentation consisted of separating
friendship from the idea of possible utility in political endeavours. Thus, John

Sheffield's contribution to the debate on equality in his essay *On Friendship* presents a bitter moralistic diagnosis of his times:

> My Lord Chancellor Bacon observes very justly, that we now see nothing of it [friendship] between *Equals*; and only a little of it sometimes where the different degrees of men render each of them useful and necessary to the other: As between a wealthy country-gentleman and his led-captain … between a great courtier and one of his dependant flatterers; whereas *inequality is quite contrary to the very nature of friendship*, which like love, either *finds people equal*, or makes them so. (Sheffield 1740: 273–274; emphasis added)

He further complements this observation with an assessment of his age as corrupt, since virtuous friendship could rarely be seen. Sheffield also compares friendships of his epoch to those of the ancients and concludes, with regret, that friendship in his time resembled more 'effeminate Love-matters' than the noble and heroic friendship of the ancients (ibid.: 275–276; for comparison of friendship and love see also Taylor 1657: 17–18).

Correspondingly, flatterers and other advantage-seeking friends were commonly made the subjects of satirical portrayals. Early modern authors defending their normative agendas no longer saw calculated advantage as falling within the frame of the concept of friendship. This is first because many authors were of the opinion that friendship springs from a natural affection that cannot be bought or purposefully cultivated. Secondly, it was argued that friendship requires that the parties make some effort, and maintain reciprocal exchanges and ceremonies (for the former view see Savile 1750: 150 and Goldsmith [1767] 1966: 201; for the latter view see Rousseau 1788: 84). As a result of this prevailing normative line of argumentation, the understanding of friendship as a means of attaining power was removed to the periphery of political theorising, and its place was occupied by arguments of a different sort, which could be illustrated well by Owen Felltham's statement that 'Policy and Friendship are scarce compatible'. Felltham's contrast of policy and friendship is typical of a moralist argument. Policy, in his understanding, incorporates all motives of utility, while friendship is assigned to a completely different realm of relations:

> As *Policy* is taken in the *general*, we hold it but a kind of crafty *wisdom*, which bows every thing to a *self-profit*. And therefore a *Politician* is one of the worst *sorts* of *men*, to make a *friend* of. Give me one, that is virtuously *wise*, not cunningly *hid*, and sconc'd in himself. *Policy* in friendship, is like *Logick* in truth: something too *subtil* for the *plainness* of open *hearts*. (Felltham 1709: 196)

With this very modern and familiar belief in the distinction between the realms of politics and friendship, moralist arguments prepared one of the key directions of the coming conceptual change. The ideas of legal contract, contingency and eventually politics expressed in the contractual concept of friendship were logically compatible with the idea of inequality. As we saw in Livy and the early modern jurists, the contingency of a political situation translating into a contract of friendship could imply unequal contributions from the parties to the arrangement, not to mention the explicit recognition of the superiority of one of the parties. Similarly, groups of friends gathering around a noble lord in the contest for power within a political community could well recognise a degree of inequality. Moralist arguments virtually closed the space for the concept of friendship to capture such political arrangements.

The worth of inter-princely friendship

The discussion in the previous section highlighted a number of noble principles that constituted the ideal of true friendship, which in the opinion of moralist authors was hardly attainable in politics in general and more particularly for a prince. The duty to care about the good of the realm, contrasted with the often incompatible interests of foreign realms, rendered inter-princely friendship desirable but highly problematic from the perspective of moralist arguments. On the one hand, the holder of supreme power within a realm was equal in this respect to the holder of supreme power within a foreign realm. In this sense, the requirement of equality for the moralists' true friendship was satisfied. On the other hand, the likeness and spontaneity of friendly feelings that two princes-as-persons could cultivate might become a source of peril for their realms, because privileging the other prince and his subjects might soon prove detrimental to the commercial, military and other concerns of one's own subjects. As Shannon noted in passing, Elizabeth I in defending her isolationist policy touched upon exactly the same problem by pointing at the danger of the subordination of the realm in 'foreign friendships' (Shannon 2002: 188, fn. 8). This apparent moral impasse, and sometimes trap, was well understood by the Humanist authors, but nonetheless fed a good number of political criticisms levelled at inter-princely relations.

In fact, this critique becomes a popular Renaissance *topos*, feeding the debate with discussions of sincere, true, feigned and unfeigned friendships. A critique of amity became one of the central themes, for instance, in Erasmus's *The Complaint of Peace* (*Querela Pacis*, 1521). Concerned with the recovery of peace in Europe, Erasmus investigated the principles upon which peace rested and attempted to fill them with different moral content. In line with the trend discussed above, he advanced a normative critique of friendship as a hierarchical relationship, focusing on the problem of sincerity in this kind of friendship (Erasmus 1917; see Nashe 1592 for a similar critique). Lack of sincerity is also a problem that corrupts the type of friendship with which Erasmus is principally concerned, namely friendship among princes. One of the main practices of 'international' friendship that comes in for major criticism from Erasmus is 'friendship by alliance' or 'marriages in amity'. This model of friendship can also be found later in

Bacon's historical account, where he mentions 'marriages in amitie' as a means employed by William the Conqueror for conjoining whole peoples, for example the Normans and the Saxons (Bacon [1630] 1969).

Erasmus, driven by the idea of permanent peace, argued that this peace cannot be established either by intermarriages of royal families or by treaties. Instead of these 'factitious ties', he proposed that the kings should be united by 'pure and sincere friendship' (Erasmus 1917). In his *The Education of a Christian Prince* (*Institutio Principis Christiani*, 1516) he wrote that the 'prince might be born and educated among the people which he is destined to rule, for friendship best germinates and flourishes when the origin of affection is nature itself' (Erasmus 1921: 21). This is also the reason why he argued against alliances by marriage: 'I do not like the accepted custom of allying the Prince by marriage with foreign, especially with remote nations. Race and nationality, and the common spirit they engender, are great aids in winning affection. It is inevitable that part of this benefit will be lost if mixed marriages disturb the native and inherent tendency' (ibid.).

In his opinion, the best choice for a marriage alliance, if it is unavoidable that a prince has to marry a foreign party, would be a spouse from a neighbouring country, which will be the most faithful friend afterwards (ibid.: 50). Otherwise, Erasmus holds a very sceptical view on the durability of marriage alliances:

> If Princes could secure peace for the world by marriage alliances, I could wish each of them six hundred wives ... The duty of Princes is lasting and general peace ... Though marriage may win peace, it assuredly cannot win perpetual peace. One party dies, and the chain of concord is broken. But if peace were concluded on the proper basis, it would be solid and lasting. (Ibid.: 51)

This, however, was just one of many views on marriage alliances. Bishop John Leslie starts and finishes his pamphlet *A Treatise* with words of amity. As a way to introduce the topic and win the approbation of the reader, he lists undoubtedly profitable things for a commonwealth, including 'the leagues of forrain Princes, with their mariages, and mutuall agreementes in loue and amitie' (Leslie 1584: 2). Towards the end of the pamphlet he writes, apparently unproblematically, about the desire of the Scottish nation to have this kind of 'coniunction in amitye', when it could have united with England as a result of the marriage of Lady Margaret with King Edward of England (ibid.: 69). Similar statements were common in other sources, such as *The Mirror for Magistrates* (1559), which reports on the release of King James I of Scotland from captivity: 'they [the English] maried me [James] to a cosin of their king ... And sworne my friendship neuer should appayre' (1960: 157).

What is even more important for this study is the way Erasmus addressed the issue of treaties concluded by princes, a matter on which his opinion was also critical. He pronounced that princes should be united merely by virtue of being

Christian, and asked rhetorically: 'Why then conclude so many treaties daily, as if everyone were the enemy to everyone else, and we must effect by conventions what Christ cannot achieve?' (Erasmus 1921: 47). This question thus introduces a moral-political horizon, in which the concept of friendship appears simultaneously to undermine the concept of contingent and purposefully made contracts. Christian princes, as Erasmus tries to convince his reader, do not need these treaties, since:

> between good and wise Princes, even where there is no treaty, there is steadfast friendship: but where Sovereigns are foolish and evil inclined, the treaties which were designed to make war impossible are the cause of war, for someone is always complaining that one or another of their innumerable articles has been violated. The usual purpose of a treaty is to end war, but nowadays the name is applied to an agreement to carry it on. (Ibid.)

Thomas More makes a very similar argument in *Utopia* (1516), written in the context of his fellow Englishman Cardinal Wolsey's diplomatic efforts to establish perpetual friendship and peace in Europe, when describing the principles of friendly relations that the Utopians establish with other nations. Granted the satirical dimension of this work, we can sense the condemning moralist overtones that More attaches to his assessment of the practice of treaty-making: 'As touching leagues, which in other places between countrey and countrey be so ofte concluded, broken and renewed, they never make none with anie nation' (More 1931: 89); because if the ties of humanity do not hold people together then all kinds of promises and the sworn agreements of princes are of no use. More at this point reproduces a maxim that love between men should exist by nature, and hence the Utopians call 'frendes' those to whom they were merely beneficial (Richard Hooker similarly emphasised the deeper meaning of 'league and amity' as a means of reciprocation and learning, in [1594] 1989, I: 97).

Erasmus and other Humanists thus privilege the ideal of 'true' and deep friendship between Christian princes, which is a product of sincere and sage attraction rather than a contract. This fairly narrow conception of friendship for obvious reasons did not fit the needs of princes in the course of European expansion in the New World and intensified commerce with non-Christians, although in certain situations it did have some moral appeal and was used pragmatically by political actors. Therefore, in practice the diplomatic convention was flexible enough to allow for friendships with non-Christian people. Anthony Munday picks up this topic by asking whether 'a Christian Prince, that beleeueth in God, may ... receiue the amitie and alliance of another Prince, different in Religion' and answering in the affirmative by giving biblical examples of such alliances (Munday 1605: Fol. 34).

Erasmus's critique of the contemporary practice of treaty-making among princes emphasises another important theme in the discussion of political friendship, namely whether these friendships are true or feigned. On the one hand, by means of the concept of friendship authors could simply register existing political associations or describe a concluded agreement; on the other, with the same concept they could criticise or, alternatively, commend the relations to which it referred. Again, authors taking the latter position were thus minimising the room for constructing arguments based on the former position, since the emphasis on true and natural friendship removes the logical space for the contractual and hence potentially conflicting concept of friendship.

This type of critique was usually directed at pretended friendships between individual political agents, as in the story about Thomas Woodstock, duke of Gloucester: 'Euin so it fared by this frendship fained, Outwardly sounde, and inwardly rotten' (*The Mirror for Magistrates* 1960: 97). But it was also levelled at 'international' agreements in general. For instance, Walter Raleigh (c. 1554–1618) asserts that 'it also importeth the peace should be simple, true, and unfeigned; for all feigned and dissembling amity is to be doubted' (Raleigh 1829: 80; on feigned league and amity see also Munday 1605). It is significant that the idea of feigned friendship was not just a trope common in moralist complaints; it was also shared by holders of high office and communicated in diplomatic correspondence. The account of the customs of foreign nations published by Johann Boemus (in 1520) contains a letter from the emperor of Ethiopia to the pope in which the former complained about the practices of the Moors, who 'faine friendship' with the aim of facilitating commercial intercourse. The emperor was not fond of this practice and for this reason called them 'hollow friends' (Boemus 1611: 528).[2]

The theme of feigned friendship comprises a collateral potential dynamic of betrayal and friends turning into enemies. Thomas More captures this potentiality in another remark on the nature of friendship between commonwealths: 'they all staye at the chiefeste doubte of all, what to do … with *Englande* … and with mooste suer and strong bandes to bynde that weake and feable *frendeshippe*, so that they muste be called *frendes*, and hadde in suspicion as enemyes' (More 1931: 35; emphasis added). Notably, in the context of this observation the bands of friendship resonate with the medieval notion of the community of law and peace (see the discussion in chapter one), which is internally regulated by multiple friendships rather than constituted by virtue of a distinction made between friends and enemies. More's concept of the friend contains an explicit potential of enmity, which arises when someone stands outside the peace. This view of

---

[2] Slingsby Bethel's account is a vivid example of a much later perception of potentially treacherous princely friendship towards the city of Geneva: '*Geneve* … thinking themselves thereby secure, entertained an intimate correspondence with *Savoy* … but that Duke in a few Years after, whilst in full Peace (with a *Hypocritical pretence of Friendship*) plotted the surprising of the City, with an intent to have put all to the Sword' (1681: 308; emphasis added).

friendship, existing in political knowledge and conduct, allowed for a country or a people called a 'friend' to at some point become an enemy or be portrayed as such. The issue of the perilous potentiality of friendships continued to be among proliferating topics of debate in the seventeenth and eighteenth centuries. For instance, Francis Osborn could afford to maintain that the greatest enemies are 'bought at the dearest rates of friendship'; therefore, according to him, the friend described by Seneca could only be taken as 'Utopian' (Osborn 1682: 66, 71; see also Savile 1750: 150–151 for the inherent links between friends and enemies). As was stressed in the previous chapter, Alberico Gentili articulated a similar opinion while rejecting ideal friendships invented by philosophers, although Gentili's argumentation differed from Osborn's in that he sought to describe a friend as a legal person recognised by law.

In light of this nature of public friendship, it is remarkable that Humanist authors noticed the utility of friendship for power-holders and power-seekers. Thus, in a story about the duke of Gloucester, Humphrey Plantagenet, included in *The Mirror for Magistrates*, the queen was told to ally with former foes in friendship in her endeavour for power (1960: 457). In a similar context, Richard Edwards finishes his play *Damon and Pithias* (1571) by wishing, in a rather didactic manner, for Queen Elizabeth to have true friends and friendships, who apart from 'sweet companion' can also serve as a shield from enemies (Edwards 2002). The recognition of the swiftness with which friends and foes change roles in political affairs could not win the approbation of moralist writers. However, regardless of the Humanist critique of the existing politics of friendship, which sometimes was labelled as rotten and feigned, they still maintained that friendship was a vital requirement for the commonwealth to survive. Even Erasmus makes this claim in the chapter on treaties:

> The good and wise Prince will make every effort to keep peace with all men, but especially with his neighbours, who, if incensed, can do most harm, but as friends are most useful; nay, without mutual intercourse with them, the State cannot even exist. Moreover, it is easy to establish and maintain friendship between peoples who are linked by community of language, propinquity of territory and similarity of character and customs … there are some [nations] so captious, so perfidious and insolent, that, even as neighbours, they are useless for purposes of friendship. (Erasmus 1921: 48)

In this passage Erasmus joins the voices of those who believe that it is essential to have friendships with neighbours surrounding the realm (see also Starkey in the previous chapter), but now this idea extends to all surrounding territories and peoples. The commonly understood utility of friendship in this respect lay in maintaining commerce and preserving alliances. Although Erasmus meant to criticise existing practices of friendship, it is notable how his Humanist dictum on neighbourhood policies and friendship resembles the notion of the community of law and the contracted concept of friendship in bringing about peace, order and mutual advantages for its members.

More important in the context of this study than recognition of the mutable and pragmatic nature of political friendship is the recognition of treaties/ contracts of friendship in moralist assessments of princely relations. The connection between the concepts of league, alliance and treaty, on the one hand, and friendship on the other is still present in the critical moralist arguments. The remaining conceptual association is what in fact frames the moralist critique: as long as friendship can be seen as a political agreement, and as such subject to potential betrayals, it is possible to criticise such political friendships by contrasting them with ideals of virtuous or true friendships. It is not surprising, then, that all deviations from the agreed terms of contracted amity, let alone outright breaches, could be assessed as marks of feigned or pretended friendship. Certainly, with the advancement of the figure of true and virtuous friendship, the freedom of choice – although it could sometimes take the form of an inevitable choice – inherent in contractual or negotiated friendship had been shrinking, even if it were preserved as a significant undesirable alternative.

The language of diplomacy, the language of ideals?

Paradoxically, the language of European diplomacy, that is, of European princes and commonwealths, which often caused much dissatisfaction among Humanist critics, was couched in the same vocabulary used to criticise questionable diplomatic conduct. As we saw in the previous chapter, the phrasing of the diplomatic agreements in the fifteenth and sixteenth centuries started to embrace self-reinforcing rhetoric emphasising the true and inviolable nature of the agreements, which by their nature could be violated, even if with some reluctance, when opportunity dictated. The linguistic expression of this transformation was reflected in the changing ratio of verbs, nouns and adjectives in diplomatic formulations. In fact, we may contend that the verb as an expression of active contractual vocabulary was giving the stage to adjectives and nouns. The driving forces of this barely visible early modern change were very different. One reason, as we have already seen, may have been the impossibility of ensuring strict observance of agreements by princes, even despite the oaths that were occasionally taken (see Epp 1999: 218–219 for a discussion of early sworn friendships). Additionally, diplomats may have tried to stress the value and sanctity of an agreement by amplifying its wording with elevated adjectives. Another reason may well have been the correspondence between the professed ethics of the Christian prince, pled by Humanist educators, and the lofty language of diplomacy; the virtue of the Christian prince and the promises he made had to be matched by the proper diplomatic language.

Thus, in early modern diplomatic agreements between European princes the range of adjectives most commonly used with 'friendship' to emphasise the strength and value of the relationship included, but was not limited to, 'universal', 'perpetual', 'strict', 'firm', 'inviolable', 'constant', 'intimate', 'sincere', 'true', 'perfect' and 'mutual'. Therefore, it is not surprising that the Westphalia peace treaties (1648),[3] which for many epitomise the start of the new era of the modern international system based on the principle of state sovereignty, follow the same linguistic diplomatic tradition. Thus, the first articles of the Westphalian peace treaties concluded in Münster and Osnabrück contain references to '*amicitia*'. For instance, the peace treaty between the holy Roman emperor and the king of France, made in Münster, postulates: '[art. I] That there shall be a Christian and Universal Peace, and a perpetual, true, and sincere Amity, between his Sacred Imperial Majesty, and his Most Christian Majesty; as also, between all and each of the Allies, and Adherents of his said Imperial Majesty' (English translation of 1710).[4] It is noteworthy that the analogous article in the peace treaty made with Sweden in Osnabrück was translated into English in 1713 using two words 'friendship' and 'amity': 'That there be a Christian, universal and perpetual Peace, and a true and sincere Friendship and Amity'.[5]

Other major peace treaties of the 'new' Westphalian epoch, to which England was a party, included similar and, in fact, customary references to friendship. For instance, the first article of the Treaty of Peace made at Westminster in 1674 between Charles II, king of England, and the United Provinces of the Netherlands to end the Third Anglo-Dutch war postulates that 'it is agreed and concluded, that from this day there shall be a firm, sincere and inviolable peace, union and friendship' and continues in the second article by stating 'to the end that the concert of amity, union, and mutual interest may not only be confirmed by the present articles' (Jenkinson 1785, I: 202). This treaty was followed by a number of treaties made in Nijmegen in 1678–1679 and involving France, the United Provinces, the Holy Roman Empire, Spain, Sweden and Münster. The first articles of these treaties also proclaim perpetual, sincere and other elevated forms of friendship (see Jenkinson 1785, I). Probably one of the most extended and hyperbolic versions of the formula can be found in the Treaty of Navigation and Commerce between Great Britain and Spain (1713), which followed the conclusion of peace and friendship treaties at Utrecht (1713):

---

[3] England was not a party to the Westphalian treaties, but nonetheless considered them an event of crucial importance in European history. The treaties also affected English treaty practice, which started to embrace references to the treaties of Münster and Osnabrück.

[4] Cf. '*Pax sit christiana, universalis et perpetua veraque et sincera amicitia inter sacram maiestatem Caesaream et sacram maiestatem Christianissimam nec non inter omnes et singulos foederatos et adhaerentes*'.

[5] See the invaluable Internet resource 'Die Westfälischen Friedensverträge vom 24. Oktober 1648. Texte und Übersetzungen', which allows the comparison of the original Latin text and its translations into vernacular languages.

[art. I] First, it is agreed and concluded, that from this day forward there shall be, between the two crowns of Great Britain and Spain, *a general, good, sincere, true, firm, and perfect amity, confederation and peace, which shall endure for ever, and be observed inviolably* ... and also between the lands, countries, kingdoms, dominions, and territories, belonging unto, or under the obedience of either of them [Princes]. And that their subjects, people, and inhabitants respectively ... shall help, assist, and shew to one another all manner of love, good offices, and friendship. (Jenkinson 1785, II: 90; emphasis added)

Such bombastic style was an inherent part of the convention prevailing in diplomatic rhetoric of the sixteenth to eighteenth centuries. In many senses it reflected the idea of a virtuous prince as a member of the European 'republic'. The lofty diplomatic rhetoric certainly facilitated the sense that the concluded pacts were trustworthy and would be observed in good faith; as such, however, it could not but accentuate the virtuousness of the agreement and the parties involved by giving it full expression using moralist vocabulary, of which adjectives that emphasise values are the best markers. In this sense, the diplomatic language framed the ethics of sovereign and primarily monarchical members of the 'republic' of crowns. Their 'virtuous' friendship in turn bound not only the princes, but also their respective realms, as is evident from the above-quoted article, which hooked onto virtuous friendship the whole complex arrangement of diplomatic relations in Europe involving territorial units and power hierarchies. Whether this bondage 'truly' matched the idea of the friendship of virtue professed by moralist critics is an altogether different issue; what matters here is that the sovereign subject explicitly embarked on the rhetoric of virtue and sought to invoke a range of corresponding commendable ideals.

The language of virtuous conduct fits well this diplomatic genre not least because of the personalised nature of reached agreements. As Lesaffer correctly observes, until the eighteenth century international treaties were private *pacta* between rulers rather than public *foedera* between political entities (Lesaffer 2000: 182). Nor does this logic of personalised ethics contradict reflections in political philosophy, in which the emergence of the concept of the state as embodying the idea of impersonal rule was recognised sometime in the seventeenth century (see, for instance, Skinner 2002b, chapter 'From the state of princes to the person of the state' and pp. 403–405 in particular). The state – which it would be difficult to imagine speaking in such an excessive language of personalised morals – did not become a legitimate party to friendship agreements until the late eighteenth/early nineteenth century. Until then the figure of the abstract sovereign state was of minimal utility to monarchs and state bureaucrats when presenting issues of friendship and order.

Appeals to friendship remained in the preambles and first articles of treaties throughout the eighteenth century. However, such elevated diplomatic language had gradually disappeared from the international stage by the early nineteenth century, when most friendship treaties were concluded with non-European peoples. In those treaties the linguistic formula of diplomatic expressions is significantly reduced, and friendship as a rule is either mentioned in the preamble or in the first article; in some cases it was not used at all, even though the engagement was named a treaty of friendship, as in the case of the Treaty of Friendship and Alliance (1817) between the British government and Nana Govind Row, an Indian ruler (BFSP, vol. 5: 905). At the beginning of its international socialisation, the United States employed similar European diplomatic expressions, but by the mid nineteenth century the references to friendship in its treaties are reduced to scant expressions of perpetual friendship or to maintain and confirm the relations of friendship. Moreover, American treaties of friendship frequently do not even allocate a separate article to the proclamation of friendship, a remarkable example of such practice being the Treaty of Amity and Commerce with Sweden, 1816 (TCIAPA, vol. II).

Another linguistic marker of the place friendship carved out in the conceptual world of the seventeenth- and eighteenth-century European 'republic' is its association with the range of nouns made in diplomatic rhetoric. Perhaps the quintessential form of expressing this association in early modern diplomacy was the handful of values that contracting sovereign parties professed in the preambles and first articles of the key treaties. In these treaties 'friendship' was commonly accompanied by such tightly linked terms as 'peace', 'alliance', 'ally', 'union', 'unity', 'defence', 'security', 'tranquillity', 'concord', 'faithful neighbourhood', 'good correspondence', 'confidence' and, less frequently, 'commerce' and 'trade' (while the antonymic range of nouns in the body of treaties included 'enmity', 'enemy', 'hostility', 'war', 'aggression', 'differences', 'misunderstanding'). Hence, the period was marked by a continued use of the terminological couples 'friendship and alliance', 'peace and friendship' and 'friendship and league/union', stemming, as identified in the previous chapter, from the late medieval custom of treaty-making. The overall tendency in the use of friendship perhaps is best captured in the crucial article II of the Utrecht Treaty of Peace and Amity between Great Britain and Spain (1713):

> And whereas, to take away all uneasiness and suspicion, concerning such conjunction, out of the minds of people, and to settle and establish *the peace and tranquility of Christendom, by equal balance of power* (which is *the best and most solid foundation of a mutual friendship, and of a concord* which will be lasting on all sides) as well the Catholic King, as the Most Christian King, have consented, that care should be taken by sufficient precautions, that the kingdoms of Spain and France should never come and be united under the same dominion, and that one and the same person should never become king of both kingdoms. (Jenkinson 1785, II: 67; emphasis added)

The treaties of Utrecht played a crucial role in setting up a new European society based on a balance of power and resolving the succession in Spain. The new

idea of the balance of power was seemingly well received in the fertile soil cultivated and prepared by the friendship–alliance couple and became associated with
'the solid foundations of mutual friendship and concord' and the 'tranquility
of Christendom'. Heinz Duchhardt points out that 'the balance of power' was
predominantly a metaphor used by publicists, but was virtually absent in international law, apart from treaties related to the question of the Spanish throne;
while the formula the 'tranquility of Europe', which appeared, for instance,
in the 1703 treaty between Great Britain and Portugal and for some time was
'ranked beside the formula of the tranquility of Christianity', becomes nearly
self-imposing and legitimating in the eighteenth century (Duchhardt 2004:
56–57). Although the concept of the balance of power did not become one of the
integral parts of peace and friendship treaties, friendship was still predominantly
used in rhetoric defending alliance-building and 'conflict resolution'; for this
reason the appeal to friendship predates the articles on the cessation of hostilities
and the promises of supplying allies with various kinds of assistance in numerous
peace and friendship treaties.

Outside formal treaty formulations, as Duchhardt notes, the link between
friendship and the balance of power became increasingly firm. Publicists thus
normally reported the friendships that princes made for the sake of alliance or
friendships aimed at preserving the balance of power.[6] The curious nature of the
balance of power lies in its two opposing purposes: on the one hand, it has to
preserve the integrity of the European political arrangement; on the other hand,
it should maintain tension and anxiety between powerful countries to contain
the risks of the system disintegrating as a result of possible deadly war and the
emergence of empires. The association of friendship with this principle indicates
that friendship does not embrace all European crowns and commonwealths
in one club of friends; conversely, it emphasises the exclusive nature of 'noble'
sovereign friendship, which strangely parallels the moralist observations on the
limited scope of 'true' friendship or friendship of virtue, something that would
certainly please the sovereign noble friends.

Treaty preambles and different declarations of friendship in this context
acquire a particular significance. Contrary to the opinion that these documents
and their parts can be nearly meaningless, they actually often provide good examples of diplomatic rhetoric, or just statements as the minimal units of delivery

---

[6] For instance, Adam Anderson reports that King William received the Russian grand prince
Peter the Great and 'cultivated his friendship and alliance, in hopes of forming an useful
balance of power against France', in Anderson (1787, II: 627); Arthur Young describes a
promiscuous English policy of making friendships and waging wars following the example
of the key allies, in Young (1772: 47); while John Bowles goes so far as to say that neutrality of certain countries towards France is 'impolitic amity' (1795: 51), echoing the debate
in the law of nations on obligations towards friends who are at war with each other, which
produced the concept of amity as neutrality.

used to justify and legitimise a course of action subsequently spelled out in particular clauses. For instance, it is crucial to identify the terms that monarchs choose to employ to build and support these justifications. King William and Queen Mary's Declaration of War against France (7 May 1689) lucidly shows how friendship can be used to justify a bellicose course of action and the provision of help to allies:

> [W]e think ourselves obliged to endeavour to the uttermost to promote the welfare of our people, which can never be effectually secured, but by preventing the miseries that threaten them from abroad. When we consider the many unjust methods the French King hath of late years taken to gratify his ambition; that he has not only invaded the territories of the Emperor, and of the empire, now *in amity with us* ... but declared war against our *allies* ... we can do no less than join with our *allies* in opposing the designs of the French King, as the disturber of the peace the *common enemy of the Christian world*. (Jenkinson 1785, I: 282–283; emphasis added)

The way friendship appears in this Declaration and in the Utrecht treaty quoted above as well as in other preambles and first articles indicates that it clearly became a recognised international good, positive value and normatively laden relationship, even if at times linked to Christian ideals. The array of adjectives described above that were used with friendship also points to attempts to promote and strengthen a normatively regulated relationship. The same could be deduced from the new character of verbs used in the treaties, in which parties resolve to 'preserve', 'cultivate', 'increase' and 'make friendship flourish'. Thus, friendship as a concept becomes linguistically and ideologically attached to shared ideals of a morally commended conduct and a desired ethical standard. The use of such a concept consequently helps to bring about desired results by justifying and legitimising the proposed actions, as exemplified by the treaty expression 'for the sake of the treaties and friendship which subsists between them' (see the Treaty of Alliance concluded between Charles II of Great Britain and Charles XI of Sweden, for the confirmation of their Friendship, and for the mutual Security of their Dominions and Trade 1661, in ibid.: 166).

The republican challenge to the 'republic' of monarchs

Apart from the assault of moralist authors highlighting the untrustworthy and, due to its sovereign nature, limited friendship of European princes, this friendship also proved liable to a more fundamental challenge anticipating further changes in the European system. The challenge concerned the very nature of the subject of public friendships and associated ethical standards, and originated from the political communities that were founded on an alternative idea of government, that is, a republican or mixed constitution. The Italian city-republics, the Dutch Republic, the English republic and a number of free cities in northern and central Europe constituted a critical mass whose survival could not but be reflected in a language of diplomatic communication and political theory that defended their alternative form of political constitution. The intellectual republican tradition binding together in one chain classical republican thought, the political thought of Florence and Venice, the English republican thinkers and the American founding fathers was well documented in John Pocock's seminal *The Machiavellian Moment* (1975). In International Relations the argument was picked up by Nicholas Onuf, who traced the origins of contemporary international political thought to two main traditions of republicanism: Atlantic (epitomised by Emer de Vattel) and Continental (epitomised by Immanuel Kant) (Onuf 1998). These major contributions overlook, each for its own reasons, the concept and associated ethics of friendship that constitute and relate the republican subjects in the international (or, in fact, adverse inter-princely) realm. This is despite clear aberrations in diplomatic language and theoretical reflections accompanying the survival of republics.

The first corruptions of the primarily monarchical diplomatic language of friendship can be detected after the English Revolution and the establishment of Cromwell's Protectorate, and after the recognition of the United Provinces as an independent sovereign agent. It would not be an overstatement to claim that England under Cromwell and the United Provinces caused a delicate problem for the rigid language of diplomatic friendship. Those few treaties of friendship concluded under Cromwell introduced into the lexicon of treaties such unwonted terms (and, accordingly, unusual agents) as 'Protector', 'republic' and 'state'.[7] A similar problem was posed by the necessity to cooperate and conclude treaties with the United Provinces. Treaty language appears to have had some difficulties in accommodating this new type of commonwealth to the principle of reciprocity. Consider, for instance, article I of the Treaty of Peace between Charles II of England and the United Provinces of the Netherlands, 1674, that brought to a conclusion the third Anglo-Dutch war: 'It is agreed and concluded, that from this day there shall be a firm, sincere and inviolable peace, union and friendship, between the most serene and potent King of Great Britain, and the high and mighty Lords the States General of the United Netherlands' (ibid.: 202). This puts the king and members of States General on the same level, that is, that of contracting parties. The presence of the States on the international

---

[7] See article I of the Treaty of Peace and Alliance between Frederick III of Denmark and Oliver Cromwell, 1654: 'there shall be *a firm friendship* and alliance *between the King* and *the Protector*, and *between the subjects of Denmark* and *the republic*'; and article VIII of the Treaty between France, England, and the United Provinces, made to oblige the Northern Kings to make Peace, 1659: 'the three *States* shall likewise use their diligence to accommodate them [differences] *amicably*, and to restore the said Elector [of Brandenburg] to a good understanding and *friendship* with the King of Sweden', in Jenkinson (1785, I: 75, 106 respectively; emphasis added).

stage seems not to have always been reflected in reciprocal diplomatic formulations. For instance, article I of the Defensive Treaty between Great Britain and
Portugal, 1703, while referring to the previous peace agreement between these
powers and the United Provinces, puts 'States' and 'kingdoms' on an equal footing: 'so that there shall be between the said *kingdoms* and *states*, their people and
subjects, *a sincere friendship and perfect amity*: they shall all of them, mutually
assist one another; and each of the said powers shall promote the interest and
advantage of the rest, as if it were his own' (ibid.: 348).

Later on, though, the diplomatic convention of using the term 'friendship'
was temporarily restored. The formulation found to substitute for the occasional
use of 'states' was 'the High and Mighty Lords the States General of the United
Netherlands' (see, for instance, the Treaty of Peace between Charles II king of
England, and the United Provinces of the Netherlands, 1674; ibid.). From that
time onwards, in England's friendship treaties with the Netherlands, the parties
to friendly relations were addressed as 'kings' on the one side and as 'lords' on the
other, so that the convention was 'personified' again.

Another series of innovative uses of friendship together with new actors relates
to the agreements that England made with peoples outside Europe and with
European powers about relations with non-Europeans. One of the first such
innovations can be found in the seventeenth century, when Charles II concluded
the Treaty of Peace with Osman Bassa and the *people* of Tripoli in 1662 (see
ibid.: 177). In 1686, James II and Louis XIV concluded The Treaty of Peace,
good Correspondence, and Neutrality in America, the first article of which proclaimed 'that there be a firm peace, re-union and amity between the British and
French *nations*' (ibid.: 261; emphasis added). Thus, the appeal to friendship in
establishing the legal and political order in America was still found expedient in
the late seventeenth century. Non-European agreements again displayed tolera-
tion of a certain asymmetry between contracting subjects: whereas agreements
made by European monarchs preserved the symmetry of the contracting parties
(e.g. monarch–monarch), in relations with non-European actors this requirement becomes relaxed. For instance, the treaty of alliance with the Cherokees
(1730) introduces the nation of the Cherokees as a counter-agent to the British
king. Similarly, but in reversed order, in a later treaty of peace and friendship
with the emperor of Morocco (1750) 'the English in general' are presented as
friends to the emperor and his subjects.

Another extension of the range of international friends coincides with the
appearance on the international stage after 1776 of the United States of America
as a compound republic (in this definition I follow Deudney's (2007: 162) res-
urrection of Madison's terminology). Most European powers, including Great
Britain, concluded treaties of peace, friendship and commerce with the United
States in the 1770s and 1780s. The texts of these treaties traditionally included
the figures of European monarchs as contracting parties, but also included an

active entity: the United States of America. Subsequently, the US adopted a more heterogeneous use of friendship in its treaty-drafting. Apart from 'the US' itself, the treaties of friendship started to include such actors as 'nation', 'country', 'power', 'republic' and 'subjects'. In this sense, the American republic brings back into international friendship-making the agency of 'nation/people' after its place in the relationship was downplayed with the collapse of the Roman Empire.

Occasionally, the European powers also resorted to proclamations of friendship with peoples and nations, and this was particularly the case in the American continent. As can be deduced from conventional treaty formulations, the newly emerged American government took up the available 'diplomatic' customs. This is especially evident in treaties concluded with the American Indian nations (tribes) in the early nineteenth century (see treaties of peace and friendship concluded in 1807 and 1814 in BFSP, vol. 3, and chapter five for more details). By the second quarter of the nineteenth century, when the texts of the treaties began to proclaim friendship between two nations, the convention basically received its modern form in the expression 'friendship among nations'.[8] Although friendship was first announced between the US and an individual monarch, later on the texts proclaimed that it subsisted between two nations.

The friendship registered in treaties with American Indian tribes was also further stretched to include the 'citizens of the US' and 'individuals' comprising these tribes, who are listed as separate subjects of friendly relations.[9] However, as specified in other clauses of certain treaties, individuals cannot damage or in any way affect the state of public friendship. For instance, article IV of the Treaty between the United States and the Assiniboine Indians postulates: 'That the friendship which is now established between The United States and the Assinaboin [sic] Tribe, shall not be interrupted by the misconduct of Individuals, it is hereby agreed, that, for injuries done by Individuals, no private revenge, or retaliation, shall take place' (ibid., vol. 14: 1213).

Despite somewhat pragmatic appeals to friendship between individuals belonging to the new contracting parties, 'international' friendship remained public and attached to the bearer of sovereignty, who was the only authority to declare public friends and enemies, even if the nature of this subject was changing under the strain of revolutionary waves. The revolutionary changes in Europe

---

[8] See, for instance, the texts of the Convention of Friendship, Commerce and Navigation concluded with Denmark, 1826; or the Treaty of Amity, Commerce and Navigation with Brasil, 1828, in TCIAPA (vol. I).

[9] See article II of the Treaty of Peace and Friendship concluded between the United States and the Pattawatima Indians, 1815, which contains the common diplomatic formula: 'There shall be perpetual Peace and Friendship between all the Citizens of The United States of America, and all the Individuals composing the said Poutawatamie Tribe or Nation' (BFSP, vol. 3: 438).

and over the Atlantic brought another agency to the realm of friendly relations: around the mid nineteenth century, as the introduction of the new term reflects, governments become common initiators and subjects to friendships with the US.[10]

In the early nineteenth century the language of the treaties concluded by Great Britain undergoes a similar transformation. Quite indicatively, this transformation only concerns treaties concluded with actors residing in the geographical and political periphery, as seen from an Old World perspective. In this period Great Britain made a number of treaties with the peoples in the Indian subcontinent (e.g. Persia, various Indian rulers), in which 'state', 'British government' and the 'East India Company' (EIC) (sometimes coupled with the adjective 'honourable') were mentioned among the main parties of established friendships (see the series of treaties in BFSP, vols 4–12). These treaties did not always follow the principle of status symmetry. Thus, friendship could be established between the authorised EIC and a rajah or between the British government and a rajah. Yet, if one of the parties to a friendship agreement were named the 'state', then the other party to the same agreement was usually named identically and the treaty texts consequently used the expression '2 states', as in article I of the Treaty of Defensive Alliance with the Rajah of Berar, 1816: 'The peace, union, and friendship so long subsisting between the 2 States, shall be promoted and increased by this Treaty' (ibid., vol. 5: 892; for more examples see other treaties from the years 1816–1818, ibid., vols 4–6). Some two decades later, friendship as proclaimed between two states was replicated in treaties with the newly independent states in the New World (predominantly republics). The preamble and first article of the Treaty of Amity, Commerce and Navigation, between Great Britain and the Oriental Republic of the Uruguay (1842) is a representative example:

> Her Majesty the Queen of the United Kingdom of Great Britain and Ireland, and his Excellency the President of the Oriental Republic of the Uruguay ... deeming it meet that the friendly relations which now subsist between the 2 States, should be acknowledged and confirmed by the signature of a Treaty of Amity, Commerce and Navigation... [art. I] There shall be perpetual peace and amity between the dominions and subjects of Her Majesty the Queen of the United Kingdom of Great Britain and Ireland, her heirs and successors, and the Oriental Republic of the Uruguay, and its citizens. (ibid., vol. 30: 343)

Until a much later point, all these transformations escaped the diplomatic language employed in relations between traditional European monarchies themselves, which continuously affirmed the old interpersonal princely friend-

---

[10] See, for instance, the Treaty of Friendship and Commerce with the Persian empire, 1856, or the Treaty of Friendship, Commerce and Navigation with the Republic of Honduras, 1864, in TCIAPA (vols 1 and 2).

ship. The diplomats in the service of monarchical courts and the principles of treaty composition proved adaptable to the changing political landscapes both in Europe and beyond, and this was reflected in the expanded range of actors that diplomatic language registered as parties to friendship (individuals, citizens, nations, states and governments). However, by virtue of its own arrival in the European 'republic' the new republican agent disturbed the conservative conventions of diplomatic language. The disturbance in itself was an important indicator of an alternative political organisation, but the reciprocal nature of diplomatic language is such that it cannot show whether an alternative subject bore a challenge to the ethos of noble princely friendship. For this reason it is instructive to turn to commentaries on diplomatic relations made by key contemporaneous exponents of republican views.

The cornerstone figures for many early modern republican thinkers were Cicero and Niccolò Machiavelli as repositories of classical and Renaissance republican wisdom for the seventeenth-century republics. In England, for instance, John Milton, James Harrington and other 'neo-roman' thinkers frequently refer to Cicero, other ancient authors and Machiavelli (see Pocock 2003: 383–401; Skinner 1998), while Cicero and Machiavelli's popularity among political and juridical philosophers in the Dutch Republic has also been well documented (see, for instance, Van Gelderen 2002: 198–202). So far as friendship is concerned, Machiavelli's writings grant us another point of access, albeit mediated by a Humanist author, to Roman political and linguistic conventions. First of all, this convention is manifested in Machiavelli's understanding of the political nature of public friendship. In both the *History of Florence* (1532) and the *Discourses* (1531), he gives many examples of friendship formed in contingent circumstances for pragmatic purposes, thereby positing the concepts of friendship and utility within the same conceptual framework. Machiavelli even shares certain tropes of moralist rhetoric when reporting 'feigned friendship' and the 'pretence of friendship' (1882, I: 18 and I: 23). However, the use of such expressions is not intended so much to arouse repugnance in his readers, but is rather a plain statement of a matter of fact. Furthermore, like many of his contemporaries Machiavelli reproduces the Roman link of friendship to alliance by invoking this terminological couple (*lega ed amicizia*) or by using the terms interchangeably, thus prompting modern translators to confuse the meaning of both.[11]

The elements of this Roman convention are then rearticulated by English

---

[11] For instance, Christian E. Detmold translates the title 'Non è partito prudente fare *amicizia* con uno principe che abbia più opinione che forze' (book II, XI) as, 'It is not wise to form an *alliance* with a prince that has more reputation than power' (emphasis added) and similarly in the body of this paragraph Italian '*amici*' and '*amicizia*' are translated with 'alliance' (Machiavelli 1882, vol. II), because this is exactly what the modern diplomatic linguistic convention and understanding suggests.

republican thinkers. James Harrington, when quoting Cicero, similarly uses the term 'amity' to designate external relations. At the same time, we can find in his text the distinction between the nation and its prince, both being significant actors in the international realm. Harrington, who drew extensively on Roman republican ideals and examples, uses the term 'amity' (once) to refer to the relations between the Sicilian cities and the people of Rome. Like Machiavelli before him, he does not use the term to underline the normative aspects of such relations; rather, he follows the convention of applying the term to descriptions of treaties and political events: 'We have so received the Sicilian cities into amity', saith Cicero, 'that they enjoy their ancient laws, and upon no other condition than of the same obedience unto the people of Rome, which they formerly yielded unto their own princes and superiors' (Harrington [1656] 1996: 226). It is notable that in this early modern context the Roman convention has not yet been adjusted to accommodate the reality of the consolidating sovereign state, and thus this abstract subject is still missing from the list of legitimate friends.[12]

However, John Milton, another prominent republican thinker, made remarkable innovations – deliberately or not – to the convention of using 'friendship', significantly broadening the range of application of the concept. This may well have been Milton's goal in his ideological battles. In his argument against the royalists, he emphasises the divide between the king and the nation, and claims that power belongs to the latter. Thus, his political uses of 'friendship' and 'amity' simply exclude the figure of the prince. The same regularity in the use of the concept is discerned in Algernon Sidney's *Discourses* (1698), although Sidney prioritises references to particular *peoples* as subjects of friendship (e.g. 'the French'), whereas 'kings', as well as 'men' or 'individuals', are not parties to public friendship (Sidney 1996b). What is remarkable in Milton's *The Tenure of Kings and Magistrates* (1650) is that the main category to which friendship is related is man in a largely Ciceronian statement comparable to the arguments put forward in *De Amicitia*: 'Who knows not that there is *a mutual bond of amity* and brotherhood between *man* and *man* over all the world, neither is it the English sea that can sever us from that duty and relation: a straiter bond yet there is between fellow-subjects, neighbours, and *friends*' (Milton 1991b: 18; emphasis added).

This is an outstanding extension and in fact universalisation of political friendship that goes beyond the Aristotelian conception of fellow citizens and engages with the Ciceronian universal society and its ascending associations (see Cicero 2003, I: 51–53; Onuf 1998: 48–51). Nonetheless, the rules of formal diplomatic correspondence proved too conservative for a republican radical. Milton's formal

---

[12] As Quentin Skinner observes, the defenders of 'free states' preferred to use the term 'commonwealth' when describing the system of civil government; the term 'state' was virtually absent from their accounts (Skinner 1989b: 113).

writing as a statesman is in sharp contrast to his proposed universalisation of friendship. Thus, the expressions used in official letters that he composed on behalf of the Parliament reveal a perfect convergence with the above-described language of the princely 'republic'. But it is against this backdrop of formal writing, the customs of which Milton as a statesman had to adopt, that his innovative Humanistic use in political treatises can be highlighted. One example of such writings can be found in a letter to Christina, queen of Sweden (1651), which uses the following expression: 'as also how earnestly we expect your friendship, and how highly we shall value the amity of so great a princess' (Milton 1847). Notably, the term 'amity' also appears in a letter to the doge of Venice (1652): 'Wherein your highness and the most serene republic will do as well what is most just in itself, as what is truly becoming the spotless amity between both republics' (Milton 1847). In accordance with the prevailing early modern convention, Milton could use 'friendship' and 'amity' in one expression, which continues to underline more personalised relations with sovereign rulers.

The extension of the Roman convention was not however the only challenge that republican reflections posed to existing practices of friendship. A greater disturbance came from praising the friendship of republics on its own merits over the friendship of princes. This line of thinking was present already in Machiavelli's *Discourses*, which proposes that league and friendship (*lega ed amicizia*) made with republics should be trusted more than those with princes. The explanation of this proposition is largely procedural: the structure of republican government is such that it will take much longer than a prince to break the faith, and for this reason it will be less prone to betray the engagements and undertake careless diplomatic moves (I, 59). In this case republics are more likely than princes to excel in the virtue of prudence. Moreover, as Machiavelli emphasises, the advantage of truly glorious republics lay in their *virtù* and in the reputation of strength that could be actualised upon a friend's request (II, 30).

The value of friendship with and between republics was later recognised by Dutch theorists, even if the prospects for such friendships seemed gloomy in the hostile neighbourhood of princes. Pieter De La Court, for example, argued against forming alliances with other European republics, such as Italian or Hanseatic, because the former are far away while a strict alliance with the latter entails greater risks of being dragged into a costly war, since they are so weak. Self-reliance and prudent policy are a much safer substitute for such friendships: 'For tho' indeed those republican allies and friends are good, yet woe to us if we stand in need of them, and ten times more woe to us if we wilfully and deliberately order matters so, as at all times, and for ever to stand in need of our neighbours and allies' (De La Court [1662] 1746: 225). However, a commitment to a weak prince would be equally dangerous and harmful for Holland. Relations with England were also uneasy, even if advisable in De La Court's opinion. As he reports, after beheading their own king, the English, 'hated by all the monarchs in the world', came to seek 'friendship between both nations'. De La Court thought that friendship with England would have benefited Dutch commerce and its fish trade, were England not 'despised' and rejected by the Orange faction (ibid.: 392–393). Overall, the protracted rivalry between England and the United Provinces until the Glorious Revolution was perceived by some as detrimental to these naval powers, while 'a firm and perpetual friendship and union' was believed to be in their true interest (Bethel 1681: 65).

A comparable sense of the distinctive nature of republican friendship was present among English republican thinkers. One example is Algernon Sidney's reflections on English foreign policy and its international treaties, which specifically touch on friendship between states. His dialogues *Court Maxims* (1665–1666) may also have been influenced by his own diplomatic experience. On the one hand, the exponent of royalist views in the dialogue simply reiterates clichés from treaty practice, and follows the same pattern of friendship between individual kings: 'if he [the prince] would keep the king of France his friend' and 'He ... control strict amity with king James' (Sidney 1996a: 154, 163 respectively). Yet, Sidney also employs a style, even if not distinctively republican, that portrays countries and peoples as subjects of friendship: '*Denmark* is our *friend*, but cannot help us' or '*a strict friendship* is to be held with *the French*' (ibid.: 177 and 152 respectively; emphasis added).

On the other hand, Sidney further shapes the conventional style by using the concept of friendship to create a satirical image of English foreign policy, its priorities and goals. The republican polemical pathos in his use of the concept is evident when he ridicules the royalist principles in foreign policy articulated by the character Philalethes. The absurdity of royalist principle and the irony of princely friendship are tackled in the tenth dialogue 'Ninth Court Maxim: Union with France and war with Holland is necessary to uphold monarchy in England, or thus, a strict friendship is to be held with the French that their customs may be introduced and the people by their example brought to beggary and slavery quietly' (ibid.: 152). As a continuation of this satire, friendship with Holland should be deemed unadvisable mainly because of its republican form of government, which could contingently be transferred to England in the event that – as Sidney very much endorsed – the two formed a friendship.

Furthermore, republican thinkers sought to undermine the opposition that emerged between friendship and enmity, and which in their opinion was abused by the royalists. For instance, Milton intervenes in the discussion of the constitutive role of the friend/enemy antithesis for politics at large by arguing that this antithesis is purposefully superficial, and that enmity is deliberately sustained in the international realm by royalist thinkers (thereby indirectly confirming the effectiveness of this antithesis at least as an ideological tool). He argues, however, that the function of this antithesis is to sustain the maximum degree of unity within the political commonwealth, and consequently to keep it more governable by cultivating the image of the enemy in the international environment. For this reason he resolutely disclaims the maxim that 'enemies are rather to be spared than friends', which some falsely, and possibly intentionally, attributed to the foreign policy priorities of the English (Milton 1991a: 133). His own idea of friendship represents an attempt to dismiss the dichotomy of friends and enemies and to suggest a concept of friendship which would include mankind as a whole.

Such republican pathos certainly had much in common with Christian values and morals, and more importantly with the concerns discussed earlier of the Christian Humanists. This can even be seen in their chosen modes of argumentation. Thus, Milton also discusses friendship in the posthumous *A Treatise on Christian Doctrine*, in which, while dealing with the subject of duties towards one's neighbour, he defines friendship as 'a most intimate union of two or more individuals, cemented by an interchange of all good offices, of a civil at least, if not of a religious kind' and supports this definition with many references to scripture (Milton 1825: 647). In the same subchapter he contrasts in an already familiar mode this type of friendship with pretended friendship, friendship with the wicked, and with enmity (ibid.: 648), with all oppositions supported with quotations from scripture.

A further 'liberal' and 'republican' wave of polemical arguments for friendship may have been invoked by Robert Filmer's *Patriarcha* (published posthumously in 1680), in which Filmer presents a critique of 'popular government' (or democracy) and argues in favour of the supreme authority of the king. While addressing the topic of friendship, Filmer makes an argument diametrically opposed to Milton's thesis on the nature of the friend/enemy opposition. Filmer argues that the eternal drive to have conflicts is in the very nature of 'popular government'. Only the constant presence of the external enemy, which a 'popular government' may start fighting any time, keeps this political entity together and serves as its genuine ruler. However, if there is not such an enemy – and here Filmer's argument becomes particularly important – then the members of this commonwealth start fighting friends at home (Filmer 1996: 29).

Thus, Filmer reiterates the old formula of interpreting 'friend' to mean a potential enemy, which echoes Thomas Hobbes's understanding of the multitude without civil government that only unites temporarily to fight foreign enemies, but dissolves when the threat is no longer there (Hobbes [1651] 1992: 119). Paradoxically, long after these debates on the principles of popular government, Alexander Hamilton appeals to nearly identical arguments while advocating the idea of federal union. He argues that un-united states 'would be subject to those *vicissitudes of peace and war*, of *friendship and enmity with each other*, which have fallen to the lot of all neighbouring nations not united under one government' (*The Federalist* 2001, No. 8, p. 32; emphasis added). The opposition is further sustained, and indeed consolidated, in the refutation of Filmer's assumptions in

Locke's *Two Treatises* (1689), which strengthens Milton's case for public friendship to include all men. Locke's application of friendship is reminiscent of the
Aristotelian concept of friendship, especially when he claims that friendship
should be a preliminary condition for people to unite into society (Locke 2003:
II, § 107: 339). The concept of friendship, as used by Locke, implies certain
knowledge of the other and sustains relations of trust, by means of which Locke
may have meant to eliminate the distance associated with the figure of the enemy.

The moralist and republican arguments discussed in this chapter converge on at
least one main point: these arguments constitute a distinct ethical perspective on
friendship in 'high' politics and diplomacy. Unlike the centrality of contingent
politics and the juridical/institutional implications of the contractual concept
of friendship explicated in the previous chapter, this perspective focuses on the
ethics and criteria of truth that are used as standards against which the actual
friendships can be assessed and, more importantly, criticised. This genre of moralist critique had little or no room in the contractual language game. It does not
mean, however, that such arguments had to annihilate the conceptual alternative entirely from the realm of the thinkable and the legitimate, had the public
endorsed their aims at once. The effect of the moralist argument was in fact to
recognise contracted friendships and the politics of inter-princely friendships
while simultaneously providing a normative evaluation of their conduct (primarily as immoral and corrupt), as the recognition offered was not value-neutral. In
the long run, this valorisation of moral norms and ideals in friendship was bound
to marginalise the contractual vocabulary and the legal concept of friendship as
an incompatible alternative, because moralist virtue is opposed to utility; natural
attraction and faithfulness to contingency and contracts; and gradual universalisation to exclusivity.

     In fact, the language of princely diplomacy remained attuned with Renaissance
moralist discourses by sharing the same vocabulary and setting similar high
moral standards for the friendships contracted by noble princes. The elevated
language of these discourses nurtured the idea of exquisite and virtuous friendship in princely society while downplaying ideas of contingency and contract.
Even the association of friendship with alliance and union was couched in lofty
expressions, as these contributed to the tranquillity of the European society
of Christian powers. However, the full and irrevocable marginalisation of the
contractual concept had to wait until the intervention of arguments on human
nature and natural design. The logic of the moralist argument – putting forward
high ethical standards and recognising diplomatic friendship – sowed the seeds
of another crucial suspicion common in modern interpretations of international
politics: if high moral expectations laid upon sovereign friends constantly fail as
friendships are broken or betrayed, is it possible to avoid being deeply sceptical
about the whole idea of international friendship?

The republican interventions paved the way for similar arguments about morality and the nature of the European 'republic'. The association of genuine, useful or simply good friendship with a form of government that republican thinkers brought to the public debate had a more profound impact on further arguments about public friendship, whether evaluative or analytical, than may appear at first glance to be the case. This association meant that the criteria of true friendship, and hence the grounds for criticism, were dangerously expanded. Previously, the conduct of a prince towards his friends could be assessed by his proven observance of obligations in friendship or by the sincerity he displayed; now, by contrast, the window was open for judgements about princely nature and behaviour to be passed before any friendship was contracted. Republics professed a different set of virtues: that is to say, their *virtù* was distinct from that of princes, including prudence and moderation as well as a passion for liberty and commerce. If critics were of the opinion that true friendship rests on a different set of assumptions than that shared in the princely 'republic', the 'republic' therefore lost its common ethical denominator, and thus its normative foundations were exposed to increasing pressure. This change had far-reaching historical implications that allowed it to re-actualise in a more recent past, when Maxim Litvinov, the Soviet commissioner for foreign relations, condemned the friendships of capitalist countries as hypocritical and argued that only Soviet friendships can be true (*Vneshnyaya Politika* 1946: 277). This particular instance of the rhetoric of 'truth' proved short-lived, but more instances deriving their criteria of truth from political ideology or religion can still be seen. Moreover, new forms of commonwealths and multiplied heterogeneous agents with whom friendships could be made in principle paved the way for the novel idea of the European republic or a society of sovereigns, imagined not only as individual princes but also as countries, nations and states. Strikingly, this gradual transition to friendship among impersonal agents in the eighteenth and nineteenth centuries was paralleled by reduced demand for elevated and moralist appeals in diplomatic rhetoric.

4

Turning friendship into a moral prescription: conceptual change in modernity

The debate over the state of nature

Thomas Hobbes and the hostile state of nature

To understand further changes in the use of friendship in juridical and political treatises, we have to turn to a crucial theoretical intervention associated with the works of Thomas Hobbes from the mid seventeenth century. If the club of sixteenth- and seventeenth-century intellectual authorities on the law of nations and nature included Gentili, Belli, Grotius and Bodin, then starting from Richard Zouche – and particularly from Samuel Pufendorf and other writers of the later seventeenth century – Hobbes became a cornerstone figure, although not always seen as praiseworthy. Hobbes's political treatises inaugurate a new era in the history of political thought. Quentin Skinner, for example, suggests that it is with Hobbes that we arrive at the idea that the indispensible end of any civil or political association is to establish over itself a supreme and sovereign power that would be independent of the association and its office-holders (Skinner 1989b: 119).

However, for understanding a conceptual change and paradigm shift in the history of friendship, Hobbes's original and powerful descriptions of human nature, the state of nature and the reasons for establishing a supreme authority are more important. As Hobbes put it in *Leviathan* (1651), human nature itself generates conflicts among men. Since men are by nature equal, there are three insuperable motives that will always cause quarrels between them: competition, diffidence and glory (Hobbes 1992: 88). With this precondition and in the absence of a common power that could keep men in awe, they end up living in the state of war – 'such a warre, as is if every man, against every man' (ibid.). He continues with the famous passage: 'In such condition, there is no place for Industry; because the fruit thereof is uncertain: and consequently no Culture of the Earth … no account of Time; no Arts; no Letters; no Society; and which is worst of all, continuall feare, and danger of violent death; And the life of man, solitary, poore, nasty, brutish, and short' (ibid.: 89).

In such a situation, according to Hobbes, there are no notions of right and wrong, just and unjust; there is no law, and force and fraud are the *cardinal* virtues. Thus, to rescue themselves from this war-prone state of nature, men transfer by a covenant all their powers onto a single person, and 'he that car-ryeth this Person, is called Sovereigne, and said to have *Sovereigne Power*; and every one besides, his Subject' (ibid.: 121). This reasoning of human nature and political association was Hobbes's 'assault' on earlier jurists and Aristotelians, who believed in man's sociable and peaceful nature (Skinner 2008: 40–41; see also Thornton 2005: 54–59), and was later countered by attacks from political moralists, ecclesiastical authors, commonwealthmen and legal scholars. The rea-soning itself became a *topos* in political arguments on the institution of the state and the principles regulating its conduct, and established the framework for the re-description of the concept of friendship.

This logic of the constitution of a sovereign power has a direct bearing on the relations between sovereigns and 'international' politics. Since the sovereign is endowed with supreme and indivisible powers, it finds itself in an uncertain environment populated with similar entities, which are not subjected to any supreme authority. The question is what sort of principles and norms should govern sovereigns' conduct towards each other. This is a question of basic atti-tude to the other, the possibility of 'international' law and, consequently, legal arbitration and enforcement. Since sovereigns embody supreme authority, any limitations or constraints imposed upon their authority in the form of 'interna-tional' law or the will of the 'international' community would compromise and thus undermine the whole idea of sovereignty. For this reason, the prospects of anything like the law of nations glossed by generations of jurists become illusive.

In Hobbes's interpretation, the same law of nature that guides the conduct of individuals who are not united into a civil association also regulates the law of nations (Hobbes 1983: XIV, 4). Hence, the sovereign cannot be bound by any new law imposed on it from above or from the external domain, except perhaps for duties to God. By analogy, sovereign entities are found in an environment in which the possibility of war is ever-present. In such conditions, artificial persons are driven by distrust and fear, producing misjudgements of security measures and consequently conflicts (Tuck 1999: 129–131). The legitimation of sovereign authority based on the fearful and hostile state of nature, as well as the increas-ing popularity of the analogy between individuals and artificial persons, that is, states, determined the rupture in juridical and political use and the evolution of the concept of 'international' friendship, as I shall show below.

Before discussing the arguments and debates that established a new conven-tion of applying the concept of friendship, a caveat must be made about the use of the metaphor of hostile state of nature to describe 'anarchical' relations among sovereign entities. A number of scholars have identified the limits of this application. Kinji Akashi, drawing on Hobbes's argumentation, stresses that the state of nature among individuals differs from the state of nature among nations (Akashi 2000: 203). The difference arises from the special status and mission of the sovereign authority. Since sovereigns are under a duty to preserve the safety of their people (Hobbes 1983: 157; 1992: 124), they are limited in their sovereignty and cannot follow the reckless logic of war of all against all, as it is contrary to their basic purpose. The nature of sovereign duty means that the external environment of commonwealths can only qualify as a modified state of nature (Akashi 2000: 205–208; on the limits of the applicability of the state of nature to international politics see also Beitz 1999: 35–50).

In his critique of the tendency of international relations scholars to misrepresent Hobbes's views on 'international politics', Noel Malcolm also emphasises this aspect of the conception of the state of nature. Hobbes maintains that the law of nations, which regulates the conduct and actions of sovereigns, is essentially the same thing as the law of nature, which dictates what men ought to do towards one another when no state authority has been established. Malcolm contends that this gives a clue as to the principles regulating the conduct of sovereigns towards one another. As their chief motive is the preservation and well-being of their people, reason would dictate that sovereigns avoid war and maintain peace (Malcolm 2002: 436–437). The same precept does not allow for Hobbes to be allied to the 'positivist' tradition of international law and some trends in 'realist' international relations scholarship (ibid.: 439).

Nevertheless, the prominence of the state-of-nature metaphor, which with some reservations could be used to grasp relations between sovereign entities, affected the value of friendship as a conceptual tool in debates about the law of nations and the law of nature. David Armitage has emphasised the significance of Hobbes's equation of the law of nations with the law of nature, because it shaped later debates between naturalism and positivism and debates about the law of nations and the international state of nature. In fact, Richard Zouche's treatise, discussed in the previous chapter, could be interpreted as a response to this equation, with *jus inter gentes* serving to foreground the difference between the law of nature and law comprising agreements that add something to the law of nature and are not derived directly from it (Armitage 2006: 229; 2013: 68). Hobbes's innovation divided previous and subsequent theorising into two main groups: those who believed that the law of nations was the same as the law of nature, and those who thought of it as positive law produced by the consent of commonwealths (Armitage 2013: 69 and the whole ch. 4).

In fact, equating the law of nations with the law of nature eliminates the distinction between the latter's general or universal character and the more particular and variable qualities of the former, which many authors had stressed before. As Francisco de Vitoria wrote: 'I answer that the *jus gentium* does not necessarily follow from the natural law, nor is it necessary simply for the conservation of the natural law, for if it should necessarily follow from the natural law, now it would be the natural law' (Vitoria 1934: cxiii; for a similar distinction made by Suárez see Scott 1934: 77–79; see also *Digest* 1, 1, 1, 3). Therefore, whereas the contractual concept of friendship could be invoked in the previous tradition of *jus gentium* thinking (belonging to the first group) in discussions of issues such as a typology of treaties, *postliminium*, and equal and unequal obligations, then with the suggested equation of the law of nations and the law of nature friendship starts to be conceived as an element or prescription of nature. The question then becomes one concerning the attributes of, or the way we understand, nature.

In light of this equation, it is crucial to take into account the stress that Armitage places on the law of nations as applying only to 'commonwealths in their capacity as artificial persons' (Armitage 2006: 224) and their situation in the state of nature as fearful individuals (ibid.: 224–228). Hobbes's peculiar account of the state of nature and commonwealths formed the groundwork for, and in fact provoked, debates on the character of persons and the state of nature. By virtue of the proposed equation of the law of nations and natural law, the latter temporarily received a 'privileged' position within the debate. Hence, authors were preoccupied with discussing the basic principles of natural law and how they could be ascertained.

If the law of nations and the law of nature are juxtaposed, it is reasonable to assume that sovereigns' behaviour would be predominantly described using the vocabulary of feelings, particularly anxiety, distrust and fear, while friendship as a benevolent virtuous affection would be an alien element. It would also be easy to imagine that the legal, contractual concept of friendship of previous epochs would not be used in Hobbes's argument, because there is no sovereign authority that could grant and impose law over other sovereigns. However, Hobbes does find a place for elements of the contractual concept of friendship that was so common in juridical writings. He needs this concept to support his theory of sovereign authority and to claim sovereign prerogative from possible challengers.

In contrast to earlier political theorists, Hobbes's theory of communal association forbids subjects to make political friendships that could have consequences for the commonwealth as a whole. It is essential for his theory that this prerogative be solely in the hands of the sovereign. In *De Cive* (translated into English in 1651) Hobbes writes:

> no Subject can privately determine who is a publique friend [*amicus* in Latin text], who an enemy, when Warre, when Peace, when Truce is to be made ... These and all like matters therefore are to be learned, if need be, from the City, that is to say, from the Sovereign powers. (Hobbes 1983: 228; compare with Hobbes 1782: 353)

This formulation shows a nascent distinction between private and public or political friendship, and implies the exclusive right of the sovereign to define the latter. In fact, the understanding of friendship as a political relationship contracted by sovereign powers is in line with the contractual convention identified in the previous chapters. Hobbes uses the concept in the same context of peace treaties, although he does not stress friendship as a particular type of treaty or as a contract that could impose unequal obligations. Hobbes also borrows the expression 'being in amity' from diplomatic vocabulary. While, for instance, Edward Coke had written three decades previously about amity between kings, Hobbes in *Leviathan* mentions amity between sovereigns: 'For whosoever entreth into anothers dominion, is Subject to all the Laws thereof, unlesse he have a privilege by *the amity of the Soveraigns*, or by speciall license' (Hobbes 1992: 154). In *Behemoth*, Hobbes employs the concept of amity in regard to peace envoys, but this is probably because the envoys were there to express the will of the sovereign who sought to sustain that amity (see Hobbes 1840).

On rare occasions when Hobbes uses the term 'friendship', he seems to refer predominantly to the sphere of private relations. These could include both the personal relations of a monarch (Hobbes 1983: ch. X, VI; p. 133) and relations between ordinary people. Hobbes mentions friends among the 'instrumental' powers of men. When making his case against natural sociability or men's love for each other, Hobbes argues that by nature men look not for friends but for the benefits (honour or advantage) they can bring (ibid.: I, 2; Hobbes 1992: 62; 1899: ch. VIII, 4; Tuck 1999: 134–135). Hobbes also uses the term 'friendship' when giving examples of diplomatic practices. In *Behemoth*, for example, he uses this term when describing negotiations in which friendship was offered and turned down by particular ambassadors (Hobbes 1840: 376, 380).

These examples show that, even if friendship is an unlikely sentiment in the state of nature and an irrelevant description of relations among sovereigns, amity or friendship as a distinct diplomatic and juridical instrument is not inconceivable to Hobbes. In this context, it differs from friendship between individuals and refers to engagements of public or artificial persons. These engagements are reciprocal instruments to secure diplomatic and commercial interaction, rather than general benevolent political relations among public persons.

Hobbes also uses the term 'amity' in the sense of civil concord common to earlier thinkers. Early modern moralists put forward the concept of amity as concord, together with the virtues of love and benevolence, to neutralise or mitigate the perils of civil factions and to achieve the ideals of the good life within a political entity. In *Leviathan*, we find a seemingly identical use of the concept: 'it is they say, impossible to entertain a constant Civill Amity with all those, with whom the Businesse of the world constrains us to converse' (Hobbes 1992: 483). However, his use of the term differs from the earlier convention, since it does not mean that kings had to have friendly relations with their subjects as a means of maintaining political order. Hobbes's innovative theory of state sovereignty postulates the transfer of all legitimacy and authority to the sovereign, eliminating this necessity alongside the need for a 'hierarchical' political friendship.

Hobbes's use of friendship in these examples is dictated by his own theory of the state as the primary political agent and bearer of supreme authority. He finds room for a diplomatic concept of amity or friendship that can only be contracted by a sovereign entity. Thus, political or diplomatic friendship appears to be linked to the transformation of political knowledge that, as Jens Bartelson notes, allows it to bestow subjectivity upon the sovereign state (Bartelson 1995: 188). But this is, perhaps, the less remarkable impact that Hobbes's writings had on the transformation of the concept of friendship. The more significant consequences arose from his description of the state of nature that evolved into a prevalent metaphor for international relations and the equation mentioned above of the law of nations and law of nature, all of which provoked a whole genre of 'confutations' of Hobbes's assumptions. These confutations attempted to re-describe Hobbes's case by redefining his concepts and by offering more commendable and easily acceptable conceptual alternatives. As I shall demonstrate below, friendship happened to be in the centre of this conceptual battlefield, which profoundly transformed our vision of the concept and related phenomena.

Amicable re-description of the state of nature

Hobbes's powerful intervention into traditions of theorising about society and the founding of commonwealths significantly rearranged the agenda of political and legal theories, as well as transforming the focus of the discussions. His assumptions about human nature and the natural condition were denounced by many, but also found many supporters. As Jon Parkin (2007: 305) shows, 'Hobbism' became an intellectual fashion in the second half of the seventeenth century. The portrayal of fearful individuals and the state of nature as the state of war of all against all, even if not always actual, is a precondition for the Hobbesian theory of sovereignty and commonwealth. Thus, to challenge the emerging authority of the immortal Leviathan and the underlying idea of the egoistic ethic, Hobbes's intellectual rivals would have to start by undermining the basic assumption of such an institution. Hence, the obvious target of many rhetorical attacks was Hobbes's picture of the nature of men and the state of nature determining the logic of further association. One of the most popular alternatives to the Hobbesian theory was the assumption about an inherent human sociability advocated from diverging theoretical and methodological viewpoints. The concept of friendship was thus used as an effective means of defending and substantiating this proposition, but a collateral effect of the new mission was a dramatic reconfiguration of its range of reference: the conditional and contractual concept of friendship of the earlier law of nations had to be sacrificed to a new cause.

One of the most ardent advocates of the new cause and an influential opponent of Hobbes was Richard Cumberland, who provided a model for many contemporaries to avoid Hobbism in discussing natural obligations (ibid.: 281). Natural law was a manifestation of God's will, and thus did not require a sovereign's command to be observed, whereas self-preservation induced natural sociability rather than the escalation of conflict. Others, like John Shafte, added that people unite into societies out of the pleasure and benefits resulting from human company. He argues that 'this is the reason that people desire to unite themselves in Commonwealths, and under Civil or Politick Governments; and a more powerful and effective reason, I think, then that of fear, which Mr. Hobbes seems only to insist upon' (1673: 37).

The pleasures in question, as well as the pillars of social life, happened to be found in human friendship. Hobbes's opponents maintained that love and friendship, rather than fear, constitute human sociability and bring people to society. Cumberland, in his treatise *De Legibus Naturae* (first published in Latin in 1672, and in translation in 1727 as *A Treatise of the Laws of Nature*), diligently refutes the assumptions of Hobbes's theory and attempts to re-describe his miserable state of nature in which men found themselves before the institution of civil government. Particularly, in the chapter 'Of the Law of Nature' he says: 'I have laid down these *Observations,* in order to *shew the Reason,* "Why I consider'd all Mankind as one Whole, whose Parts are in some measure connected, by an obvious Resemblance of Nature and Necessities; and that there is a Probability of procuring Friendship among them"' (Cumberland 2005: 642).

In the same chapter he writes that it is natural reason that makes men assist one another out of benevolence, and that this natural reason also stands behind the establishment of friendships 'on which the Foundations of *Societies* may be laid' (ibid.). In this sense, Cumberland subscribes to the same 'Aristotelian' interpretation that could be identified in John Locke's work and in previous moralist literature, which defended the argument that there must be some degree of acquaintance, trust and friendship for people to unite into society.

Originally written in Latin, Cumberland's treatise was soon conveniently paraphrased, translated and abridged for the wider English-speaking audience by Samuel Parker in 1681 and James Tyrrell in 1692. Both Parker and Tyrrell emphasised the argument that friendship binds people together in the pre-political condition and thereby facilitates the institution of 'civil' societies. Thus, Tyrrell, in the part entitled 'Mr. Hobbs's Principles Considered, and Confuted', argues that 'Common Amity or Benevolence, cannot be omitted to be first supposed, even in the very constitution of Common wealths: Since those who founded them, must have been before united' (Tyrrell 1693: 263). For him this common and general amity is not the same as civil society, which can result from a stricter amity and is a narrower social unity.

Parker also argues that it is natural for people to be concerned about the happiness of their posterity, and that this consideration makes them secure 'Peace and Amity'. For this purpose they arrange for 'the establishments of Government and standing Laws and prescriptions of Justice' (Parker 1681: 54). Parker concedes that there are 'bad' people who fail to preserve nature and God's designs:

> This then is the proper end and usefulness of Society, to institute a *common Amity and Friendship* amongst men, to unite multitudes together into *combinations of Friendship*, to endear them to each other by mutuall Offices of *love and kindness*, and by a joynt defence …; and were Mankind as faithfull to one another as the condition of their Nature requires, and the Author of it expects, there would be *no need of civil Laws and Penalties, that are onely a second and subsidiary help* to force a few bad men to *preserve that amity and friendship,* which, were they good and vertuous, they would choose of their own accord, as most reasonable in it self, and most agreeable to humane nature. (ibid.: 27; emphasis added)

Thus, the point that these authors were making was that man is a 'Creature designed by God for Society' (Tyrrell 1693: 259), and that the laws of nature and reason oblige him to be friendly and sociable, rather than spiteful and hostile. They denounced Hobbes's assumptions as Epicurean and offered a religious alternative, deriving from a totally different starting point: human friendship and sociability are predetermined by nature (and God). According to them, this is not only a matter of belief; but it is also what reason dictates. It is rational for people to be sociable and friendly, because it is the only true way to safety. As Parker argues against the 'Philosopher of Malmsbury' (Hobbes):

> for nothing is more plainly so [contradictory to safety] than a State of perpetuall war and enmity … So that if it be most naturall to Mankind to love their own ease and happiness … then it follows unavoidably that nothing is more naturall than *to seek peace and friendship* without which the life of Man must of necessity be sadly unsafe and uncomfortable. (Parker 1681: 30; emphasis added)

God granted man mental faculties to understand such nature of things and see that 'engagements of mutual Love and Friendship' are the means to avoid troubles, war and misery (ibid.: 58). A similar argument is made against the assumption that natural equality can be a cause of violence by virtue of men's equal ability to kill. Tyrrell concurs with Hobbes that men are equal by nature, and that the law of nature instructs 'to do to others, as we would have others do to us'. However, he insists on a diametrically opposite conclusion, namely that such a situation 'rather purswades to amity and concord' (Tyrrell 1693: 267). Note that, in making these arguments, the seventeenth-century authors still use expressions typical of more technical juridical writings, such as 'league of amity' or 'amity and friendship', implying a distinction between two types of relations (see Gale 1671 for the constantly used combination of 'amitie and [/or] friendship').

John Locke, a key figure in the history of competing social contract theories, also locates friendship in the realm of natural law. This is evident in his early unpublished essays on the law of nature (around 1664). In these essays, he finished his argument against the sceptical position and the principle of individual utility as the basis of natural law, the articulation of which he ascribed to the ancient Greek author Carneades, by stating that 'it is impossible for any principle to be the basis of natural law [*legis naturae*], whereby, if it is laid down as true, all justice, friendship, and generosity [*justitia, amicitia, liberalitas*] are taken away from life' (Locke 2002: 212–215). In his *Two Treatises of Government* (1689) he postulates that the state of nature is governed by the law of nature, which is also the reason that teaches people that they are all servants of an omnipotent God and equal among themselves, that they live in one community of nature and ought not to harm each other. Thereby Locke provides a theological substantiation, and also an anti-utilitarian one, of the law of nature and human 'sociability' (see also Dunn 2001: 48–50 for the argument on Locke's theological interpretation of the law of nature).

In a similar polemical argument, albeit one critical of Cumberland, about human nature and the drive for association, Lord Bolingbroke in *Fragments or Minutes of Essays* (c. 1740) repudiates considerations of utility in friendship and the sceptical position as a whole. This argument is a constituent part of his overall proposition about natural sociability as a principle of civic association. He summarises a set of theoretical propositions that explain the establishment of societies and laws:

> There is a sort of *genealogy of law*, in which nature begets natural law, *natural law sociability, sociability union of societies by consent, and this union by consent the obligation of civil laws* … *Self-love*, the original spring of human actions, directs us necessarily to *sociability* … That *friendships* may be formed, and maintained, *without any consideration of utility*, I agree, and I hope I have proved … Society cannot be maintained without benevolence, justice, and the other moral virtues … Self-love operates in all these stages. We love ourselves, we love our families, we love the particular societies to which we belong, and our benevolence extends at last to the whole race of mankind. (Bolingbroke 1809: 376–378; emphasis added)

In this argument, friendship along with self-love and sociability are inserted in a law-like axiomatic sequence of conditions determining the development of political societies. Even if not all possible audiences perceived friendship as such an ironlaw natural relationship, for the natural law tradition it becomes intimately linked to the vocabulary of virtues and affections.

Hobbes's references to empirical evidence for the state of nature are also rebutted on the grounds of natural friendship and human sociability. Tyrrell points out that '[Hobbes's] instances from the Savage People of America make rather against, than for him' (Tyrrell 1693: 242). As David Hume later observed, also in a counter-Hobbesian fashion, in the American tribes '*men live in concord and amity* among themselves without any established government and never pay submission to any of their fellows, except in time of war, when their captain enjoys a shadow of authority' (Hume [1738–1740] 1826: book III, II, VIII: 319; emphasis added). Hume here supports the existing account of natural human relations in terms of concord and amity with a type of empirical observation.

This effort was carried further by Anthony Ashley Cooper, the third earl of Shaftesbury, who developed some of Cumberland's ideas in his *Characteristicks* (1699), which subsequently had an important influence in the eighteenth century. Shaftesbury puts forward an argument against the anti-social nature of men and the state of nature by means of illustrating an admittedly unacceptable situation:

> And the more we are thus sensibly disjoin'd every day from Society and our Fellows; the worse Opinion we shall have of those uniting *Passions*, which *bind us in strict Alliance and Amity* with others. Upon these Terms we must of course endeavour to silence and suppress our *natural* and good *Affections*: since they are such as wou'd carry us to the good of Society, against what we fondly conceive to be our private Good and Interest; as has been shewn. (Shaftesbury 2001: II, part II, sec. II; emphasis added)

Such arguments present the natural human condition in a light that would delegitimise the Hobbesian justification of sovereign authority. The flipside of this argumentation was that friendship, as a part of nature's design, became not just a descriptive but also a prescriptive concept as a response to the critique of the actual, rather than original, social order. Many dissenting voices lamented the lack of true Christian friendship in the present world, despite the hypothetical dictates of natural law. For them, all true human friendship must follow the pattern of 'amitie or friendship with Christ', which would be based on excellence in virtue and choice rather than on mere natural demands (Gale 1671: 4, 9). Other thinkers, taking into consideration existing possibilities in the real world, allowed for a variation in social practices greater than a presupposition of natural amity. Thus, Adam Ferguson contributes to the debate observations on the principles of union and dissention guiding 'factual' human behaviour and informing alternative social theories:

> Thus, in treating of human affairs, we would draw every consequence from a principle of union, or a principle of dissension. *The state of nature is a state of war, or of amity,* and men are made to unite from *a principle of affection, or from a principle of fear,* as is most suitable to the system of different writers. (Ferguson [1767] 1782: part. I, sec. III; emphasis added)

He admits that people are frequently full of hatred and rage, but he also adds that these feelings of animosity mix with 'sentiments of affection and friendship' (ibid.: I, IV; see also Gordon and Trenchard 1995: 156; Letter 31, 1721). Otherwise, the scale of dissention would be horrifying. Indicatively, both Shaftesbury and Ferguson ascribe friendship to the list of affections immanent to human nature. Whereas 'amity' previously was used conventionally to designate public political relations, both Shaftesbury and Ferguson use the word 'amity' to

designate this positively valued affection, although Ferguson uses it interchangeably with 'friendship'.

An alternative vision of the state of nature is all the more important from the
perspective of international relations and the law of nations. In this field a key
contribution was made by Samuel Pufendorf, one of the most subtle interpreters
of Hobbes's works among late seventeenth-century jurists and a central figure in
the history of international law (Skinner 1966: 290–291; Tuck 1999: 140–165).
As Richard Tuck points out, Pufendorf showed that the practice of international
politics refutes Hobbes's assumption about sovereigns existing in a state of war,
because there are cases of states living peacefully alongside each other, and the
emergence of a global Leviathan seems improbable (Tuck 1999: 142, 150–151).
Hobbes, in Pufendorf's interpretation in *De Jure Naturae et Gentium* (1672),
abuses the limits of a pure and unrealisable hypothesis that pictures masses of
men as 'risen out of the Earth like a Mushroom' and having no 'Obligation to
each other', by applying it to existing relations among sovereign communities
(Pufendorf 1749: II, 2, VII). According to Pufendorf, 'the contrary Opinion
seems more reasonable'. It is worthwhile reproducing here Pufendorf's famous
denunciation of Hobbes's premises:

> Hobbes is the more inexcusable for maintaining that his natural State cannot be
> remov'd and broken up, but by letting in the Sovereignty of another, and by uniting
> in the same Commonwealth: For that those Commonwealths, how distinct soever,
> which are allied by *Friendship and by Leagues*, should still continue in a State of
> mutual War, is *a Contradiction evident to the common Sense of Mankind*. (Ibid.: II,
> 2, VIII; 110; emphasis added)

The reason why Pufendorf considers it to be a contradiction derives not only
from his observations on actual interactions between foreign realms and distinct
political entities, but also from his disagreement with Hobbes's interpretation of
the nature of men, the state of nature and what it is reasonable to do under this
condition. As in the case of Hobbes's other intellectual opponents, friendship
appeared to be at the heart of the arguments that Pufendorf levelled against the
Hobbesian state of nature, and this had a profound impact on the use of the
concept in the domain of the law of nations.

Pufendorf supports his case by defending the theory of inherent human
sociability that brings people together and determines the prevalence of non-
conflictual behaviour. He goes back to the mythological origins of mankind and
presents 'the natural State of Man, not hostile, but peaceful, and shew that Men,
in their true Condition, are rather hearty Friends than spiteful Foes' (ibid.: II,
2, VII). Pufendorf admits that this applies to the first couple,[1] but given that

---

[1] This line of argument is hardly accidental, for there are reasons to believe that Hobbes's
account of the state of nature incorporated, albeit implicitly, a vision of the Fall (see
Thornton 2005: 164–168).

mankind descended from them: 'we may conceive Mankind mutually engaged, not only by such a vulgar *Friendship* as might result from *Similitude of Nature*, but also by such a *tender Affection* as endears Persons allied by a Nearness of Race, and of Blood' (Pufendorf 1749: II, 2, VII ; emphasis added).

He also notes that this sense has 'almost worn off amongst the Descendants' due to their increased numbers and distance from each other. However, this does not necessarily prevent men from realising that friendship should prevail over enmity. As Pufendorf puts it: 'And that therefore, since the first Mortals were placed in such a State as inspired them with *Love*, and not with Enmity, and since from this State all the rest of Mankind descended, it is plain, if Men were mindful of their first Original, they might be rather accounted *Friends than Foes*' (ibid.; emphasis added).

Apart from being just mindful of their first origin, men have the experience of banding together for the purposes of sustenance, protection and the perpetuation of the species. Hence, the state of nature as a possible condition in which men are dissociated and hostile to each other appears unlikely. Even in the context of relations between distant communities or among sovereign entities it makes little sense to believe, as Pufendorf suggests, that these agents are enemies who are necessarily trying to hurt each other. In his argument against Hobbes, he insists that: 'those cannot immediately hurt one another, who are divided by Distance of Place'. Moreover, the 'Equality of Strength which Hobbes asserts' in fact restrains 'the Desire of hurting'. And when there is no will to hurt each other, the term 'friendship', according to Pufendorf, can be applied to describe this relationship (ibid.: II, 2, VIII).

Taking his cue from Cicero, Pufendorf introduces a fundamental law of nature according to which every man ought to be peaceful and sociable with all others, and that this disposition should extend to all of mankind (on equal obligation to obey natural law see Saastamoinen 2010). In his understanding of the basic premise of the law of nature, Pufendorf expressly concurs with Richard Cumberland, whose treatise was published in the same year as Pufendorf's Latin original:

> We would have it observed, that the fundamental Law of Nature, established by us, doth not disagree with that which *Dr. Cumberland* hath laid down in his Work on that Subject, concerning the Study and Endeavour after the common Good, and the demonstrating all possible Benevolence towards all Men. For we, when we maintain that *a Man ought to be sociable*, do at the same time intimate, that he ought not to make his own separate Good the Mark of his Proceedings, but the Benefit of Mankind in common. (1749: II, 3, XV; 136; emphasis added)

We have already noted that, in proclaiming general human sociability, Pufendorf was supporting Grotius's idea, drawn from Cicero, of universal human society. The point of debate here is whether such sociability is explained by pragmatic calculations of individuals trying to maximise their profits and satisfy their

goods by joining in society with others (Hont 1990: 266). However, as Kari
Saastamoinen argues, Pufendorf attempted to ground his natural law theory not
on the principle of individual utility and motives of self-preservation, but on
the assumption that sociability was made an inherent part of human nature and
mankind as a whole by the will of God. Thus, human friendliness derives not
from calculated advantages that advance personal security, 'but from common
humanity' (see Saastamoinen 1995: particularly 62–69; 2002; also Tuck 1999:
151–152; on the confusion arising from Pufendorf's identification of the origins
of sociability in both law and nature see Haakonssen 1996: 42–43).

Therefore, in opposition to Hobbesian hostile men, Pufendorf puts forward
the view that sociability and friendship are intrinsic qualities of human nature.
He observes: 'Nature having … really constituted a general Friendship amongst
Men, from which no Person is excluded' (Pufendorf 1749: II, 3, XVIII; 138).
Pufendorf develops a largely moral argument about natural law and political
association; it is no accident, therefore, that he admits correspondence between
his theory and Richard Cumberland's theory of common good and obligation.[2]
The proclaimed sociability and consequent friendship of mankind does not
mean that there can be no instances of hostile behaviour or, otherwise, situations in which a man loves one person more than another (Pufendorf 1749: II,
3, XVIII). Despite these variations, friendship remains an effect of social human
nature or an affection of varying degrees rather than a particular contract.

It must be stressed that, despite important differences with Grotius over
kinds of rights (Tuck 1999: 152–158), Pufendorf's theory of natural sociability
and friendship is also limited. German Aristotelians criticised Grotius for this,
but it could also apply to Pufendorf's understanding of friendship. Even if it
is in the nature of men to be mutually sociable and friendly, such friendliness
for Pufendorf is restricted to forbearing from doing violence to others. When
elaborating the above-mentioned argument on equality as restraining force, he
explains that 'the Term Friendship maybe fairly applied, where there is neither
Will nor Power to injure'. He immediately admits that this understanding of
the concept differs substantially from that offered by Aristotle. Aristotelian
friendship, according to Pufendorf, requires true 'performance of kindness'
(Pufendorf 1749: II, 2, VIII; 109). Thus, the universal extension of friendship
as a basic human relationship had to be predicated on the loosening of ethical
standards and obligations constituting a close and intimate friendship between
individuals.

Nevertheless, the challenge posed to the link between morality and law by
Hobbesian notions of the state of nature and natural law was met by attempts

---

[2] For the ways in which Pufendorf's theory relied on those of Cumberland and Hobbes see
Parkin (2003: 43–45); for the elaboration of Pufendorf's moral arguments regarding
natural law and civil association see also Carr and Seidler (1996).

to restate this state of nature on different grounds with recourse to stronger alternative moral arguments. Proponents of alternative conceptions of the state of nature and political association readily adopted a normative concept of friendship modelled on the ethics of personal relations. Instead of an egoistic conception of natural right and the fearful state of nature, the debate offered inherent human sociability and friendship as the foundations of natural law, while the appeal to such friendship was meant to invoke a number of general moral duties that help people to build a better society. These duties, which should be interpreted as feelings and qualities, such as benevolence, love and a disposition towards common good, are in turn presupposed by God's ordained nature.

This change of perspective managed to entrench the concept of friendship in the realm of natural law. In turn, the attachment to this realm affected the concept's range of reference. The contractual concept of friendship described in the previous chapters that designates written and unwritten compacts between particular political agents thus appeared to be a less effective armour in this type of rhetorical warfare. The natural law arguments mentioned above virtually eliminated the possibility of interpreting friendship as something contracted as well as something that may be used to legitimate inequality. As opposed to a number of specific duties that earlier jurists spelled out by resorting to friendship, in this account friendship is understood as 'already being there' by nature. For this reason, it would make little sense to use friendship in arguments facilitating the realisation of sovereign rights and duties by rulers themselves. Instead, it is used to promote a specific view of the primordial condition of civil association that in turn legitimates a particular theory of the state. The next section will demonstrate how this polemical use of concepts in debates over the state of nature and natural law affects the application of the concept of friendship in the law of treaties and international relations.

Friendship: natural vs legal obligation

The change in the structure of argumentative positions and range of reference of the concept consequently affects the use of friendship in descriptions of international treaties. Pufendorf's treatise *De Jure Naturae et Gentium* contains a chapter 'Of Leagues', which dwells on a subject conventional for this genre of works, namely the typology of treaties, and contains a subchapter titled 'Leagues that establish nothing but what was due by the Laws of Nature' (1749: VIII, 9, II). It is in this subchapter that Pufendorf addresses treaties of friendship. In his view, friendship treaties constitute an archaic diplomatic practice popular among the ancient nations, many of whom 'had lost the Sense of that *Law of Nature, that there was a Sort of Natural Kindred between Men*'. In contrast, friendship treaties could be just an unnecessary element for the conduct of civilised nations, which, Pufendorf believes, have learned the law of nature better and have no need of special treaties that simply reiterate and confirm this law. They only make sense at the stage of acquaintance and do not embody specific obligations:

> Such Leagues [that are aimed simply at preserving the Law of Nature] indeed are commonly called no more than *Treaties of Friendship*; but certainly the strict proper *Notion of Friendship* also includes much more than the common *Offices* of *Humanity*. For tho' the *Actions* due to *Friendship* are not so determinate, as those due by *Compact*; yet in general, every Man will allow that it is the *Duty* of one *Friend* to impart himself and his *Fortunes* to the Relief of the other. (Ibid.)

This is a restatement of an earlier observation in the same treatise where Pufendorf remarks that, if common leagues are made between nations without spelling out any particular conditions, they should be considered to be leagues 'for the Establishment of Friendship, which is reckon'd to imply a closer Union, than is produc'd by that general Peace of Nature' (ibid.: II, 2, XI; 112). Note that in this context Pufendorf's attachment of friendship to the leagues that add nothing to the laws of nature is less equivocal than seen in Grotius. In his later *The Two Books on the Duty of Man and Citizen According to Natural Law* [1673] (Pufendorf 1964), these statements are replicated in a more refined and concise form. In an identically titled chapter, Pufendorf draws a distinction between leagues or alliances 'which are made with a view to the mutual performance of some duty *already enjoined* by the natural law; and those which *add something over and above* the natural law'. The former concern 'the mere exercise of simple humanity' and include only the confirmations of friendship without any particular obligations (Pufendorf 1964: ch. XVII; emphasis added).

This precept of the law of nature has a universal application; hence, friendship as the mere exercise of humanity is only possible on grounds of equality. This logic therefore rules out friendships that confirm inequality, as well as those securing the parties' concrete rights and duties. Friendship and issues of equality and inequality thus become logically separated in Pufendorf's theory of the law of nature, although he shows awareness of the link between equality and friendship-as-treaty, as follows from his reference to Quintus Curtius's observation on the firmness of friendship concluded between equals (Pufendorf 1749: II, 2, VIII; 109). For this reason, the discussion of formal international equality and inequality is found under the category of leagues of the second type, that is, those that add something to the law of nature. In this type of league, inequality is not so much about symbolic affirmation of superiority. Instead, as Pufendorf highlights, inequality means unequal performances and promises; and it could well be the case that the superior party bears more responsibilities towards the inferior one than *vice versa* (ibid.: II, 17, III–V; VIII, 9, III–IV).

As mentioned above, Pufendorf also admits friendships of varying degrees. Friendship, in his theory, might be conceived of as less of a universal quality than 'particular *Ties* of *Kindness* and *Respect*'. However, even when pointing out this aspect, he emphasises that there are no express articles of treaty that promise favourable treatment and attachment, and that concern for a friend might be limited by some stricter obligations, such as those of an ally (ibid.: VIII, 6, XIV). Hence, the 'particular' dimension of friendship concerns the intensity of the basic precepts of the law of nature and human sociability, rather than its legal and contractual aspects.

Pufendorf's use of friendship is one of the first influential examples of polemical re-descriptions of the concept in the law of nature and of nations. As well as implying a very particular state of nature, by presenting friendship as something favoured by the law of nature, and thus not needing to be contracted for particular purposes, he posits a new normative framework for further juridical theorising and use of the concept. Not only does it separate problems of inequality, the various political strategies that actors could pursue by using friendship in international politics, and the establishment of specific legal regimes: but such a rhetorical move also attaches the concept to a different intellectual and argumentative tradition.

If earlier jurists could invoke those classical authorities that allowed speaking of heterogeneous politics of friendship, Pufendorf on most occasions chooses to refer to very peculiar normative statements about what friends ought to do. This intellectual development was already being reflected upon by the early eighteenth century. For instance, Gershom Carmichael noted that such an interpretation of the law of nature conditions the choice of intellectual authorities in discussions of friendship. He pointed out that Pufendorf, and Grotius before him, had preferred to quote Cicero's *De Amicitia* and *De Officiis* on this matter (Carmichael 1724: 76), even though both authors were well acquainted with Roman history. This is partly due to Pufendorf's eclectic method, which allowed him to refer to ancient sources not to invoke certain eternal truths and commonplaces, but to make new suggestions and arguments based on selective and creative use of sources. Thus, in defending his theory of sociability against sceptic and 'Epicurean' (i.e. Hobbesian) accounts, Pufendorf drew on the Stoics and Cicero (see Hochstrasser 2000: 6, 42). This determined his range of reference and intellectual authorities in the discussion of friendship and the law of nature. The implication for his classification of treaties or 'leagues' was to dissociate friendship from the idea of contract and unequal obligations. Pufendorf mentions established *loci classici* such as Livy and other authors (e.g. Thucydides), but not verbatim; this allows him to omit previous links of friendship to a type of compact (Pufendorf 1749: VIII, 9, III–IV).

Subsequent legal writers in the law of nations and natural law tradition, even those who did not embrace Pufendorf's method and vision of sovereign entities, continued to dissociate the concept of friendship from the idea of contracted obligations that could be enshrined in a special type of international treaty. Such conceptual re-description also implied that friendship could no longer be negotiated, compromised or used to create contingent political associations and leagues. Possible theoretical controversies notwithstanding, the use of friendship by different agents in the debate and their understanding of the phenomenon appear to converge when it comes to the *topos* of friendship treaties and the duties of friends. For instance, in Johann Gottlieb Heineccius's treatise on the law of nature and nations (1737), we find the proposition that leagues or treaties of friendship stipulate the good offices that the parties owe to each other by 'natural obligation' and *do not* include anything *particular*. However, Heineccius stresses that these treaties are not 'unnecessary', since: 'there is no other way of securing another's performance to us of *the duties of humanity*, but by pacts. And it often happens, that war puts an end to all the duties of humanity, and therefore it is absolutely necessary that *friendship should be renewed by pacts and covenants*' (Heineccius 1763: 200–201; emphasis added).

Likewise, the belief that a treaty of friendship presupposes only universal human duties and obligations not to do injury was upheld by prominent eighteenth-century thinkers such as Christian Wolff in *Jus Gentium* (1749), to which I shall return below, and Jean-Jacques Burlamaqui, who borrowed many insights from Pufendorf, even if he disagreed with his interpretation of the reasons for human sociability. Burlamaqui maintains this opinion in *Principes du Droit Politique* (1751), in which he distinguishes between assistance emanating from the nature of friendship and assistance determined by formal treaty (Burlamaqui 2006: 464). He even emphasises that any acts in the spirit of a treaty of alliance that continue after the treaty expires should be interpreted more as 'simple marks of friendship and benevolence, than as a tacit renovation of the treaty' (ibid.: 524).

In the same vein, Thomas Rutherforth writes about the law of nature that exists among nations. He argues against Grotius's proposition that the privileges of ambassadors are only due to positive law of nations by pointing out that an exchange of ambassadors is 'a matter of mutual convenience' or 'friendship or kindness'. Moreover, such 'good offices is due to mankind in general' and therefore 'it would be unkind and unfriendly, as well as imprudent, to refuse' to admit ambassadors (Rutherforth 1754–1756: 600–601). Later, Robert Ward makes this case even stronger by noting that, while the contemporary custom of exchanging ambassadors surely 'cannot be demanded as a matter of law', it was so widespread that friendship between states depended on ambassadors to such an extent that 'not to send them therefore has been sometimes regarded as an affront' (Ward 1795: 291). In this kind of argument, the concept is deprived of any contractual specificity and acquires traits that allow it to be called a 'floating signifier' or a catch-all concept for anything related to the benevolent laws of nature. Friendship becomes just a general 'affect' or feeling that can easily be appealed to in different justificatory arguments. As such, it can only be used to appeal to some ethical duties, rather than legal obligations. This marks a fundamental change in the application of the concept, which henceforth loses its place in the legal vocabulary. Thomas Wood thus paradigmatically asserts this dissociation of friendship from the legal order in his 1704 treatise at the level of understanding the meaning of obligation:

> *Friendships* ... ought not to be reckon'd among *Obligations*, because they are of a nature distinguishable from them by these two Characters. One is, that there can be *no Friendship* where there is *not mutual Love*, whereas in Obligations the Love, which ought to be mutual, is not always so: The other is, That *Friendships do not make any particular kind of Obligation*, but are the consequents that proceed from it. (Wood 1721: 33; emphasis added)

This conceptual transformation marks a key point in removing friendship from the vocabulary of law and contracts and its irreversible assignation to the language of ethics and emotions. In fact, this dissociation was at the heart of a development that eventually deprived the modern subject of conceptual means to conceive of law and friendship as similar social orders. Such a distinctively modern attitude is summarised by Heinrich Rommen in *The Natural Law: A Study in Legal and Social History and Philosophy* (1936), which underlines the essential difference between friendship and the legal order. He observes that 'there is no such thing as forced love, friendship and love freely embrace the special quality of the friend or loved one: the core of his person as wholly unique, as this "you."' Law does not penetrate so deeply', and continues by arguing that the legal order can only set up 'a network of rules around the person' that would not be dependent on that person's unique character (Rommen 1998: 165).

As a continuation of changes related to universalisation and emancipation from legal obligations, the *topos* of the friendship treaty also transforms in terms of its discussions of equality and inequality in friendship. Similarly to Pufendorf and Heineccius, Christian Wolff separates the discussion of friendship treaties from the discussion of equal and unequal treaties, as they, according to him, represent a different subject, even though he discusses them immediately after the chapter on friendship (see Wolff 1934b: §§ 394–398, pp. 204–206). Admittedly, international equality and inequality are also dealt with separately by Textor, who, while citing Livy's classification of treaties, criticises it and proposes his own classification, which includes both equal and unequal treaties. However, he does not mention friendship in this context (Textor 1916b: 253). Emer de Vattel in *Le Droit des Gens* (1758), considered to be one of the major contributions in international law in the second half of the eighteenth century (see Beaulac 2003: 241; Koskenniemi 1989: 89–98), follows the same 'convention' in providing a classification of treaties. He does so by distinguishing 'simple treaties of peace and friendship', which make no addition to 'those duties that men owe to each other as brethren, and as members of the human society', from those that deal with extra engagements. Such simple treaties of friendship, according to Vattel, only help to *demand* what otherwise could have been just requested 'as an office of humanity' (Vattel 2008: II, XII, § 169).

Vattel's treatise demonstrates yet another attempt to break away from the idea of 'ancient' friendship. Subduing another nation by means of force and a friendship treaty, which would be in line with Livy's account, appears incongruent with the values of a 'universal society'. Thus, Vattel uses friendship to underline the equal footing of the nations. Even if one were conquered by another, the liberties of the former's subjects should be preserved and not diminished by a friendship compact. As a rhetorical means of conveying this idea, he cites the Scythians who said to Alexander the Great: 'there is never any friendship between the master and slave: in the midst of peace the rights of war still subsist' (*inter dominum et servum nulla amicitia est*; ibid.: III, XIII § 201).

In a way, this change in the description of friendship was predetermined. By previous convention, a friendship agreement could have been dictated by a superior party or requested by a party in need of help. The political deal that followed could have produced a formal misbalance of legal obligations and inequality in political statuses. However, if friendship is ascribed to the domain of nature as a universal regulator of social relations, then it must be removed from the domain of particular political situations and the sphere of limited legal contracts, whether reciprocal or not.

The next collateral effect of the conceptual change is the connection to the ancient juridical concept of *postliminium*, which remained on the agenda of early modern juridical discussions. In his opening thesis on the subject, Wolff defines it as 'the restoration to their original condition of property and persons captured by the enemy and their return into the power of their nations' (Wolff 1934b: § 896, p. 460). He proceeds to argue that *postliminium* belongs to both 'the law of nature' and 'the voluntary law'. But in contrast to previous scholarship, even when Wolff suggests that there is *postliminium* with 'allied nations' (ibid.: § 898, p. 461) or that there is no *postliminium* with neutral nations (ibid.: § 899, p. 461), he does not invoke the concept of friendship, although he was aware of Pomponius's and Paulus's definitions of *postliminium* and the difference between them. In this sense, the change in the concept's links to contractual, negotiated and hence political aspects of relations among sovereign entities could be said to be total. All of its links to the vocabulary of contracts and political regimes identified in previous chapters were removed as a result of this 'naturalisation' of friendship and its use in the conceptualisation and justification of international society.

All of this would have been just a matter of antiquarian interest in localised and highly moralised debates on the origins of political community, had the spill-over effect of the conceptual re-description not reached other sub-fields of international law and international relations and affected our means of conceiving of existing power relations. Having been formulated in a specific historical context, 'naturalised' and 'moralised' friendship was then employed with ease by proponents of approaches and theories far removed from the original debates on the state of nature. For instance, this concept of friendship could be found in the vocabulary of 'positivist' scholarship around the end of the eighteenth century. This is particularly indicative of Georg Friedrich von Martens's *Precis du Droit des Gens Modernes de l'Europe* (1789), which mentions friendship in passing while presenting and justifying certain customs, acts and obligations of European princes. Thus, von Martens occasionally employs remarks such as 'in way of friendship', 'motives of friendship' and 'ties of friendship' without assigning much significance to the phenomenon itself (see Martens 1795: 71, 78, 175). The 'natural law' conventional usage of friendship thus interferes in positivist and custom-based thinking, transfiguring its precepts as well.

Von Martens also uses friendship in his description of the treaties, though his use of the concept in this context is very different from previous conventions, and could even be a mark of accepted scholarly understanding of developments in European treaty-making customs. The convention described in the previous chapter of using friendship in treaties between European princes in the eighteenth century and in most nineteenth-century American treaties appears in the section 'Of definitive treaties of peace'. In this section von Martens draws a distinction between general and specific articles of peace treaties: 'After the introduction, usually follow the general articles, respecting the re-establishment of peace and friendship, the cessation of hostilities … Then follow the principal particular articles' (ibid.: 333–334).

With this conventional description we basically arrive at the modern understanding of international friendship both as a part of treaty practice, in which it occupies a rather marginal place among ignored proclamations of a general nature, and as a moral imperative. Von Martens does not explicitly seek to promote the latter; rather, he is engaged in presenting international customs. As Martti Koskenniemi has demonstrated, von Martens's project was about 'completely procedural law', and had no normative conception of society or culture. Koskenniemi argues that von Martens's and Johan Ludwig Klüber's conception of international law became 'old-fashioned' very quickly, as it basically pictured history as a history of dynasties regulated by balances of power, and in this sense seemed very conservative (Koskenniemi 2002: 19–23). However, alongside his 'empirical' observations on friendship in the structure of peace treaties, von Martens also somewhat unreflectively uses the concept as normatively justifying certain conduct. This normativity would in turn be lodged in what could already be termed 'commonsensical' human duties.

Friendship as the normative foundation of international society

By becoming an obligation and an element of nature, the concept of friendship was transformed in one more important dimension that had a profound and enduring impact on contemporary views of what it meant to have friendship among nations. As shown earlier, the result of equating friendship with universally applicable precepts of natural law was to remove it from discussions of particular and conditional obligations. In previous political and juridical accounts, the concept of friendship could be used to reflect inequality, international leagues and unions. Thus, it was part of the conceptual means of understanding dissensual politics involving ideas of competition, rivalry, conflicts of interest and instruments of conflict resolution. The polemical efforts of natural law theories ascribed friendship to the conceptual apparatus of politics, understood as management of social harmony originally dictated by human nature. In this perspective on society and politics, friendship played a crucial role in describing the basic social relations that ensured the integrity of societies and in justifying the institution of all other political structures.

Hobbes's portrayal of commonwealths as artificial persons and Pufendorf's description of them as moral persons stirred up intense debate over how to conceive of the sum of such artificial persons and the relations between them. The Hobbesian solution was to treat relations between aggregate entities as though they existed in the state of nature – that is, in a state of war – even if limited and hypothetical. The alternative suggestion was to extend the idea of inherent human sociability to the aggregate level and to conceive of nations as moral persons in relation to each other. This required the transformation of the concept of society to allow its application to the international realm, and the understanding of this realm as society similar to the natural society of sociable and benevolent individuals.

Thus, it is no accident that the concept of society also undergoes a covariant transformation in this period. As Keith Michael Baker demonstrated in his survey of French seventeenth- and eighteenth-century dictionaries and encyclopaedias, essentialist and ethical meanings were added to and further prevailed over existing voluntaristic and contractual meanings of the term 'société'. In fact, Baker notes that an article on société in Diderot and d'Alembert's *Encyclopédie* (1751–1761) treats it as a primarily moral concept, and draws substantially on Jean-Jacques Burlamaqui's *Principes du Droit Naturel* (Baker 2001: 84–90). The same is true of the trajectory that the concept of *societas* follows from sixteenth- and seventeenth-century treatises on the law of nations through Pufendorf's reinterpretation to its use by Wolff and later generations. In Grotius, Zouche and Pufendorf there are many instances of *societas* being used to describe a purposeful association of sovereigns or individuals. For example, in Pufendorf we can still find an entire chapter titled 'De Societate' (1749: V, VII), which discusses commercial partnerships or companies (for more on this see Roshchin 2013). Wolff's generation of jurists discusses *societas* of nations, which does not require a contract and is itself a product of nature.

In his *Jus Gentium Methodo Scientifica Pertractatum* (1749), Wolff starts with the assumption that by nature all human beings are united into society, allowing him to draw a distinction between natural and voluntary law. In the logic of his argument, nations then have to be regarded as individuals. By virtue of this equation, the dictates of natural society are transferred onto the international realm:

> For nature herself has established society among men [*societatem inter homines*] and *binds them to preserve it*. Therefore, since this obligation, as coming from the law of nature ... it cannot be changed for the reason that nations have united into a state. Therefore *society* [*societas*], which nature has established among individuals, still *exists among nations* [*subsistit inter Gentes*] and consequently, after states have been established ... *nature herself also must be said to have established society among all nations and bound them to preserve society*. (Wolff 1934b: Prolegomena § 7; emphasis added)

This is a foundational definition for Wolff and for subsequent debates. First, such an understanding of a society of *nations* provides an avenue to envisioning a kind of world state, analogous to the states into which nations united. This kind of state could have been Wolff's *civitas maxima* (see Tuck 1999: 187–189). As Jens Bartelson observes, this *civitas maxima* combined both nations and individuals and was itself embedded within the community of mankind, and was perhaps one of the last attempts to understand this community as a single world community (Bartelson 2009: 142–143). Such a construction of society and supreme state could be attributed to the 'tradition' that Nicholas Onuf termed 'continental republicanism', stemming from Cicero's understanding of the world as a series of ascending associations, which could be topped by the Wolffian supreme state (Onuf 1998: 48, 58–75). Secondly, the idea of *civitas maxima* as built upon the society of nations and individuals could have blurred the difference between the natural and voluntary law of nations had it not been discarded by many commentators, including Emer de Vattel, the main populariser of Wolff's ideas. Vattel, nonetheless, remained loyal to the idea of the existence of natural society among *states* (ibid.: 77–81; Tuck 1999: 192).

Thus, inter-national society was a prerequisite for future arguments about relations among nations or states. It performed a similar function for the international realm to the Hobbesian Leviathan: the latter provided an efficient tool to handle social friction and civil strife, while the former could have been appealed to mitigate and regulate international conflict, and more importantly to legitimate the very existence of a system of distinct and sovereign political entities. An aversion to conflict and the war of all against all, as well as concern for the prosperity and recognition of similar members of inter-national society, dictated the turn to a range of sociable and benevolent attitudes most natural to the idea of human nature to conceptualise the symbiosis and interaction of aggregate units. As we saw earlier, a number of leading thinkers chose friendship to describe the most basic social bond and principle of cooperation for such society. However, a mere observation that it is friendship that in fact directs international conduct might have contradicted a common-sense understanding and lacked credibility. Thus, many struggled to offer a means of arriving at such a conclusion, given the decreasing popularity of eclectic methods and theological explanations. One solution was found by delegating this task to human reason, which was capable of understanding the laws of nature.

Francis Hutcheson's argument is a good example of how the design of nature is normally deduced from individual perceptions of kind affections. Hutcheson argues against those who denied human capacity to foresee the remote effects of actions and insisted on following proclaimed propositions of God without reasoning about them:

> We should not take upon us, antecedently to revelation, to form any conclusions as laws of nature; but follow every particular affection of kind passion, which we naturally approve, such as pity, gratitude, *friendship*, at all hazards; without considering its distant effects, about which, they argue, we are not competent judges. (Hutcheson 1755: 128, emphasis added; for the analogy with men's social affections or sentiments see also Burlamaqui 2006: 49, 155)

Having presented this opinion, Hutcheson insists that it is precisely these human affections and reasoning about tendencies of action that allow men to discover certain laws of nature, which are not explained through revelation (for more on the connection between the perception of action and its moral evaluation see Haakonssen 1996: 78–81). In discussing in *Principes du Droit Naturel* (1747) the principles from which reason may deduce the law of nature, Jean-Jacques Burlamaqui maintained that 'nothing is more agreeable to humanity, or more useful to society, than compassion, lenity, beneficence, and generosity' and continued with reference to Cicero's *De Officiis* (I, 7) that 'we *ought* … to comply with the design of nature … by employing all our care and industry … *to strengthen that love and friendship* which *should always prevail* in human society' (Burlamaqui 2006: 158; emphasis added). In the spirit of a conceptual innovator, Burlamaqui cites Cicero while creatively adjusting the source to his own cause, as Cicero uses neither *amor* nor *amicitia* in his original passage.

With these theoretical and moral constructions, friendship occupied a stable place among the values and duties of humanity that natural law and philosophically minded jurists of the eighteenth century sought to affirm, advocate or just take for granted. We could contend that friendship had gradually become a necessary background condition of the proposed systems of the law of nature – even though, as Otto von Gierke suggests, Pufendorf's idea of the state of nature, with sovereigns as *personae morales*, had no following among proponents of the ideal of a natural society of states described as *societas aequalis*, or even *civitas maxima* in Wolff, and who in turn built their theories in opposition to that offered by Pufendorf (see Gierke 1957: 195–197).

However, the discovery of basic and, for many, obvious conclusions about sociable, peaceable and friendly co-existence in the international realm was not perhaps immediately possible for all the political agents concerned. Therefore, we can see a discrepancy between political practice and the conclusions dictated by reason. The conclusions arrived at by way of abstract reasoning had to be couched in prescriptive normative language; thus, *oughts* and *shoulds* would frame the overall tenor of subsequent discussions of friendship in international politics.

Prescriptive statements derived from the association of friendship with the dictates of nature and the good of society were first applied to the relations between individuals and then translated into similar statements about the proper conduct of nations. For instance, the use of friendship in Wolff's *Jus Gentium* already forms part of a largely normative statement 'that nations [*gentes*] ought to cultivate friendship with each other' (Wolff 1934b: § 172, p. 90). Wolff makes the statement even stronger by proposing that the nations 'ought to love one another as themselves'. Then, having suggested that friendship consists of mutual love ('*Quamobrem cum in mutuo amore amicitia consistat*'; Wolff 1934a: § 172, p. 62), he extends this thesis to substantiate the claim that nations ought to cultivate friendship for that very reason (Wolff 1934b: § 172, p. 90). In his account, friendship is already conventionally prescribed by the law of nature; for one nation to injure the friendship of others would be contrary to the law of nature (ibid.).

Wolff's formulation sets a standard for a new conventional use of friendship in international law and international politics. It was further developed by Emer de Vattel in *Le Droit des Gens*, which was a channel for many of Wolff's ideas to wider European and trans-Atlantic audiences (see Hochstrasser 2000: 177; Onuf 1998: 58–59). Vattel was also a critic of Wolff's ideas, as he rejected the Wolffian supreme state and other propositions as redundant (Tuck 1999: 192–193). As mentioned above, he also maintained the idea of natural international society populated by moral persons (Vattel 2008: Prolegomena § 11). This society differed from the Wolffian natural society of nations. As an 'Atlantic' republican, in Onuf's terminology, Vattel could not foresee an international compact that would give some supreme authority the power to impair the authority of constituent powers. Nature provides a law regulating the conduct of these powers towards each other, rather than a constitution (Onuf 1998: 164–166). These powers can in principle create a sort of republic that would allow them to excel in their statist virtues but would not be detrimental to those virtues. In fact, as Stéphane Beaulac suggests, Vattel's international society was a society of particular units: it was basically a modern society of sovereign states. Vattel's society allowed for the individualisation of nations as sovereign states, the sole representatives of their constitutive publics and independent of all others – an idea that is associated with his milestone treatise (Beaulac 2004: 133–149).

Despite this key difference with Wolff, Vattel ranks friendship among the proper basic relations that should facilitate individualisation and peaceful interaction among sovereign states. He almost reiterates Wolff's dictum about friendship in the section titled 'Each nation ought to cultivate the friendship of others' (Vattel 2008: II, I, § 12), and even claims that 'every nation is obliged' to do so. This is the logic that, according to Vattel, drives the conduct of wise and prudent nations, which also seek in this way to avoid giving any reasons for enmity towards them.

In his work on the structure of international legal argument, Martti Koskenniemi highlights that Vattel, much in line with classical discourse, treats states by analogy with 'super-individuals', whose conduct is determined by the pursuit of self-interest (Koskenniemi 1989: 90). This analogy between individuals subject to the laws of nature and nations figures strongly in the use of friendship. Vattel reasserts the precept that nature prescribes men to love each other, and by analogy rhetorically transposes this prescription onto relations among nations:

> If it be incontestable that men *must love* each other in order to answer the views of *nature* and discharge the *duties* which *she prescribes* them, as well as for their own private advantage, – can it be doubted that nations are under the like *reciprocal obligation?* Is it in the power of men, on dividing themselves into different political bodies, to break *the ties of that universal society which nature has established amongst them?* (Vattel 2008: II, I, § 12; emphasis added)

Such a rhetorical move depicts friendship and love prescribed by nature as the constitutive bonds of 'universal society'. In contrast to the links that Pufendorf makes between friendship and man's sociable nature, Vattel mentions universal society, which, as will become evident from subsequent argumentation, also bears a teleological normative component, when he contrasts the ancients and 'civilized nations'. As he states, like Pufendorf, in the section 'Bad customs of the ancients', 'the ancients had no notion of any duty they owed to nations with whom they were not united by treaties of friendship' (II, I, § 20). Once again, his argument thus breaks away from the particularistic and contracted notion of friendship, and replaces it with a concept that introduces a universal humanistic standard prescribed and justified by the law of nature. He then continues in the same section: 'the voice of nature came to be heard among civilized nations; they perceived that all men are brethren' (ibid.). Thus, the opposition between the ancients and civilised nations includes an opposition of particularistic and contracted friendship against universal friendship. Hence, on another occasion he also tries to dismiss particular friendship, which might be selectively advantageous or disadvantageous, in favour of universal, when emphasising that 'the private laws of friendship' must not contradict 'the common duties of humanity' (IV, IV, § 45.2).

With this theoretical and rhetorical intervention, Vattel fixes the idea of a new friendship for universal society: friendship is already presupposed as a condition of that society's existence, while at the same time every possible appeal to friendship bears with it the moral imperative that nations ought to cultivate friendship. But Vattel apparently realises that there is a certain gap between the idea of a universal society and the actual behaviour of nations. Hence, he relies on the treaty of friendship in an attempt to put this idea into practice or as an instrument to enforce a normative imperative. It is worth stressing once again that, in such an argument, a friendship treaty cannot be specific and does not add anything to human duties, and as such becomes a purely rhetorical instrument of political reinforcement. It is in fact in line with the argument that the law of nature, with its normative postulates in Vattel's interpretation, applied only to the consciences of sovereigns, while the voluntary Law of Nations, comprising specific rules and particular agreements, was free from moral arguments. Such a separation owes much to Hobbes's treatment of states as *magni homines*, which recognise each other as free *personae morales* (see Koselleck 1988: 41–50, 155 fn. 43 on the exclusion of natural law morality from international politics and the effects of the personification of states).

These examples from the literature on the law of nature and nations reflect a major re-description of the concept of friendship, whereby the contractual understanding was removed from the scope of legitimate discussion, while the concept became inextricably linked to the realm of natural dispositions and affections and as such extended to the sphere of relations among nations by means of analogy with individuals. By that time a similar convention had been established in the genre of political pamphlets and treatises that could be said to have continued the work initiated by the Humanist moralist literature of the sixteenth century discussed in the previous chapter.

It is perhaps no accident that eighteenth-century British moralists rearticulated Erasmus's efforts to condemn wars and contentious princely conduct. For instance, Vicesimus Knox made an English translation (occasionally paraphrased) of Erasmus's fragment on war entitled *Antipolemus; or the Plea of Reason, Religion, and Humanity, against War* (1795). In the preface, he indicates that he is writing to denounce war and support the idea of universal and perpetual peace. In this text, peace is directly equated to amity in a rhetorical question: 'Yet what is peace, but love and amity subsisting between great numbers?' (Knox 1824). Using another rhetorical question, the author casts the ideals of personal friendship onto the sphere of international politics:

But it is the nature of all good, that the more it is extended, the greater the good becomes, the more benign its influence; therefore, if *the amicable union of individuals* is so sweet and so salutary, how much will the sum total of happiness be augmented, if *kingdom with kingdom, and nation with nation*, coalesce in this *amicable union?* (ibid.; emphasis added)

Seemingly, it was Edmund Burke who made the most striking analogy between personal and international friendships in his *Letters on a Regicide Peace* (1790s) when discussing the politics of alliances and balancing. However, this analogy in itself sows the seeds of contradiction in the argument for general friendship, since it accentuates affinity between particular nations and thus differs from ideas of universal friendship:

Entirely to trust to either, is to disregard our own safety, or not to know mankind. Men are not tied to one another by papers and seals. They are led to associate by resemblances, by conformities, by sympathies. *It is with nations as with individuals.* Nothing is so strong *a tie of amity* between nation and nation as correspondence in laws, customs, manners, and habits of life. (Burke 1999: Letter No. I; emphasis added)

Setting the debate on the institution of civil authority around the question of whether or not the nature of mankind – and consequently the state of nature – should be interpreted as originally amicable and sociable or as egoistic and hostile in effect allowed the concept of international friendship to be restated predominantly in anthropomorphic terms. Any reference to friendship would conventionally invoke a number of normative imperatives regarding relations among individuals, although some, like Montesquieu, highlighted the limits of the analogy between natural individuals and nations, being asexual entities driven less by amiable affection than by fear (for this caveat, see Tuck 1999: 186).

The collateral consequence of this development was that, with the emerging conceptual consensus about state sovereignty, the concept of friendship, which was used to designate a means of gaining and consolidating political power, became marginalised in political discourse. Defenders of perpetual peace such as Erasmus and Knox made attempts to stretch the normative understanding of individual friendships to relations among nations by appealing to the nature of mankind and the state of nature. They thereby also ultimately downplayed an alternative conventional understanding of friendship as a political compact aimed at establishing and maintaining an international political and legal order.

This conceptual transformation had at least two important implications for contemporary *topoi* of friendship. First, it led to an explicit commendation of personal friendships between individual monarchs, as in William Penn's peace project (1693):

The Seventh Advantage, of an *European, Imperial Dyet, Parliament,* or *Estates,* is, *That it will beget and increase Personal Friendship between Princes and States,* which tends to the Rooting up of Wars, and Planting Peace in a Deep and Fruitful Soil. For Princes have the Curiosity of seeing the Courts and Cities of other Countries, as well as Private Men, if they could as securely and familiarly gratify their Inclinations. (Penn 2002: sect. X)

Many conflicts and wars, according to Penn, were the outcome of princely insincerity and unkindness. Once the discussion focuses on personal friendship, then questions can legitimately be asked about the sincerity and reciprocity of the relations, and participants condemned for feigning and betrayals. This corresponds to a familiar modern-day belief in the positive outcomes that friendly personal relations between heads of governments might have for their respective countries. Today it is customary to think that meetings at various diplomatic forums such as the G8, G20 or EU summits and bilateral visits can help to develop friendly attitudes and thus facilitate mutual understanding and, perhaps, speed up and favour certain decisions.

Secondly, the normative imperatives of personal friendships, as in natural law arguments, were stretched to apply to relations among more abstract entities (e.g. peoples, nations, kingdoms and states). This type of argumentation can be found in Thomas Paine's treatises *Common Sense* (1776) and *The American Crisis* (1776–1783), which contained a number of important rhetorical arguments on international politics just as the United States was emerging as an independent power. Paine's arguments in defence of American states in *Common Sense* were predicated on a more universal concept of friendship by attaching it to a kind of 'internationalist' outlook:

In this extensive quarter of the globe, we forget the narrow limits of three hundred and sixty miles (the extent of England) and carry our *friendship* on a larger scale; we claim *brotherhood* with every European Christian, and triumph in the *generosity of the sentiment.* (Paine 1894a 'Thoughts on the present state of American affairs'; emphasis added)

In Paine's exposition, the policies and friendship of England represent an ideal example of limitedness and restraint. In contrast, the Americans, according to Paine, live in a world that surmounts the boundaries and superstitions of an island and are therefore able to 'hold out the right hand of friendship to all the universe' (Paine 1894b: part VI). He uses a similar figure of speech, although addressed to immediate neighbours, when finishing *Common Sense*. Moreover, an identical universalising concept was laid down in the *Declaration of Independence* (1776): 'as we hold the rest of mankind, Enemies in War, in Peace Friends' (see *The Federalist* 2001, No. 6, p. 498).

In Paine's opposition of English and American politics, we can see the changing range of references of the concept of friendship. As opposed to a contractual understanding, Paine draws a parallel between friendship and Christian ideals of universal brotherhood and non-selective generosity. In terms of rhetorical application of the concept, this type of argument was just one step away from the twentieth-century Wilsonian idealist and Soviet internationalist projects, both of which proclaimed, however sincerely, the goal and value of cultivating and strengthening friendships with immediate neighbours and worldwide.

The inherent sceptical argument

By the late seventeenth and early eighteenth centuries, both legal and political discourses on relations among sovereign entities asserted a prevailing perspective on friendship as an 'ethical' and 'normative' concept. The concept was usually applied, as today, in two main contexts. One embraced closer and friendly relations between particular nations, and allowed them to be described in anthropomorphic terms, emphasising sentiments, fidelity and the similitude of the agents. The other included cases of normative proclamation and appeals to universal friendship, informed by the logic of a universal law of nature. The latter cases could also draw on the ethics of personal friendship, but not all protagonists and agents of friendship could easily accept this line of analogy, because the idea of personal friendship implies limitations derived from individual preferences, choices and virtues specific to particular friends. The arguments made for friendship in both types of situation are amenable to inherent criticisms. Normative prescriptions and speculations about universal friendship could be restated as wishful thinking against the background of continuing power politics and wars between countries.

When political treatises predominantly employ rhetorical figures or tropes to praise friendship among countries using traditional virtues such as sincerity, honesty and affection, it cannot but invite the use of opposite, lamenting tropes by the offended parties in disrupted friendships. This general rhetorical disposition determines the prevalence of a popular *topos* of pretended friendships in accusatory rhetoric levelled against those seen as breaching faith (see, for instance, Paine's warning of the pretend friendship of the British in Paine 1894a; for a similar critique of feigned friendship in political conduct see Godwin 1793: book V, ch. xviii). The negative qualification of pretended friendship allows Paine to advocate policies against friendships that are prone to treachery. This use of the concept in the context of the foreign relations of the American states allows him to argue that friendships with those who have already 'wounded affections' would be folly and even madness (Paine 1894a). Thus, the maxims of early modern moralist pamphlets and treatises that approved virtuous friendships and condemned feigned ones were re-employed in arguments over international politics in a way that allowed the author to win the support of the audience by appealing to common-sense truths.

As far as the general picture of friendly international politics is concerned, the 'sceptical' counter-argument is derived from a quasi-empirical observation on the actual conduct of princes and states largely guided by egoistic motives of enrichment, jealousy, their own security and balances of power, among other reasons. Burke provides a good example of this 'realist' argument in his bitter diagnosis of international politics, which nonetheless encapsulates the whole attitude:

> In looking over any State to form a Judgment on it; it presents itself in two Lights, the external and the internal. The first, that Relation which it bears in point of *Friendship or Enmity to other States.* The second, that Relation its component Parts, the Governing, and the Governed, bear to each other. The *first Part of the external View* of all States, their *Relation as Friends*, makes so trifling a Figure in History, that I am very sorry to say, it affords me but little Matter on which to expatiate. The good Offices done by one Nation to its Neighbour … would afford a very ample and very pleasing Subject for History. But, alas! all the History of all Times, concerning all Nations, does not afford Matter enough to fill ten Pages, though it should be spun out by the Wire-drawing Amplification of a Guicciardini himself. *The glaring Side is that of Enmity.* War is the Matter which fills all History, and consequently the only, or almost the only View in which we can see the External of political Society, is in a hostile Shape … War, says Machiavel, ought to be the only Study of a Prince … A Meditation on the Conduct of political Societies made old Hobbes imagine, that War was the State of Nature; and truly, if a Man judged of the Individuals of our Race by their Conduct when united and packed into Nations and Kingdoms, he might imagine that every sort of Virtue was unnatural and foreign to the Mind of Man. (Burke [1756] 1993: 16–17; emphasis added)

In this passage, Burke articulates what now might seem a traditional image of international relations as understood in terms of friendship and enmity. This understanding in turn is based on two alternative conceptions of the state of nature discussed above. For the sake of a rhetorical argument, Burke presents simplified versions of these conceptions. Therefore, the concept of friendship is reduced to all the good things that nations do to each other. In saying that these things occur in insignificant numbers, Burke makes a strong case for the Hobbesian conception of the state of nature as a state of war transferred onto the sphere of international politics. The crucial element in this analogy is the emphasis that he puts on the virtue of man. This emphasis once again indicates that the criteria for making an evaluative judgement of international conduct are derived from the normative imperatives of moral philosophy regarding interpersonal relations. Consequently, appeals to universal brotherhood and friendship render themselves liable to immediate criticisms based on mere observations of past and present conflicts.

In *Letters on a Regicide Peace*, and particularly the second letter 'On the Genius and Character of the French Revolution as it regards other Nations', Burke detaches the concept of friendship even further from the actual conduct of the nations. In this sense, his political arguments are aimed at condemning the conduct of the French nation, and resonate with developments in juridical discourse, including ascribing friendship treaties to mere confirmations of benevolent relations that add nothing to the existing law of nations. When speaking about the possibility of fraternity with the French nation he suggests with despising overtones that it should be put out of sight or substituted with:

> a sort of periphrasis, something of an ambiguous quality, and describing such a connection under the terms of 'the usual relations of peace and amity.' By this means the proposed fraternity is hustled in the crowd of those treaties, which imply no change in the public law of Europe, and which do not upon system affect the interior condition of nations. (Burke 1999: 168)

Burke then argues that the idea of these 'usual relations of peace and amity' could be accessed in the voluminous collection 'the corps diplomatique', which included documents pertaining to relations in 'civilized Europe' (including 'ancient France'). He finds it doubtful that France after the revolution could be treated the same as the 'ancient France' with which 'relations of peace and amity' could be maintained. Burke observes that the revolution changed the nature of relations that France had with other nations; France, according to him, sought to be not 'a neighbor, but a mistress', not 'observant of laws, but to put her in a condition to impose them' (ibid.). In this argumentation, France's call for universal fraternity and friendship is contrasted with the old relations of 'peace and amity', regardless of how meaningless they might have been.

Such downplaying of international friendship could effectively be countered with diametrically opposed arguments, as the oppositional logic of the re-described concept suggests. Joseph Towers, who took a critical stance towards Burke's reflections on the French Revolution, uses the term 'friendship' in line with the convention forged by moralist authors. For instance, he reports that many Frenchmen desired peace with England, and 'have even appeared extremely solicitous, that *real friendship and harmony may subsist between the two nations*'. As a response to this attitude, he expresses the wish 'that these *sentiments* may be cordially cherished on our part, and that *perpetual peace and friendship may be established* between Great Britain and France, and the general welfare and freedom of *the human race* promoted by their united efforts' (Towers 1796: 177–178; emphasis added).

None of these arguments could be said to have won the day. The concept of friendship thus appeared to be a powerful rhetorical instrument used either to denounce or advocate some policy options or general states of affairs. It could also be used to undermine an opponent's position or, alternatively, to support the position of an ally. Towers thus frequently uses such titles as 'the true friends of liberty', 'the friends of despotism', 'sincere friends to the rights of mankind' (ibid.: 82, 115, 180 respectively) to commend friendship between the French and English nations and to rule out the arguments of those who oppose this idea (for similar moves see Swift 1824: 316). The same rhetorical strategies were applied in putting forward and justifying commercial interests. As will be demonstrated in the following chapter, the ideals and values of commercial society were commended by attachment to a normatively loaded concept of friendship. Therefore, what dominated in these rhetorical battles was the restatement of the debate on international friendship almost exclusively on moral grounds, with collateral marginalisation of contracted political friendship as a means of establishing and maintaining the international political order.

This may have been one of the reasons why the concept was of marginal utility in influential peace projects aimed at creating institutional conditions to preserve peace and prevent war. Thus, in *Perpetual Peace* (1795), Immanuel Kant discussed the possibility of a federation of free states, but not universal friendship or friendship between particular states (on the significance of Kant's project for international relations see Brown 2005; Doyle 1983, a, b). Interestingly, we find his discussion of friendship in *The Metaphysics of Ethics* (in the 'Conclusion of the Elementology' [1796]; see Kant 1886).

This range of available rhetorical ways of using the concept of friendship marks the stabilisation of the modern convention. The episode in the conceptual history of friendship that highlights debates on the state of nature and natural law and explicates the rationality of eliding the contractual and contingent political connotations of friendship, while simultaneously affirming its natural, ethical and normative meanings, seems to be a milestone in the formation of our means to conceptualise friendship among nations and states. The re-description of the concept discussed above made it a convenient tool for justifying, commending and reinforcing, or for condemning, criticising and disapproving of, certain policy choices and developments in international politics. This conceptual change could be said to continue informing approaches to friendship in contemporary debates in international relations and political theory, ranging from constructivist attempts to portray it as an ideal role structure modelled on individual, preferably virtuous, relations, to normative arguments advocating the agenda of universal friendship as a way out of an egoistic and conflict-prone international system.

This was just one of the factors contributing to conceptual change. It is important to remember that the valorisation of ethical perspectives on friendship and the simultaneous marginalisation of its political regulatory functions took place against a background of an emerging international order that brought about institutions such as state sovereignty, international law and the balance of power. In fact, demand for contracted friendships might have decreased due to the growing specialisation of regimes of international trade, navigation, and so forth. But the discussed episode of conceptual change helps us to understand how friendship is transformed from a concept used to initiate and regulate such regimes into a popular instrument in rhetorical attacks on these regimes and the overall political order.

This, in fact, raises more fundamental questions of the relationship between concepts and the political practices they designate, and whether change in one element of this couple means an immediate change in the other. The examples given above of how the concept was used were taken from rather abstract philosophical and juridical discussions of how nations should behave towards each other. The extent to which changes in this peculiar argumentative domain and the theoretical means of conceptualising international politics correspond to actual ways in which diplomacy used the concept is one of the questions that will be addressed in the final part of this book. However, to anticipate that discussion, it could be said that the conceptual change that took place in the fields of natural law and the law of nations produced a concept of friendship that is not always the most effective instrument for understanding or analysing diplomatic friendships.

5

The unknown friendship of the modern international order

To finish the story of international friendship with the conceptual transformation that tailored the 'naturalist' and normative perspective to our conceptions of international friendship would be to overlook the obvious – namely, the exceedingly popular practice of bilateral friendship agreements, which are *par excellence* voluntary contractual instruments, between countries. Despite the loss of lexicon indicating the contracted nature of this friendship, such agreements remained a key instrument in early modern and contemporary diplomatic practice. Therefore, it is reasonable to suppose that the study of such documents is likely to uncover linguistic conventions and political practices that are antithetical to natural and ethical interpretations. The unintended consequence of the conceptual transformation in philosophical debate was to divert the attention of students of international politics from one of the most salient and possibly most political functions of friendship in diplomatic communication. In this way, early modern discourse of and about international politics contained a paradoxical combination of at least two language games prescribing the rules for using the concept of friendship: one game embedded friendship in a normatively loaded discussion, while the other associated the concept with pragmatic contexts of establishing juridical and political regimes in inter-state relations. Despite their shared terminology these two games did not aggravate the conceptual conflict, because the first for internal reasons preferred to view friendship treaties as unimportant, while the second held friendship as a *value* used to justify the contracted treaties and their goals, and thus excluded the opposition to 'natural' and normative interpretations. This peaceful co-existence of two linguistic and political conventions resulted in a gap in our understanding of friendship in modern diplomacy. While philosophers, jurists and political theorists managed to re-describe the concept of friendship as a demand of nature and moral obligation, the following three centuries witnessed countless examples of friendships made for the purpose of commerce, colonisation and state-building. These examples can only be made intelligible from the perspective of linguistic conventions and modes of argumentation recovered in the first and second chapters of this book. In this chapter I shall attempt to recover this largely unnoticed background of normative and 'naturalist' consensual understanding by scrutinising the justificatory functions of friendship in diplomatic agreements.

Friendship and international commerce: from relations of determination to in-distinction

One of the central elements of inter-national life that would remain unaccounted for were we to accept friendship as a natural and universal ethical obligation is commerce, and the often exclusive nature of agreements contracted by trading partners. This would indeed be a puzzling effect of conceptual re-description, not least because friendship contracts have regulated property rights and trade with foreigners since early times, as chapter two demonstrates, but also because friendship and commerce remained tightly intertwined and widely spread as such in diplomatic instruments in the epoch following the theoretical re-description of friendship. Had we excluded friendly engagements under the pressure of a new theoretico-ethical convention, many of the factors that contributed to the growth of commercial powers and the expansion of empires in the eighteenth and nineteenth centuries would remain inexplicable. As I shall demonstrate below, the diplomatic instrument of friendship was an inextricable element in the toolkit of this commercially and politically driven European expansion.

An Historical and Chronological Deduction of the Origin of Commerce (1762) by Scottish economist Adam Anderson provides an account of the history of commerce that from the very beginning is intertwined with the history of friendship treaties. Anderson maintains that 'The first record that we meet to our purpose in the thirteenth volume of *Foedera*, is in the year 1502, p. 6: It is a treaty of friendship and intercourse of commerce between King Henry VII of England and Maximilian King of the Romans, &c. wherein it is in general terms stipulated, "That the merchants on both sides may freely resort and trade to each other dominions"' (Anderson 1787, II: 7). Anderson's work commences with a treaty of friendship and commerce, and continues as both history of commerce and of friendly engagements securing commercial exchanges. Anderson couches friendship in the language of the law of nations when referring to alleged Elizabethan regulations concerning freedom and safety of navigation for ships of 'potentates in amity', and relates back to the famous debate between Selden and Grotius on the limits of the freedom of the sea (ibid.: 194, 208).

The contractual concept of friendship is perhaps key to understanding the dynamics of and justifications for the expansion of the commercial interests of major European powers. In Europe itself, diplomatic uses of friendship often linked the concept to political alliances. The other side of this Janus-faced concept reflected a close connection to commercial relations. Even the idea of balancing other nations held commercial appeal in addition to military and political dimensions. Slingsby Bethel (1617–1697), while favouring peace and amity between England and Holland as two trading and naval nations, stressed that it would be of great benefit for England to maintain friendship with Spain, first because Spain was 'little inclinable to Commerce', and secondly because it could be used 'for the balancing of France' (Bethel 1681: 71–72). Anderson also points out that the Dutch Republic at times, such as during the first Anglo-Dutch war, realised the losses incurred by going to war with England, and sought to re-establish friendship and commerce (Anderson 1787, II: 424). This, however, did not mean that trading countries could not abandon their friendship duties when contingent windows of opportunity opened. On such occasions, friendship could conveniently be turned into a rhetorical tool of disapprobation. For instance, Jonathan Swift, in his remarks on the First Barrier Treaty (1709) between Great Britain and the United Provinces, used the expression 'our good friends and allies' as an ironic figure to express disapproval of the ungrateful conduct of those allies: 'But what is very surprising, in the very same article, where *our good friends and allies* are wholly shutting us out from trading in those towns we have conquered for them with so much blood and treasure' (Swift 1824: 390; emphasis added). Thus, the maximisation of a country's own interests could easily prevail in determining the usefulness of a particular friendship. Nonetheless, a country would be unlikely to get away with failure to meet the expectations of a friend or to fulfil a contracted duty; in this case, as a rule, friendship was used to mount a rhetorical diplomatic assault, not to mention that a formal severing of a friendship would be detrimental to the privileges accorded in amity to the country's subjects.

'Trading countries' – and trading republics in particular – made great diplomatic efforts to put friendship at the service of furthering their exclusive commercial and political interests. The most dramatic association of friendship and commerce was conditioned by expansion overseas. This is already evident from Anderson's investigation of the origins of commerce, which while accounting for the trade and colonial activities of the Dutch East India Company in the seventeenth century, for example in South Africa, did not fail to mention that such activities required cultivating/contracting friendship with 'savage natives' (Anderson 1787: 417, 423). Likewise, the English realised relatively early the utility of friendship for commercial engagements overseas. Queen Elizabeth's message to the kings of Sumatra is one such diplomatic historical source that indicates the nature of a relationship binding together friendship and commerce:

> God having so ordained that no place should enjoy all things appertaining to man's use, but that one country should have need of another, by which means men of remote countries have *commerce* one with another, and by their interchange of commodities are linked together in *amity and friendship*, the Queen has been moved to grant licence to divers of her subjects to visit his territories and dominions, and to offer *commerce* according to the course of merchants. (*Calendar of State Papers* 1864: Jan. 1601 (?), pp. 120–121; emphasis added)

This message provides a clue to a different understanding of friendship from the proclaimed/contracted relations of international treaties. Nevertheless, in this context friendship also requires a purposeful effort to germinate. This effort, as the quote indicates, commences with commercial exchanges, which if successful may produce friendship. In a way this statement suggests a derivative nature for friendship that is conditional upon prior achievements.

Certainly, this was not the only diplomatic convention regulating appeals to friendship. Contractual friendship could determine commercial relations by means of sanctioning or legitimisation, which was a common trait of seventeenth- and eighteenth-century treaties. In this period, peace and friendship treaties sometimes contained separate clauses regarding commerce, and sometimes treaties of peace were followed by separate treaties of commerce that also made references to friendship. In the context of these treaties, friendship was commonly used to sanction the establishment and confirmation of commercial relations with the implications that they bore for levying duties, admitting vessels to ports, property rights, and so on. The Treaty of Commerce that Charles II of England concluded with Turkish sultan Mahomet IV (1675) is a clear example of such diplomatic 'rhetorical' legitimation. Once the parties agreed to be in 'peace and amity' under the terms of this treaty, the English were granted access to Turkish ports and assigned the same 'privileges' that 'had been granted to the French, the Venetians, or any other Christian nation whatever, whose king was in peace and friendship with the Porte' (art. XVIII). This treaty also shows that the term 'friendship', when applied to a specific state of affairs, could combine contract-related accounts and value-ascribing proclamations, thereby making the very contract of friendship something that in itself was worthy of commendation by the parties and the public. The use of 'friendship' in this particular context thus contributes to the moral reinforcement of the legally binding international agreements.

This type of friendship is hardly wholehearted or practised for its own sake, as even polite diplomatic convention permits the establishment of conditions under which friendship may last. On the one hand, the conditions agreed with the sultan stress the need to conform to 'the treaty of friendship' and proclaim that 'articles of peace and friendship above declared, have been concluded, signed, agreed to, and confirmed' (art. XX). On the other hand, in the same article the sultan promises to endeavour to 'with the utmost respect cultivate the friendship and good correspondence', and states by way of a caveat: 'as long as Charles the second King of England … shall maintain a good friendship and correspondence with us … we will not fail on our part to preserve that friendship with all the tenderness possible' (see Jenkinson 1785, I: 228–256).[1]

---

[1] Such a condition was not novel in diplomatic practice, and in fact reiterates clauses from earlier agreements. This treaty reconfirms a treaty made by Elizabeth I that contained a

The conditionality of the contracted friendship was essential to preserving commercial interests. The ancient maxim that 'friends have all things in common' was thus alien to commercial rationality, while the lexicon of friendship was not. Daniel Defoe, in his discussion of the state of Spanish trade in America, noted that the Spaniards had managed in previous treaties to secure commercial privileges in their American colonies for themselves alone. However, these privileges were totally dependent on the 'Justice and Friendship of the rest of the Powers of Europe' and had these powers wished to 'withdraw that Friendship' they could launch unimpeded trade with New Spain (Defoe 1727: 22). In this Defoe's observation echoes Swift, for they both seem to share an assumption that friendships are made to secure certain commercial advantages for a limited number of participants, and sometimes one party alone.[2] When commercial interest is at stake, fairness to a friend could well be compromised in the name of advantage. Even if a friend is at war, this is no reason to prohibit trade with an enemy of the friend. Typical in this respect is the Treaty of Alliance between Sweden and Great Britain (1720), which seeks to preserve commercial interests with the help of friendship in such a way as to avoid detrimental effects on trade by subjects of either side with enemies of the other party.[3] As we saw in chapter two, the legal argument defending such a course of action was formed in debates regarding the status of friends and allies and translated into the concept of amity as neutrality in the eighteenth century.

Colonial trade is another key chapter in the history of mutual engagements of friendship and commerce. David Armitage's work on the early ideological origins of the British Empire shows how discourses of political economy initially compelled commercial republics to seek profits from their colonies and bound 'the colonies to the metropolis within a single trading system' (Armitage 2000: 180).[4] Once these discourses translated into legal and diplomatic languages in the context of the foundation of colonies and their gradual expansion, they inextricably intertwined with the rhetoric of friendship. The complex web of issues embracing the shifting balance of power, diverse commercial interests and a void

---

similar expression: 'so long as the said Queen of England shall in peace, friendship and alliance shew herself firm, constant and sincere to us, conformably to the present treaty of friendship, and a hearty good correspondence, we promise likewise on our part reciprocally' (ibid.).

[2] For the reference to friendship as a means of protecting British commerce see also Postlethwayt (1757: 235, 498).

[3] See article XVIII of the treaty: 'yet that obligation shall not be so far extended, as that all friendship and mutual correspondence shall be taken away and prohibited with the enemies of the other confederate: ... it shall be free for his subjects and inhabitants to have trade and navigation with the enemies of that ally who is engaged in the war' (Jenkinson 1785, II: 263).

[4] See also chapters 6 and 7 of Armitage; for a discussion of discourses on trade in early modern England see Knorr (1963).

of legal order created a fertile context for appeals to friendship as a diplomatic and legal instrument. As this was a central rhetorical and juridical practice to expanding European empires and emerging states in the New World, I shall consider the use of friendship in imperial history in greater detail in the next two sections. Here it is enough to note that through colonial political and commercial engagements, diplomatic friendship was transferred to the New World, eagerly absorbed and multiplied by the newly independent states in their foreign policies.

However, before I move on to mapping the trajectory of diplomatic friendship from early modern to nearly contemporary legal instruments regulating commercial regimes by key powers and inheritors of British linguistic and legal traditions such as the United States, it is essential to highlight the bifurcation of the rhetorical convention that bound together friendship and commerce. The historical examples mentioned above generally followed the pattern of determination, that is, diplomatic friendship was used or appealed to sanction and launch a commercial agreement. Growing appreciation of the value of commerce with colonies and foreign nations dictated the inclusion of commerce into the horizon of things natural. In the previous chapter, we saw the process by which theoretical reflection described friendship exclusively as a fruit of nature. In itself the belief that nature begets social relations is as old as the hills. The normative empowerment of concepts that inclusion into natural argument brings is a process that we can still witness in socio-political debates, when new interests and phenomena need to be legitimised before the public.

Commerce is no exception to this chain of reasoning and legitimation. The eighteenth-century theoretical argument was also transformed to insert commerce into the chain of determination flowing from nature to friendship and thus conditioning the latter. Since the moral authority of naturally produced friendship was already unchallenged, portraying commerce as a causal mediator linking two moral phenomena in natural succession was bound to be a successful rhetorical strategy. Adam Smith, who in his seminal book *The Wealth of Nations* (1776) put forward the idea that commerce is there to foster the ties of universal international friendship, is one of the key proponents of this strategy. In an ironic portrayal of international politics he demonstrates the tendency to abuse the benefits of commerce, which becomes a problem for 'true' international peace and friendship:

> *Commerce*, which ought naturally to be, *among nations, as among individuals, a bond of union and friendship*, has become the most fertile source of discord and animosity. The capricious ambition of kings and ministers has not, during the present and the preceding century, been more fatal to the repose of Europe than the impertinent jealousy of merchants and manufacturers. The violence and injustice of the rulers of mankind is an ancient evil, for which, I am afraid, the nature of human affairs can scarce admit of a remedy. (Smith 1904: book IV, III, II; emphasis added)

In this and the following quotation Smith uses ironic figures to highlight the value of commerce in maintaining international friendship, which itself is no longer understood as a type of political contract:

> But the very same circumstances which would have rendered an open and free commerce between the two countries [France and Great Britain] so advantageous to both, have occasioned the principal obstructions to that *commerce*. Being neighbours, they are necessarily enemies, and the *wealth and power* of each becomes, upon that account, more formidable to the other; and *what would increase the advantage of national friendship serves only to inflame the violence of national animosity*. (ibid.; emphasis added)

Evidently in this context friendship is turned into a value for which sake certain policies should be adopted and others abandoned.[5] Smith thus juxtaposes the practice of balancing adopted by the European powers against an ideal order based on the development of commerce. Here the balance of power, which not long before had commonly been associated with the idea of diplomatic friendship, is set against the 'liberal' argument favouring commerce and its collateral effect, that is, friendship of nations. This representation of the advantages of commercial conduct almost completely removes any possible doubts about the very causal relationship between a value-laden idea of international friendship and commerce.

David Ramsay, one of the greatest authorities on the American Revolution, in his historical narrative of relations between the British metropolis and its American colonies presents it as an already self-evident truth that commerce leads to friendship between countries:

> That mercantile intercourse, which connects different countries, was in the early periods of the English Colonies, far short of that degree, which is necessary to perpetuate a *friendly union*. Had the first great colonial establishments been made in the Southern Provinces, where the suitableness of native commodities would have maintained a brisk and direct trade with England – the constant exchange of good offices between the two countries, would have been more likely to perpetuate their *friendship*. But as the Eastern Provinces were the first ... their descendants speedily lost the fond attachment, which their forefathers felt to their Parent State. (Ramsay 1990: 48; emphasis added)

A similar line of determination is evident in arguments explaining the need to preserve 'the relations of amity' between major metropolises by means of favourable treaties and privileged treatment in order to ensure uninterrupted trade with important colonies, for example Portuguese Brazil.[6] In such arguments, levels of

---

[5] For signs of an emerging convention of equating friendship with international commerce and the positive implications for peace and prosperity, see analogous statements in The Federalist 2001 No. 6, p. 23; Hopkinson (1792: 14) and Paine (1894a).

[6] See Brougham (1803: 484) explaining the necessity of amity between Great Britain and Portugal for this precise purpose.

trade and mercantile intercourse are presented as sources of friendship, which itself then appears as a derivative relationship invoked to praise and legitimise its alleged and overlooked causes, thereby casting these causes in a positive moral light. The effect is produced by rhetorical strategies that invoke a positively valued relationship or state of affairs, often designated with the term 'friendship', and then present something as an essential condition of this state of affairs. In the case of commerce, the requirements of its successful representation as a condition of friendship seem to have been met: the corresponding term 'friendship' had long been used in legal contexts to sanction commercial intercourse; friendship was no longer understood by theorists as a princely contract or sovereign sanction of commercial activities, but presented as a universally benevolent and affectionate relationship among nations that appeared beneficial to observers; and commerce presented as a source of prosperity showed its benefits to the public. This is an important politico-economic twist in the discursive framing of friendship that constitutes the bifurcation of the rhetorical use of friendship: on the one hand, the diplomatic and legal context still articulated a linguistic convention endowing friendship with the power to sanction and promote commerce; on the other, politico-economic argument aimed at integrating commerce deeper into the fabric of legitimate social norms and conventions, implying a change in the public perception of friendship and individual friendships.

Drawing on Smith, Alan Silver argues that, with the development of commerce and the emergence of universal civil and commercial society with its endorsement of voluntary relations and natural sympathy, the ancient tradition of understanding friendship in terms of necessity and utility disappears (Silver 1997: 50). This also follows from David Hume's *Treatise of Human Nature*, to which Silver's title 'Two Different Sorts of Commerce' refers. Reflecting on societal changes, Hume observes that the 'self-interested commerce' dominant in society does not necessarily 'abolish the more generous and noble intercourse of friendship and good offices'. He argues that the distinction between these 'two different sorts of commerce, the interested and the disinterested' is even reflected in the form of words associated with the former (the words that make the promise of certain actions binding) (Hume 1826: book III, II, V: 297). In light of these arguments, it is worth noting that Smith, in the first passage quoted above, does not emphasise this distinction. In fact, in his argument the concepts are in a way compounded, as friendship is produced by commerce. However, what is more illuminating about this type of friendship is his equation of friendship among nations and friendship among individuals that makes the former as noble and generous as the latter, irrespective of its dependence on commerce.

This reverted chain of determination had little negative effect, or none at all, on the use of friendship in diplomatic rhetoric, which only benefited from the stronger and mutually reinforcing association between commerce and friendship. Against the background of an overall preoccupation with commerce, treaties of friendship and commerce started to dominate among other peace and friendship/alliance treaties in the late eighteenth and early nineteenth centuries. Indeed, commercial republics actively employed friendship in the service of their primary cause. The classical European custom of making friendships for the purpose of alliance becomes largely a custom of making friendship for the purpose of furthering commerce. Friendship in this period becomes a commonly used instrument mediating and putting forward commercial legal regimes that accompany growth in trade with foreign countries, especially newly independent states. Friendship and commerce treaties of this era typically contained specific clauses on freedom of trade, the levying of duties and taxes, rules of navigation, the registration of trade vessels and provision of security (see, for instance, British treaties of amity and commerce with Colombia, 1825; the United Provinces of Rio de la Plata, 1825; the United States of Mexico, 1826; Brazil, 1827 in BFSP vols 12 and 14). The preamble and the first article of the Treaty of Amity and Commerce between the king of Shoa (a region in modern Ethiopia) and Great Britain (1841) is one of the most remarkable examples of the new intrinsic connection between commerce and friendship:

> Whereas *commerce is a source of great wealth and prosperity to all those nations who are firmly united in the bonds of reciprocal friendship*; and whereas the conclusion of a Treaty of perpetual Amity and Commerce betwixt Shoa and Great Britain … would tend to the mutual advantage of both nations … [art. I] That *a firm, free, and lasting friendship shall subsist* between His Majesty Sahela Selassie, King of Shoa … and between Her Most Gracious Majesty Victoria, Queen of Great Britain. (BFSP, vol. 29: 156; emphasis added)

Nothing, however, compares to the degree of association between friendship and commerce in American treaties. Since independence, most US treaties had been treaties of amity, commerce and navigation (commonly abbreviated as FCN – friendship, commerce and navigation), containing detailed articles on freedom of trade, freedom of travel and navigation, duties on vessels or tonnage, protection of citizens and property rights, and equal treatment (see the collection of US treaties in TCIAPA). This valorisation of friendship and commerce may stem from the self-understanding of the new polity as a commercial republic fighting for its liberties and commercial rights. It is in the American context that the re-described concept of friendship as neutrality (see chapter two) falls on fertile soil. Amity was put to use by Americans to defend the cause of commerce. As war was a constant factor in early American foreign policy and trade, tools were needed to preclude any disruption that conflict with one power could cause to commerce with other powers. James Madison thus famously proclaimed in 1806 that 'a nation not engaged in the war remains in the same relations of amity and of commercial pursuits, with each of the belligerent nations' and can continue trade with each of them uninterrupted (Madison 1900).

Despite the number of American friendship and commerce treaties following independence, these treaties may seem rather disappointing for those trying to recover the meaning of the term 'friendship'. Firstly, there were no treaties solely about friendship. Secondly, existing treaties were dominated by commercial issues to the extent that some bearing the title 'Treaty of Amity, Commerce and Navigation' do not even mention friendship in the body of the text (see for instance the Treaty of Amity, Commerce and Navigation with Congo 1891; TCIAPA, vol. II). Indeed, the majority of US treaties in the period between 1782 and 1891 were treaties of friendship and commerce or FCN (see the same collection). This development in the ways in which treaties were phrased corresponds to the overall process of the dissolution of traditional European international law and the formulation of a new international law and order based, *inter alia*, on a belief in a free global trade. Thus, Carl Schmitt's observation about a free economy running through territorially organised states and conceivable as 'a modern type of amity line' receives a new type of support from rhetorical quarters (Schmitt 2003: 227–236).

The new world order and commercial ideology could not but be reflected in the use of friendship – as one of the most popular diplomatic instruments –, which only retained its name to inaugurate the content of negotiated treaties while losing the previous rhetoric of elevated friendship values. By the 1950s, scholarly discourse was already unambiguous in interpreting FCN treaties. Thus, the American diplomat Herman Walker Jr, writing in this period, showed no scruples about the nature and purpose of the FCN treaty, which for him was synonymous with 'commercial treaty' (1956: 230). He even referred to the *Encyclopaedia of the Social Sciences* (1930) for the entry on commercial treaties, thus omitting the friendship part, which was not considered in that entry (Walker 1957–1958: 805, fn. 2; compare to *Encyclopaedia of the Social Sciences* 1953: 24–31). In Walker's interpretation, FCN treaties in the twentieth century developed into an investment instrument. In contrast to a specialised investment instrument, 'broad-gauged' FCN treaties were more beneficial to international trade because their framework ensured protection in several areas amounting to a desired investment 'climate' (Walker 1956: 243–244).[7]

Thus, on the one hand, the concept of friendship could be claimed to have become extremely diffuse in the American commercial treaties. On the other hand, looking at the usage and application of the term, one could contend that its sanctioning power, which inaugurates legal commercial regimes just by virtue of being mentioned as one of the names of such a regime, had reached its climax. Consequently, this shift in the diplomatic focus had implications for the lan-

---

[7] For a reappraisal of the role of FCN treaties in the contemporary law of treaties see Coyle (2013); for the use of friendship treaties in twentieth-century great power politics see Roshchin (2011).

guage of friendship. It applied both to the composition of adjectives and verbs as well as to the range of relative and synonymous terms used together with the concept. As I mentioned above, the early modern extended diplomatic formula was eventually buried in oblivion; American treaties of the nineteenth century show that the term 'most favored nation' became nearly an exclusive synonym for friend. This term implied that friendly powers would grant each other the same trade privileges they accord any other nation with 'most favored nation' status. The term appears in American treaties soon after independence, but with the Monroe doctrine proclaimed in the presidential message to Congress in 1823, it became an element of most friendship and commerce treaties, particularly those concluded with Latin American countries. The family of terms that emerges from this association in American diplomatic rhetoric of bilateral engagements also includes, but is not limited to, 'commercial intercourse', 'advantage', 'equal treatment', '(non)discrimination', 'good understanding', 'harmony' and 'religious liberty'.

The relationship of the terms 'friendship' and 'most favoured nation', and the policies they describe and justify, was brilliantly noted by the eminent Scottish jurist James Lorimer as a question: 'Is a "favoured nation's clause" in a treaty, for example, by which the goods of the favoured nation are admitted on easier terms than those of other nations, an injury to non-favoured nations and a breach of international friendship?' As is evident from the way this question is formulated, the two concepts are closely related, but there is room for appealing to friendship as a means of criticising 'most favoured nation' policies. In his answer to this admittedly legitimate question, Lorimer argues that states, like individuals, can favour those 'which lie nearest' to them in all senses, and in 'proportion to their nearness' states should do all they can to aid other states. But what the states should not do is favour those who are near beyond their nearness or to favour more one of two equidistant states (Lorimer 1883–1884: 235). In the late nineteenth century, Lorimer was already operating with a background understanding of scholarly discourse on friendship as a universal and ethical relationship, which, however, still allows him to differentiate friendships depending on the degree of proximity. In the context of US efforts to preserve its own independence and countervail European influence in the Americas, the terminological couple of friendship and most favoured nation appears as a predominantly bilateral and contractual instrument for building politico-legal regimes, particularly if contrasted with the stronger emphasis on universal values of peace and friendship in European diplomatic rhetoric.

Perhaps to the uneasiness of both proponents of international friendship and international trade, this analysis shows that the contemporary valorised culture and discourse of international commerce and foreign investment – often accompanied by a sense of exclusivity, competition and inclination of governments to preferential treatment in the near past – was to a large degree the fruit of friendship agreements. It demonstrates that the commercial cause and the striving for prosperity as a new factor in international politics could not but be legitimised and sanctioned by references to friendship. In fact, commerce may have been even unintelligible without the accompanying relations of friendship. Due to its historical record in the field of international law and diplomacy, it was to friendship that contracting parties looked in order to enforce and popularise the idea of a commercial treaty as an exclusive instrument. At the same time, seen from the angle of early treaties of commerce and friendship, the concept of diplomatic friendship displays a unique, even if possibly disturbing, combination of the values ascribed to it in ethical discourses and a contingently negotiated contract, which is profit-driven and naturally exclusive of others. This in turn relates us back to the Aristotelian theme of the first chapter, giving a new twist to the history of the Janus-faced friendship of virtue and utility in the era of thriving international commerce.

Friendship and English colonisation of North America from the 1640s onwards

Equally overlooked is the role of friendship in a context closely related to commerce – the history of colonisation and the foundation of new states – despite the popularity and instrumentality of the term in early encounters with native peoples in many parts of the New World. This part of the history of friendship in international politics may indeed be the least convenient for its contemporary proponents, but it deserves to be put under the microscope as it opens an important perspective on understanding the ways in which regimes of power were established and legitimated in the colonised world. The British Empire represents the classical and most prominent example for the Anglo-Saxon story of colonialism. Anthony Pagden's study of the ideologies of empire in Spain, Britain and France showed that Spanish expansion was motivated by the idea of the conquest of settled civilisations sanctioned by the authority of the pope. The French and British approach was different, even if it eventually led to large-scale dispossession of native Americans from their traditional lands. This approach to colonisation, Pagden maintains, rested on the argument of *res nullius* applied to land, as many of the tribes of North America were nomads. Thus, the British and French tended either to exclude the natives or turn them into trading partners instead of gaining privileges by right of conquest (Pagden 1995: 65). This more intricate approach, which nonetheless was not immune to military confrontation and subjugation, required a range of instruments to ensure that the exclusion of the natives would look acceptable to them and not detrimental to the settlers, while the sanctity of trade agreements was observed and a means of settling disputes provided. Given these ideological differences, as well as the decline of the French and Dutch colonisation projects in North

America, in this chapter I shall consider two paradigmatic examples of British colonial expansion. In the following section I shall focus on the use of friendship in the establishment of colonies in North America and negotiating with peoples unfamiliar with European legal customs and constitutions of political societies. In the next, I shall consider the use of friendship in a qualitatively different setting, namely diplomatic exchanges with the rulers of India and the acceptance of a position of inferiority in existing hierarchies and organised political societies.

One of the key British instruments for encountering and negotiating with native peoples was friendship. This is not to say that other powers did not use this concept of European diplomacy. Although the evidence of the treaties concluded, for instance, during the first Spanish encounters is scarce, those extracts and letters that have survived provide a clue as to the ways in which the first explorers and settlers employed the concept of friendship. For instance, the extracts from a reported friendship treaty,[8] *paz y amistad*, concluded during the Magellan expedition with the 'kings of Moluccas' (1521), today an archipelago in Indonesia, appear to be very much in line with the ancient Roman convention of using friendship treaties, since the kings acknowledge their status as friends and servants of the Spanish king.[9] However, about a century later the English colonisation of America already provides abundant examples of friendship-making with native peoples, revealing functions of friendship that had by that time disappeared from the formal language of intra-European diplomacy. These functions included the legitimisation of subjection to the English king, securing peace with those tribes that could stand on equal terms with the settlers, and imposing the idea of contract and its sanctity on the native American peoples. The terminology and some of the metaphors of friendship that facilitated this process were clearly European in origin and carried specific ideas of subjection and obligation. However, translations into the languages and practices of the native peoples could not but take into account their traditions of 'diplomacy'. Therefore, the use of friendship and associated metaphors in early British encounters with native American peoples is key to understanding the sorts of values that were attached to friendship and the power relations to which it was tailored further.

Friendship in treaty's clothing
The rhetoric of friendship used in communications between native American tribes and the English colonists varied across the different political contexts in

---

[8] Below I shall use 'treaty' as a generic term that includes agreements, articles of agreements, minutes of negotiations and treaties *per se*.

[9] '*Convino en ser* amigo y servidor *del rey, dió cuatrocientas medidas de arroz, veinte cabras, veinte puercos, ciento y cincuenta gallinas dentro de ocho dias*', see *Colección de los viages* (1837: 296).

which the parties found themselves. It could well stress the appealing value of the relations designated by the concept. But what it illustrates most clearly is the contractual and political nature of relations labelled as friendship. The European colonisers chose to employ the concept of friendship to deliver abstract notions such as order, law, obligation and its binding force to cultures unfamiliar with European legal and diplomatic traditions. The political contexts in which friendships were made with native American tribes varied both geographically (across the North-East, West and South-East geographical regions of tribal habitation and Dutch, French and English colonial possessions) and historically throughout the seventeenth and eighteenth centuries (with the expansion of the English colonies, the demise of French power and changes in the native confederacies). Situations in which the appeal to friendship was made were highly varied, from the establishment of alliances on the basis of equality and those registering the subjected status of a native tribe, to multilateral and bilateral agreements, to the conclusion of new agreements and the renewal of old ones. However, most of these situations shared the basic purposes of concluded friendships: they are *political*, in the sense of seeking peace, making alliance and subjecting certain tribes; and *orderly*, in the sense of enacting legal regimes to secure commercial transactions and settlement.

The history of colonial encounters in America is probably as complex as any other case of colonisation not based solely on military conquest. The English settlements and colonial administration in the North-East, effectively running from the first half of the seventeenth century, pursued their business in a region encircled to the north and west by vast French colonies and rivalled inside by the Dutch colonists of New Netherland (its capital, New Amsterdam, was seized by the English in 1664 and the colony renamed New York, provoking the Second Anglo-Dutch War). This region also fell within the sphere of interest and habitation for tribes of varying degrees of power including the Cayuga, Mohawk, Oneida, Onondaga and Seneca tribes, known collectively as the Iroquois League. The Iroquois League increased its military might after receiving arms supplies from European traders during the so-called Beaver wars of the mid seventeenth century. All of these factors constitute background conditions to which the forms of friendship and accompanying rhetorical tropes had to be adjusted. Thus, by the mid seventeenth century, when the English colonists intensified their treaty-making, their tribal counterparts already had some knowledge of European diplomatic customs and language. In some of these cases, existing power structures and confederacies meant that the colonists were unable to impose conditions on tribes that outnumbered them, and had instead to seek mutually favourable and equal agreements; on other occasions, when the balance of power changed and the colonists prevailed over local tribes – for example, when the colony of Virginia prevailed over some neighbouring Sioux and Iroquois tribes and made them its tributaries in the second half of the seventeenth century – the rhetoric and metaphors of inequality were employed in full strength to record and legitimise such hierarchies.

Despite some familiarity with native and European diplomatic customs, scholars have observed that even the texts of later treaties were 'written as simply as possible' (Kvasnicka 1988: 198). This, however, does not mean the colonial negotiators did not use dubious formulations to temporarily satisfy local chiefs while leading in practice to major concessions of land to the colonists (e.g. the famous Walking Purchase of 1737 that gave Delaware land to Pennsylvania, or Onondaga leader Canasatego making a deal that granted 'half a continent' to Virginia in 1744; see Jennings 1985: 46). Whatever tactics and tricks the treaty negotiators tried to use, such 'simple' foreign terms as 'peace' and 'friendship' still had to have some moral and political appeal to the native Americans, and to correlate with their experiences and ideas of diplomatic conduct. Indeed, for many basic diplomatic terms, corresponding native American diplomatic practices and symbols were found: a tree or the smoking of a peace pipe for peace; a number of images such as 'one body' for unity; and a rope for alliance (Jennings et al. 1985: 121–122).[10] It is a commonplace nowadays to interpret friendships made with North American tribes, particularly in the form of a 'chain of friendship', as standing for bilateral and multilateral alliances (ibid.: 116). Making such friendships also corresponded to native American wampum-belt diplomacy, to which I shall turn below. As such, this correspondence facilitated the translation of European ideas of order and diplomacy into a new context, while the simplification and decoding of concepts necessarily required by any translation once again highlight their meaning in use.

The contractual and treaty-like nature of friendships that the colonists made with various American tribes is reflected in the language in which the agreements were expressed. Seventeenth-century documents made with American tribes often copy European diplomatic rhetoric by stating that they seek to have or continue 'feirme peace and settled frendship' (Treaty between the Narragansett tribe and Massachusetts and Connecticut colonies, 1675, in EAID, 19: Doc. 36, 440); that they declare friendship (the Mahicans confirming loyalty to Connecticut, 1678, ibid.: Doc. 59, 471); that they renew and continue ancient alliance and friendship (in a Dutch proposal of gifts to the 'River Indians' made in New Amsterdam in the presence of the Mohawks, 1647, EAID, 7: Doc. 30, 109). These formulas are already familiar to us from analysis of treaties made between European powers, but friendship and peace agreements with American

---

[10] Nancy L. Hagedorn emphasises the key role played by interpreters in negotiations between the English and the Iroquois. She shows that finding proper translations of the rhetoric and terms employed required a degree of learning on both sides and the ability of interpreters to find terms grasping the deeply metaphorical Indian language, implying the possibility of discrepancy between the selected terms and wider meaning of the Indian metaphors (1988: 61–65).

tribes are similar to some European treaties also in that they could be extended to include a third party: 'Included in this peace shall be all, not only the afore-mentioned tribes of savages, but also all others, who are in friendship with the Director-General [of New Netherland]' (art. 8 of the Treaty of Peace with the Esopus tribe, 1660; EAID, 7: Doc. 38, 223). In this respect, textual expressions make salient a connection between friendship and formal alliance, and between friendship and treaty, thereby imposing European ideas of order as the balance of power and alliances onto a new environment.

As I have noted throughout this book, such friendship of utility is conducive to appeals to the precious value of concluded friendships, and thus naturally is not free of complaints that follow any breaches of friendship. Agreements with American tribes are no exception to this rule. Concluded friendships could be used to justify certain types of conduct, to appeal to positively valued affections and to support accusatory arguments. Thus, both sides could express 'desire' for and 'will' to have 'frendshippe'.[11] Some of the most brutal massacres of native Americans were ordered under the pretext that they had disrespected the 'friend-ship and kindness which has continually been bestowed upon them'.[12] On other occasions following conflict incidents, the agreements reached and normalised relations were described as if nations were speaking in 'frindship' with each other.[13] In line with this rhetorical convention, the parties were demanded 'to show' their friendship, while any professed friendship could always be put on rhetorical trial. These and similar expressions emphasising the value of friendship were common throughout the early period of relations with American tribes.

As conflicts resulting from deception and treacherous conduct by one or both parties were frequent between the colonists and American tribes or between the rival tribes, so too were complaints over breaches of the terms of friendships so highly praised by the friends previously. In fact, the enumeration of injuries and even accusations against the other parties were quite customary in early agree-ments. For instance, the Mohawks in their recorded complaint (1660) about the insulting behaviour of the Dutch demanded that the latter be forbidden from roaming in the woods and molesting the Mohawks, as a condition for the latter not breaking the old friendship between the two (EAID, 7: Doc. 36, 218). Then, when renewing their recently made friendship with the Iroquois League and Virginia (July 1684), the Mohawks colourfully reproached three other members

---

[11] This is an example from the records of the Sachem (a chief) of the Pequot tribe seeking friendship, and hence help, from Massachusetts after incidents involving the Dutch and the Narragansett that caused casualties and – apparently more important – disturbed trade in 1634. See EAID (19: Doc. 2, 56–57).

[12] Such was the pretext of a reported massacre in the territory of New Netherland in February 1643; see EAID (7: 74).

[13] See a confirmation of the Covenant Chain by Iroquois representatives at Albany in 1677, EAID (4: Doc. 2, 271).

of the league – the Oneida, Onondaga and Cayuga nations: 'but ye are stupid and brutish, and have no Understanding, we must stamp Understanding into you' (EAID, 4: Doc. 17, 290). These agreements once again emphasise the conditionality of concluded friendships and the inevitable collapse of orderly commercial transactions and political relations when the conditions of the friendship are not satisfied, arousing the wrath and complaints of the parties.

The conditionality of friendship in relations with tribes in itself allows for conditions to be unevenly undertaken by the contracting parties; the diplomatic formulas do not always have to be symmetrical, as the parties' interests might often lie in achieving different goals (i.e. if I do A for you, you do B for me). In the practice of colonial relations this often meant that friendships were arrangements in which tribes consented to giving up lands and a subservient status in exchange for money, gifts, military aid and protection. Thus, the conditionality and contingency of the agreements help us recognise the ways in which political friendship brings about and fixes imperial hierarchies and colonial expansion. The conditions attached to concluded friendships sometimes plainly stipulated the subjection of one of the parties to the other; for example, a message from Massachusetts to the 'Sachem of Naamhok' (1675) reads: 'conclude with you: upon such meet termes And articles of friendship Amity [sic] and Subjection as were formerly made and concluded betweene the Englise and old Passaconaway your father and his sonns and people' (EAID, 19: Doc. 24, 433). This observation first and foremost concerned the so-called tributary tribes, which were obliged by treaties to be '*faithful* to her Majestys Government' and 'maintain a Strict Peace, friendship and amity with all her Majestys Subjects' (see art. 3 of the 1714 treaty between Virginia and the Nottoways in EAID, 4: Doc. 32, 217).[14] However, relations of subjection and submission based on strictly defined terms would perhaps have left little room for manoeuvre to allow the contracting parties to exploit the relationship to their own benefit had they not been open to appeal to extra-juridical terms. This type of rhetorical situation is not specific to the colonisation of the New World; we have already encountered such appeals in Roman history and early modern European politics and diplomacy. Similarly,

---

[14] See similar clauses in the 1677 treaty between Virginia, acting in the name of Charles II, and its tributary tribes, which first proclaims 'Mutual League and Amity' and then promises land and safety for tribes 'in amity' with the English king on condition that they 'keep and maintain their due Obedience and Subjection to His Majesty ... and Amity and Friendship towards the English', see EAID (4: Doc. 5, 83). A number of other documents indicate the protected status of the native American people in friendship with the English, and the extension of friendship to third parties with which the superior party makes new contracts. See, for example, the terms of the meeting between Virginia and Pennsylvania governors discussing friendship between their tributary tribes in 1721: 'settling a firm Peace and Friendship between our Indians and those under protection of that Government, and all the other Indians to the Southward in Alliance and Amity with them' (EAID, 4: Doc. 42, 337).

native American leaders attempted to mould relations by appealing to family ties between the superior and inferior party as between a father and his children, or simply to love, which is presented as an inherent part of the engagement and their submission to the English king. One such instance is a letter sent to Massachusetts by the Sachems of the Narragansett (1644):

> And the rather because we have subjected our selves … unto that famous and honourable government, of that Royall King Charles, and that state of Old-England … not doubting of the continuance of that former love that hath been betwixt you and us, but rather to have it increased hereby, *being subjects now (and that with joynt and voluntary consent) unto the same King and State your selves are.* (Force 1947: 93, Doc. 6)

Regardless of the ultimate goal of such rhetorical strategies, once the parties had mutually embarked on extra-juridical values, including activating the dimension of virtue in contracted friendships, they certainly amplified the legitimacy of the engagements, but at the same time also exposed them to a much wider spectrum of political challenges. Relations between the colonies and powerful tribes such as the Iroquois confederacy were harder to represent in terms of subjection, but they nevertheless also turned to thick symbolism to increase the legitimacy of concluded agreements. The choice of metaphors and symbols involved in this process provides us with exclusive insights not only into the nature of friendship but also the foundations of European legal and diplomatic practice.

Chains of friendship

A key concept and metaphor enacting the idea of law and political order in the history of relations between the English and native American tribes is the chain of friendship. Also known as the Covenant Chain, this was a name for a multilateral alliance between the Iroquois nations and their dependants on the one side and the English colonies on the other, thus covering vast areas of the American North-East (see Jennings 1985: 38). The great alliance was formed in the 1670s, and its significance for its members was reflected in the symbolic quality of the chain, which was proclaimed 'silver' in contrast to earlier alliances, which were iron or even rope-bound. The alliance helped English colonies to balance France's influence in the region of the Great Lakes and Mississippi valley and to control neighbouring tribes, while the Iroquois used it to expand their control over the large territories and tribes of the North-West. Regardless of the Iroquois failure to prevail over the French in the long run, examination of their agreements with the English is instructive for understanding the binding and political nature of friendship.

The governor of New York, Edmund Adros was, Francis Jennings maintains, the originator of the multilateral agreement with the Iroquois, most likely concluded in 1677 after New Netherland had been retaken from the Dutch in

1674 (Jennings 1984: 167). Sometimes the origin of 'the chain of friendship' with the Iroquois is attributed to the earlier 1613 Tawagonshi treaty with the Dutch, but the authenticity of this document has been convincingly disputed (see Gehring and Starna 2012).[15] I am, however, less concerned with the precise date of origin of this name than with the ways in which the idea of a binding law was delivered to and accepted by the contracting parties. The mythology of the forging of the chain of friendship/Covenant Chain seemingly formed much later than the original agreements and served the purpose of renewing and confirming past agreements. It is this myth and accompanying rhetoric that highlight the performative functions of the chain of friendship.

According to the myth, the Indians fastened the ship of the first English settlers to the shore, and thus was the first friendship treaty concluded. The content of the eighteenth-century agreements exhibits a peculiar use of friendship and the myth as such. However, one caveat is first due concerning a very special structure found in agreements with the native Americans. Such agreements consisted of proceedings that could last several weeks, and include the enumeration of the wrongs committed by the sides, along with apologies and proposals and discussion of them (*Documents* 1999: 9). Thus, sometimes these agreements are termed treaty events or treaty conferences rather than treaties in the usual sense. The 1722 treaty conferences during negotiations of a grand alliance between New York, Virginia, Pennsylvania, the Iroquois nations and other tribes offer a variety of uses for the chain of friendship. One of the chain's functions was to affirm, where possible, a political hierarchy in relations with the tribes. Thus, in his address to the Mahican nation, Governor William Burnet of New York made the following suggestion to renew the Covenant Chain (Albany, August 1722):

> … Which *Chain of Friendship* I am informed by the Inhabitants of this Place has been kept inviolable by your Ancestors from the first time that Christians settled here in this River & since you have always been *obedient children* & *observed the commands* of my Predecessors & been protected by this Government, I do assure you of the same Protection of the Great King, *so long as you prove obedient children.* (O'Callaghan 1855: 662; emphasis added)

The family metaphor used in this address reflects a specific hierarchical arrangement of roles in the colonial political order, in which the obedience of children was purchased in exchange for the protection of a stronger father. The metaphor was indeed widely circulated in the region even among the tribes (e.g. the

---

[15] Nevertheless, the practice of making friendships with the tribes was very familiar to the Dutch. In the 1640s–1650s, they effectively sought friendship from the more powerful Mohawk tribe and less powerful tribes in the immediate vicinity of New Netherland. Thus, appeals to 'friendship' and mentions of the 'chain' were recorded at their meetings with the Mohawks, though the appearance of the 'chain' might be due to the later English translation of the documents. See O'Callaghan (1848: 390–393).

Delaware were forced to call the Iroquois their 'uncles', thereby emphasising the latter's superiority, but at the same time accentuating a degree of independence for the former). The Iroquois, for instance, tried to avoid the role of children in relation to the colonial administration, particularly at their most powerful, and preferred for themselves the status of 'brethren'. But by the time of the Treaty of Utrecht (1713), the Europeans considered them subjects of Great Britain (see Jennings et al. 1985: 161–169).

In another case in 1722 of a sequence of treaty conferences, the five Iroquois nations, in reply to proposals put forward by Governor Alexander Spotswood of Virginia and aimed at setting the frontiers between Virginia's tributary tribes and the tributaries of the five nations, recapitulate one of the versions of the myth that highlights the binding function of political agreement (at Albany, September 1722):

> When the Christians first came here, they came in a great ship, & we were glad of their coming & fastened the Ship behind a great Tree & our business then was trading and Merchandize
>
> And considering the benefit thereof & that the Tree to which the Ship was fastn^d might rot, & so let the Ship go we carried the Anchor behind a great Mountain, that so we might keep it forever, and it was we that desired the Christians to come to settle among us & not they
>
> The third thing that was done by the Christians & our Ancestors, after they understood one an other was to enter into a Covenant of Friendship which they called the Covenant Chain & to the best of our Knowledge that Covenant has been kept by both parties from that time to this, And both our Ancestors were so prudent that they stipulated and agreed that if any bad accidents or mischeif should happen on either side it should be forgot & forgiven and not make a Breach in ye Covenant Chain. (O'Callaghan 1855: 671)

The use and sequence of particular terms can certainly be questioned in this case, as the tribes' reply was first interpreted into Dutch and then rendered into English, but the complex translation route cannot conceal the fact of covenanting/contracting and the particular emphasis on binding as chaining. The materiality, and thus reality, of the chain was emphasised in different ways: first it was rope that had to rot to be replaced with iron chain as a symbol of stronger relations; then the iron chain became rusty as a result of misconduct among friends; eventually even iron does not last and had to be replaced with silver to ensure solid relations; the chain may jingle when one party molests the other, or may need to be polished when damaged by conflict. However figuratively these 'physical' transformations are reflected in diplomatic rhetoric, they indicate that forged chains of friendship do bind political agents and that their weight does circumscribe action.

Further to this interpretation is the American Indian diplomatic tradition according to which every part of the agreement or important message was followed by an exchange of wampum belts.[16] Exchanging belts as special symbols after an important clause or message helped the abstract idea of a contract to become nearly physically binding for both parties.[17] This tradition persisted throughout seventeenth- and eighteenth-century relations with native American tribes. For instance, according to the minutes of the council of representatives of the six nations (the Tuscarora tribe became the sixth nation in the Iroquois League) and Virginia (4 July 1775), while ritually polishing the chain of friendship, the Virginian representative pronounced 'we deliver into their hands [the Delaware] this Belt of Friendship', which was followed by the actual delivery of 'a Large Belt representing the chain of Friendship' (*Documents* 1999: 21).[18]

Wampum diplomacy, with its belt-based mechanics of friendship, was not only the product of Iroquois culture, but also spread across the wider American East and was familiar to large tribes including the Cherokee and Creek. Thus, the chain of friendship figures in the treaty of alliance and commerce with the people of Cherokee (1730):

> the chain of friendship which is betwixt him and the Indians of the Cherokees, is like the sun which gives light, both here and upon the high mountains they inhabit, and which warms the hearts both of the Indians and the English. And as we see no spots in the sun, so there is no rust nor dirt on this chain: and as the Great King holds one end of it fastened to his breast, 'tis his intention that you should take up the other end of the chain, and fix it to the breast of Moytoy Telliquo, and to those of your wise men, your captains and your people, in such a manner that it may never be broke nor loosed. (Jenkinson 1785, II: 316)

Here the chain of friendship with a similar physicality ties together the British king and the Indian tribe in a peculiar political order that ascribes familial roles of father (to the king) and children (to the Cherokee). The binding function of friendship was occasionally further reinforced by a range of additional metaphors: diplomatic rhetoric suggested that the chain of friendship/Covenant Chain united parties into 'one Body and one Soul' and 'one People'. Thus, as links in the same chain, the tribes and colonies were supposed to turn into one

---

[16] Wampum belts are woven strings of cylindrical shell beads that may carry messages or denote important treaties. The larger the belt, the more important it is. Strings of beads or belts could also be used as presents.

[17] Hagedorn argues that in fact the passing of a wampum string could accompany each proposal or speech made at the meetings (1988: 66).

[18] Similarly, a century earlier, in 1675, Governor Andros of New York renewed friendship with the Delaware according to the same ritual. The minutes of that meeting described the exchange with the analogous expression 'the two belts shall be kept as bands of friendship between them', see EAID (7: Doc. 6, 360). Indeed, this type of communication mediated by material objects containing meaning, such as the wampum belt, offered a convenient vantage point for redefining diplomacy by looking at the actual 'practices' that produce meaning and constitute actors (Andersen and Neumann 2012: 473, 477).

body. As long as the parts constitute one body, it should be inconceivable for them to rebel against this body and its head's desires. This type of logic can be found in social contract theory and the constitution of the sovereign commonwealth in Hobbes's *Leviathan*. Certainly, the degree of political unity was much lower among the tribes, even if the colonists would have wished for greater subordination and obedience. Moreover, the hierarchy imposed by the chains implied subordination of the tribes only to a remote British king whose will cannot be known other than through his agents. Powerful tribes such as the Iroquois would always consider themselves brethren to the colonists; they were prepared to share the role of children with the colonial authorities, which should be equally obedient to the virtually present king, who thereby performed the role of arbiter between his children – who naturally argue from time to time.[19]

This metaphorical construction, in which friendship was one of the main constitutive principles enacting legal obligations, allowed the colonists to exercise a certain degree of control over the new territories, the acquired status of which remained rather precarious, to regulate commercial relations with the American natives and build a much desired, hierarchical political order. Thus, the explicit aim of the proposal voiced in the 1730 treaty with the Cherokee was to provide secure commerce and passage through territories inhabited by native Americans as well as to guarantee peace among the tribal people themselves. In J.G.A. Pocock's words, the colonists on entering the wilderness entered the state of nature (Pocock 2005: 152), and in this state of nature they found it expedient to employ an array of metaphors built around the chain of friendship as a means of affirming royal sovereignty and its inherent social and legal organisation. Dorothy Jones even maintains that treaties that dealt with matters such as 'acts and offices of friendship' were neither more nor less than 'conscious attempts to create out of the chaos of a warring "state of nature" a universe of intelligible discourse and predictable behaviour, of rights and responsibilities'. Meanwhile, tribal diplomatic rituals, shaped by ceremony, imagery and symbolism, helped to create a new state of affairs in the course of negotiations on the agreement (Jones 1988: 186–188).

Jones also points out that the Covenant Chain was a unique diplomatic instrument, rooted in the tradition of the wampum belt and employed pre-

---

[19] See, for instance, the 1744 grand treaty at Lancaster between Pennsylvania, Virginia, Maryland and the six nations, which the Iroquois saw as a success while in fact it led to them losing their dominant position among other tribes. In this treaty event both Canasatego, a speaker of the Indian nations, and the governor of Virginia and other commissioners all appealed to the chain of friendship and referred to 'one soul and one body'. Colonists and tribal nations alike were called 'brethren' in relation to each other, while in relation to the 'Great King of England' the Indian nations were represented as 'children' of their 'father'. Wampum belts were exchanged, as was traditional practice. See Van Doren and Boyd (1938: 43–50).

dominantly in relations with the League of Iroquois in the specific locale of the Middle Atlantic in the late seventeenth to late eighteenth centuries (ibid.: 186, 188). For the purpose of this book, however, this tradition is central, as it frames early colonial encounters with the most important tribes from North-East to South-East and highlights the nature of friendly engagements. The choice of the 'chain of friendship' metaphor and its constitutive terms is hardly accidental. In the absence of shared ideas of law in general and law among nations in particular, friendship is the most basic social and political engagement that parties could understand and embark on to render the regime of law operative. The image of the chain indeed reinforces the idea of friendly ties, but it also appears instrumental in showing the seriousness and solidness of the proposed relations, and also sits well with the native tradition of wampum-belt diplomacy and other ceremonies and imageries. This, however, does not mean that the chain metaphor originated from tribal culture to merge with the European concept of friendship. This is evident even from comparisons drawn by tribal representatives. For instance, a leader from the Creek (a large South-East tribe) in a speech from 1765 delivered his understanding of the chain metaphor: 'I observe that among the white People Friendship is compared to a chain which links people together … In our Nation friendship is compared to a Grape Vine' (quoted in ibid.: 187).

In fact, 'the chain of friendship' is likely to be a European invention that tells us more about European legal and diplomatic culture than it does about relations with the tribes to which it was contingently adapted. Indeed, it furthers the argument of this book by linking friendship more firmly to the idea of a political and legal contract and its binding nature. Thomas Hobbes in *Leviathan* (1651), written not much earlier than when the first chains of friendship were being forged between the English and the Iroquois, employs the chain metaphor to designate voluntary subjection to laws as a result of the institution of the commonwealth. In the critical chapter XXI he explains:

> But as men, for the attaining of peace, and conservation of themselves thereby, have made an artificial man, which we call a commonwealth; so also have they made *artificial chains* [*ita etiam vincula excogitarunt artificilia*], called civil laws, which they themselves, by *mutual covenants*, have fastened at one end, to the lips of that man, or assembly, to whom they have given the sovereign power; and at the other end to their own ears. These *bonds* [*vincula*], in their own nature but weak, may nevertheless be made to hold, by the danger, though not by the difficulty of breaking them. (Hobbes 1992: 147; emphasis added)

This is a striking correspondence in language, metaphors and purpose with the 'treaties' made with the American tribes. However, it is hardly accidental, for Hobbes himself envisioned America as a quasi state of nature (see Aravamudan 2009; Malcolm 2002: 75). And if something reminiscent of the Hobbesian social contract were to take place in reality, it was allegedly taking place in America when colonists and tribes, both at times exposed to hardships and insecurities, tried to bind each other in chains of friendship so that a political and legal order could be instituted and security offered. In fact, Hobbes's work also helps us to understand why the colonists used 'chain of friendship' and 'Covenant Chain' almost interchangeably in their treaties with the tribes. If for Hobbes a contract is a mutual and immediate transfer of rights, then a covenant is a promise to transfer rights in future, which as in all regular contracts imposes obligations and in which one or both parties are trusted to comply in the meantime (see chapter XIV of *Leviathan* for definitions of contract and covenant). Such politico-jurid-ical reasoning makes the interchangeable use of 'Covenant Chain' and 'chain of friendship' all the more intelligible, as it posits both terms and metaphors within the same conceptual framework of law, contract and obligation. Hobbes's for-mulations in *Leviathan* are not peculiar to his theory of social contract and state, but rather point towards an older and wider European legal tradition of inter-preting the concept of obligation, which is evident from his use of '*vinculum*' in the Latin version of *Leviathan* (on how the use of *vinculum* ties Hobbes to the debate over the distinction of *lex* and *ius* in European scholastic and juridical thought see Brett 2011: 83). It is from Roman law that generations of European jurists borrowed the understanding of obligation as a chain. The paradigmatic source of this understanding is *The Institutes of Justinian*, which defines obliga-tion as a tie or chain of law (*obligatio est iuris vinculum*) compelling a person to do some act (*Institutiones* III, XIII).[20]

Thus, while European legal circles debated the specific obligations owed by political friends to each other, the unique situation of the New World furthered colonial authorities and crown agents to use friendship as a means of activat-ing the foundational, but by nature metaphorical, legal idea of obligation. As we saw in previous chapters, Roman and later political and legal thought often included the idea of contracted friendships and the liabilities they generate. However, as the diplomatic systems and political regimes in which such ideas originally germinated came to maturity, the emphasis gradually shifted to praise the imagined or desired virtue of existing friendships, which as an alternative concept has also been available since time immemorial. Crises such as wars or radical transformations of the established system provide contingent opportu-nities to rhetorically re-describe the relations in which the agents previously engaged, by showing the contractual nature of the existing friendship and pos-sibly re-negotiating unfavourable terms. In this sense, the political situation in the New World was a kind of ideal type, for it offered a unique opportunity for diplomatic rhetoric to couple friendship with the ancient legal idea of

---

[20] Indeed, the term is central to Roman juridical and political thought. For instance, the cen-trality of *vinculum iuris* for Cicero's understanding of *res publica* (*De Re Publica* III, 43) has already been noted (see Kharkhordin 2010).

obligation-as-chain and to continuously highlight the liabilities of the parties bound by the chain.

Colonies and metropolis

Another condition that facilitated this association was demand for political friendship between rival colonies and attempts to conceptualise the relations between colonies and their respective metropolises. This demand is reflected in agreements concluded by colonies for the purposes of alliance and for producing political regimes of cooperation. Thus, the Articles of Confederation of the United Colonies of Massachusetts, New Plymouth, New Haven and Connecticut, establishing the alliance known as the United Colonies of New England (1643) and aimed at creating a system of collective defence against threats emanating from the Dutch and local tribes, declared that these colonies would 'enter into into [sic] a firme and perpetuall league of Frendship and amytie for offence and defence' (EAID, 19: Doc. 26, p. 152). This diplomatic expression is much more similar in style to conventions used in treaties between European powers. Nonetheless, it is also deviant, as it merges the concepts of league and friendship/amity in a very Roman fashion, and postulates the function of political friendship in pure and simple terms, namely 'offence and defence'. A later agreement with the Dutch not coincidentally shares the terminology of the Articles: 'Concerning the proposition of nearer union of friendship and amity betwixt the English and Dutch nation in these parts, especially against a common enemy, we judge [it] worthy of due and serious consideration' (Article of agreement between the United English Colonies and New Netherland, 1650, in O'Callaghan 1848: 154). A shared European diplomatic heritage, continual treaty-making between metropolises and the training of colonial officials help to explain the dissemination of key political terms and their norms of application in official language, even of different national origins, while the need to constantly adapt to the shifting balance of power and territorial order constituted a condition for a strong conceptual association between friendship and league/alliance.

It comes as no surprise that in the Articles of Confederation (1777) the American states proclaimed that they 'enter into a firm league of friendship with each other, for their common defence' (see *The Federalist* 2001, Art. III, p. 500). From that point and until the US Constitution came into force in 1789, the confederacy of the United States of America was practically held together by contracted friendship. The novel function that the league of friendship was assigned to perform in the context of grave conflict with Britain and the affirmation of the colonies' independence from the metropolis was to secure the liberty, trade and sovereignty of the United States. This is a key conceptual association of friendship with sovereignty and union that determined further American engagements with both local tribes and European powers. The eventual treaty of peace and friendship between the British king and the United States (1783) thus also recognised the sovereignty and independence of the US (Jenkinson 1785, III). The conceptual association is also central to an understanding of the nature of the 'league of friendship' or union created between the States. For upon realising how detrimental the sovereignty of the independent States could be to the future of the union, James Madison, one of the key supporters of the federalist stance, complained that the union was a mere treaty of amity, commerce and alliance, and advocated the adoption of the constitution. The union was considered a defective organisation even by comparison with the European system that the revolutionaries sought to supplant, and had to be replaced with a 'compound republic' (see Onuf and Onuf 1993: 124–129; Deudney 2007, in his analysis of the republican 'Philadelphian system', overlooks its origins in such a contract of friendship).

The examples above emphasise the centrality of friendship to the institution of the foundations of political order in the American continent. Making friendship thus facilitated orderly relations with the native Americans, the legal regimes that mediated transactions among colonists and natives, and the political alliances that were key to survival in an environment affected by the conflicting interests of colonial powers and powerful tribes. If such precarious political arrangements were deeply entrenched in networks of political friendships, it would be counter-intuitive to suppose that the metropolises were excluded from the very friendships that cemented the colonial structure – even though their relations with their colonies were regulated by charters and grants issued by the crowns rather than treaties concluded between two parties. And indeed they were not. However, their inclusion in such friendship was reflected in discourses of a different sort. The famous Charter granted to Sir Walter Raleigh by Elizabeth I in 1584 posits the early relations between the mother country and its colonies within the framework of friendly relations by setting the aim of 'uniting in more perfect league and amity' the 'Countreis, lands and territories' and the 'Realmes of Englande' (see *Charter to Sir Walter Raleigh*). However, further conceptualisations of such friendly relations are better explicated in political and legal theory of the period.

Given that the colonists were subjects of the crown and ventured to the New World by authorisation of the sovereign, the treaty could not be the appropriate framework for their friendship with the authority that had despatched them. At the very least, it could not be the same contractual friendship as with nations 'never met before' or with independent powers with which the terms of contract had to be re-negotiated for some reason. Therefore, their relations were conceived rather as a hierarchical political friendship of the type that we earlier saw in the works of More and Bodin. The primary function of such friendship is to cement a single political order within one hierarchically organised entity. Friendship was not aimed at legitimising simple subjection in this order; rather, legitimacy grew out of the reciprocity that implied allegiance in exchange for security, honours and other benefits. However, the recognition of supreme or sovereign power is also an essential issue that such friendship had to ensure.

Perhaps nowhere is the nature of this function better explicated than in Hobbes's *Leviathan*. Hobbes addresses the issue in chapter XXIV, which deals with the 'nutrition and procreation' of the commonwealth. He singles out two principal forms for relations with the metropolis, the watershed between the two being the possession of sovereignty, and hence status as a commonwealth:

> The Procreation, or Children of a Common-wealth, are those we call *Plantations*, or *Colonies*; which are numbers of men sent out from the Common-wealth ... to inhabit a Forraign Country, either formerly voyd of Inhabitants, or made voyd then, by warre. And when a Colony is setled, they are either a Common-wealth of themselves, discharged of their subjection to their Soveraign that sent them (as hath been done by many Common-wealths of antient time,) in which case the Common-wealth from which they went was called their Metropolis, or Mother, and requires no more of them, then Fathers require of the Children, whom they emancipate, and make free from their domestique government, which is Honour, and Friendship; or else they remain united to their Metropolis, as were the Colonies of the people of *Rome*; and then they are no Common-wealths themselves, but Provinces, and parts of the Common-wealth that sent them. So that the Right of Colonies (saving Honour, and League with their Metropolis,) dependeth wholly on their License, or Letters, by which their Soveraign authorised them to Plant. (Hobbes 1992: 175–176)

English colonies in North America did not perfectly fit one of these two ideal types. On the one hand, they had the authority granted by royal charter to dispose of their own business and territories, but on the other the subjects who received such charters were not thereby released from their allegiance to the crown or from their obligation to pay duties. However, as the political status of the colonies gradually evolved in the direction of the first type, Hobbes's account is instructive, as it emphasises the importance for the new commonwealths to show honour and friendship to their 'mother country' (on Hobbes's relationship to the Virginia Company and suspicion of merchants, see Malcolm 2002: 53–79). Comparing relations between the 'mother country' and its colonies with those between a father and his children also implies the symbolic superiority of the former much in line with the definition of a free people in the *Digest* (see chapter one), as *de jure* both are independent commonwealths.

A little more than a century later, the Hobbesian typology of colonial relations was reasserted in Thomas Reid's *Lectures on the rights and duties of states* (1766), although Reid emphasised that the second type better captured the contemporary practice of planting colonies, and thus privileged direct subordination over symbolic superiority:

> The Laws of Colonization in ancient and in Modern times very Different. In Ancient Times a Colony commonly became a new State and resembled a Child that

is foris familiate. So that no other Connection remained between them but that of alliance and Friendship … The Colonies conceived themselves obliged to regard the Honour & Interest of the State from which they sprung next to their own … In modern Times the manner of planting Colonies is quite different. A Colony planted abroad is still subject to the Mother Country they still enjoy all the rights of Subjects of the State. (Reid 2007: 159–160)

In application to British colonies in North America, this argument was later effectively disputed by the colonists and those sympathetic to the rights of colonies, while the symbolic power structure maintained by friendship and the family metaphor appeared a much more functional diplomatic instrument that the colonists eventually twisted to their own advantage. As we have already seen, the family metaphor proved instrumental in forging the chain of friendship with native American tribes. In that context, the king was represented as a father to both the tribes and the colonists, giving him authority to mediate conflicts and thereby 'polish' the chain of friendship. However, it produced a degree of confusion in the conceptual underpinnings of this tripartite political arrangement: while relations between colonists and the tribes were contractual and relations between the crown and the tribes could be interpreted analogously by virtue of the created chains, relations between the king and colonists evaded such an interpretation. Were such a perspective on colonial relations accepted, then the matter could have been simply solved by the sovereign enforcement of the king's will and licences. In reality, however, the colonists possessed a degree of political agency, and were in fact often the source of initiative in adopting policies vis-à-vis the American nations and other colonies (see Deudney 2007: 170). This led some authors to defend the first, contractual, perspective on relations between colonies and metropolis. The motivation to defend this perspective became particularly acute with the end of the war with France in 1763 and the imposition of new taxes on the colonies by the British Parliament as compensation for the costs it had incurred – that is, the events that led to the American Revolution.

Richard Bland made a strong case for a validity of the first perspective on colonialism in his defence of the rights of British subjects to be taxed by the authority of their representatives. He argued that the colonists lived under a regular government that ran its internal affairs independently, which practically made it a distinct state (Bland was primarily referring to Virginia) even though externally it was still united with England (Bland [1766] 1922: 20). This status, according to Bland, could have only been due to the original 'compact' between sovereign and subjects, who under the terms of this compact moved to a new country and established a new political society. He discovers this compact in the Charter granted to Sir Walter Raleigh, according to which 'the country was to be united to the Realm of England in perfect League and Amity, was to be within the

Allegiance of the Crown of England' (ibid.: 16).[21] This argument puts a radically different perspective on colonial relations to mere subordination of the colonists to the will of the sovereign. Now the colonies and the metropolis are found to have a special relationship originating from the contract of friendship. Whether the terms of friendship applied to the original institution of a new political society and distinct state, or to all subsequent relations between the 'child' and the 'mother country', was a matter of contingent contestation.

The American revolutionaries seemed to have preferred the opinion shared by Hobbes and Reid that a new political society was a distinct commonwealth and owed no more than honour and friendship to its country of origin. This is a move away from contractual obligation in friendship, which in theory can be legitimately enforced either by an appeal to a third party or by resorting to force. If the political friendship binding together two parties is dissociated from a contract, then its binding power can only originate from an appeal to virtue with its accompanying ideals. However, as I have already demonstrated, once political relations between the two parties are cast in terms of virtue, they immediately render themselves amenable to bitter reproaches and complaints with consequent re-description of the situation and legitimation of the cause of the allegedly offended party. Thomas Paine's rhetorical attack on British colonial policy epitomises such an opportunity, as he famously denounced the unfaithful and 'pretended' friendship of Britain, which in practice sought conquest and subjugation (Paine 1894a: ch. 'Of the Present Ability of America'; see chapter four). Similarly, the authority of the family metaphor is doomed to fail once the 'child' starts to rebel against the father. The state of dependency that this metaphor presupposes runs counter to the idea of liberty that other British subjects enjoyed, and for Americans largely meant slavery, as they were forced to live under laws enacted by others (see Pagden 1995: 135–136; for a detailed republican argument on the incompatibility of liberty and dependency see Pettit 2010; Skinner 1998). Paine and others fiercely accused King George III of 'parental abuse' and the vicious use of the idea of 'parent or mother country' against Americans (see Godbeer 2009: 146–148; Pagden 1995: 155), and with this republican argument undermined the legitimacy of the friendship that secured hierarchical relations. This is not to argue that, had friendship continued to be conceived in terms of contract, it would be harder for Americans to declare it void, for instance on the grounds of the crown's non-compliance with its terms. However, once talk about the contracted conditions of friendship is abandoned, opportunities to either normalise and depoliticise relations between polities by appeal to nature and virtue, or otherwise to criticise and denounce them by reference to the corruption of virtue, evade any rules of the game.

[21] See also Pocock (2005: 152) for a discussion of the effects of the wilderness or state of nature on the rights of Englishmen and their ability to generate civil sovereignty.

The US conceptual interception

While the revolt of Britain's American colonies rested on republican arguments and a consequent challenging of friendship with the metropolis, relations
between the colonies and their native American neighbours continued to employ
the same diplomatic rhetoric that had been practised since the forging of the first
chains of friendship in the seventeenth century between tribes, colonies and the
king. The newly founded United States saw potential threats to its security not
only from the British crown, but also from its allies on the American continent
(i.e. tribes such as the Iroquois confederation). Thus, the American States sought
to redirect loyalties in existing friendships solely towards themselves, or to forge
new chains.

One of the first attempts at such an agreement was the address to the six
Iroquois nations at the second Continental Congress on 13 July 1775 (see
Documents 1999: 13). The native Americans were exhorted to hold fast to their
'Covenant Chain'; to remain in peace with the colonists, in the light of the
conflict with 'Old England'; and a proposal was made to 'rekindle the council
fire, which [our] ancestors sat round in great friendship' (ibid.: 25–28). After
the proclamation of independence, Thomas Jefferson similarly advised the
Wyattanons and other Indian nations (June 1781) to 'hold fast the chain of
friendship which binds us together, keep it bright as the sun, and let them,
you and us, live together in perpetual love' (see Jefferson 1781).[22] The Iroquois
nations, anxious about colonial expansion, eventually remained loyal to the old
chains of friendship, and joined the British forces in war against the American
States. It proved a fatal decision in the long run, as it split the League, with the
Oneida and Tuscarora tribes siding with the Americans, and put an end to the
system of tributary relations with subordinated tribes (see Jennings 1985: 58).
In fact, the United States promptly filled the void of authority and became a
new power to which such tribes were soon chained. Following the Peace of Paris
(1783), under which Britain ceded to the US all territories south of the Great
Lakes, the defeated Iroquois were also forced to cede their lands to the US (the
chains of friendship between Britain and the Iroquois proved lasting, and the
defeated tribes were granted territories for habitation within British possessions
in Canada; see Willig 2008: 5, 17).

Therefore, the logic of the situation and existing tradition suggested that
it would be expedient for the US to seize control of 'the chain of friendship'
as a conceptual tool to erect its own political and territorial order. Thus, the
Delawares, who had previously considered the Iroquois their 'uncles', in 1778
negotiated a treaty with the Americans that also employed the metaphor of the

---

[22] In fact, the argument is sometimes made that the symbolism of chain and unity entered the
writings of colonists and lay at the basis of the identity of united colonies; see Johansen and
Grinde (1990): 'A New Chapter' (ch. 8).

chain, despite being considered the first treaty written in formal diplomatic and legal language (*Documents* 1999: 8, 12). The last article of this treaty proclaims:

> [art. 6] Whereas the enemies of the United States have endeavored ... to possess the Indians in general with an opinion, that it is the design of the States aforesaid, to extirpate the Indians and take possession of their country: to obviate such false suggestion ... to guarantee to the aforesaid nation of Delawares ... all their territorial rights ... as it hath been bounded by former treaties, as long as they the said Delaware nation shall abide by, and *hold fast the chain of friendship now entered into*.[23]

The treaty starts with the mutual forgiving of offences and cessation of hostilities, and a declaration of perpetual peace and friendship. However, in light of subsequent developments in treaty practice, it is worth drawing attention to a clause in the fifth article that renders the Delawares *dependent* on the United States for various provisions of war. The affirmation of this dependence became one of the main innovations in diplomatic rhetoric and the application of friendship. In treaties of the 1780s and 1790s, this clause was transformed into more explicit proclamations of US dominance. As noted by Robert Kvasnicka, treaties made during the revolution emphasised amity and alliance, while treaties made after the War of Independence merely extended US protection to the tribes (Kvasnicka 1988: 196). In this respect, the third article of a 1785 treaty with the Cherokees – 'do acknowledge all the Cherokees to be under the protection of the United States of America, and of no other sovereign whosoever' – represents a typical clause regarding the submission of a tribe to the power of the US.[24] Such early treaties commonly ended with promises to bury the hatchet and establish perpetual friendship (see, for instance, article 11 of the 1786 treaty with the Chickasaw nation). However, submission to the protection of the US soon became interlinked with proclamations of friendship. One of the first examples appears in article five of the treaty with the Shawnees (1786): 'The United States do grant peace to the Shawanoe nation, and do receive them into their friendship and protection.'[25] In making this linkage, the US in fact resurrected the old practice of colonial agreements with so-called tributary tribes of granting friendship together with protection.

After being used in the first political and legal agreements with indigenous

---

[23] Reproduced at the the Kappler Project of Oklahoma State University Library; source: Kappler (1904): http://digital.library.okstate.edu/kappler/vol2/treaties/del0003.htm. It is worth noting that, while appealing to the chain of friendship in the early revolutionary period, the Americans abandoned the metaphor after their victory over Britain and its allies and switched to more conventional European vocabulary.

[24] Kappler (1904): http://digital.library.okstate.edu/kappler/Vol2/treaties/che0008.htm; see also the Treaty of Peace and Friendship with the Creek nation, 1790.

[25] Kappler (1904): http://digital.library.okstate.edu/kappler/Vol2/treaties/sha0016.htm.

peoples, the concept of friendship slowly became one of the instruments that facilitated the recognition of supreme authority over certain territories and peoples, as well as the demarcation of the borders of the States. In this friendly setting the parties – that is, the union striving to affirm its sovereignty, and the tribes – obviously lacked parity in status and in the services they were able to provide each other. Therefore, the native peoples could only occupy an inferior position in unequal friendships with the United States. Thus, whereas the joining of the States into one union and their fight for independence from the metropolis were supported by republican arguments for liberty as the absence of dependency, on the other side of this coin we find treaties of friendship affirming the exact opposite as a condition of the existence of such a union.

The formulation mentioned above from the treaty with the Shawnees becomes a conventional formula in early nineteenth-century treaties, marking a further process of US expansion. In these treaties, friendship took the form of protection granted by the US, as postulated in, for example, the first article of the treaty between the United States and the Sac and Fox Indians (1804): 'The United States *receive* the United Sac and Fox tribes into their *friendship and protection*, and the said Tribes agree to consider themselves under the protection of The United States, and of no other Power whatsoever'[26] (emphasis added; see also the 1825 treaty with the Crow tribe and the 1825 treaty with the Makah tribe).

However, diplomatic convention did allow for slight variations in the enunciation of these effects. Proclamations of friendship and acknowledgements of US protection were sometimes separated into different articles. In some cases, treaties only postulated friendship and peace, and dealt with border disputes, trade and 'misconduct' by the parties. But the effect remained the same.

Tribal resistance to US expansion continued in the late eighteenth and nineteenth centuries, thus generating further conflicts and consequently treaties. The so-called Treaty of Greenville concluded between the United States and the Wyandot, Delaware and other Indians in 1795 without consultation with their former leaders the Iroquois (Jennings 1985: 59) happened to become the model treaty for subsequent practice. As such, it contained a further innovation in diplomatic convention, since it suggested that the terms of friendship *require* that 'the said Indian tribes do also cede to The United States the following pieces of land'.[27] Paradoxically, the compilers of treaty formulations did not hesitate to supply this and similar demands with proclamations of the sincerity of their friendship. As we have seen in European treaties, such a rhetorical move is anything but new in diplomacy. But it once again highlights the interplay of virtuous ideas and expediency/contract in relations of political friendship. The

---

[26] Ibid.: http://digital.library.okstate.edu/kappler/Vol2/treaties/sau0074.htm.
[27] Kappler (1904): http://digital.library.okstate.edu/kappler/Vol2/treaties/wya0039.htm.

latter component still had to be emphasised, even in the absence of the 'chain of friendship', by the use of legal jargon, that is, the verb 'bind':

> To confirm and perpetuate the *friendship*, which happily subsists between The United States and the Nations aforesaid, to manifest *the sincerity of that friendship*, and to settle arrangements mutually beneficial to the Parties … the following *Articles* are agreed to … shall be *binding* on them, and the respective Nations of Indians. (see the 1807 treaty between the United States and the Ottoway, Chippeway, Wyandotte and Pottawatamie Indians; emphasis added)[28]

Such American policies inaugurated by the confirmations of friendship, including treaties with clauses on protection, had important implications for US constitutional development. In 1830 the Cherokee nation, following the Indian Removal Act and President Andrew Jackson's policy of resettling the Cherokee, brought its grievances in a case against the State of Georgia and tried to argue for the status of a foreign nation; the US Supreme Court resolved that it should rather be defined as a 'denominated domestic dependent nation' since in treaties the Cherokee had acknowledged the protection of the US and admitted an exclusive right to trade with them. The Court further substantiated its decision by the lack of foreign recognition for the Cherokee, claiming that 'they and their country are considered by foreign nations, as well as by ourselves, as being so completely under the sovereignty and dominion of the United States' (The Cherokee Nation v. The State of Georgia, 30 U.S. 1, 1831).

From the 1820s and early 1830s onwards, most treaties with native peoples abandoned the use of friendship. By this time, the diplomatic concept of friendship seems to have fulfilled its contingently determined purpose. Together with other engagements and policies, the body of friendship treaties thus effectively deprived Indian nations of a number of freedoms and placed them into a state of dependency within the compound republic of American States. In many respects political friendship, represented by that concept that selectively accentuated elements of contract and virtue, facilitated the introduction of the principle of sovereignty by legitimising the hierarchical structure and supreme authority of the US government, its relationship to a fixed territory, and its prerogative to enact and enforce binding laws.

This is certainly a crucial framework for applying the concept of friendship, but by no means the only one. Discourses of friendship were prolific among the Americans, penetrating interpersonal relations and various civic associations (see Godbeer 2009). Thus, the diplomat Joel Barlow paradigmatically asserted to his fellow citizens that commercial intercourse and travelling 'would have a powerful

---

[28] Currently referred to as Ottawa, Chippewa, and Potawatomi. Various spellings of the latter are in use including Pottawatomie and Pottawattomie. For the source see ibid.: http://digital.library.okstate.edu/kappler/Vol2/treaties/ott0092.htm.

effect in ... inspiring that confidence and friendship so necessary to the political union' (1983: 1120). Commerce and independence, as we have seen, were also key motivations of the new republic in its 'external' relations with European powers. Therefore, the revolutionaries sought treaties of alliance and amity with European powers to put them on an equal footing vis-à-vis Britain and integrate them into a new system of balance of power (see Onuf and Onuf 1993: 104–113). However, this 'external' context constituted a qualitatively different framework of agents and policies; consequently, diplomatic rhetoric contingent upon this qualitative difference adapted the concept of friendship to securing the new set of values discussed in previous chapters.

Friendship and empire in India

Seeking friendship: the embassy of Sir Thomas Roe to the Mughal emperor
I shall now turn to another major chapter in the history of the British Empire – expansion in India. This chapter contains plenty of material illustrating how the British actively employed the rhetoric of friendship and friendship treaties to establish commercial ties, and eventually to institute imperial administration in the region. As was the case with expansion in America, this political-linguistic context highlights the utility of political friendship in establishing hierarchy, exercising power, instituting and circumscribing regimes of sovereignty, and eventually creating imperial machinery. However, this context is also instrumental for showing variation in the diplomatic use of friendship that reflects the encounter with established and powerful political societies familiar with European and Arabic diplomatic customs and capable of enforcing them, as well as the gradual change in power positions that led to the establishment of a new imperial pattern adapted to Indian circumstances.[29]

Regular English contacts with the 'East Indies' started in the early seventeenth century. Chronologically this coincided with English expansion in North America. However, the two processes were driven by different ideologies. Whereas colonists in America occupied 'vacant' lands and turned certain indigenous people into tributaries, in India English embassies and merchants encountered Hindu and Muslim cultures and 'developed' political societies. The Mughal Empire (1526–1761) was becoming more powerful and expanding across the Indian subcontinent when the first English embassies arrived to establish firmer diplomatic and commercial ties. As Charles Alexandrowicz emphasises, the Europeans were allowed to come and settle due to existing ancient

---

[29] Treaties concluded with indigenous peoples during nineteenth-century expansion in Africa are brilliantly analysed by Edward Keene (2007). British expansion in the Pacific did not produce a comparable body of friendship treaties. For a number of exceptions in this region see Devere (2014).

traditions of how foreigners should be treated (1967: 94–98). Thus, the aim of the early contacts of the European East India companies (British, Dutch and later French) was to ask for and negotiate with the emperors treaties and concessions that would permit the companies to establish a stronger foothold in the subcontinent. No such idea as planting new colonies in India was at stake. Expansion to this region was a commercially driven project that was meant to be facilitated by agreements on friendship or at least by the 'friendly' disposition of the hosting side. Thus, the Charter granted by Elizabeth I (1601) to merchants trading in the East Indies instructed them to trade with those who were in 'League and Amity' with Her Majesty (*Charters* 1773: 25). In 1609 the Charter granted by James I reiterated this provision. However, the treaties that would secure this status were not easy to negotiate with the Moghuls. Alexandrowicz suggests that the Moghuls' reluctance to conclude treaties with the Europeans could have been 'a manifestation of imperial superiority' over the Europeans, who managed to obtain only *firmans* ('permissions') and thus had to come to terms with their 'inferiority' (Alexandrowicz 1967: 93; see also Keene 2002: 79).[30]

Sir Thomas Roe's embassy to the court of the Moghul emperor in 1615–1619 illustrates an attempt to win favour in the form of a commercial and friendship treaty granting exclusive commercial rights to the English, and shows how rhetoric of friendship could be adapted to this cause.[31] On Roe's departure, King James I instructed him to explain to the emperor the curious nature of the conflict between England and Portugal in that part of the world: despite being in 'general league and amity' with the king of Spain, who reigned over Portugal at the time, the English were fighting the Portuguese because the latter had allegedly tried to deprive them of the right to conduct commerce in the East Indies. However, once the Portuguese encroachments had been repelled, the English did not intend to continue hostilities out of respect for their 'general amity' with that nation (Foster 1899: 552). James I's rhetoric indicates the contingency of existing friendships with other nations: while loose contract and peace are preferable, the advancement of commerce with the main economic player in the region should be the chief purpose of all political friendship.

Roe was also commissioned to convey the preliminaries of a treaty of friendship and commerce to Emperor Jahangir, who had previously by *firmans* granted to his subjects rights, 'Libertyes and Privileges for their peaceable Trade and Commerce'. In exchange for such favours to his merchants, James I expresses

---

[30] How reliable such legal instruments were is difficult to determine, but some were certainly not. As follows from Sir Thomas Roe's letters to the East India Company: 'Ordinary *firmans* not worth a halfpenny' (January 1616, *Calendar of State Papers* 1864: 453–457: www.british-history.ac.uk/report.aspx?compid=68784.

[31] Alexandrowicz (1967: 192) maintains that Roe, a graduate of Oxford, was in all likelihood familiar with the writings of Oxford Professor of Law Alberico Gentili, whose arguments on juridical friendship were analysed in chapter two.

the desire to 'correspond in the lyke Offices of Frendshippe' and for this purpose to agree upon the 'Maintaynance and Continuance of the Amity and Course of Merchandiz' and to 'compound and covenant … Articles, Covenants and Conditions'. At the end of the preliminaries, James I does not fail to mention the instruction for his subjects to abstain from injuring subjects of the king of Spain and other 'Confederats Frendes or Allyes' (Rymer VII, II, 206, 1615). All of this posits the discussion back to the framework of the contemporaneous debates held by Alberico Gentili and others on the duties of friends within the emerging legal regime of 'global' commerce. In such diplomatic messages we can see how the whole idea of friendly contract is tailored to the main purpose of promoting commerce. Thus, the much desired amity was aimed at securing certain commercial rights and privileges (e.g. protection of property) and eventually at winning concessions in the form of jurisdiction over sites of commercial settlement. English diplomats and the EIC were not in a position to demand or impose such amity. Therefore, the advancement of the cause required much time and diplomatic effort.

Roe's diplomatic correspondence while in residence in India further demonstrates how ideas of political friendship were intertwined with the logic of commerce. While his main concern was the port and factory in Surat, Roe also consulted the EIC on other issues and sources of profit. Thus, in 1616 he advised the EIC to explore opportunities for trade in the Red Sea in the company of the Gujarats, which would be 'the best securityes of our frendship' (Foster 1899: 348). Then, in a letter of 1619 to the governor of Mocha, he wrote: 'wheras entercourse and trafique is the Principall bond of Ametye, wee doe desier on our Parts to resort yearly to your Port, ther to trade in loue and frendship as honest Merchants' (ibid.: 515). Hence, for a diplomat in the region the security that flowed from established amity was inalienable from the growth of trade with local powers. However, Roe did not fail to notice how contingent such friendships were. The (in)stability of established friendship was not a matter of faith or sincerity, but a product of pragmatic calculation of various factors, including the emperor's peace or conflict with the Portuguese or the state of relationships with the Persians. Thus, in 1616 Roe lamented: 'The friendship we have here is fickle, the trade unsettled, one day a grant to us, the next to the Portugal, as they are false so they fear both, and would and will at last join with the strongest' (*Calendar of State Papers* 1864: January, p. 456).

While failing to conclude a commercial treaty with the emperor, Roe succeeded in soliciting letters of reply from the emperor to the English king (1618; see Alexandrowicz 1967: 196). In these letters the emperor confirms the reception of 'the lettre of frendship', thereby giving his own perspective on the English preliminaries. He informs the king that he has ordered his subjects to receive English merchants as subjects of a friend in safety in his dominion, and to grant them all liberties to trade together with protection. For further 'confirmation of our loue and frendship', however, the emperor wished that the king should command his merchants to bring 'rareties and rich goods' for his palace (Foster 1899: 557–560).[32] Thus, the concept of friendship proved instrumental to enacting a new legal regime for commercial intercourse with a mighty power. In fact, it was central to the diplomatic language that justified, described and legitimised such regime. Indeed, this language became an empirical condition for making possible conceptual innovations such as Adam Smith's intrinsic linkage of commerce and friendship. However, the concept as such resists any essentialist definition, since its application varied from expressing affection to an agent never met in person to designating a commercial agreement depending on the contingent circumstances of a particular case. Soon afterwards the EIC received permission to set up trading posts and factories along the Indian coast. Later in the seventeenth century it was also authorised to make political treaties, which gradually turned it into a powerful political agent affirming its rule over vast Indian territories.

Fighting the Marathas: friendship and subordination
During the eighteenth century, the power of the Mughal Empire evaporated in its conflict with the growing Maratha Confederacy, which emerged victorious to become the dominant power in the Indian subcontinent. In the second half of the eighteenth century, the Marathas were a confederacy of princedoms often driven by the conflicting interests of their leaders. This was a qualitatively different situation from initial British attempts to solicit commercial privileges from the mighty imperial court. The window of opportunity was now open for much broader action to expand British and EIC interests further into the continent. The result was the three Anglo-Maratha wars (1778–1782, 1803–1805 and 1817–1818), as well as wars with Mysore and other powers. These wars, which resulted in the establishment of British control over various princedoms and eventually the whole of India, were ended by a number of treaties that provided a new framework for the use of political friendship.

Many eighteenth-century friendship treaties were concluded on the basis of parity and sought to affirm EIC strongholds in key regions of expansion by displaying unity with local rulers. Thus, early EIC treaties with the rulers of Bengal, although meant to impose the Company's will, did not yet make use of friendship as an instrument legitimising its superiority, but rather represented the engagement as mutual assistance. For instance, the 1760 treaty with Meer Mahomed Cossim Khawn states that: (art. 3) 'Betwixt us and Meer Mahomed Cossim Khawn Bahader a firm friendship and union is established, his enemies are our enemies, and his friends are our friends' (Bolts 1772: appendix No. VIII).

---

[32] These letters certainly reflect the linguistic conventions and terminology available to a translator, but they also reflect the context and purposes for which the sender used the original synonymic expressions.

A nearly identical clause is contained in the 1765 Treaty of Allahabad between the Mughal emperor (albeit one reduced in power) and the EIC, granting the latter the right to collect taxes in Bengal and other provinces. In the treaty the parties undertook to establish and maintain sincere and reciprocal friendship as well as perpetual and universal peace and union (ibid.: No. XVII).

The concept of friendship was used to serve essentially different goals in the context of the Marathas wars. The rationale of its application changed to explicitly legitimise the political superiority and supreme power of the EIC and Great Britain. Even if this were contingent upon a changing balance of power and the EIC's foreign policy goals in India, after considering the American case and being mindful of the Roman intellectual heritage, we can see that the utility of friendship in this context was at least not novel, and possibly even conventional. However, the form of imperialism brought about and legitimised by friendship treaties differed from the political orders observed in North America. The treaty with the Nizam (1798), the treaty of friendship and alliance imposed on Mysore (1799) or the famous treaty with the peshwa of the Maratha Confederacy (1802) that provoked the Second Anglo-Maratha War all paved the way for the system of so-called subsidiary alliances that were at the centre of the British imperial project in India. Such engagements prescribed that the ruler of a particular state should maintain a portion of British troops in his territory and recognise the supremacy/'paramountcy' of the EIC, and in several other ways circumscribed his power to carry out an independent foreign policy.[33] This was not entirely new to the political history of India. Indeed, the British, as Keene suggested, 'plugged into' an existing structure of ideas about the Mughal Empire and affirmed the idea of their own 'paramountcy' (Keene 2002: 90–91). However, the role of friendship and treaties of friendship and alliance (as many of these engagements were entitled) in establishing this type of imperial regime is rarely recognised.

Friendship, in fact, was a key concept in the political vocabulary of expansion and indirect rule. At the end of the Anglo-Maratha wars, treaties of friendship and alliance were the legal instruments regulating the transfer of authority from princely states to the EIC and British government with respect to their foreign relations. In some cases these treaties were just formal registrations of an existing political setting, while in others they presented the superior party as kindly granting friendship. One such bold proclamation of superiority by means of a treaty of friendship is the Treaty of Friendship made between the EIC and the rajah of Karauli (formerly Kerowlee) in 1817:

> Art. II. The British Government *takes under its protection* the Dominions of the Rajah of Kerowlee.

---

[33] As Andrea Major has argued, this system diminished the political authority of princely states and led to the decline of their overall effectiveness (see Major 2011: 7–9).

> Art. III. The Rajah of Kerowlee *acknowledges the supremacy* of, and will cooperate with, the British Government for ever. (BFSP, vol. 5: 913; emphasis added)[34]

In light of my analysis of treaties made with native American nations, it is not difficult to notice parallels between tropes of diplomatic rhetoric employed during the same historical period. For instance, we can find a similar formulation in the US treaty with the Assiniboine Indians (1825):

> Art. II. It is admitted by the Assinaboin [sic] Tribe of Indians, that they reside within the territorial limits of The United States, *acknowledge their supremacy*, and claim their protection …
> Art. III. The United States *agree to receive* the Assinaboin [sic] Tribe of Indians *into their friendship, and under their protection*. (ibid., vol. 14: 1212; emphasis added)

The similarity of the formulations is striking given the different political contexts in which the two treaties were made. This, however, is an indication of how conventional treaties of friendship or contracted political friendship were as a diplomatic tool. Notwithstanding differences in the goals of North American and Indian treaties, political agents clearly found it expedient to employ friendship. The reasons for such choice may be different. The most obvious is the power of the diplomatic tradition, which determines the range of instruments for a particular foreign policy issue. In this case we once again encounter the old juridical approach to friendship. Another reason is that the term 'friendship' may be used to present the engagement in a commendable and accepted light to the contracting parties and their immediate audiences. In this case, however, we cannot but ask what makes it so important for the parties to appeal to friendship and related values and practices when there is an option for at least one of the parties to lose its position of power and independent voice on a number of issues related to its political identity. One explanation for many historical junctures is that parties reinforced their contracted relationship by appealing to a set of moral values and extra-contractual language. This explanation, however, implies a questionable degree of idealism and naïvety, given the available knowledge of past friendships and their not always fortunate implications, that agents should uphold in a highly pragmatic situation of political treaty.

A more plausible explanation for an 'imperial' context consists in a sense of reciprocation that parties sought to stress by inserting the term 'friendship' into the text of agreements. And this is indeed something that can increase the legitimacy of agreement: while the situation of a contracting party sometimes does not even include an option of rejecting a treaty (for it would incur deadly losses), the use of friendship may stress the intention of the superior party not to resort

---

[34] See also a range of other treaties with similar provisions concluded with Indian princely states in 1817–1818 in ibid. (vol. 5).

to further violence or other types of behaviour that would aggravate the condition of the inferior; the reciprocal intention of the inferior party would consist in complying in good faith with the conditions, even if they are detrimental to political liberties that it previously enjoyed. In other words, the use of friendship in this context seems to convey not so much the idea of emotional attachment or preferential disposition, but a reciprocal exchange of intentions and mutual compliance with negotiated terms, thereby rhetorically highlighting its contractual nature and its sources of legitimacy. Furthermore, the whole notion of a hierarchy might be effectively subsumed by the concept of friendship and slip away from sight in agents' self-representation in terms of friendship.

The terms of reciprocity, however, are contingent on the specifics of each case. The function of early nineteenth-century 'imperial' friendships in India was to limit the power of princely states in foreign policy, and to establish the indirect rule of the EIC.[35] Thus, the political system of subsidiary alliances was founded by treaties of friendship or friendship and alliance. For instance, the provision of troops for EIC-led operations could have been demanded by an appeal to existing friendship. The fifth point of an address to the rulers of Malwa and Sirhind (1809) prescribes that 'should an enemy approach from any quarter, for the purpose of conquering this Country, friendship and mutual interest *require* that the Chiefs join the British Army with their forces, and, exerting themselves in expelling the enemy, *act under discipline and obedience*' (BFSP, vol. 23: 1081; emphasis added). Friendships with the EIC involved other restrictions on the exercise of a key sovereign power – the making of war and peace. Militarily, this meant limitations on the contingents maintained by princes. Thus, the treaty with Lahore contains a common provision regulating this aspect of military powers: 'the Rajah will never maintain, in the Territory occupied by him and his Dependants ... more Troops than are necessary for the internal duties of that Territory' (Treaty with Runjit Singh, the Rajah of Lahore, 1809, ibid., vol. 1: 267). This provision was often accompanied by the requirement of friendship to provide free passage to British troops and companies through the lands and waters belonging to local rulers. Further, friendship treaties commonly emphasise that the British government would have no concern with the territories and subjects of local rulers. However, these treaties simultaneously delineate the borders of the territories and postulate that friendship requires that certain territories should be allocated to the British government or the EIC.

This division of authority became one of the foundations of indirect rule in India. To some extent, the instituted legal and political setting could be understood through the theory of 'divisible sovereignty', which, according to Keene, stems from Grotius and contradicts the theories elaborated by Bodin

---

[35] For the institutions of indirect rule, such as residency of the British officials within the local administrations, see Fisher (1984) and Alexandrowicz (1967: 202).

and Hobbes. Divisible sovereignty in this case could imply that the British acknowledged the sovereignty of local rulers in respect to their internal affairs, while retaining for themselves the rights to manage their foreign relations as well as preserving some important rights concerning commerce (see Keene 2002: 82, 90–93 and the whole of chapter three). But authority over the foreign relations and thus the 'relational' identity of the Indian princely states became the prerogative of the EIC and had to be legitimised using the concept of friendship.

In his study of international hierarchy, Edward Keene observes some of these elements in British treaties of the nineteenth century with African rulers. Those treaties generally aimed at securing territorial concessions and commercial privileges, but at the same time their provisions postulated that local peoples were brought under British protection. Keene points out that, in the early nineteenth century, the treaties with the Barbary States employed generous language of friendship and 'stressed the equality of contracting parties', but in just two decades the British were no longer accepting the competence of African rulers to make treaties. The change, Keene maintains, was related to a shift in the understanding of the difference between 'civilised' nations and 'barbarous' chiefs (see Keene 2007: 325–329). Although the denial of competence to make law could have been part of a strategy to construct an international hierarchy, the language of friendship and brotherhood, as argued above, did not necessarily preclude building an international hierarchy even before the exclusion from lawmaking took place. This perspective on friendship offers ways to resolve the contradiction that Keene seems to see between such language and the fact that local rulers came under British protection (see ibid.: 324–326). It suggests that appeals to friendship are taken not as a mere sentiment arising out of the proximity and parity of the involved parties, but rather as a repertoire of conventional expressions that could be used as effective tools for legitimating disparate relations and as limitations imposed on and undertaken by the inferior party. In this sense, what could have been seen as dictates and humiliation could in fact be represented as a strategy of saving face and generating legitimacy for concluded agreements.

In India, the context of the Anglo-Maratha wars and efforts to preclude anti-British alliances of subdued princely states can explain the British preoccupation with limiting the military capacity and foreign policy of these states. With these treaties Britain also sought to ensure the loyalty of princely states as a way to counter rival imperial interests in the subcontinent. In particular, northern Indian and Afghan states were conceived of as buffer states in the so-called Great Game played out in the region by the British and the Russian empires.[36]

---

[36] For such an account of British policies towards Afghanistan and the Russian reaction towards Khiva see *The Cambridge History of British Foreign Policy* (vol. II: 201–208), Gillard (1977: 20–27, 180–181) and Hyam (2002: 287).

In maintaining such a complex spatial geopolitical order of divided sovereignties, friendship was made to play another crucial role: circumscribed sovereignty in the sphere of foreign relations was reinforced and legitimised by means of friendships exclusive towards third parties. Contracted friendships were used to emphasise the identity of the foreign policy interests of the imperial power and Indian rulers, and thus their firm unity against the outside world. As in agreements with native American nations that employed the metaphor of the chain, British treaties with Indian princely states contained a number of performative speech acts invoking metaphors from outside the contractual framework and thereby producing a sense of particularly tight unity. These treaties do not necessarily imply a complete formal unification; neither do they mean that the parties share crucial norms, values and ideas that could indeed allow them to be conceived as one political community.

Thus, the Treaty of Perpetual and General Defensive Alliance with the Peshwa (1802), which provoked the Second Anglo-Maratha War, postulates that the friendship and union of these 'two states' ties them so closely together that they might be considered 'one and the same' (BFSP, vol. 4: 191). The 'one and the same' formula became a proliferating element in friendships between Great Britain and Indian princely states. By contrast, European powers in their friendly engagements hardly ever tried to accentuate so strongly the lack of difference between the parties. European agents could only afford themselves to claim brotherhood, unity and concord, while emphasising their distinct sovereign roles.

The rhetorical emphasis on unity had further performative implications for the proclaimed friendships. Making friendship with Great Britain in certain cases involved a total redefinition of the political reality of the counter-agents by stating who their friends and enemies were and what ought to be done with respect to them. The typical rhetorical formula for organising political reality according to the friend/enemy distinction is found in many treaties with Indian rulers, and is commonly worded as follows: 'the friends and enemies of either of the contracting parties shall be considered as the friends and enemies of both'. However, the Agreement made in 1798 between the powerful imam (sultan) of Muscat and the EIC as an attempt to strengthen British control over the Gulf of Oman and to protect India from alleged French and Russian ambitions, represents one of the most vivid exercises in friendly and orderly naming. Article II of the Agreement reads:

> From the recital of the said Nawab my heart has become disposed to an increase of the friendship with that State; from this day forth the friend of that Sirkar is the friend of this, and the friend of this Sirkar is to be the friend of that Sirkar, and the enemy of this to be the enemy of that. (*A Collection of Treaties, Engagements,* 1865: 209)

Rhetorically this is an exceptionally sumptuous formulation, but at the same time it evidently and elaborately demonstrates the mechanism of assigning the roles of friends and enemies upon entering a new relationship. By means of this rhetorical act, the imam agrees to conduct all his foreign policy through a resident British officer (see Mehr 1997: 39–40). The unification of the parties and the division of the world into friends and enemies is commonly reflected in subsequent treaty stipulations. The EIC and Great Britain as a rule agree to afford their protection to a local ruler, whereas the latter promises 'sole reliance on the protection of the British Government' and 'not to employ in his service any Foreigner … not to allow such Foreigner to reside within his Dominions without the permission of the British Government' (see the Treaty with the Colaba State, 1818; BFSP, vol. 12: 506). However, what seems even more important is that the Indian ruler assumes an obligation not to conclude any other treaties, and often relegates the right to communicate with other powers to his superior friend, that is, the EIC.[37]

The rhetoric of later British imperialism anticipated in a way Carl Schmitt's famous understanding of the political (Schmitt 1996). Schmitt's concept, defined by the antithesis of friendship and enmity, corresponds to the actual linguistic formulas employed in support of British imperial policies and for the structuring of the political space in the Indian subcontinent. However, such examples of the diplomatic rhetoric of friendship pertain to a particular historical and political juncture, and can by no means be universalised by extending these observations to other parts of the world. After all, friendship in India was employed to facilitate a type of imperial order different from that in North America. The vertical distribution of power and monopolisation of external relations by the metropolis was captured by Johan Galtung's theory of imperialism (Galtung 1971). In addition, further studies of imperial policies in India have also shown that British expansion was possibly due to local collaborators who, in exchange for their loyalty, often were granted autonomy in running internal affairs (see, for instance, Hyam 2002: 4–5; Johnson 2003: 29–31; Lieven 2001: 90; Strang 1996: 35–36).

As we saw earlier, this process was effectively mediated by the diplomatic rhetoric of friendship. However, in the seventeenth and eighteenth centuries in North America, appeals to friendship helped to build a system that bound together the 'peripheries' – that is, plantations, colonies and indigenous people – into one political order that deprived the centre of its monopoly on 'foreign' relations, even if technically these relations were not 'foreign'. Thus, the created ties of friendship or chains of friendship helped to produce an independent

---

[37] See, for example, the Treaty of Perpetual Friendship and Alliance with the Rajah of Mysore, 1799 (ibid., vol. 4: 177–178) and the Treaty of Friendship and Alliance with Nana Govind Row (ruler of Kalpi, in BFSP referred to as Kalpee), 1817 (ibid., vol. 5: 906).

polity that successfully challenged the authority of the centre. Despite the similarity of the terms employed in the diplomatic rhetoric of British expansion in these two remote parts of the world, they constituted distinct concepts of order, necessitated by different language games and different concerns with legitimacy that were contingent upon the respective political situations.

However, as the nineteenth-century empire did not expand for the sake of winning honour, but for the sake of intensifying commerce and multiplying profit, multiple friendship arrangements maintaining an imperial order were not aimed exclusively at the affirmation of sovereignty, securing territories, providing military help and appeasing 'war-prone' peoples. Friendship treaties concluded by the parties in that period dealt with the issues of sovereignty *and* commerce. If local rulers received protection, secured their authority and won other related advantages, the fruits of friendships for Great Britain included opening up the territories of those rulers for commerce and free passage. Hence, friendship treaties of the period contained concrete clauses on free trade, levying duties, principles of taxation, navigation rules, registration of commercial vessels and security for British merchants.[38] While friendship and commerce under the early system of indirect rule in India were often detrimental to foreign powers, British treaties of friendship and commerce with other independent nations were regulated by the 'most favoured nation' clause.[39] Both patterns, however, encapsulate generally overlooked convention in the use of friendship and the strong conceptual linkage between friendship and commerce advocated by Adam Smith.

[38] For a good illustration of this thesis see, for instance, the treaty between the EIC and Nawab Mahommad Bahawal Khan of Bahawalpur, 1833, creating a 'subsidiary' alliance with this princely state, which emerged after the collapse of the Afghan Durrani Empire. The first article of this treaty proclaimed 'eternal friendship and alliance'; then the authority of the nawab was confirmed in regard to his internal affairs; while articles 5–16 regulated various commercial rights and issues; the treaty concluded (art. 16) by stating that the articles concerning authority and commerce will 'form an everlasting bond of friendship between the 2 States' (BFSP, vol. 22: 1177–1178).

[39] See, for instance, the clauses of the Treaty of Friendship and Commerce between Great Britain and Borneo, 1847 (ibid., vol. 35: 14–17), or friendship treaties with South American states such as Columbia 1825, the United Provinces of Rio de la Plata 1825, the United States of Mexico 1826 and Brazil 1827, in ibid. (vols. 12 and 14).

Conclusion

Today any serious discussion of friendship between states or nations aims to show that international politics can be arranged differently, or perhaps that it is already different if viewed not in terms of power-maximisation, economic self-interest, military rivalry and conflict, but rather from the perspective of friendship bringing together networks of people, individual organisations, cities, regions and states. This benign effect of friendship is what prompts us to think of ways to extrapolate it to relations between states in order to remove obstacles and anxieties and create unprecedented levels of social, democratic and cooperative international organisation. Such a motive was behind the recent revival of interest in friendship among IR theorists. This interest, however, grew against the background of a sceptical/realist view that denies the reality for true and sincere friendship between states and nations since states are inherently egoistic and are mainly concerned with their own interest and security. This genealogical study of the concept of friendship has demonstrated that the opposition of ethical/moralist and sceptical/realist perspectives is a product of 'the social construction' of knowledge. The construction can be traced back to early modern theoretical, and hence rhetorical, debate over the principles upon which relations among sovereign polities in international society are built. Making a successful and convincing contribution to the debate required re-describing the concept of friendship in naturalistic and ethical terms. Thenceforth, the naturalistic and ethical concept of friendship established itself as dominant and effectively foreclosed theoretical reflection on its alternatives.

This genealogical investigation into the history of friendship has offered a number of critical insights into the constructivist understanding of knowledge, international society, rules and law. Highlighting the role of power in the construction of contemporary knowledge about friendship also helps us uncover the alternatives, that is, concepts discarded in theoretical debates and the now-overlooked practices of international friendship that had been previously captured by the concept. The recovery of the lost concept can move IR debates beyond the opposition of normative and sceptical understandings of friendship by showing that there can be more than one concept of friendship. The recovered alternative is of critical importance to IR scholarship as it uncovers one of the popular diplomatic means to maintain equal and unequal relations, build political and social hierarchies, and preserve status asymmetries in international politics. To understand the ways these practices are shared and legitimised is to understand the modern international society beyond its formal institutional façade.

The recovery of the alternative concept expands our conceptualisation of the role of friends in international politics in yet another aspect. Up until now the conceptualisation, and particularly attempts to theorise the 'Kantian' tradition of international political culture, revolved around the Aristotelian concept of *virtuous friendship*, also referred to as *true* or *genuine* friendship. This genealogical history of friendship reconstitutes another type of friendship that Aristotle saw as being legitimately practised in politics, namely the *friendship of utility*. With the reconstruction of the Roman political and legal concept and its early modern reception IR theory acquires an alternative concept of political friendship. This concept of international friendship exhibits contractual elements and captures motives of utility, power and status that friends might have. As such, this concept renders meaningless the sceptical argument and, more importantly, makes intelligible power politics within the complex of contracted socio-political relationships. Thus, equipped with this concept students of IR can pursue a novel avenue in empirical research on particular cases of friendship among nations.

This study has shown that such a concept is not a matter of philosophical speculation but was a widespread linguistic and diplomatic practice, the residual elements of which can still be discovered in the field of treaty-making. The genealogical investigation had to identify the discarded perspectives and peripheries of political practice to show in which regimes and formative junctures the concept was most actively utilised. Going beyond the canonical figures of international political thought helped us see that friendship can boast an outstanding record in the history of international politics: until the seventeenth and eighteenth centuries it was employed in political, juridical and diplomatic discourse to designate a political, negotiated and contracted relationship binding two or more parties. Classical and early modern sources in the history of 'international' encounters indicate that entering relations of friendship could entail a number of further obligations, with varying degrees of formality, pertaining to the provision of succour in alliance-related engagements, to the protection or subjection of weaker parties, to promises of safe entry for merchants and their goods and many other practical issues that polities have to arrange when launching or restoring relations. Only as such political and contingent relationships could friendship be part and parcel of diplomatic discourse, even if moralists did not always dare marvel at what the corresponding diplomatic practice involved. If recognised as a practical element of the international order, friendship could in fact claim its place among the institutions of early modern European international society, because ideas of the individuality of polities, sovereign state and empire were often predicated on political friendship.

As this book has sought to demonstrate, the uncovered concept of political friendship may contribute to the debates on international law. Nicholas Onuf (2012) and Friedrich Kratochwil (2014) recently drew attention to law as a performative language game. In this study of friendship in diplomacy, and particularly in historical, geographical and political junctures devoid of accepted rules and laws, we saw how friendship was frequently used to work out the idea of obligation that would be shared by parties to friendly relations. Attempts to oblige, to make rule-following normative and the relations binding, were all parts of the diplomatic rhetoric of friendship. The more peripheral geographically or historically such diplomatic instances are, the more overt and obvious such functions of friendly rhetoric become. Thus, it is hard to overestimate the role political friendship played in language games corresponding to the institution of international commerce or imperial and statist forms. The recognition of such language games can give us cues for interpretation of novelties and transformations in contemporary doctrines of international law.

In making rule-following normative, political actors were keen to capitalise on an alternative ancient concept of 'ethical' and highly moralised friendship, especially when legal and political arrangements were disturbed and the window of rhetorical opportunity was open. Until early modernity, two distinct concepts of political friendship – 'ethical' and 'contractual' – were available in discourse about 'international' relations, but they could be interchanged and intertwined for the purpose of specific political and legal arguments. The interplay of these perspectives in diplomacy is what the use of the Aristotelian 'friendship of utility' can unravel. As a result of conceptual change necessitated by the intellectual debates on the state of nature, these diplomatic and international practices were gradually lost from our focus.

In recovering the lost perspective on political and contractual friendship, this study has focused on past diplomatic customs and examples of juridical glosses. On these grounds it may be deemed positivistic, and thus conservative, because it speaks from the perspective of the past international political order and its practices, whereas contemporary normative theorising on friendship, as its opposite, may represent a reformist argument reflecting developing standards of international morality. However, the aim of writing effective, genealogical history consists not in reproducing past practices but rather in reconstructing means to conceptualise neglected political practices and showing how currently prevailing perspectives are informed by past political choices so that we preserve opportunities to account for heterogeneity of friendship and interrogate those forms that might appear marginal and strange. Thus, the main aim of the approach pursued in this study was in questioning all assumptions of the natural essence of friendship and friendship as a natural spring of affection, while highlighting aspects of power in contracted relations such as international recognition or the launch of certain institutions and practices.

Finally, this study has raised a number of methodological issues concerning the object of analysis and the degree of contextualism and genealogy that such research can afford to remain relevant to contemporary debates about international politics. The problems that IR students usually experience with contextualism relate to the scope of questions that can be raised in a detailed contextualist reading of particular debates and periods. If one were interested in the origins and legitimacy of a particular international institution, IR theory would expect something more analytically abstract and longitudinal than a nuanced analysis of specific arguments made by a few contemporaneous authors in the distant past. In assembling a number of discursive episodes in this study, I have made an attempt to combine contextualist analysis with a diachronic perspective on conceptual usage and change. Certainly, this combination could not have been achieved at no cost to both components. Nevertheless, it demonstrates that contextualism and conceptual history can effectively address questions pertaining to IR and international political theory.

As a contribution to the field of history of concepts, this study offers an insight for the understanding of rhetorical re-description of concepts. Re-description normally implies a conscious attempt by an actor to use a rhetorical technique, for example *paradiastole*, to change the meaning or application of a concept to gain a political advantage. This study has shown that understanding conceptual change, which takes place across different contexts, may also require studying the argumentative contexts in which the concept is not the main target of intentional re-description, but rather is a part of a package of ongoing conceptual changes. Thus, the change in the concept of friendship was predicated on seventeenth- and eighteenth-century debates on the nature of the state, the state of nature and human society. Last but not least, studying conceptual change across contexts may also require attention being paid to incremental changes in the use of relevant terms in less personalised and routinised contexts, such as the corpus of legal documents – something that is not always done in contextualist research.

In no way have I wished to argue in this book that the recovered contractual perspective on political friendship is *the* missing perspective or the only way forward in studies of friendship. Following the Weberian understanding of objectivity as the recognition of perspectivism in one's own research (Weber 2004), this study offers just one possible perspective, while many others still await discovery. For instance, it remains to be explained how far the ideology of internationalism propelled by the Soviet Union, which was also the chief advocate of friendship among peoples, transformed or discredited the idea of international friendship; whether friendship is a discriminatory institution and whether the rhetoric of friendship among many without foundations, as sought in Jacques Derrida's *Politics of Friendship* (1997), would be meaningful in the realm of international politics; and whether friendship was instrumental only in installing various institutions of the modern international system, whereas its role in 'post-modern' world politics may be circumscribed. Finally, this study does not claim that the understanding of friendship as a contingent, negotiated and contracted engagement is a more adequate means of grasping the contemporary practices which condition the international order than the moralist understanding. However, based on the assumption of its unquestionable value, emotional dynamics and moral codes, it can contribute to normative debates about international friendship the idea that the prospects of such relations may be forged out of the originally pragmatic contracts from which contracting parties sought mutual advantage.

Bibliography

Documents

A Collection of Treaties, Engagements and Sunnuds Relating to India and Neighbouring Countries. 1865. Compiled by C.U. Aitchison. Vol. VII. Calcutta: Military Orphan Press.

An Ordinance of the Lords and Commons. 30 August 1644. London: Printed for John Wright in the Old-baily. Available at EEBO.

Bolts, William. 1772. *Considerations on India Affairs; Particularly Respecting the Present State of Bengal and Its Dependencies. To which is Prefixed a Map of Those Countries, Chiefly From Actual Surveys.* 2nd ed. London: Printed for J. Almon in Piccadilly, P. Elmsly in the Strand and Brotherton and Sewell in Cornhill.

British and Foreign State Papers. London: H.M.S.O, 1839–1861. Vols 1–36.

Calendar of State Papers, Colonial Series, East Indies, Vol. 2, edited by W.N. Sainsbury. London: Longmans, H.M.S.O., 1864. Available at www.british-history.ac.uk/source.aspx?pubid=759 (accessed on 31 July 2017).

Charter to Sir Walter Raleigh. 1584. Elizabeth I. Available at the Avalon Project website: http://avalon.law.yale.edu/16th_century/raleigh.asp (accessed on 31 July 2017).

Charters granted to the East-India Company, from 1601; Also the Treaties and Grants, made with, or Obtained from, the Princes and Powers in India, from the year 1756 to 1772. London, 1773.

Colección de los viages y descubrimientos, que hicieron por mar los españoles desde fines del siglo XV, con varios documentos inéditos concernientes á la historia de la marina castellana y de los establecimientos españoles en Indias. Coordinada é illustrada por D. Martín Fernández de Navarrete. Vol. IV 'Expediciones al Maluco: Viage de Magallanes y de Elcano'. Madrid en la Imprenta Nacíonal, 1837.

Davenport, Frances Gardiner (ed.). 1917. *European Treaties bearing on the History of the United States and its Dependencies.* Vol. I. Washington, DC: The Carnegie Institution of Washington, Gloucester, MA: P. Smith.

Die Westfälischen Friedensverträge vom 24. Oktober 1648. Texte und Übersetzungen (*Acta Pacis Westphalicae. Supplementa electronica,* 1). Available at www.pax-westphalica.de/ (accessed on 31 July 2017).

Documents of American Indian Diplomacy: Treaties, Agreements and Conventions, 1775–1979. 1999. Compiled by Vine Deloria, Jr, and Raymond J. DeMallie; with a foreword by D. Inouye. Vol. I. Norman: University of Oklahoma Press.

Early American Indian Documents: Treaties and Laws, 1607–1789. 1979. (Gen. ed.) Alden T. Vaughan. Vol. IV 'Virginia Treaties, 1607–1722'. (ed.) W. Stitt Robinson. Washington, DC: University Publications of America.

Early American Indian Documents: Treaties and Laws, 1607–1789. 1979. (Gen. ed.) Alden T. Vaughan. Vol. VII 'New York and New Jersey Treaties, 1609–1682'. (ed.) Barbara Graymont. Washington, DC: University Publications of America.

Early American Indian Documents: Treaties and Laws, 1607–1789. 1979. (Gen. ed.) Alden T. Vaughan. Vol. XIX 'New England Treaties, Southeast, 1524–1761'. (ed.) Daniel R. Mandell. Washington, DC: University Publications of America.

Edict. James I. 23 June 1603. Imprinted at London by Robert Baker. Available at EEBO.

Fontes Historiae Iuris Gentium. Sources Relating to the History of the Law of Nations. 1995. (ed.) Wilhelm G. Grewe. Berlin and New York: Walter de Gruyter.

Force, Peter (collect.). 1947. *Tracts and Other Papers, Relating Principally to the Origin, Settlement, and Progress of the Colonies in North America, from the Discovery of the Country to the Year 1776.* Vol. IV. New York: Peter Smith.

Foster, William (ed.). *The Embassy of Sir Thomas Roe to the court of the Great Mogul, 1615–1619, as narrated in his journal and correspondence.* Vol. II. London: The Hakluyt Society, 1899.

Jenkinson, Charles. 1785. *A Collection of all the Treaties of Peace, Alliance, and Commerce, between Great-Britain and Other Powers, From the Treaty signed at Munster in 1648, to the Treaties signed at Paris 1783.* 3 vols. London.

Kappler, Charles J. *Indian Affairs: Laws and Treaties.* 1904. Vol. II (Treaties) in part. Compiled and edited by Charles J. Kappler. Washington: Government Printing Office. Available at 'The Kappler project' of Oklahoma State University Library website: http://digital.library.okstate.edu/kappler/Vol2/Toc.htm (accessed on 31 July 2017).

O'Callaghan, E.B. 1848. *History of New Netherland; or New York under the Dutch.* Vol. 2. New York: Bartlett and Welford.

O'Callaghan, E.B. (ed.). 1855. *Documents Relative to the Colonial History of the State of New York.* Vol. 5. Albany, NY: Weed, Parsons and Co.

Rymer, Thomas. *Fœdera, conventiones, literæ, et cujuscunque generis acta publica, inter reges Angliæ, et alios quosvis imperatores, reges, pontifices, principes, vel communitates ab ineunte sæculo duodecimo.* 1967. (ed.) R. Sanderson. 10 vols. Farnborough (Hants): Gregg Press.

The Cherokee Nation v. The State of Georgia, 30 U.S. 1, 1831. Available at the FindLaw website: http://caselaw.lp.findlaw.com/scripts/getcase.pl?court=US&vol=30&invol=1 (accessed on 31 July 2017).

The Peace of Augsburg. 1555. Available at the Internet-Portal 'Westfälische Geschichte': www.lwl.org/westfaelische-geschichte/portal/Internet/finde/langDatensatz. php?urlID=739&url_tabelle=tab_quelle (accessed on 31 July 2017).

The Statuses at Large, From Magna Charta, to the End of the Reign of the King Henry the Sixth. 1763. (ed.) Owen Ruffhead. Vol. I. London: Mark Basket.

Treaties, Conventions, International Acts, Protocols and Agreements between the United States and Other Powers, 1776–1909. 3 vols. Washington: Government Printing Office, 1910–1923.

Vneshnyaya Politika. 1946. Vneshnyaya Politika SSSR. Sbornik Dokumentov. (Foreign Policy of the USSR. A Collection of Documents.) Vol. IV (1935–Iyun' 1941). (ed.) S.A. Lozovskii. Moskva.

Primary sources

Agathius Myrinaeus. 1967. Agathiae Myrinaei Historiarum Libri Quinque. In R. Keydell (ed.) *Corpus Fontium Historiae Byzantinae*. Vol. II. Washington: Trustees for Harvard University.

Anderson, Adam. 1787. *An Historical and Chronological Deduction of the Origin of Commerce From the Earliest Accounts, Containing an History of the Great Commercial Interests of the British Empire*. Vol. II. London.

Andocides. 1968. On the Peace with Sparta. In *Minor Attic Orators*. Vol. I. Translated by Maidment KJ. London: William Heinemann Ltd and Cambridge, MA: Harvard University Press.

Aristotle. 1947. The Nicomachean Ethics. In *Aristotle in Twenty-three Volumes*. Vol. XIX. With an English translation by H. Rackham. Cambridge, MA and London: Harvard University Press (The Loeb Classical Library), William Heinemann Ltd (repr. 1982).

Aristotle. 1984. *The Complete Works of Aristotle. The Revised Oxford Translation*. (ed.) Jonathan Barnes. Vol. II. Princeton, NJ: Princeton University Press.

Ascham, Roger. 1904. *English Works*. (ed.) William A. Wright. Cambridge: University Press.

Augustine. 2002. *The City of God against the Pagans*. Edited and translated. by R.W. Dyson. 1st publ 1998. Cambridge: Cambridge University Press. Latin original is available at the Latin Library: www.thelatinlibrary.com/august.html (accessed on 9 May 2017).

Augustus. *Res Gestae Divi Augusti*. Available at the Latin Library website: www.thelatin-library.com/resgestae.html#32 (accessed on 23 October 2013).

Ayala, Balthazar. 1912. *De Jure et Officiis Bellicis et Disciplina Militari Libri III*. (ed.) J. Westlake. Vol. I. 1582 1st ed. Washington, DC: Carnegie Institution of Washington.

Bacon, Francis. 1964. *Bacon's Essays*. (ed.) J.M. McNeill. London: Macmillan.

Bacon, Francis. 1969. *The Elements of the Common Lawes of England*. Amsterdam and New York: Theatrum Orbis Terrarum Ltd, Da Capo Press. Available at the Constitution Society Home Page: www.constitution.org/bacon/ecle.htm (accessed on 23 October 2013).

Bacon, Francis. 1998. The History of the Reign of King Henry the Eighth. In Brian Vickers (ed.) *The History of the Reign of King Henry VII and Selected Works*. Cambridge: Cambridge University Press, pp. 221–222.

Barclay, John. 1631. *The Mirror of Minds: Icon Animorum*. London: John Norton.

Barlow, Joel. 1983. To His Fellow Citizens of the United States. Letter II: On Certain Political Measures Proposed to Their Consideration (1801). In Charles S. Hyneman and Donald Lutz (eds) *American Political Writing During the Founding Era: 1760–1805*. Vol. 2. Indianapolis, IN: Liberty Fund, pp. 1099–1125.

Beacon, Richard. 1996. Solon *His Follie, or a Politique Discourse Touching the Reformation of Common-weales Conquered, Declined or Corrupted*. (eds) Clare Caroll and Vincent Carey. Binghamton, NY: Medieval & Renaissance Texts & Studies.

Belli, Pierino. 1936a. *De Re Militari et Bello Tractatus*. Vol. I 'A Photographic Reproduction of the Edition of 1563'. Oxford: The Clarendon Press and London: Humphrey Milford.

Belli, Pierino. 1936b. *A Treatise on Military Matters and Warfare, In Eleven Parts*. Vol. II. Translation by Herbert C. Nutting. Oxford: The Clarendon Press and London: Humphrey Milford.

Bethel, Slingsby. 1681. *The Interest of the Princes and States of Europe*, 2nd ed. with additions, London.

Blackstone, William and Tucker, George. 1996. *William Blackstone's Commentaries: with Notes of Reference, to the Constitution and Laws, of the Federal Government of the United States; and of the Commonwealth of Virginia. In five volumes. By George Tucker.* Originally published in Philadelphia, 1803. With an Introduction by P. Finkelman and D. Cobin. Vol. V. Union: The Lawbook Exchange, Ltd.

Bland, Richard. 1922. *An Inquiry into the Right of the British Colonies*. (ed.) Earl Gregg Swem. Richmond: The William Parks Club.

Bodin, Jean. 1962. *The Six Bookes of a Commonweale. A Facsimile reprint of the English translation of 1606, Corrected and supplemented in the light of a new comparison with the French and Latin texts.* (ed.) Kenneth Douglas McRae. Cambridge, MA: Harvard University Press.

Bodin, Jean. 1986. *Les Six Livres de la République*. Livre Cinquième. (eds) Ch. Frémont, M.-D. Couzinet and H. Rochais. Paris: Fayard.

Boemus, Joannes. 1611. *The Manners, Lawes, and Customes of All Nations Collected Out of the Best Writers by Ioannes Boemus*. Translated into English by Ed. Aston. London. Available at EEBO.

Bolingbroke. 1997. *Political Writings*. (ed.) D. Armitage. Edition 1754. Cambridge: Cambridge University Press.

Bolingbroke, Henry St. John. 1809. Fragments, or Minutes of Essays. In Kenneth Douglas McRae (ed.) *The Works of the Late Right Honourable Henry St. John, Lord Viscount Bolingbroke. In eight volumes.* Vol. VII. London: Printed for J. Johnson, etc.

Bowles, John. 1795. *The Dangers of Premature Peace*. London: printed for T.N. Longman.

Brinsley, John. 1612. *Cato Translated Grammatically Directing for Understanding, Construing, Parsing, Making, and Proouing the Same Latine: and so for Continuall Practice of the Grammaticall Analysis and Genesis*. London: H.L.

Brougham, Henry. 1803. *An Inquiry into the Colonial Policy of the European Powers.* 2 vols. Edinburgh: printed by D. Willison for E. Balfour, Manners & Miller.

Burke, Edmund. 1993. A Vindication of Natural Society: or, A View of the Miseries and Evils sharing to Mankind from every Species or Artificial Society. In a Letter to Lord by a late Noble Writer. In Ian Harris (ed.) *Pre-Revolutionary Writings*. Cambridge: Cambridge University Press, pp. 8–57.

Burke, Edmund. 1999. Letters on a Regicide Peace. In *Select Works of Edmund Burke*. A New Imprint of the Payne Edition. Foreword and Biographical Note by Francis Canavan. Vol. III. 4 vols. Indianapolis, IN: Liberty Fund.

Burlamaqui, Jean-Jacques. 2006. *The Principles of Natural and Politic Law*. (ed.) Peter Korkman. Translated by Thomas Nugent (based on 1763 translation). Indianapolis, IN: Liberty Fund.

Bynkershoek, Cornelius van. 1923. *On the Sovereignty of the Sea*. Translated by Ralph Van Deman Magoffin. New York: Oxford University Press.

Bynkershoek, Cornelius van. 1930a. *Quaestionum Juris Publici Libri Duo*. Vol. I 'The Photographic reproduction of the edition of 1737'. Oxford: The Clarendon Press and London: Humphrey Milford.

Bynkershoek, Cornelius van. 1930b. *Quaestionum Juris Publici Libri Duo*. Vol. II 'The Translation' by Tenney Frank. Oxford: The Clarendon Press and London: Humphrey Milford.

Caesar, Caius Iulius. 1896. *Caesar's Commentaries on the Gallic War: First Six Books*. Translated by Edward Brooks. Philadelphia, PA: David McKay.

Caesar, Caius Iulius. *Commentariorum Libri VII de Bello Gallico*. Available at the Latin Library website: www.thelatinlibrary.com/caesar/gall4.shtml#16 (accessed on 23 October 2013).

Carmichael, Gershom. 1724. *Supplements and Observations upon The Two Books of Samuel Pufendorf's On the Duty of Man and Citizen according to the Law of Nature*. 2nd ed. Edinburgh: John Mosman and Partners.

Cassiodorus. *Variae*. Available at the Latin Library website: www.thelatinlibrary.com/cassiodorus.html (accessed on 23 October 2013).

Charron, Pierre. 1608 [?]. *Of Wisdome Three Bookes Written in French by Peter Charron Doctr of Lawe in Paris*. Translated by Samson Lennard. London: Printed for Edward Blount & Will: Aspley. Available at EEBO.

Churchyard, Thomas. 1580. *A Pleasaunte Laborinth Called Churchyardes Chance Framed on Fancies*. London: Ihon Kyngston. Available at EEBO.

Cicero. 2003. *On Duties*. (eds) M.T. Griffin and E.M. Atkins. 1st publ. 1991. Cambridge: Cambridge University Press. Latin original *De Officiis* available at the Latin Library website: www.thelatinlibrary.com/cicero/off.shtml (accessed on 23 October 2013).

Cicero, Marcus Tullius. 1913–21. *The Orations of Marcus Tullius Cicero*. Translated by C.D. Yonge. London: G. Bell and Sons. Vol. 1. Available at OLL: http://oll.libertyfund.org/index.php?option=com_staticxt&staticfile=show.php%3Ftitle=570&Itemid=28 (accessed on 23 October 2013).

Cicero, Marcus Tullius. 2001. On Friendship. In Charles W. Eliot (ed.) *The Harvard Classics*. Vol. 9 (1). Translated by E.S. Shuckburgh. New York: P.F. Collier & Son, 1909–14. Available at Bartleby.com, 2001 (accessed on 24 February 2009). Latin original *Laelius de Amicitia* available at the Latin Library website: www.thelatinlibrary.com/cicero/amic.shtml (accessed on 23 October 2013).

Cicero, Marcus Tullius. *Orationes in Verrum*. Available at the Latin Library website: www.thelatinlibrary.com/cicero/ver.shtml (accessed on 23 October 2013).

Coke, Edward. 2003. *Excerpts from the 'Institutes'*. In Steve Sheppard (ed.) *The Selected Writings of Sir Edward Coke*. Vol. II. Indianapolis, IN: Liberty Fund, pp. 573–1183.

Constantine Porphyrogenitus. 1967. De Administrando Imperio. In *Corpus Fontium Historiae Byzantinae*. Vol. I. Greek text ed. by G. Moravcsik, English translation by R.J.H. Jenkins. Washington, DC: Trustees for Harvard University.

Cornwallis, William. *Essayes*. 1600–1601. London: Printed for Edmund Mattes. Available at EEBO.

Corrozet, Gilles. 1602. *Memorable Conceits of Diuers Noble and Famous Personages of Christendome, of This Our Moderne Time*. London: Printed for Iames Shaw. Available at EEBO.

Crouch, Humphrey. 1642. *The Parliament of Graces*. London. Available at EEBO.

Cumberland, Richard. 2005. *A Treatise of the Laws of Nature*. Translated by John Maxwell (1727). (ed.) Jon Parkin. Indianapolis, IN: Liberty Fund.

Curtius Rufus, Quintus. 1956. *History of Alexander*. Translated by John C. Rolfe. 2 vols. London: William Heinemann Ltd and Cambridge, MA: Harvard University Press.

Dawson, George. 1694. *Origo Legum or a Treatise of the Origin of Laws and Their Obliging Power*. London.

De La Court, Pieter. 1746. *The True Interest and Political Maxims of the Republic of Holland*. Translated by John De Witt. London: John Campbell, Esq, [1662].

Defoe, Daniel. 1727. *The Evident Advantages to Great Britain and Its Allies from the Approaching War: Especially in Matters of Trade. To Which Is Added Two Curious Plans, One of the Port and Bay of Havana; the Other of Porto-Belo*. London. Available at ECCO.

Dio Chrysostom. 1946. *Dio Chrysostom*. Vol. IV. With an English translation by H.L. Crosby. London: William Heinemann Ltd.

Dionysius of Halicarnassus. *Roman Antiquities*, Vols II–IV. Translated by Earnest Cary. Cambridge, MA: Harvard University Press and London: William Heinemann Ltd, 1993, 1971, 1986. 7 vols.

Dorke, Walter. 1589. *Tipe or Figure of Friendship*. London: imprinted by Thomas Orwin and Henry Kirkham. Available at EEBO.

Edwards, Richard. 2002. *Damon and Pithias*. The text was transcribed by R.S. Bear, March 2002 from the 1571 edition. Available at the Renascence Editions website: https://scholarsbank.uoregon.edu/xmlui/bitstream/handle/1794/674/damon.pdf?sequence=1 (accessed on 23 October 2013).

Elyot, Thomas. 1992. *A Critical Edition of Sir Thomas Elyot's 'The Boke named the Governour'*. (ed.) Donald W. Rude. New York and London: Garland Publishing, Inc.

Erasmus. 1917. *The Complaint of Peace*. Translated by Thomas Paynell. Chicago, IL: Open Court. Available at OLL: http://oll.libertyfund.org/?option=com_staticxt&staticfile=show.php%3Ftitle=87 (accessed 23 October 2013).

Erasmus. 1921. Institutio Principis Christiani. Chapters III–XI. In *The Grotius Society Publications. Texts for Students of International Relations*. No. 1. Translated by Percy Ellwood Corbett. London: Sweet and Maxwell, Ltd.

Felltham, Owen. 1709. *Resolves: Divine, Moral, Political*. 12th ed. London: Printed by B. Motte, etc.

Ferguson, Adam. 1782. *An Essay on the History of Civil Society*. 5th ed. London: T. Cadell (first publ. 1767). Available at OLL: http://oll.libertyfund.org/?option=com_staticxt&staticfile=show.php%3Ftitle=1428&chapter=19708&layout=html&Itemid=27 (accessed on 23 October 2013).

Filmer, Robert. 1996. Patriarcha. In J. Sommerville (ed.) *Patriarcha and Other Writings*. 1st ed. 1991. Cambridge: Cambridge University Press.

Gale, Theophilus. 1671. *Theophilie: Or a Discourse of the Saints Amitie with God in Christ*. London.

Garatus Laudensis, Martinus. 2004. Tractatus de confederatione, pace, & conventionibus principum. In Randall Lesaffer (ed.) *Peace Treaties and International Law in European History: From the Late Middle Ages to World War One*. Edited by Alain Wijffels based on 1584 ed. Cambridge: Cambridge University Press, pp. 412–447.

Gent, E.G. 1676. *A Discourse of Friendship*. London: Printed by J.B. Available at EEBO.

Gentili, Alberico. 1585. *De Legationibus, libri tres*. London. Available at EEBO.

Gentili, Alberico. 1921a. *Hispanicae Advocationis Libri Duo*. Vol. I 'The Photographic reproduction of the edition of 1661'. New York: Oxford University Press.

Gentili, Alberico. 1921b. *Hispanicae Advocationis Libri Duo*. Vol. II. The Translation by Frank Frost Abbot. New York: Oxford University Press.

Gentili, Alberico. 1933a. *De Iure Belli Libri Tres*. Vol. I 'The Photographic reproduction of the edition of 1612'. Oxford: The Clarendon Press and London: Humphrey Milford.

Gentili, Alberico. 1933b. *De Iure Belli Libri Tres*. Vol. II. Translation by John C. Rolfe. Oxford: The Clarendon Press and London: Humphrey Milford.

Gibbon, Edward. 1906. *The History of the Decline and Fall of the Roman Empire*. (ed.) J.B. Bury. 12 vols. New York: Fred de Fau and Co. Available at OLL: http://oll.libertyfund. org/index.php?option=com_staticxt&staticfile=show.php?title=1681&Itemid=9999 9999 (accessed on 23 October 2013).

Godwin, William. 1793. *An Enquiry Concerning Political Justice, and its Influence on General Virtue and Happiness*. Vol. 2. London: G.G.J. and J. Robinson. Available at OLL: http://oll.libertyfund.org/index.php?option=com_staticxt&staticfile=show. php%3Ftitle=236&Itemid=28 (accessed on 23 October 2013).

Goldsmith, Oliver. 1966. *Collected Works of Oliver Goldsmith*. (ed.) Arthur Friedman. Vol. III. Oxford: The Clarendon Press.

Gordon, Thomas and Trenchard, John. 1995. *Cato's Letters, or Essays on Liberty, Civil and Religious, and Other Important Subjects*. (ed.) R. Hamowy. Vol. I. Indianapolis, IN: Liberty Fund.

Grotius, Hugo. 1625. *De Jure Belli ac Pacis Libris Tres in Quibus Ius Naturae & Gentium*. Paris. Available at the French National Library website: http://gallica.bnf.fr/ ark:/12148/bpt6k580227.capture (accessed on 23 October 2013).

Grotius, Hugo. 2005. *The Rights of War and Peace*. (ed.) Richard Tuck, from the edition by Jean Barbeyrac. 3 vols. Indianapolis, IN: Liberty Fund.

Hakluyt, Richard. 1903. *The Principal Navigations Voyages Traffiques & Discoveries of the English Nation. Made by Sea or Over-land to the Remote and Farthest Distant Quarters of the Earth at any time within the compasse of these 1600 Yeeres*. Vol. I. Glasgow: James MacLehose and Sons, Publishers to the University.

Hale, Matthew. 1736. *Historia placitorum coronæ. The history of the pleas of the crown*. London.

Harrington, James. 1996. The Commonwealth of Oceana. In J.G.A. Pocock (ed.) *The Commonwealth of Oceana and A System of Politics*. 1st ed. 1992. Cambridge: Cambridge University Press.

Heineccius, Johann Gottlieb. 1763. *A Methodical System of Universal Law: or, the Laws of Nature and Nations Deduced from Certain Principles, and Applied to Proper Cases*.

Translated by George Turnbull. Vol. II. London: printed for George Keith. Available at ECCO.

Henry VIII. 1545. *Speech before Parliament.* Available at the 'Tudor England: 1485 to 1603' website: http://englishhistory.net/tudor/h8speech.html (accessed on 31 July 2017).

Herodotus 1960.. *The Persian Wars.* Vol. I. Translated by A.D. Godley. 1st publ. 1920. London: William Heinemann Ltd.

Hobbes, Thomas. 1782. *Elementa Philosophica De Cive.* Basel: Johan. Jac. Flick. Digitised and made available by Google at: https://books.google.nl/books?id=IuURAAAAIAAJ (accessed on 9 May 2017).

Hobbes, Thomas. 1840. Behemoth: the History of the Causes of the Civil Was of England. In Sir William Molesworth (ed.) *The English Works of Thomas Hobbes of Malmesbury.* Vol. VI. London: John Bohn, pp. 161–418.

Hobbes, Thomas. 1899. *The Elements of Law Natural and Politic.* (ed.) F. Tonnies. London: Simpkin, Marshall and Co. Available at Liberty Library of Constitutional Classics: www.constitution.org/th/elements.htm (accessed on 31 July 2017).

Hobbes, Thomas. 1983. *De Cive. The English Version Entitled in the First Edition: Philosophical Rudiments Concerning Government and Society.* A critical edition by Howard Warrender. Oxford: The Clarendon Press.

Hobbes, Thomas. 1992 (repr.). *Leviathan.* (ed.) Richard Tuck. 1991 1st ed. Cambridge: Cambridge University Press.

Hoby, Thomas. 1900. *The Book of the Courtier from the Italian of Count Baldassare Castiglione.* London: published by David Nutt.

Hooker, Richard. 1989 (repr. 1994). *Of the Laws of Ecclesiastical Polity.* (ed.) A. McGrade. Cambridge: Cambridge University Press.

Hopkinson, Francis. 1792. *The Miscellaneous Essays and Occasional Writings of Francis Hopkinson.* Vol. II. Philadelphia: Printed by T. Dobson.

Hume, David. 1826. A Treatise of Human Nature. In *The Philosophical Works of David Hume. In Four Volumes.* Vol. 2. Edinburgh: Adam Black and William Tait. Available at OLL: http://files.libertyfund.org/files/1482/0221–02_Bk.pdf (accessed on 24 March 2009).

Hume, David. 1983. *The History of England from the Invasion of Julius Caesar to the Revolution in 1688.* Foreword by William B. Todd. 6 vols. Indianapolis, IN: Liberty Fund.

Hutcheson, Francis. 1755. *A system of moral philosophy, in three books; written by the late Francis Hutcheson, … To which is prefixed some account of the life, writings, and character of the author, by the Reverend William Leechman.* Vol. 2. 3 vols. Glasgow. Available at ECCO.

Institutiones Justiniani. Available at the Latin Library website: www.thelatinlibrary.com/justinian.html (accessed on 8 May 2017).

James I. 2001. Basilikon Doron or His Maiesties Instructions to His Dearest Sonne, Henry the Prince. In Johann P. Sommerville (ed.) *King James VI and I. Political Writings.* 1st ed. 1994. Cambridge: Cambridge University Press.

Jefferson, Thomas. Indian Address. Available at the The Avalon Project: http://avalon.law.yale.edu/18th_century/jeffind1.asp (accessed on 28 May 2013).

Johnson, Samuel. 1792. *The Works of Samuel Johnson, in Twelve Volumes*. Vol. IV. London: Printed for T. Longman, etc.

Kant, Immanuel. 1886. *The Metaphysics of Ethics*. (ed.) Rev. Henry Calderwood. Translated by J.W. Semple. 3rd ed. Edinburgh: T. & T. Clark. Available at OLL: http://oll.libertyfund.org/index.php?option=com_staticxt&staticfile=show.php& title=1443&search=%22friendship%22&chapter=56343&layout=html#a_1352134 (accessed on 23 March 2009).

Knox, Vicesimus. 1824. Antipolemus; or the Plea of Reason, Religion, and Humanity, against War. A Fragment. In *The Works of Vicesimus Knox, In Seven Volumes*. Vol. V. London: J. Mawman. Available at OLL: http://oll.libertyfund.org/?option=com_ staticxt&staticfile=show.php%3Ftitle=630&chapter=82331&layout=html&Ite mid=27 (accessed on 19 March 2009).

Lamond, Elizabeth (ed.). 1929. *A Discourse of the Common Weal of this Realm of England*. 1st ed. 1893. Cambridge: Cambridge University Press. Available at the Internet Archive website: www.archive.org/details/discourseofcommo00lamouoft (accessed on 23 October 2013).

Leibniz, Gottfried Wilhelm von. 1981. Portrait of the Prince. In Patrick Riley (transl. and ed.) *The Political Writings of Leibniz*. Cambridge: Cambridge University Press, pp. 85–103.

Leslie, John. 1584. *A Treatise Tovvching the Right, Title, and Interest of the most Excellent Princesse Marie, Queene of Scotland, And of the most Noble King Iames. Her Graces sonne, to the succession of the Croune of England. With an exhortation of them selues in a true league of Amitie*. Rouen: Printed by G. L'Oyselet. Available at EEBO.

Lignano, Ioannis. 1584. De Amicitia. In *Tractatus Illustrium in utraque Tum Pontificii, Tum Caesarei iuris facultate Iurisconsultorum, etc*. Tomus XII. Venice. ff. 227–242.

Livius, Titus. *Ab Urbe Condita*. Available at the Latin Library website: www.thelatin library.com/liv.html (accessed on 23 October 2013).

Livy, Titus. 1600. *The Romane historie written by T. Livius of Padua. Also, the Breviaries of L. Florus: with a chronologie to the whole historie: and the Topographie of Rome in old time*. Translated by Philemon Holland. London. Available at EEBO.

Livy, Titus. 1686. *The Roman history written in Latine by Titus Livius. With the supplements of John Freinshemius and John Dujatius from the foundation of Rome to the middle of the reign of Augustus*. London: Printed for Awnsham Churchill. Available at EEBO.

Livy, Titus. 1905. *History of Rome*. (ed.) Ernest Rhys. Translated by Rev. Canon Roberts. London: J.M. Dent & Sons, Ltd. Available at the Ancient History, Archaeology and Biblical Studies website: http://mcadams.posc.mu.edu/txt/ah/Livy/index.html (accessed on 23 October 2013).

Locke, John. 2002 (repr.). *Essays on the Law of Nature*. (ed.) W. von Leyden. 1st publ.1954. Oxford: The Clarendon Press.

Locke, John. 2003. *Two Treatises of Government*. (ed.) P. Laslett. Student edition 1998. Cambridge: Cambridge University Press.

Lorimer, James. 1883–1884. *The Institutes of the Law of Nations. A Treatise of the Jural Relations of Separate Political Communities. In Two Volumes*. Edinburgh and London: William Blackwood and Sons.

Lyly, John. 1902a. Endimion, The Man in the Moone. In Warwick Bond (ed.) *The Complete Works of John Lyly*. Vol. III 'The Plays. Anti-Martinist Work. Poems. Glossary and General Index'. Oxford: Clarendon Press.

Lyly, John. 1902b. Euphues and his England. In Warwick Bond (ed.) *The Complete Works of John Lyly*. Vol. II 'Euphues and his England. The Plays'. Oxford: Clarendon Press.

Machiavelli, Niccolo. 1882. *The Historical, Political, and Diplomatic Writings of Niccolo Machiavelli*. Translated from the Italian by Christian E. Detmold. Vol. 1. *History of Florence*. Available at OLL: http://oll.libertyfund.org/?option=com_ staticxt&staticfile=show.php%3Ftitle=774&chapter=75806&layout=html&Ite mid=27. Vol. 2 *Discourses on the First Ten Books of Titus Livius*. Boston, J.R. Osgood and company. Available at OLL: http://oll.libertyfund.org/?option=com_ staticxt&staticfile=show.php%3Ftitle=775 (accessed on 23 October 2013).

Madison, James. 1900. An Examination of the British Doctrine, Which Subjects to Capture a Legal Trade, Not Open in Time of Peace. In Gaillard Hunt (ed.) *The Writings of James Madison, comprising his Public Papers and his Private Correspondence, including his numerous letters and documents now for the first time printed*. Vol. 7. New York: G.P. Putnam's Sons. Available at OLL: http://oll.libertyfund.org/?option=com_ staticxt & staticfile = show . php%3Ftitle = 1938&chapter = 119003&layout = html&Ite mid=27 (accessed on 9 May 2017).

Marcellinus, Ammianus. *Res Gestae a Fine Corneli Taciti*. Available at the Forum Romanum website: www.forumromanum.org/literature/ammianus17.html (accessed on 23 October 2013).

Martens, Georg Friedrich von. 1795. *Summary of the Law of Nations, Founded on the Treaties and Customs of the Modern Nations of Europe; with a List of the Principal Treaties, Concluded since the Year 1748 down to the Present Time, Indicating the Works in Which They are to be Found*. Translated by William Cobbett. Philadelphia: Published by Thomas Bradford. Available at ECCO.

Meadows, Philip. 1689. *Observations on the Dominion and Sovereignty of the Seas*. London: printed by Edw. Jones.

Milton, John. 1825. *A Treatise on Christian Doctrine, Compiled from the Holy Scriptures Alone*. Translated by Charles R. Sumner. Cambridge University Press, J. Smith.

Milton, John. 1847. Letter to the most Serene Christiana, Queen of the Swedes, Goths, and Vandals; Letter to the most Serene Prince, the Duke of Venice, and the most Illustrious Senate. In *The Prose Works of John Milton*. Vol. 2. 2 vols. Philadelphia: John W. Moore. Available at OLL: http://oll.libertyfund.org/?option=com_staticxt&staticfile=show. php%3Ftitle=1210&chapter=78277&layout=html&Itemid=27 (accessed on 23 October 2013).

Milton, John. 1991a. A Defence of the People of England, in reply to a Defence of the King by Claudius Anonymous, alias Salmasius. In M. Dzelzainis (ed.) *John Milton. Political Writings*. Cambridge: Cambridge University Press, pp. 51–254.

Milton, John. 1991b. The Tenure of Kings and Magistrates. In M. Dzelzainis (ed.) *John Milton. Political Writings*. Cambridge: Cambridge University Press, pp. 3–50.

Montaigne, Michel. 1613. *Essays written in French by Michael Lord of Montaigne, Knight of the Order of S. Michael, gentleman of the French Kings chamber*. Translated by John Florio. London: Printed by Melch. Bradwood. Available at EEBO.

Montesquieu, Charles Louis. 1777. Persian Letters. In *The Complete Works of M. de Montesquieu*. Vol. 3. 4 vols. London: T. Evans. Available at OLL: http://oll.liberty-fund.org/title/1338/74815/1826186 (accessed on 23 October 2013).

More, Thomas. 1931. *Utopia*. With an introduction by J. O'Hagan. 1st ed. 1910. London and Toronto: J.M. Dent and Sons.

More, Thomas. 1997. *The History of King Richard the Third*. Based on the Rastell edition of 1557. Renascence Editions. The University of Oregon. Available at: www.luminarium. org/renascence-editions/r3.html (accessed on 23 October 2013).

Munday, Anthony. 1605. *Falsehood in Friendship, or Unions Vizard: or Wolves in Lambskins*. London: printed for Nathaniell Fosbroke. Originally published in 1592. Available at EEBO.

Nashe, Thomas. 1592. *Pierce Penniless, His Supplication to the Devil*. London: Imprinted by Richard Jones. Available at the Oxford Authorship Site: www.oxford-shakespeare. com/Nashe/Pierce_Penilesse.pdf (accessed on 23 October 2013).

Osborn, Francis. 1682. Advice to a Son. In *The Works Francis Osborn. Divine. Moral. Historical. Political*. 8th ed. London: A. Banks, pp. 1–24.

Paine, Thomas. 1894a. Common Sense. In M. Conway (ed.) *The Writings of Thomas Paine*. Vol. I. New York: G.P. Putnam's Sons. Available at OLL: http://oll.libertyfund. org/?option=com_staticxt&staticfile=show.php%3Ftitle=343&chapter=17023&layo ut=html&Itemid=27 (accessed on 23 October 2013).

Paine, Thomas. 1894b. The American Crisis. In M. Conway (ed.) *The Writings of Thomas Paine*. Vol. I. New York: G.P. Putnam's Sons. Available at OLL: http://oll.libertyfund. org/?option=com_staticxt&staticfile=show.php%3Ftitle=343&chapter=17046& layout=html&Itemid=27 (accessed on 23 October 2013).

Parker, Samuel. 1681. *A Demonstration of the Divine Authority of the Law of Nature, and the Christian Religion*. London: printed for R. Royston.

Penn, William. 2002. An Essay towards the Present and Future Peace of Europe by the Establishment of an European Dyet, Parliament, or Estates. In *The Political Writings of William Penn*. Introduction by A.R. Murphy. Indianapolis, IN: Liberty Fund, pp. 401–420.

Plutarch. Solon. 1967. In *Plutarch's Lives. In eleven volumes*. Vol. I with an English trans-lation by Bernadotte Perrin. London and Cambridge, MA: William Heinemann Ltd and Harvard University Press (The Loeb Classical Library), pp. 403–499.

Plutarch. Theseus. 1967. In *Plutarch's Lives. In eleven volumes*. Vol. I. with an English translation by Bernadotte Perrin. London and Cambridge, MA: William Heinemann Ltd and Harvard University Press (The Loeb Classical Library), pp. 1–87.

Polybius. 1967. *The Histories. In six volumes*. With an English translation by W.R. Paton. Vols. I, II, V. Cambridge, MA and London: Harvard University Press (The Loeb Classical Library) and William Heinemann Ltd.

Postlethwayt, Malachy. 1757. *Britain's Commercial Interest Explained and Improved; in a Series of Dissertations on Several Important Branches of Her Trade and Police*. Vol. II. London: Printed for D. Browne. 2 vols. Available at ECCO.

Procopius of Caesarea. 1954. *Procopius in seven volumes*. Vols. I, IV with an English translation by H.B. Dewing. Cambridge, MA and London: Harvard University Press and William Heinemann Ltd.

Pufendorf, Samuel. 1749. *The Law of Nature and Nations: or, a General system of the most important principles of morality, jurisprudence, and politics. In eight books.* Translated by B. Kennet. 5th ed. London: Printed for J. and J. Bonwicke [and others]. Available at ECCO.

Pufendorf, Samuel. 1964. *The Two Books on the Duty of Man and Citizen According to the Natural Law.* Vol. II 'The Translation' by F.G. Moore. New York: Oceana Publications Inc. Available at www.constitution.org/puf/puf-dut.htm (accessed on 23 October 2013).

Raleigh, Walter. 1829. The Cabinet-Council: Containing the Chief Arts of Empire, and Mysteries of State (published by John Milton). In *The Works of Sir Walter Raleigh in Eight Volumes.* Vol. VIII 'Miscellaneous works'. Oxford: The University Press, pp. 37–156.

Ramsay, David. 1990. *The History of the American Revolution.* Vol. 1. Foreword by Lester H. Cohen. Indianapolis, IN: Liberty Fund.

Reid, Thomas. 2007. *Thomas Reid On Practical Ethics. Lectures and Papers On Natural Religion, Self-Government, Natural Jurisprudence and the Law of Nations.* (ed.) Knud Haakonssen. Edinburgh: Edinburgh University Press.

Rousseau, Jean-Jacques [1788]. *Thoughts of Jean-Jacques Rousseau,…* Selected from his writings by an anonymous editor. Translated by Miss Henrietta Colebrooke. Vol. I. 2 vols. London: printed for the author. Available at ECCO.

Rutherforth, Thomas. 1754–1756. *Institutes of natural law being the substance of a course of lectures on Grotius de Jure belli et pacis … by T. Rutherforth.* Vol. 2. 2 vols. Cambridge: printed by J. Bentham. Available at ECCO.

Sallust. 1965. *The War with Catiline; The War with Jugurtha.* Translated by John C. Rolfe. London: William Heinemann Ltd and Cambridge, MA: Harvard University Press.

Savile, George, Marquis of Halifax. 1750. *A Character of King Charles the Second: and political, moral and miscellaneous thoughts and reflections.* London: printed for J. and R. Tonson and S. Draper. Available at ECCO.

Selden, John. 1652. *Of the Dominion, or, Ownership of the Sea.* London: William Du Gard.

Selden, John. 1771. *The dissertation of John Selden, annexed to Fleta.* Translated, with notes, by the editor of Britton. London: Sold by J. Worrall and B. Tovey. Available at ECCO.

Seneca. *Moral Epistles.* Translated by Richard M. Gummere. 3 vols. Cambridge, MA: Harvard University Press (The Loeb Classical Library), 1917–1925. Vol. I available at www.stoics.com/seneca_epistles_book_1.html (accessed on 9 May 2017).

Shafte, John. 1673. *The Great Law of Nature, or Self Preservation Examined, Asserted and Vindicated from Mr. Hobbes his Abuses.* London: printed for the author. Available at EEBO.

Shaftesbury (Anthony Ashley Cooper). 2001. *Characteristicks of Men, Manners, Opinions, Times.* (ed.) Douglas den Uyl. Vol. 2. 3 vols. Indianapolis, IN: Liberty Fund.

Sheffield, John. 1740. *The Works of John Sheffield, Earl of Mulgrave, Marquis of Normanby, and Duke of Buckingham.* Vol. II. 3rd edition, corrected. London: Printed for T. Wotton, etc.

Sidney, Algernon. 1996a. *Court Maxims.* (eds) H.W. Blom, E.H. Mulier and R. Janse. Cambridge: Cambridge University Press.

Sidney, Algernon. 1996b. *Discourses Concerning Government.* (ed.) Thomas G. West. Indianapolis, IN: Liberty Fund.

Silius Italicus. 1961. *Punica*. Translated by J.D. Duff. Vol. II. London: William Heinemann Ltd and Cambridge, MA: Harvard University Press.

Smith, Adam. 1904. *An Inquiry into the Nature and Causes of the Wealth of Nations by Adam Smith*. (ed.) Edwin Cannan. Vol. 1. London: Methuen. Available at OLL: http://oll.libertyfund.org/?option=com_staticxt&staticfile=show.php%3Ftitle=237& chapter=39449&layout=html&Itemid=27 (accessed on 23 October 2013).

Spenser, Edmund. 1935. *The Faerie Queene*. (ed.) Ray Heffner. Baltimore, MD: The Johns Hopkins Press.

Stanley, Thomas. 1655. *The History of Philosophy in eight parts*. London: printed for H. Moseley and Th. Dring.

Starkey, Thomas. 1871. *England in the Reign of King Henry the Eighth. A Dialogue between Cardinal Pole and Thomas Lupset, Lecturer in Rhetoric at Oxford*. (ed.) J.M. Cowper. London: Early English Text Society.

Suárez, Francisco. 1944a. *Selections from Three Works*. Vol. I 'A Photographic Reproduction of the Selections from the Original Editions'. Oxford: The Clarendon Press and London: Humphrey Milford.

Suárez, Francisco. 1944b. *Selections from Three Works*. Vol. II 'The Translation'. Prepared by G. Williams, A. Brown and J. Waldron. Oxford: The Clarendon Press and London: Humphrey Milford.

Swift, Jonathan. 1824. *The Works of Jonathan Swift, D.D.* (ed.) Walter Scott. 2nd ed. Vol. IV 'Tracts Historical and Political, During the Reign of Queen Anne'. Edinburgh: Printed for Archibald Constable and Co, etc.

Tacitus. 1970. *The Annals. In five volumes*. With an English translation by John Jackson. Vol. IV. London and Cambridge, MA: William Heinemann Ltd and Harvard University Press (The Loeb Classical Library).

Taylor, Jeremy. 1657. *A Discourse of the Nature, Offices and Measures of Friendship, with Rules of conducting it*. London: Printed for R. Royston at the Angel in Ovie-lane. Available at EEBO.

Textor, Johan Wolfgang. 1916a. *Synopseos Juris Gentium*. Vol. I. Washington, DC: The Carnegie Institution of Washington.

Textor, Johan Wolfgang. 1916b. *Synopsis of the Law of Nations*. Vol. II 'The Translation' by John Pawley Bay. Washington, DC: The Carnegie Institution of Washington.

The Digest of Justinian. 1998. Vol. II. Translated by A. Watson. Philadelphia, PA: University of Pennsylvania Press.

The Federalist, by Alexander Hamilton, John Jay and James Madison. 2001. (eds) George W. Carey and James McClellan. The Gideon Edition. Indianapolis, IN: Liberty Fund.

The Mirror for Magistrates. 1960. (ed.) Lily B. Campbell. 1st ed. in 1938 by Cambridge University Press. Reprinted in New York: Barnes & Noble, Inc. Available at the Internet Archive website: www.archive.org/details/mirrorformagistr007312mbp (accessed on 23 October 2013).

Thucydides. 1992. *History of the Peloponnesian War*. Vols II, III. With an English translation by Charles Forster Smith. Cambridge, MA and London: Harvard University Press (The Loeb Classical Library). First published 1921.

Towers, Joseph. 1796. *Tracts on Political and Other Subjects*. Vol. III. 3 vols. London: Printed for Cadell and Davies.

Tyrrell, James. 1693. *Brief Disquisition of the Law of Nature*. London: Printed by Richard Baldwin. Available at EEBO.

Vattel, Emer de. 2008. *The Law of Nations, Or, Principles of the Law of Nature, Applied to the Conduct and Affairs of Nations and Sovereigns, with Three Early Essays on the Origin and Nature of Natural Law and on Luxury*. (eds) Béla Kapossy and Richard Whitmore. Indianapolis, IN: Liberty Fund.

Victoria, Franciscus de. 1917. *De Indis et de Iure Belli Relectiones*. (ed.) Ernest Nys. Translated by John Pawley Bate. Washington, DC: Carnegie Institution.

Vitoria, Francisco de. 1934. De Jure Gentium et Naturali. In James Brown Scott. *The Spanish Origin of International Law. Francisco de Vitoria and His Law of Nations*. Oxford: Clarendon Press, Appendix E.

Ward, Robert Plumer. 1795. *An Enquiry into the Foundation and History of the Law of Nations in Europe, from the Time of the Greeks and Romans, to the Age of Grotius*. Vol. 2. Dublin: Printed by P. Wogan and others. Available at ECCO.

Wheaton, Henry. 1878. *Elements of International Law*. (ed.) A.C. Boyd. 1st publ. 1836. London: Stevens & Sons, Law Publishers and Book Sellers. Available at the Internet Archive website: www.archive.org/stream/elementsinterna00boydgoog#page/n7/mode/1up (accessed on 23 October 2013).

Wither, George. 1653. *Friendship*. Available at EEBO.

Wolff, Christian. 1934a. *Jus Gentium Methodo Scientifica Pertractatum*. Vol. I 'The Reproduction of the Edition of 1764'. Oxford: The Clarendon Press and London: Humphrey Milford.

Wolff, Christian. 1934b. *Jus Gentium Methodo Scientifica Pertractatum*. Vol. II 'The Translation' by Joseph H. Drake. Oxford: The Clarendon Press and London: Humphrey Milford.

Wood, Thomas. 1721. *A New Institute of the Imperial or, Civil Law*. 3rd ed. London: printed for Richard Sare.

Xenophon. 1863. *The Anabasis; or, Expedition of Cyrus, and the Memorabilis of Socrates*. Translated by J.S. Watson. New York: Harper and Brothers.

Xenophon. 2008. *Hellenica*. Translation by H.G. Dakyns. The Project Gutenberg Ebook. Available at www.gutenberg.org/files/1174/1174-h/1174-h.htm (accessed on 23 October 2013).

Xenophon. 2009. *Cyropaedia*. Translation by H.G. Dakyns. The Project Gutenberg Ebook. Available at www.gutenberg.org/files/2085/2085-h/2085-h.htm#2H_4_0006 (accessed on 23 October 2013).

Young, Arthur. 1772. *Political Essays Concerning the Present State of the British Empire*. London: Printed for W. Strahan, and T. Cadell.

Zouche, Richard. 1911. *Juris et Judiciis fecialis, sive Juris inter Gentes et Quaestionum de eodem explicates*. (ed.) Th. Holland. Baltimore, MD: The Carnegie Institution.

Secondary literature

Acemoglu, Daron and Robinson, James. 2013. *Why Nations Fail: The Origins of Power, Prosperity, and Poverty*. Reprinted ed. New York: Crown Business.

Agamben, Giorgio. 1998. *Homo Sacer: Sovereign Power and Bare Life*. Translated by Daniel Heller-Roazen. 1st ed. Stanford, CA: Stanford University Press.

Agamben, Giorgio. 2005. *State of Exception*. Chicago: University of Chicago Press.

Akashi, Kinji. 2000. Hobbes's Relevance to the Modern Law of Nations. *Journal of the History of International Law* 2, pp. 199–216.

Alexandrowicz, Charles H. 1967. *An Introduction to the History of the Law of Nations in the East Indies (16th, 17th and 18th Centuries)*. Oxford: Clarendon Press.

Althoff, Gerd. 1999. Friendship and Political Order. In J. Haseldine (ed.) *Friendship in Medieval Europe*. Stroud: Phoenix Mill, pp. 91–105.

Andersen, Morten Skumsrud and Neumann, Iver B. 2012. Practices as Models: A Methodology with an Illustration Concerning Wampum Diplomacy. *Millennium: Journal of International Studies* 40 (3), pp. 457–481.

Angell, Norman. 1913. *A Study of the Relation of Military Power to National Advantage*. 4th ed. New York and London: G.P. Putnam's Sons.

Aravamudan, Srinivas. 2009. Hobbes and America.I In Daniel Carey and Lynn Festa (eds) *The Postcolonial Enlightenment: Eighteenth-Century Colonialism and Postcolonial Theory*. New York: Oxford University Press, pp. 37–70.

Armitage, David. 2000. *The Ideological Origins of the British Empire*. Cambridge: Cambridge University Press.

Armitage, David. 2006. Hobbes and the Foundations of Modern International Thought. In Annabel Brett, James Tully and Holly Hamilton-Bleakley (eds) *Rethinking the Foundations of Modern Political Thought*. New York: Cambridge University Press, pp. 219–235.

Armitage, David. 2013. *Foundations of Modern International Thought*. New York: Cambridge University Press.

Austin, J.L. 1956–1957. A Plea for Excuses. *Proceedings of the Aristotelian Society*. Available at the Digital Texts International (by Andrew Chrucky) webpage: http://www.ditext.com/austin/plea.html (accessed on 30 May 2009).

Austin, J.L. 1975. *How to Do Things with Words*. 2nd rev. edition. Cambridge, MA: Harvard University Press.

Austin, John. 1885. *Lectures on Jurisprudence; Or, The Philosophy of Positive Law*. Edited by Robert Campbell. 5th ed. Vol. 1. 2 vols. London: J. Murray. Available at http://archive.org/details/lecturesonjuris02austgoog (accessed on 9 May 2017).

Baker, Keith Michael. 2001. Enlightenment and the Institution of Society: Notes for a Conceptual History. In Sudipta Kaviraj and Sunil Khilnani (eds) *Civil Society: History and Possibilities*. Cambridge: Cambridge University Press, pp. 84–104.

Baldus, Christian. 2004. The Roman Peace Treaty. In Randall Lesaffer (ed.) *Peace Treaties and International Law in European History: From the Late Middle Ages to World War One*. Cambridge: Cambridge University Press, pp. 103–146.

Ball, Terence. 1997. Political Theory and Conceptual Change. In Andrew Vincent (ed.) *Political Theory: Tradition and Diversity*. Cambridge: Cambridge University Press, pp. 28–44.

Bartelson, Jens. 1995. *A Genealogy of Sovereignty*. Cambridge: Cambridge University Press.

Bartelson, Jens. 2009. *Visions of World Community*. Cambridge: Cambridge University Press.

Beaulac, Stéphane. 2000. The Westphalian Legal Orthodoxy – Myth or Reality? *Journal of the History of International Law* 2, pp. 148–177.

Beaulac, Stéphane. 2003. Emer de Vattel and the Externalization of Sovereignty. *Journal of the History of International Law* 5, pp. 237–292.

Beaulac, Stéphane. 2004. *The Power of Language in the Making of International Law: The Word Sovereignty in Bodin and Vattel and the Myth of Westphalia*. Leiden and Boston: Martinus Nijhoff Publishers.

Bederman, David. 2001. *International Law in Antiquity*. Port Chester, NY: Cambridge University Press.

Beitz, Charles R. 1999. *Political Theory and International Relations*. 2nd ed. Princeton, NJ: Princeton University Press.

Bell, Duncan S.A. 2002. Language, Legitimacy, and the Project of Critique. *Alternatives: Global, Local, Political* 27 (3), pp. 327–350.

Bell, Duncan (ed.). 2007. *Victorian Visions of Global Order: Empire and International Relations in Nineteenth Century Political Thought*. New York: Cambridge University Press.

Berenskoetter, Felix. 2007. Friends, There Are No Friends? An Intimate Reframing of the International. *Millennium: Journal of International Studies* 35 (3), pp. 647–676.

Brett, Annabel S. 2011. *Changes of State: Nature and the Limits of the City in Early Modern Natural Law*. Princeton, NJ: Princeton University Press.

Brown, G.W. 2005. State Sovereignty, Federation and Kantian Cosmopolitanism. *European Journal of International Relations* 11 (4), pp. 495–522.

Brunner, Otto. 1992. *Land and Lordship: Structures of Governance in Medieval Austria*. Translated from the fourth, revised edition by Howard Kaminsky and James Van Horn Melton. Philadelphia, PA: University of Pennsylvania Press.

Bull, Hedley. 2002. *The Anarchical Society: A Study of Order in World Politics*. 3rd ed. London: Macmillan.

Bull, Hedley and Watson, Adam. 1984. *The Expansion of International Society*. Oxford: Oxford University Press.

Burton, Paul. 2003. *Clientela* or *Amicitia*? Modeling Roman International Behavior in the Middle Republic (264–146 B.C.). *Klio* 85 (2), pp. 333–369.

Butterfield, Herbert. 1965. *The Whig Interpretation of History*. New York: W.W. Norton & Company.

Carr, Craig L. and Seidler, Michael J. 1996. Pufendorf, Sociality and the Modern State. *History of Political Thought* XVII (3), pp. 354–378.

Carr, E.H. 2001. *The Twenty Years' Crisis, 1919–1939: Reissued with New Introduction: An Introduction to the Study of International Relations* (ed.) Michael Cox. Basingstoke, Hampshire and New York: Palgrave Macmillan.

Cimma, Maria Rosa. 1976. *Reges Socii et Amici Populi Romani*. Milan: Dott. A. Guiffrè Editore.

'Commercial treaties'. *Encyclopaedia of the Social Sciences*. Tenth printing 1953 (1st publ. 1930). (ed.) Edwin R.A. Seligman, vol. 4, pp. 24–31.

Coyle, John F. 2013. The Treaty of Friendship, Commerce and Navigation in the Modern Era. *Columbia Journal of Transnational Law* 51, pp. 302–359.

Derrida, Jacques. 1997. *Politics of Friendship*. London and New York: Verso.

Deudney, Daniel. 2007. *Bounding Power: Republican Security Theory from the Polis to the Global Village*. Princeton, NJ: Princeton University Press.

Devere, Heather. 2014. Friendship in International Treaties. In Simon Koschut and Andrea Oelsner (eds) *Friendship in International Relations*. Basingstoke: Palgrave Macmillan, pp. 182–198.

Devere, Heather and Smith, Graham M. 2010. Friendship and Politics. *Political Studies Review* 8 (3), pp. 341–356.

Dewald, Jonathan. 1993. *Aristocratic Experience and the Origins of Modern Culture: France, 1570–1715*. Berkeley, CA: University of California Press.

Dickinson, Willoughby. 1927. International Friendship. *The Hibbert Journal* 25 (3), pp. 439–452.

Digeser, P.E. 2009a. Friendship between States. *British Journal of Political Science* 39, pp. 323–344.

Digeser, P.E. 2009b. Public Reason and International Friendship. *Journal of International Political Theory* 5 (1), pp. 22–40.

Donnelly, Jack. 2013. Realism. In Scott Burchill and Andrew Linklater (eds) *Theories of International Relations*. 5th ed. Basingstoke, Hampshire and New York: Palgrave Macmillan, pp. 32–56.

Doyle, Michael W. 1983a. Kant, Liberal Legacies, and Foreign Affairs. *Philosophy and Public Affairs* 12 (3), pp. 205–235.

Doyle, Michael W. 1983b. Kant, Liberal Legacies, and Foreign Affairs, Part 2. *Philosophy and Public Affairs* 12 (4), pp. 323–353.

Duchhardt, Heinz. 2004. From Westphalia to the Revolutionary Era. In Randall Lesaffer (ed.) *Peace Treaties and International Law in European History: From the Late Middle Ages to World War One*. Cambridge: Cambridge University Press, pp. 45–58.

Dunn, John. 2001. John Locke's Conception of Civil Society. In Sudipta Kaviraj and Sunil Khilnani (eds) *Civil Society: History and Possibilities*. Cambridge: Cambridge University Press, pp. 39–57.

Dunne T. and Schmidt B. 2001. Realism. In J. Baylis and S. Smith (eds) *The Globalization of World Politics*. Oxford and New York: Oxford University Press, pp. 141–161.

Eikema Hommes, Hendrik van. 1983. Grotius on Natural and International Law. *Netherlands International Law Review* 30, pp. 61–71.

Elwyn, Sue. 1993. Interstate Kinship and Roman Foreign Policy. *Transactions of the American Philological Association* 123, pp. 261–286.

Epp, Verena. 1999. *Amicitia: zur Geschichte personaler, sozialer, politischer und geistlicher Beziehungen im frühen Mittelalter*. Stuttgart: Hiersemann.

Eznack, Lucile, and Koschut, Simon. 2014. The Sources of Affect in Interstate Friendship. In Simon Koschut and Andrea Oelsner (eds) *Friendship and International Relations*. Basingstoke and New York: Palgrave Macmillan, pp. 72–88.

Fernández-Santamaria, J.A. 1977. *The State, War and Peace: Spanish Political Thought in the Renaissance 1516–1559*. Cambridge: Cambridge University Press.

Fisher, Michael H. 1984. Indirect Rule in the British Empire: The Foundations of the Residency System in India (1764–1858). *Modern Asian Studies* 18 (3), pp. 393–428.

Foucault, Michel. 1991. Nietzsche, Genealogy, History. In Paul Rabinow (ed.) *The Foucault Reader: An Introduction to Foucault's Thought.* London: Penguin Books, pp. 76–100.

Foucault, Michel. 2002. Questions of Method.I In James D. Faubion (ed.) *Michel Foucault: Essential Works of Foucault 1954–1984.* Vol. 3 'Power'. London: Penguin Books, pp. 223–238.

Fulton, Thomas Wemyss. 2005. *The Sovereignty of the Sea: An Historical Account of the Claims of England to the Dominion of the British Seas, and of the Evolution of Territorial Waters, with Special Reference to the Rights of Fishing and the Naval Salute.* 3rd printing. Clark, NJ: The Law Book Exchange, Ltd. (first published in 1911).

Galtung, Johan. 1971. A Structural Theory of Imperialism. *Journal of Peace Research* 8 (2), pp. 81–117.

Gehring, Charles and Starna, William. 2012. Revisiting the Fake Tawagonshi Treaty of 1613. *New York History* Winter, pp. 95–101.

Gellner, Ernest. 1983. *Nations and Nationalism.* Ithaca, NY: Cornell University Press.

Gierke, Otto. 1957. *Natural Law and the Theory of Society, 1500 to 1800.* Translated by E. Barker. 2nd printing edition. Boston, MA: Beacon Press.

Gillard, David. 1977. *The Struggle for Asia 1828–1914: A Study in British and Russian Imperialism.* London: Methuen & Co Ltd.

Godbeer, Richard. 2009. *The Overflowing of Friendship: Love between Men and the Creation of the American Republic.* Baltimore, MD: The Johns Hopkins University Press.

Gruen, Erich S. 1986. *The Hellenistic World and the Coming of Rome.* reprint ed. 1984. Berkeley, CA: University of California Press.

Gulick, Edward Vose. 1967. *Europe's Classical Balance of Power.* New York: W.W. Norton and Company, Inc.

Haakonssen, Knud. 1996. *Natural Law and Moral Philosophy: From Grotius to the Scottish Enlightenment.* Cambridge: Cambridge University Press.

Hagedorn, Nancy L. 1988. 'A Friend to go between Them': The Interpreter as Cultural Broker during Anglo-Iroquois Councils, 1740–70. *Ethnohistory* 35 (1), pp. 60–80.

Haldén, Peter. 2011. *Stability without Statehood: Lessons from Europe's History before the Sovereign State.* Basingstoke: Palgrave.

Herman, Gabriel. 2002. *Ritualised Friendship and the Greek City.* Cambridge: Cambridge University Press.

Hobsbawm, Eric John. 1990. *Nations and Nationalism Since 1780: Programme, Myth, Reality.* Cambridge: Cambridge University Press.

Hochstrasser, Tim J. 2000. *Natural Law Theories in the Early Enlightenment.* West Nyack, NY: Cambridge University Press.

Holden, Gerard. 2002. Who Contextualizes the Contextualizers? Disciplinary History and the Discourse about IR Discourse. *Review of International Studies* 28, pp. 253–270.

Holland, Ben. 2010. Sovereignty as *Dominium*? Reconstructing the Constructivist Roman Law Thesis. *International Studies Quarterly* 5 (2), pp. 449–480.

Hont, Istvan. 1990. The Language of Sociability and Commerce: Samuel Pufendorf and the Theoretical Foundations of 'Four-Stages Theory'. In Anthony Pagden (ed.) *The Languages of Political Theory in Early-Modern Europe.* 1st publ. 1987. Cambridge: Cambridge University Press, pp. 253–276.

Hutter, Horst. 1978. *Politics as Friendship: The Origins of Classical Notions of Politics in the Theory and Practice of Friendship.* Waterloo, Ontario: Wilfrid Laurier University Press.

Hyam, Ronald. 2002. *Britain's Imperial Century, 1815–1914: A Study of Empire and Expansion.* 3rd ed. New York: Palgrave Macmillan.

Jackson, Robert H. 2007. *Sovereignty: Evolution of an Idea.* Cambridge: Polity Press.

Jackson, Robert H. and Sørensen, Georg. 2010. *Introduction to International Relations: Theories and Approaches.* 4th ed. Oxford: Oxford University Press.

Jahn, Beate (ed.). 2006. *Classical Theory in International Relations.* Cambridge: Cambridge University Press.

Jennings, Francis. 1984. *The Ambiguous Iroquois Empire: The Covenant Chain Confederation of Indian Tribes with English Colonies.* New York: Norton.

Jennings, Francis. 1985. Iroquois Alliances in American History. In F. Jennings, W. Fenton, M. Druke and D. Miller (eds) *The History and Culture of Iroquois Diplomacy: An Interdisciplinary Guide to the Treaties of the Six Nations and Their League.* Syracuse, NY: Syracuse University Press, pp. 37–65.

Jennings F., Fenton W., Druke M. and Miller D. (eds). 1985. *The History and Culture of Iroquois Diplomacy: An Interdisciplinary Guide to the Treaties of the Six Nations and Their League.* Syracuse, NY: Syracuse University Press.

Johansen, Bruce E. and Grinde, Donald A. 1990. *Exemplar of Liberty: Native America and the Evolution of Democracy.* Available at www.ratical.org/many_worlds/6Nations/EoL/chp8.html (accessed on 9 May 2017).

Johnson, Robert. 2003. *British Imperialism.* Gordonsville, VA: Palgrave Macmillan.

Jones, Dorothy. 1988. British Colonial Indian Treaties. In Wilcomb E. Washburn (ed.) *Handbook of North American Indians.* Vol. 4 'History of Indian–White Relations'. Washington, DC: Smithsonian Institute, pp. 185–194.

Kantorowicz, Ernst H. 1957. *The King's Two Bodies: A Study in Mediaeval Political Theology.* Princeton, NJ: Princeton University Press.

Keene, Edward. 2001. The Development of the Concept of International Society: An Essay on Political Argument in International Relations Theory. In B. Neufeld and M. Ebata (eds) *Confronting the Political: International Relations at the Millennium.* London: Macmillan Press, pp. 17–46.

Keene, Edward. 2002. *Beyond the Anarchical Society: Grotius, Colonialism and Order in World Politics.* Port Chester, NY: Cambridge University Press.

Keene, Edward. 2005. *International Political Thought: A Historical Introduction.* Cambridge: Polity Press.

Keene, Edward. 2007. A Case Study of the Construction of International Hierarchy: British Treaty-Making Against the Slave Trade in the Early Nineteenth Century. *International Organization* 61 (2), pp. 311–339.

Keller, Simon. 2009. Against Friendship between Countries. *Journal of International Political Theory* 5 (1), pp. 59–74.

Kharkhordin, Oleg. 2010. Why Res Publica is not a State: The Stoic Grammar and Discursive Practices in Cicero's Conception. *History of Political Thought* 31 (2), pp. 221–246.

Knorr, Klaus E. 1963. *British Colonial Theories, 1570–1850.* London: Frank Cass & Co Ltd.

Konstan, David. 1997. *Friendship in the Classical World*. Cambridge: Cambridge University Press.

Koselleck, Reinhart. 1988. *Critique and Crisis: Enlightenment and the Pathogenesis of Modern Society*. Oxford, New York and Hamburg: Berg Publishers Ltd.

Koselleck, Reinhart. 2004. The Historical Political Semantics of Asymmetric Counterconcepts. In *Future's Past*. Translated by K. Tribe. New York: Columbia University Press, pp. 155–191.

Koskenniemi, Martti. 1989. *From Apology to Utopia: The Structure of International Legal Argument*. Helsinki: Finnish Lawyers' Publishing Company.

Koskenniemi, Martti. 2002. *Gentle Civilizer of Nations*. Port Chester, NY: Cambridge University Press.

Krasner, Stephen D. 1999. *Sovereignty: Organized Hypocrisy*. Princeton, NJ: Princeton University Press.

Kratochwil, Friedrich. 1995. Sovereignty as Dominium. In Gene M. Lyons and Michael Mastanduno (eds) *Beyond Westphalia? State Sovereignty and International Intervention*. Baltimore, MD: Johns Hopkins University Press, pp. 21–42.

Kratochwil, Friedrich. 2014. *The Status of Law in World Society: Meditations on the Role and Rule of Law*. Cambridge and New York: Cambridge University Press.

Kvasnicka, Robert. 1988. United States Indian Treaties and Agreements. In E. Wilcomb Washburn (ed.) *Handbook of North American Indians*. Vol. 4 'History of Indian–White Relations'. Washington, DC: Smithsonian Institute, pp. 195–201.

Lake, David A. 2009. *Hierarchy in International Relations*. Cornell Studies in Political Economy. Ithaca, NY: Cornell University Press.

Lane, Melissa. 2012. Doing Our Own Thinking for Ourselves: On Quentin Skinner's Genealogical Turn. *Journal of the History of Ideas* 73 (1), pp. 71–82.

Lebow, Richard Ned. 2013. Classical Realism. In Tim Dunne, Milja Kurki and Steve Smith (eds) *International Relations Theories: Discipline and Diversity*. 3rd ed. Oxford: Oxford University Press, pp. 59–76.

Lesaffer, Randall. 1997. The Westphalia Peace Treaties and the Development of the Tradition of Great European Peace Settlements Prior to 1648. *Grotiana* 18, pp. 71–95.

Lesaffer, Randall. 2000. The Medieval Canon Law of Contract and Early Modern Treaty Law. *Journal of the History of International Law* 2, pp. 178–198.

Lesaffer, Randall. 2002. Amicitia in Renaissance Peace and Alliance Treaties. *Journal of the History of International Law* 4, pp. 77–99.

Lesaffer, Randall. 2004. Peace Treaties from Lodi to Westphalia. In Randall Lesaffer (ed.) *Peace Treaties and International Law in European History: From the Late Middle Ages to World War One*. Cambridge: Cambridge University Press, pp. 9–44.

Lieven, Dominic. 2001. *Empire: The Russian Empire and Its Rivals*. New Haven, CT and London: Yale University Press.

Lu, Catherine. 2009. Political Friendship among Peoples. *Journal of International Political Theory* 5 (1), pp. 41–58.

Mack, Peter. 2002. *Elizabethan Rhetoric: Theory and Practice*. New York: Cambridge University Press.

Major, Andrea. 2011. *Sovereignty and Social Reform in India: British Colonialism and the Campaign Against Sati, 1830–60*. New York: Routledge.

Malcolm, Noel. 2002. *Aspects of Hobbes*. New York: Oxford University Press Inc.

Mattingly, Garrett. 1988. *Renaissance Diplomacy*. Or. published 1955. New York: Dover Publications, Inc.

Mauriac, Henry M. de. 1949. Alexander the Great and the Politics of 'Homonoia'. *Journal of the History of Ideas* 10 (1), pp. 104–114.

Mehr, Farhang. 1997. *A Colonial Legacy: The Dispute Over the Islands of Abu Musa, and the Greater and Lesser Tumbs*. Lanham, MD: University Press of America.

Mills, Laurens J. 1937. *One Soul in Bodies Twain: Friendship in Tudor Literature and Stuart Drama*. Bloomington, IN: The Principia Press, Inc.

Morgenthau, Hans. J. 2005. *Politics Among Nations: The Struggle for Power and Peace*. 7th ed. Revised by Kenneth W. Thompson. Boston: McGraw-Hill Higher Education.

Nardin, Terry. 1999. Legal Positivism as a Theory of International Society. In David R. Mapel and Terry Nardin (eds) *International Society: Diverse Ethical Perspectives*. New edition. Princeton, NJ: Princeton University Press, pp. 17–35.

Nussbaum, Arthur. 1952. The Significance of Roman Law in the History of International Law. *University of Pennsylvania Law Review* 100, pp. 678–687.

Oelsner, Andrea. 2007. Friendship, Mutual Trust and the Evolution of Regional Peace in the International System. *Critical Review of International and Social Political Philosophy* 10 (2), pp. 257–279.

Ojakangas, Mika. 2011. Becoming Whosoever: Re-examining Pauline Universalism. *The Bible and Critical Theory* 7 (2), pp. 17–26.

Onuf, Nicholas. 1989. *World of Our Making: Rules and Rule in Social Theory and International Relations*. Columbia, SC: University of South Carolina Press.

Onuf, Nicholas. 1998. *The Republican Legacy in International Theory*. Cambridge: Cambridge University Press.

Onuf, Nicholas. 2009. Friendship and Hospitality: Some Conceptual Preliminaries. *Journal of International Political Theory* 5 (1), pp. 1–21.

Onuf, Nicholas. 2012. *Making Sense, Making Worlds: Constructivism in Social Theory and International Relations*. London and New York: Routledge.

Onuf, Peter and Onuf, Nicholas. 1993. *Federal Union, Modern World: The Law of Nations in an Age of Revolutions, 1776–1814*. Madison, WI: Madison House Publishers, Inc.

Oppenheim, Lassa. 1905. *International Law: A Treatise*. Vol. 1. 2 vols. London and New York: Longmans, Green, and Co.

Osiander, Andreas. 2001. Sovereignty, International Relations, and the Westphalian Myth. *International Organization* 55 (2), pp. 251–287.

Oxford English Dictionary. 1989. 2nd ed. Prepared by J.A. Simpson and E.S.C. Weiner. Vols. I, VI. Oxford: Clarendon Press.

Pagden, Anthony. 1995. *Lords of all the World: Ideologies of Empire in Spain, Britain and France c. 1500–c. 1800*. New Haven, CT and London: Yale University Press.

Pagden, Anthony. 2013. *The Enlightenment and Why It Still Matters*. Oxford: Oxford University Press.

Palonen, Kari. 2002. The History of Concepts as a Style of Political Theorizing: Quentin Skinner's and Reinhart Koselleck's Subversion of Normative Theory. *European Journal of Political Theory* I (1), pp. 91–106.

Palonen, Kari. 2003. *Quentin Skinner: History, Politics, Rhetoric.* Cambridge: Polity Press.

Palonen, Kari. 2005. Political Theorizing as a Dimension of Political Life. *European Journal of Political Theory* 4 (4), pp. 351–366.

Paradisi, Bruno. 1951. L'amitie internationale: les phases critiques de son ancienne histoire. *Recueil des Cours de l'Academie de Droit International* 78, pp. 329–377.

Paradisi, Bruno. 1974. 'L'amicitia internazionale nella storia antica' and 'L'amicitia nell'alto medio evo. In *Civitas Maxima. Studi di storia del diritto internazionale* I. Florence: Olschki, pp. 296–397.

Parkin, Jon. 2003. Taming the Leviathan: Reading Hobbes in Seventeenth-Century Europe. In Tim J. Hochstrasser and Peter Schröder (eds) *Early Modern Natural Law Theories: Contexts and Strategies in the Early Enlightenment.* Boston: Kluwer, pp. 31–52.

Parkin, Jon. 2007. *Taming the Leviathan: The Reception of the Political and Religious Ideas of Thomas Hobbes in England 1640–1700.* Cambridge: Cambridge University Press.

Pettit, Philip. 2010. A Republican Law of Peoples. *European Journal of Political Theory* 9 (1), pp. 70–94.

Pitkin, Hanna. 1972. *Wittgenstein and Justice: On the Significance of Ludwig Wittgenstein for Social and Political Thought.* Berkeley, CA: University of California Press.

Pocock, J.G.A. 2003. *The Machiavellian Moment: Florentine Political Thought and the Atlantic Republican Tradition.* 2nd ed. Princeton, NJ and Oxford: Princeton University Press.

Pocock, J.G.A. 2005. *The Discovery of Islands: Essays in British History.* Cambridge: Cambridge University Press.

Reus-Smit, Christian. 2009. *The Moral Purpose of the State: Culture, Social Identity, and Institutional Rationality in International Relations.* Princeton, NJ: Princeton University Press.

Richter, Melvin. 1995. *The History of Political and Social Concepts: A Critical Introduction.* New York and Oxford: Oxford University Press.

Roelofsen, Cornelius G. 1997. Grotius and the Development of International Relations Theory: The 'Long Seventeenth Century' and the Elaboration of a European States System. *Grotiana* 18, pp. 97–120.

Rommen, Heinrich. 1998. *The Natural Law: A Study in Legal and Social History and Philosophy.* Translated by Thomas R. Hanley. Introduction and Bibliography by Russell Hittinger. 1st ed. 1936. Indianapolis, IN: Liberty Fund.

Rorty, Richard. 1989. *Contingency, Irony, and Solidarity.* Cambridge and New York: Cambridge University Press.

Roshchin, Evgeny. 2009. Supplanting Love, Accepting Friendship: A History of the Russian Diplomatic Concepts. *Redescriptions* 13, pp. 125–146.

Roshchin, Evgeny. 2011. Friendship of the Enemies: 20th Century Treaties of the United Kingdom and the USSR. *International Politics* 48 (1), pp. 71–91.

Roshchin, Evgeny. 2013. (Un)Natural and Contractual International Society: A Conceptual Inquiry. *European Journal of International Relations* 19 (2), pp. 257–279.

Saar, Martin. 2008. Understanding Genealogy: History, Power and the Self. *Journal of the Philosophy of History* 2, pp. 295–314.

Saastamoinen, Kari. 1995. *The Morality of the Fallen Man: Samuel Pufendorf on Natural Law.* Helsinki: SHS.

Saastamoinen, Kari. 2002. Hobbes and Pufendorf on Natural Equality and Civil Sovereignty. In Ian Hunter (ed.) *Natural Law and Civil Sovereignty: Moral Right and State Authority in Early Modern Political Thought*. Gordonsville: Palgrave Macmillan, pp. 189–203.

Saastamoinen, Kari. 2010. Pufendorf on Natural Equality, Human Dignity, and Self-Esteem. *Journal of the History of Ideas* 71 (1), pp. 39–62.

Schmitt, Carl. 1996. *The Concept of the Political*. Chicago, IL: University of Chicago Press.

Schmitt, Carl. 2003. *The Nomos of the Earth in the International Law of the Jus Publicum Europaeum*. Translated by G.L. Ulmen. New York: Telos Press.

Schwarzenbach, Sibyl A. 2009. *On Civic Friendship: Including Women in the State*. New York: Columbia University Press.

Scott, James Brown. 1934. *The Spanish Conception of International Law and of Sanctions*. Washington, DC: Carnegie Endowment for International Peace.

Setton, Kenneth. 1976. *The Papacy and the Levant, 1204–1571*. Vol. 3. Philadelphia, PA: American Philosophical Society.

Shannon, Laurie. 2002. *Sovereign Amity: Figures of Friendship in Shakespearean Contexts*. Chicago and London: The University of Chicago Press.

Silver, Allan. 1997. Two Different Sorts of Commerce – Friendship and Strangership in Civil Society. In J. Weinstraub and K. Kumar (eds) *Public and Private in Thought and Practice: Perspectives on a Grand Dichotomy*. Chicago, IL and London: The University of Chicago Press, pp. 43–74.

Skinner, Quentin. 1966. The Ideological Context of Hobbes's Political Thought. *Historical Journal* IX (3), pp. 286–317.

Skinner, Quentin. 1989a. Language and Political Change. In Terence Ball, James Farr and Russell L. Hanson (eds) *Political Innovation and Conceptual Change*. Cambridge and New York: Cambridge University Press, pp. 6–23.

Skinner, Quentin. 1989b. The State. In T. Ball, J. Farr and R.L. Hanson (eds) *Political Innovation and Conceptual Change*. Cambridge: Cambridge University Press, pp. 90–131.

Skinner, Quentin. 1996. *Reason and Rhetoric in the Philosophy of Hobbes*. Reprinted 2004. Cambridge: Cambridge University Press.

Skinner, Quentin. 1998. *Liberty before Liberalism*. Cambridge: Cambridge University Press.

Skinner, Quentin. 1999. Rhetoric and Conceptual Change. *Finnish Yearbook of Political Thought* 3, pp. 60–73.

Skinner, Quentin. 2000a. *The Foundations of Modern Political Thought. Vol. 1: The Renaissance*. 1st publ. 1978. Cambridge: Cambridge University Press.

Skinner, Quentin. 2000b. *The Foundations of Modern Political Thought. Vol. 2: The Age of Reformation*. 1st publ. 1978. Cambridge: Cambridge University Press.

Skinner, Quentin. 2002a. *Visions of Politics Vol. 1: Regarding Method*. New York: Cambridge University Press.

Skinner, Quentin. 2002b. *Visions of Politics Vol. 2: Renaissance Virtues*. West Nyack, NY: Cambridge University Press.

Skinner, Quentin. 2006. Surveying the Foundations. In Annabel Brett, James Tully and Holly Hamilton-Bleakley (eds) *Rethinking the Foundations of Modern Political Thought*. New York: Cambridge University Press, pp. 236–261.

Skinner, Quentin. 2007. Paradiastole: Redescribing the Vices as Virtues. In Sylvia Adamson, Gavin Alexander and Katrin Ettenhuber (eds) *Renaissance Figures of Speech*. Cambridge: Cambridge University Press, pp. 149–163.

Skinner, Quentin. 2008. *Hobbes and Republican Liberty*. Cambridge: Cambridge University Press.

Skinner, Quentin. 2009. A Genealogy of the Modern State. *Proceedings of the British Academy* 162, pp. 325–370.

Skinner, Quentin. 2012. On the Liberty of the Ancients and the Moderns: A Reply to My Critics. *Journal of the History of Ideas* 73 (1), pp. 127–146.

Smith, Graham M. 2011. Friendship and the World of States. *International Politics* 48, pp. 10–27.

Smith Pangle, Lorraine. 2003. *Aristotle and the Philosophy of Friendship*. Cambridge: Cambridge University Press.

Snyder, Glenn H. 1997. *Alliance Politics*. Ithaca, NY: Cornell University Press.

Spruyt, Hendrik. 1994. *The Sovereign State and Its Competitors*. Princeton, NJ: Princeton University Press.

Spruyt, Hendrik. 2006. Genealogy, Territorial Acquisition and the Capitalist State. *International Politics* 43, pp. 511–518.

Stirk, Peter. 2005. The Westphalian Model, Sovereignty and Law in Fin-de-siècle German International Theory. *International Relations* 19 (2), pp. 153–172.

Strang, David. 1996. Contested Sovereignty: The Social Construction of Colonial Imperialism. In Th. Biersteker and C. Weber (eds) *State Sovereignty as Social Construct*. Cambridge: Cambridge University Press, pp. 22–49.

Suganami, Hidemi. 1992. Grotius and International Equality. In H. Bull, B. Kingsbury and A. Roberts (eds) *Hugo Grotius and International Relations*. Oxford: Clarendon Press, pp. 221–240.

Suganami, Hidemi. 2008. *The Domestic Analogy and World Order Proposals*. 1st ed. Cambridge: Cambridge University Press.

Syrjämäki, Sami. 2011. *Sins of a Historian: Perspectives to the Problem of Anachronism*. Doctoral Dissertation. Tampere: Tampere University Press.

The Cambridge History of British Foreign Policy, 1783–1919. 1923. (eds) A.W. Ward and G.P. Gooch. Vol. II '1815–1866'. Cambridge: Cambridge University Press.

Thornton, Helen. 2005. *State of Nature or Eden? Thomas Hobbes and His Contemporaries on the Natural Condition of Human Beings*. Rochester, NY: University of Rochester Press.

Tuck, Richard. 1987. The 'Modern' Theory of Natural Law. In Anthony Pagden (ed.) *The Languages of Political Theory in Early-Modern Europe*. Cambridge: Cambridge University Press, pp. 99–119.

Tuck, Richard. 1991. Grotius and Selden. In J.H. Burns (ed.) *The Cambridge History of Political Thought 1450–1700*. Cambridge: Cambridge University Press, pp. 499–529.

Tuck, Richard. 1993. *Philosophy and Government, 1572–1651*. Cambridge: Cambridge University Press.

Tuck, Richard. 1999. *The Rights of War and Peace: Political Thought and the International Order from Grotius to Kant*. Repr. 2009. New York: Oxford University Press.

Van Doren, C. and Boyd, J.P. (eds). 1938. *Indian Treaties Printed by Benjamin Franklin, 1736–1762*. Philadelphia, PA: The Historical Society of Pennsylvania.

Van Gelderen, Martin. 2002. Aristotelians, Monarchomachs and Republicans: Sovereignty and Respublica Mixta in Dutch and German Political Thought, 1580–1650. In Martin van Gelderen and Quentin Skinner (eds) *Republicanism: A Shared European Heritage. Volume 1: Republicanism and Constitutionalism in Early Modern Europe*. Cambridge: Cambridge University Press, pp. 195–218.

Vucetic, Srdjan. 2011. Genealogy as a Research Tool in International Relations. *Review of International Studies* 37 (3), pp. 1295–1312.

Walker, Herman Jr. 1956. Treaties for the Encouragement and Protection of Foreign Investment: Present United States Practice. *American Journal of Comparative Law* 5 (2), pp. 229–247.

Walker, Herman Jr. 1957–1958. Modern Treaties of Friendship, Commerce and Navigation. *Minnesota Law Review* 42, pp. 805–824.

Waltz, Kenneth N. 1979. *Theory of International Politics*. Reading, MA: Addison-Wesley Publishing Company.

Waltz, Kenneth. 2000. Structural Realism after the Cold War. *International Security* 25 (1), pp. 5–41.

Weber, Max. 1978. *Economy and Society*. (eds) Guenther Roth and Claus Wittich. 2 vols. Berkeley, CA: University of California Press.

Weber, Max. 2004. The 'Objectivity' of Knowledge in Social Science and Social Policy. In Sam Whimster (ed.) *The Essential Weber: A Reader*. Translated by Keith Tribe. London and New York: Routledge, pp. 359–404.

Wendt, Alexander. 1999. *Social Theory of International Politics*. Cambridge: Cambridge University Press.

White, Peter. 1978. *Amicitia* and the Profession of Poetry in Early Imperial Rome. *Journal of Roman Studies* 68, pp. 74–92.

Wight, Martin. 1966. Western Values in International Relations. In H. Butterfield and M. Wight (eds) *Diplomatic Investigations: Essays in the Theory of International Politics*. London: George Allen & Unwin Ltd, pp. 89–131.

Wight, Martin. 1991. *International Theory: The Three Traditions*. (eds) G. Wight and B. Porter. Leicester and London: Leicester University Press and The Royal Institute of International Affairs.

Wight, Martin. 2005. *Four Seminal Thinkers in International Theory: Machiavelli, Grotius, Kant, and Mazzini*. (eds) G. Wight and B. Porter Oxford: Oxford University Press.

Willig, Timothy. 2008. *Restoring the Chain of Friendship: British Policy and the Indians of the Great Lakes, 1783–1815*. Lincoln, NE: University of Nebraska Press.

Winch, Peter. 1990. *The Idea of a Social Science: And Its Relation to Philosophy*. 2nd ed. London: Routledge.

Wittgenstein, Ludwig. 2001. *Philosophical Investigations: The German Text with a Revised English Translation*. Translated by G.E.M. Anscombe. Reprint 2003. Oxford: Blackwell Publishing Ltd.

Wolfers, Arnold. 1962. *Discord and Collaboration: Essays on International Politics*. Baltimore, MD: The Johns Hopkins Press.

Ziegler, Karl-Heinz. 2004. The Influence of Medieval Roman Law on Peace Treaties. In Randall Lesaffer (ed.) *Peace Treaties and International Law in European History: From the Late Middle Ages to World War One.* Cambridge: Cambridge University Press, pp. 147–161.

Index

EU authorised representative for GPSR:
Easy Access System Europe, Mustamäe tee 50,
10621 Tallinn, Estonia
gpsr.requests@easproject.com

www.ingramcontent.com/pod-product-compliance
Lightning Source LLC
Chambersburg PA
CBHW051958270326
41929CB00015B/2697